Training Wheels

An Experienced Guide to the Lessons of
A Course in Miracles

Training Wheels

An Experienced Guide to the Lessons of
A Course in Miracles

Amy Haible

BOOKS

Winchester, UK
Washington, USA

First published by O-Books, 2019
O-Books is an imprint of John Hunt Publishing Ltd., 3 East St., Alresford,
Hampshire SO24 9EE, UK
office1@jhpbooks.net
www.johnhuntpublishing.com

For distributor details and how to order please visit the 'Ordering' section on our website.

ISBN: 978 1 78904 024 1
978 1 78904 025 8 (ebook)
Library of Congress Control Number: 2018936099

A CIP catalogue record for this book is available from the British Library.

Design: Stuart Davies

Printed and bound by CPI Group (UK) Ltd, Croydon, CR0 4YY, UK

We operate a distinctive and ethical publishing philosophy in
all areas of our business, from our global network of authors to
production and worldwide distribution.

Contents

Review II

Review IV

Review V

Review VI

Part II

Focus Questions

1. What is Forgiveness?

5. What is the Body?

6. What is the Christ?

7. What is the Holy Spirit?

8. What is the Real World?

9. What is the Second Coming?

13. What is a Miracle?

14. What am I?

Final Lessons

Chapter 7: Continuing the Ride

Acknowledgements

With deep gratitude to Helen Schucman and William Thetford for bringing forth *A Course in Miracles*, and to all those whose work supports their original effort.

Special thanks to Sally and John Moulton who have made the Octagon a lighthouse for so many. To Ara Gillett, a fellow traveler, and to Zoe Marae who taught us how to step out of the sandbox and helped prepare my mind to accept the teachings of *A Course*.

To my husband Spike. Without your patience and support I could not have written a word. And to my girls, Renault, Ali, and Skyla, in the hope of a better world.

Introduction

It is ironic to say we live in unprecedented times for the word itself has become a commonplace description of the human state. Even so it is true. Never before has so much been available to so many, yet the pace and scope of change is frightening. The world seems poised at some unknown edge. Much of it is dying. Do we move forward or go back? Do we even have a choice? Are we evolving into something better or devolving into chaos? If the birth of the new requires the death of the old, this old is not letting go easily.

The evolution of the spiritual self is not necessarily pretty or neat. Indeed, like any creation it can be very messy. While each of us is living our own unique experience of transformation, it is the whole of humanity that is shifting now. A major lesson of *A Course in Miracles* is that all minds are joined. This is a literal truth. Consciousness is collective.

Some of you may know about *A Course in Miracles* (ACIM). You may have heard about it from a friend or even picked it up and thumbed through it. Some have been put off by the language which can come across as overly Christian and patriarchal. Others find the writing style difficult. I understand. I almost put the book down myself. But I believe ACIM is the most profound spiritual text of our times. Indeed, it is far ahead of its time. Part of my goal in this book is to make its language accessible to more people who will then tackle the original material.

This is my journey through one year of the daily lessons found in the *Workbook* of *A Course in Miracles*. It is something I would have liked when I began the work. I share it in the hope that it will help make your coming transformation more gentle, purposeful, and peaceful. If you are looking for guidance, comfort, and reassurance coping with a world in transition, you'll find it here.

Chapter 1

A Course in Miracles is Scribed

The date is 1965; the place, Columbia University's College of Physicians and Surgeons. Helen Schucman, PhD, is an associate professor of psychology, and William "Bill" Thetford, PhD, directs the Psychology Department. Each is a conservative educator and researcher heavily invested in their reputation.

According to both, their relationship is strained. They work as colleagues but the atmosphere is highly competitive. Status and position are paramount. Just before they are about to attend a professional meeting together Bill Thetford does something very out of character. In an impassioned plea he asks for an end to their aggressiveness and quarrelling. "There must be another way," he says to Helen. What Bill means is there must be some way to get along without the backstabbing, judgment and ego games that have become all too common. Equally out of character, Helen agrees to help. Unbeknownst to either of them, their joint willingness to find another way opens a door to the miraculous.

For three months after their initial agreement to work together Helen has vivid, precognitive dreams and other experiences that challenge her empirical "hard-headed" training. Acting on Bill's suggestion, Helen begins to record these dreams and experiences until one evening she hears an inner Voice insistently repeating, "This is a course in miracles. Please take notes." Thus begins Helen's role as scribe for the Voice.

What develops is a joint effort that lasts for seven years. Helen is the scribe for the Voice who identifies itself as Jesus. She brings her notes in and Bill types them up. Helen is able to turn the mental dictation on and off at will, picking up exactly where she last left off. This is impressive because many sections of the material are written in iambic pentameter, a complicated form of Shakespearean blank verse. The result of this joint effort is an unearthly masterpiece of spiritual truth titled, *A Course in Miracles*.

ACIM is a challenging channeled work. It contains a *Text* of nearly 700 pages, the contents of which are miraculous in any form, a *Workbook* for Students, a *Manual for Teachers*, Clarification of Terms, the *Song of Prayer*, and an extension on the practice of psychotherapy. The *Workbook* contains 365 daily lessons. The book you are holding is my interpretation of each lesson along with commentary and scientific information that back up the metaphysical teachings of ACIM.

Written over 50 years ago, ACIM is the spiritual truth of what new physics is discovering: we exist in a unified multidimensional field of consciousness; our thoughts directly affect our reality; linear time is a limited, three-dimensional construct; and what we see with the body's eyes is only a fraction of what is available for us to perceive.

If you are happy with the contents of your mind, ACIM might not interest you. But sooner or later, most of us come to the point where we cannot buy another thing, change our job or our partner, exercise harder, travel further, or take another class that ends our confusion and suffering. We realize we must go inward, and when we do we realize nothing "out there" can ever be enough again. As ACIM says, there are many forms of the curriculum, but the curriculum itself is a requirement. Sooner or later, everyone must learn its lessons.

This is a course in miracles. It is a required course. Only the time you take it is voluntary. Free will does not mean that you can establish the curriculum. It means only that you can elect what you want to take at a given time.
– ACIM

Chapter 2

Working with the Lessons

The daily lessons are ACIM in action. Practiced as directed, their effect is both immediate and lasting. Many of us have read wonderfully inspiring spiritual texts. They make us feel great when we are reading them and some create lasting changes. But if you can image a stone skipping across a pond, you will see that while most books or workshops may produce ripples, nothing really changes beneath the surface. This is because only the surface has been touched.

To go beneath the surface, one has to be willing to commit. Your commitment, should you choose, is to explore and work with these lessons. They will take you through all the necessary steps. You do not have to believe or fully understand each lesson. You might even actively resist a few. That's okay. But I promise you this: the student who commits to the daily lessons cannot NOT experience a transformation.

The way to do the lessons can be summed up in a single word: consistency. Begin each day with a lesson. Have a cup of tea or coffee in a quiet place and read it. Then practice the daily lesson as directed. Sometimes this will mean sitting for a couple of minutes in reflection. Other times you will be asked to quiet your mind multiple times during the day. There are many ways to remember to practice. Set your watch or cell phone. Wear a special piece of jewelry. I have tried to just remember, which has its own pluses and minuses.

Do not do more than one lesson a day and do not skip ahead. These lessons hold quantum information. They build upon each other and they are meant to be experienced at a gentle pace. Read each day's lesson slowly and purposefully. Feel its words reverberate in your body. Sense your way into the meaning.

Some words will elicit feelings or sensations. Be aware, but do not be overly concerned. Some lessons might seem outlandish or even silly. That is fine. Accept your own response, but do the lesson anyway. Do not deny yourself the experience of it or your response to it.

The original lessons were meant to begin on January 1 and some of their content paid small attention to traditional Christian holidays. I don't think it matters when you start the lessons. In fact, if you've found your way to this book on July 4 and want to begin, I suggest you trust that Source has guided you to exactly the right moment.

There is one final point. It is the concept upon which ACIM is founded: forgiveness. If you forget a lesson or cannot practice in the prescribed way, just pick up where you left off, and continue on. ACIM is experiential. It is almost as if the daily lessons are structured as opportunities to forgive yourself. Forgive yourself over and over again. Forgiveness is limitless, as is the freedom it brings.

Chapter 3

Some Fundamentals

There are several fundamental concepts in the Workbook of Daily Lessons. Understanding them will help you get the most out of each one.

1. Forgiveness.
Forgiveness is the grease in the wheels of spiritual transformation. We cannot transcend this reality without it. Forgiveness is a form of spiritual alchemy that transmutes all that is not in alignment with Source. Hatred is not aligned with Source. Judgment is not aligned with It. Fear is not in alignment with It. Forgiveness is multidimensional. It can heal the past and the future. However, forgiveness is not about overlooking a wrong or hurt. It does not imply pity or moral superiority. Forgiveness says, "I am an eternal being. I cannot be harmed, nor can I cause harm. Only in illusions can hurt seem to be real. What is there to forgive in illusion? Only the mistaken belief that suffering exists at all." It is radical to say there is nothing and no one who is not forgivable, but you will understand this more deeply as the lessons unfold.

2. Knowing through direct experience.
Miracles cannot be explained by the linear, rational mind. The rational mind is often incapable of going beyond what it "thinks it thinks it knows." Be willing to trust in your experience with the lessons. It is through experience that you will know. Wisdom is the willingness to remain open in the face of not knowing.

3. Mind is the builder.
Edgar Cayce coined this phrase. It represents not only spiritual truth, but is increasingly recognized as a foundation of quantum

physics, which recognizes the elemental building block of form is thought. Material form arises from immaterial consciousness: the "substantial" is born of the "insubstantial." This is the complete opposite of what we have been taught and its general acceptance will change the way we experience our world. Can you imagine we fought over the idea the earth is round? Galileo was labeled a "heretic" and spent the last eight years of his life under house arrest because he promulgated the idea of a heliocentric universe. Some ideas are considered too radical because they challenge accepted dogma. In a sense, this is where we are today with the idea that consciousness creates the "reality" of form.

4. Ego, or personal mind, and the Self.
Very generally, ACIM speaks of two levels of mind: the personal mind (also called the self, or ego) and the Self. The personal mind is unhealed because it believes it is separated from Source and all other personal minds. It values linear time, rational thinking, and the physical world. It believes itself to be a product of a physical brain housed in a physical body. However, Self knows its Oneness with all other minds and with its Creator. Access to the Self most often comes through peace and stillness, but Self is always available because it IS who we are. The daily lessons pointedly connect us with the Self. They help us wear a path to It through conscious connection. Practiced daily, this connection becomes almost effortlessly second nature. But do be aware, the personal mind will always try to interpret your reality. This is why ACIM calls the lessons "mind training."

5. The Holy Instant.
Now is the only "time" there is. Linear time is the product of three-dimensional perception. It is true only at its level. Quantum physics tells us that past, present, and future all happen simultaneously in "space/time." This is a very challenging concept because our entire "reality" is based on linear time and

we have completely agreed to its precepts. Again, it is as though we still believed the earth is flat and sits at the center of the solar system. Humanity has yet to correct its thinking about something that we know is not absolute truth. There is only the present moment. Past is gone and future is not arrived. You will play with this idea in one of the first daily lessons.

6. Feelings and Thoughts are Things.

Thoughts and feelings are energetic forms and have creative power. ACIM teaches everything that appears as form is generated first as a thought or feeling. The body is a product of thought. The world is a product of thought. The universe is a product of thought. This is why the contents of the mind must be explored and known because an unhealed mind creates an unhealed world. The daily lessons of ACIM gently correct perception by showing how we project our thoughts onto the world and then respond as if we had no connection to them whatsoever. The recognition that we create our reality is one we must all come to in time. It offers the most potent freedom we can know.

Chapter 4

The practice of Contemplation and Meditation

Contemplation and meditation are fundamental aspects of most spiritual practices. ACIM does not spend much time describing either, so here is a little primer for those unfamiliar with them.

Contemplation is the art of sitting quietly and holding a phrase or word in your awareness. As the phrase or word is gently repeated, the mind effortlessly sinks deeper into its meaning. There is no need to analyze or philosophize. One simply sits, breathes, repeats the phrase, and watches. The germination happens on its own. The famous seer Edgar Cayce placed great value on contemplative meditation as a way to raise the frequency of the mental body.

ACIM also emphasizes what is called "open awareness meditation." In open awareness meditation a lesson, or part of a lesson, may be repeated in the beginning, but this gives way to simply watching the breath and noticing all thoughts, feelings, and bodily sensations that arise. Open awareness trusts the Holy Spirit, or your higher self, to be in charge of your inner journey.

You can imagine open awareness meditation in the following metaphor about a boat at anchor. In this metaphor, a boat is the mind. The anchor is the breath. The line between the anchor and the boat is the lesson, or words of the lesson.

As you sit, the breath anchors the mind to the "now" moment. It keeps it from drifting around aimlessly. You set the anchor (breath) and trust the boat (mind) will not drift off into the horizon. Hold to your natural breath. If you drift off, come back to it.

The lesson, like the anchor line, uses words to connect your mind and your breath. If you repeat the lesson over and over, like a mantra, then you are keeping the line short. Along with the breath, the words hold the mind and prevent it from drifting too far off.

If you feel ready to explore a bit, you can lengthen the line. In this case you repeat the lesson once or twice and then, using the breath as your anchor, allow thoughts to arise. You watch each thought, noticing bodily sensations, emotions, and feelings as they come up, peak, and then fall away. When you find your mind drifting too much, you hold to the anchor of breath and shorten the line by refocusing on the words of the lesson.

If you have the foundation of a good practice, and feel ready, you may lengthen the line. In this case, you remain connected to the breath, but allow the tide to carry your boat further out. A whole series of thoughts might arise. You might have a waking dream. You might "see" a little story in your mind. Images and strange forms might crop up. But you always remain anchored to the breath and aware of your thoughts. This practice allows the experience of exploring the mind at work. The longer you sit watching your thoughts, coming back to the breath, and then allowing more thoughts, the further out you can go. You peel back layers of thought, going deeper and deeper. This is where profound connections are made, insights are discovered, and visions arise.

If you are just beginning to meditate, stay close to the shore. Don't allow thoughts to carry you out into the open ocean. Always remain anchored with the breath and keep the lesson close. Even the most experienced meditators routinely rely on this most basic practice. Enjoy your time in seated meditation and contemplation. Avoid making it "work." It is a gift of time you give to yourself.

Chapter 5

A word on the language

The language of ACIM can be challenging and its phrasing unusual. Although scribed by a woman, ACIM seems to leave women completely out of the picture – at least on first reading. ACIM refers to God as Father, and all of creation as the Holy Son of God. But is it not true that both the son and father depend upon motherhood to be at all? Jesus himself brought the highest feminine qualities of love, compassion, gentleness, and forgiveness to his teachings. So, in my mind, it is not improper to consider the Father as the Mother also.

This said, ACIM states clearly that God is not human, and in Reality, neither are we. Indeed, what it calls the Holy Son of God includes everything, even what we consider to be inanimate objects. There is nothing that is not a Holy Son of God. Every man, woman, dog, cat, fish, tree, blade of grass, boson or quark qualifies. When all is One, there is no gender, there are no separate physical forms, and nothing is better than anything else. Oneness has no hierarchy. We are One with the Christ and Mother/Father/Source/Creator/First Cause/God.

The term ego also features predominantly in ACIM. I interchange ego, the self, and personal mind. Traditional psychotherapy views a healthy ego as necessary for resiliency and the maintenance of good relationships. However, ACIM views the ego, or personal mind, as the unhealed product of a split mind – a mind that has created the illusion of separation from its Source. A mind that experiences its self separated from Source is literally living an illusion because nothing can be separated from the One. To be healed, the personal mind must be relinquished as the sole arbiter of reality. The healed mind is the Self.

11

ACIM uses the term Holy Spirit throughout. The Holy Spirit is the Whole-I-Spirit and It is our eternal link with Source. You can think of It as a Key Code or a Universal Translator. Source is within each of us, but Its Vastness has become almost unknowable to the unhealed mind. The Holy Spirit, as the Voice for God, reaches through the ego's illusion of separation and communicates as an experience of Knowing. The Holy Spirit is a bridge between Source and the unhealed, personal mind.

The words "holiness," "holy," and "atonement" are synonymous with Wholeness or Oneness. We are holy because we are whole. I am Whole-I. My Whole-I-Ness is in At-One-Ment with yours.

Atonement is not associated with sin. In Mind of God, there is nothing to atone for because all sin is illusion. At-One-Ment is the recognition of sinlessness through Oneness.

Sin is defined as lack of love. It is the unhealed mind's perception of separation from Source. Sin means to be without. It is an illusion because we can never be without Source and we are never separated from each other. All minds are joined and all minds are Innocent – except in the illusion of separation. Sin does not exist in Reality.

All this said, ACIM is quite clear that words are a poor substitute for the direct knowing of the heart. Trust your heart, for this is a journey Home. Take your time. Do not rush. Savor the words of each day's lesson and use them as safe harbor when you go out into the world. Enjoy this year of lessons and be patient with yourself. Are you ready to enter Reality? Let's begin.

Chapter 6

The Daily Lessons

Part I

Lesson 1

Nothing I see in this room (on this street, from this window, in this place) means anything.

Welcome to your first lesson. It is very simple. Yet like most simple lessons, it has the potential for great depth.

All you are asked to do in this first lesson is to take a seat and look with a light focus upon things within your view. Gently, without judgment, look around at specific things, (there is no order or limit to the things) and in a quiet, unhurried manner say about each thing, "Nothing I see means anything."

What does it mean to consider that nothing I see has meaning? How disorienting! Does a table have no meaning? Does the bus have no meaning? Does the person in front of me have no meaning? If nothing I see has any meaning what does that say about my world?

There is a reason nothing you see means anything. The reason will be made clear in upcoming lessons. For now, trust in the words and give yourself the experience of simply saying them. You don't have to believe them but do be open to their possibility.

When I first explored this lesson it left me feeling a little off balance. I look at the world around and say it means nothing. I feel a jolt inside. There is so much in this world to which I am attached! How could it not have meaning?

And yet, if I think about it, saying these words makes me feel a bit freer as well. After all, there is also so much in this world that I associate with pain, fear, and judgment. To say these things have no meaning releases me from past associations with them. Maybe the antique desk my sister and I fought over isn't quite what I thought it was.

Quantum physics seems to be telling us that there is an invisible field that gives substance to everything in our universe. It even suggests that we draw from this invisible field to create what appears to be physical matter. The "God particle" or Higgs Boson was thought to be the smallest particle but now we are looking for something even smaller. What exactly is this world I see made of?

This first lesson asks us to consider something we may never have considered before. What I think I see is just a perception made with the body's eyes. Yet beyond the body is a whole world of unseen things that move, vibrate, and even pass right through me! Perhaps nothing I see is actually as I see it! If it is not as I see it, then how can I know what it truly means?

How does this lesson feel for you?

Lesson 2

Yesterday you told yourself that nothing you saw in your world has any meaning. Now you go just a step beyond. The second lesson of the year begins much like the first – it is simple and easy to read. Yet its meaning will challenge the way you see your world.

> *I have given everything I see in this room (on this street, from this window, in this place) all the meaning it has for me.*

What does it mean that I give all the things of my world all the meaning they have? One might ask, "Am I to take this literally? Can it be true that I have given everything its meaning?" The answer is Yes. But for now, take the implications of this lesson lightly. Play with it, explore it with an open mind, but do not allow it to cause you any discomfort.

You may agree that each of us has our own perspective, our own reality. If twenty people gather in a room, each person brings something unique to the space. If these twenty people discuss a common topic, each person will leave with their own unique take on the subject, even if we "think" we generally agree.

In the movie *What the Bleep Do We Know?* the first European ship sets anchor in an American harbor, but the Native Americans literally don't see it. A vessel of its size and shape has no contextual meaning for them. Like the Native Americans, we do not see what we do not expect to see. We see what we DO expect to see. What do you expect?

Remember, ACIM is about mind training. In order to learn anew, we must sometimes let go of what we think is true. The first two lessons ask us to begin to open our minds to new possibilities. Lesson one asks us to consider that nothing we see has any meaning. Lesson two builds on the first. Not only does nothing I see have any meaning, but any meaning I think it has, I have given to it.

Sit quietly at your desk or in a chair for a minute or two in the morning and evening. Just look around, glance easily on what you see, and say to yourself, "I have given everything I see all the meaning it has for me." Don't concentrate on anything in particular and don't exclude anything in particular. Don't stress or over-focus. Flow with it. Be aware of what comes up for you. Is it disconcerting? Is it freeing?

Lesson 3

How gently does ACIM engage us in mind training! Gentleness is a hallmark of universal love for without gentleness, resistance arises, and resistance causes all learning to cease.

> *I do not understand anything I see in this room (on this street, from this window, in this place).*

Twice a day, take a seat. For a few minutes, look without judgment or distinction upon all that surrounds you. Slowly, with an open mind, let your vision rest a bit on one particular thing in your field and repeat the lesson. For example, you might say, "I do not understand this pencil." "I do not understand this tree." Notice if there is any resistance or emotional response when you say the words. That is all there is to it.

In thinking about today's lesson, it might be informative to consider the work of Sir Isaac Newton. Newton's work with the properties of light confirmed that what we perceive as color is merely a reflection of light waves. Different things reflect light differently. Blue is the reflection of one wavelength. Red is the reflection of another. So it is perfectly true to say, "I do not understand the light I see."

Here is another thought: the color of an object is not actually within the object itself. It is within the light that shines upon it. We really do not see what we think we see! The human eye perceives only a limited range of possible colors. Do we really understand what we think we see? We do not see infrared, yet there it is. We do not see ultraviolet, yet it is there as well. How does it feel to know you are not seeing all there is in front of you?

Lesson 4

Welcome to lesson four, one that begins your journey into mindfulness or meditation. Worry not, this exercise is simple and gentle. It asks very little of you. Indeed, the most difficult thing about this lesson is that you are required to lay all judgments aside. "Judgment about what?" you might ask. The answer is, "Judgment about yourself."

Set aside a few minutes, three or four times today and sit quietly. I suggest first thing in the morning, at noontime, later in the afternoon, and then before bed. You may wish to begin by taking two or three centering breaths. Just allow yourself to relax wherever you are. You may keep your eyes open or closed.

Now place your awareness gently upon the thoughts that come into your mind. Don't judge the thought. Don't hang onto the thought. Just notice and say softly to yourself:

These thoughts do not mean anything. They are like the things I see in this room (on this street, from this window, in this place).

The first three lessons asked you to focus on the world outside. You opened to the possibility that what you see in the outer world may not be all there is Lesson four takes you inside. You look now at what arises in your mind.

A great teacher once described the process of meditation. He said, "Meditating is like pulling a chair into the center of an empty room. Then you sit in the chair and watch all the characters that parade in front of you." This is your practice today.

Practice for about three minutes, four times today – in the morning, at noon, in the late afternoon, and before bed. Find a quiet place and take a seat. Breathe naturally, close your eyes, and watch what comes up. For each thought say to yourself, "This thought does not mean anything." Give yourself three or four minutes of being aware of your thoughts, and then go about your business. Can you remember to remember? It's only twelve minutes of your day!

Lesson 5

Most of us spend all day, each day, reacting to events that are seemingly outside us. In later lessons, you will be asked to consider whether these events are outside you, or of your own creation. But for today you are only asked to look a bit more closely at the things that seem to upset you. You are encouraged to be aware of moments during the day when you feel stressed, upset, or even mildly disgruntled. Use your body as an internal barometer. Today's lesson is:

I am never upset for the reasons I think.

Try to find four periods of quiet today. I suggest the a.m., noontime, the afternoon, and evening. Begin by centering yourself with a few deep breaths. Allow your body to relax, close your eyes, and let the outside world fade away.

Then allow your thoughts to arise naturally. Simply watch them come up. If you are like most people, some of your thoughts will contain feelings of stress, annoyance, resistance, or even anger or depression. When an upsetting thought arises, simply notice it and say to yourself, "I am not (annoyed, afraid, angry, or even mildly disgruntled) at (fill in the blank_____) for the reasons I think." This is all you need to do.

As you sit, allowing thoughts to arise, avoid efforts to search for the "real" reason why you are upset. The point here is to lightly touch the feeling or thought, and then repeat, "I am never upset for the reasons I think." Then move on!

During the day, use this phrase for any upset you might notice. I often register my upsets in my body, particularly in the area of my stomach, or solar plexus. When I feel this area tighten, it's a signal for me to notice my thoughts.

If you miss a practice period, or forget to notice, DO NOT WORRY. It's okay! Just do the exercise and try to remember next time. These exercises are not a forced march.

One more thing. Many of us feel we should not be upset about anything. We unconsciously chastise ourselves for not being "happy" all the time. The truth is, all upsets, no matter how mild or strong, are the same. Each upset is a form resistance to what is in front of you. We will talk more about this later. Enjoy the day. Notice gently. Forgive.

Lesson 6

Welcome to lesson six. Yesterday you spent time noticing your feelings, specifically ones that made you uncomfortable. You may have noticed that there are actually many times during the day when uncomfortable thoughts or feelings arise. These may range from mild irritation to anger or even fear. What did you notice, and what did you think or feel about what you noticed? One of the key ingredients of wisdom is the simple act of paying attention.

Today's lesson follows yesterday's, asking again that you notice your feelings. Even the tiniest upset is relevant because all sources of irritation come from the same source: resistance to what is happening in front of you. Today you are asked to reconsider what lies behind this resistance. Today's lesson is:

I am upset because I see something that is not there.

"What is not there?" you might ask. For now, don't worry about this. Just be open to the possibility that your upset might be about something other than what it seems to be on the surface. If you begin to notice how often your peace is disturbed during the day, you are well on your way with these lessons. Most of us unconsciously give up our peace.

Take a minute, three or four times today, and sit quietly. Allow thoughts and feelings to arise. Close your eyes if you like and notice how you feel right now. Do not force anything. When a disquieting thought arises, say to yourself, "I am upset because I see something that is not there." Don't analyze or go into thinking mode. This lesson is not about doing anything with your thoughts. It is about paying attention. When you notice, repeat the lesson, and move into the next moment.

All feelings of discomfort come from the mind. You may attribute a feeling to some particular person, thing, or event that lies outside of you, but the truth is, it is your feeling, which means it is in you. Do you see this? Be gentle with yourself about it.

Here's a personal example. Yesterday I found myself in slow

traffic on the way to an appointment. Looking ahead I saw a school bus with a long line of cars behind it. As we inched along, stopping every 50 feet, I found my hands gripping the steering wheel. "That damned bus is going to make me late," I complained to myself. Then I remembered today's lesson. "I am upset because I see something that is not there." What was I really upset about? I wasn't late yet; it was just a thought in my mind. My whole body was responding to an idea about a possible future event that wasn't true. I'd made up a story in the moment and then believed my own thoughts about it. This may seem like a small thing, but incidents like this happen over and over during the day. Noticing just one of them can change everything.

Lesson 7

Yesterday you were asked to take a few quiet moments and notice any upsetting thoughts. You were asked to respond to your thoughts with the idea, "I am upset because I see something that is not there." "Yes," you may have said to yourself, "but WHAT is not there?" Today's lesson begins to answer this question in a big way.

Today's lesson is:

I see only the past.

"Oh no," you might say. "I see this room. I see this person in front of me. What I see is happening right now!" True, but what you perceive is based on your past experience with it. You hold a pencil and remember the smell of lead. You see a loaf of bread and remember you enjoy it toasted with butter and jam.

We consistently carry the past into the present moment. This habitual, unconscious practice prevents us from experiencing things as they are now. A baby delights in a new thing because she experiences it for the first time. It matters little what the thing is – it is exciting to her! Seeing things with fresh eyes is a vital component to growth and aliveness.

ACIM tells us that this lesson is the reason for all the preceding lessons. "It is the reason why nothing we see means anything. It is the reason why we have given everything we see all the meaning it has. It is the reason we do not understand anything we see. It is the reason we are never upset for the reasons we think. And it explains why we are upset because we see something that is not there."

The past is not here unless you bring it into the present with your mind. Almost all present thoughts carry the burden of past experiences, coloring all we think, feel, and believe. This is a major realization.

Today's lesson is quite simple. Just take a minute, three or four times today, and look around. I suggest morning, noon, afternoon, and evening. Without effort, focus on something in front of you and repeat the lesson. For example, you might say, "I see only the past in this cup." Or, "I see only the past in this shoe." Or, "I see only the past in that door."

Don't be selective about what you focus upon. It can be anything at all! When you say the lesson to yourself, FEEL what it is like to say the words. Gently let the idea behind the words sink in. There is no right or wrong way to do this. And by the way, if this lesson feels silly, just try it anyway. All ACIM asks of us is "a little willingness."

Lesson 8

My mind is preoccupied with past thoughts.

I see only the past and my entire mind is preoccupied with it. This is true if you think about it all. Even my expectations of the future are created out of past experiences.

You may recall an old cereal commercial that showed people

with a bathroom scale chained to their ankle. It dragged behind as they walked down the street, waited for the bus, and met each other in the grocery aisle. When someone knocks on a woman's door and offers to exchange the scale for a box of cereal, she gladly hands over the scale. That scale is the past and we are all dragging it around all the time.

Like the scale that prevents us from moving freely, our preoccupation with the past prevents us from being in the present moment. The problem is, the present moment is the only moment we have. The past is gone. The future has not arrived. When we live with past thoughts, we literally live in an illusion of time. ACIM tells us, "The one wholly true thought one can hold about the past is that it is not here."

Today's exercise puts us well on the path of mind training. When we carry the past into the present moment, we are not truly seeing. The potential in the present moment is hidden by memory. The memory itself is illusion because it literally is not there. Today, we practice letting go of illusion.

Four or five times today, sit quietly and close your eyes. You may wish to begin with a few deep, cleansing breaths. Allow each breath to deepen your relaxation. Feel your whole body soften. Allow thoughts to arise naturally. Gently notice the content of the thought as it arises. You might say to yourself, "I'm thinking about (a person, a feeling, a thing, or an event)." Spend about a minute or two sitting quietly like this. At the end of your sitting, say in your mind, "My mind is preoccupied with past thoughts."

If you find yourself annoyed, irritated, or burdened by these practice periods, please notice and allow the feeling. Resistance to this work is natural. Feeling guilty about it will only stop you from doing it. Notice the resistance, the guilt, and sit anyway. The decision to sit is an act of forgiveness. These practice sessions are a gift you are giving to yourself.

Lesson 9

I see nothing as it is now.

We journey into metaphysical territory with the next few lessons. For those who are firmly rooted in rational thinking, this may create a bit of discomfort, or challenge your sense of "reality." You are learning that what you think is real may not be as solid as you believe it to be.

Lessons seven and eight taught that you "see only the past" and your mind is "preoccupied with past thoughts." Now you are asked to sit with the idea: "I see nothing as it is now." You are not asked to understand all that these lessons mean at this point. But you are asked to be open to the possibility that you do not really know anything. Remember, this is a course in mind training. You are releasing what you think you think you know.

Take your seat and close your eyes. Take three deep, cleansing breaths. Settle quietly in your body. Relax. When you are ready, open your eyes and look around. Begin with the things nearest you, like the pencil on your desk, your hand or shoe, or even your computer screen. In your mind say, "I see nothing as it is now." For example, you might say, "I do not see this (pencil, hand, shoe, screen) as it is now." Then slowly expand your vision to objects around you and repeat the lesson for each object. Don't specifically exclude anything and don't linger too long on anything. Just look gently and repeat the lesson with each object your eyes light upon.

When practicing this lesson you might find a sense of freedom arise as you realize how often you look, but do not *see*. There may be a small sense of joy as your awareness clears – even for a brief moment. You are looking with the eyes of a child now and that lifts a burden of the past. We are only as old as our thoughts.

Look softly upon all you see today.

Lesson 10

My thoughts do not mean anything.

Yesterday you played with the idea that you see nothing as it is NOW. This lesson extends the thought by saying, "If I don't see anything in the present moment, I'm really not seeing at all. I'm just taking the past into the present and seeing that." This thinking is revolutionary. But don't worry about it! You are not expected to "get" these concepts right now. Indeed, if they are confusing – all the better!

Still, there is a serious point to be made. The thoughts "we think we think" must be questioned if we are to align with spirit. We ARE our thoughts. We are being asked now to realize that the thoughts we think are meaningless because they are always rooted in past events, and past events do not exist. This idea, that my thoughts do not mean anything, will be seen as a direct threat to the personal mind because it uses the past to keep the present moment from your awareness. You are not your personal mind. You are the mind behind your thoughts and it is this mind you are uncovering in each moment of NOW.

Practice today in this way: take your seat and close your eyes. Relax. Take a few deep, cleansing breaths and then breathe naturally. Place your awareness inside your body. How does it feel? Just notice. You might sense energy or vibration. This is normal. Try to relax with it and breathe.

Now, allow the thoughts in your mind to arise, noting each one. It might help to imagine that you have moved a chair to the center of the room, taken the seat, and are watching all thoughts as they parade in front of you. Witness their coming and going.

As each thought arises, briefly note the content or feeling, and say to yourself, "My thought about (_____) does not mean anything." Go back to the breath and then watch the next thought arise. Again, say to yourself, "This thought about (_____) does not mean anything."

Do this exercise for a minute or so, five times today. Set your cell phone or use some other reminder. It's only five minutes of your day. And, of course, if you forget, forgive yourself!

We cannot plant seeds in a fertile field until we have cleared away the weeds. These exercises are preparing the field of our mind. We are not using heavy equipment or machinery to clear these fields. We are doing it slowly, gently, and by hand. We are not alone clearing the field either. We have help. That is something to consider.

Lesson 11

My meaningless thoughts are showing me a meaningless world.

You see nothing as it is now because you associate everything you see with the past. If everything you see is associated with the past, how can you see it as it is now? And if you don't see it as it is now, does it really mean anything?

This lesson challenges our thinking yet again. The idea that meaningless thoughts create a meaningless world rests on the four fundamentals, two of which are very clear here: mind is the builder, and thoughts are things – energetic forms that have consequences.

We live in a world of thought and it is only as meaningful as our thoughts are. Everything begins and ends in the mind. How is this so? Let me give you an example.

Imagine you are in a room with several other people. You have entered the room thinking about what you will make for dinner, the place you will do your shopping, whether it will have all the ingredients you need, etc. The person on your right entered the room thinking about getting her car repaired. It has been making strange noises. She wonders whether she remembered to get her regular oil change last month. The person on your left is thinking about his wife. She has been away and he needs to pick her up at the airport in two hours. He is telling himself to remember to check the flight schedule before he leaves to make sure the plane is on time.

What is really going on here? First, no one is living in the moment. Each person is either reviewing her past, or anticipating his future. Second, each person's experience is interior. They are their own small mind having a completely different experience of being in the same room. In a very real sense, each person has created his or her own universe and is living separately within it.

"But my world is full of meaning!" you might think. "I care for my friends, my family, my coworkers!" To hear you live in a meaningless world can be threatening, but do not let this lesson cause you any fear or discomfort. The world IS full of meaning, but until you are conscious of your thoughts you miss so much of it.

This lesson should be practiced for a minute or so, three times today. Take your seat and close your eyes. Take a few deep, cleansing breaths. Relax your tummy and shoulders. Let all things go. When you feel ready, open your eyes, letting your gaze be soft. Now, look around the room without lingering on anything particular and, in your mind, say to yourself, "My meaningless thoughts are showing me a meaningless world." Be casual about this – even leisurely. Relax and let yourself feel supported as you look slowly around and repeat the words. When you've spent a minute or so looking, close your eyes again and relax. Silently, in your mind, repeat the lesson once more. Then take a few more breaths and open your eyes.

As with the past exercises, this is all about training the mind to be present in the moment. Until you are conscious of the thoughts you think you cannot be fully present.

Lesson 12

Our meaningless thoughts create a meaningless world. How can we not be fearful about this idea? Indeed, these next couple of lessons might feel "in your face," especially for those who have established a very comfortable sense of the world as it is now. For others, these lessons might offer a sense of freedom and expansiveness.

Most of us would agree that this world is in a state of chaos. War, weather, geopolitical and financial instability, earthquakes – all of these are "in our face" daily and they seem to be getting worse. Many people live with a chronic sense of low-grade worry about the state of their own lives and the world we live in. Something is clearly happening but we are unable to name it. Lesson 12 tells us exactly what it is.

I am upset because I see a meaningless world.

The world appears to be meaningless because we have forgotten who we are and what our purpose is. In our forgetting we have attached meaning to things that are meaningless.

For this practice, take your seat, close your eyes, and take three deep, cleansing breaths. Relax your shoulders. Now, open your eyes and slowly look around. Give all objects equal attention while you say, in your mind, "I think I see a fearful world, a hostile world, a chaotic world (you may choose another word here). I am upset because I see a meaningless world."

After a minute, end the practice by saying in your mind, "A meaningless world is upsetting." Relax and be comfortable before you move on with your day. Practice sessions should be done three times today and should last no more than a minute. If the session begins to feel uncomfortable, be gentle with yourself and allow it to end there.

Yesterday's lesson told you your thoughts are largely about meaningless things. This lesson takes you further. Whether you think of your world as "good" or "bad" does not matter – both are false. The truth is, we give the world all the meaning it has, and it is not based in the Reality of Source. There is meaning in this world but we must let go of the false before we can see the true. It is this we seek to find.

When we are willing to open our minds to the reality we have created, Reality itself becomes available. Slowly and gently, we are reaching toward this vision. It is as if we are on a trapeze. We must let go of one bar to reach the next. We fear the chasm below, but in Reality, there is no chasm.

Lesson 13

Basic physics tells us nature abhors a vacuum. In the last two days, our lessons have spoken of meaningless thoughts and a meaningless world. To think of a meaningless world creates anxiety. It leaves an empty space within. Only two things can fill this empty space: Source or the personal mind, also called the ego.

A meaningless world engenders fear.

What gives meaning to the world? For most people it is whatever the personal mind gives value. Indeed, the values of the personal mind are the foundation of this world. To let go of the values of the personal mind we must recognize they are meaninglessness. This means we must also face the fear that arises when we let go of a comfortable thought system.

Is this world meaningless? No, it most certainly is not. But its meaning is not what the personal mind would have us believe. The values of the personal mind are upside down. This is a completely accurate statement. The ego has created a world based on separate bodies, separate needs, and a hierarchy of order in which some deserve abundance while others do not. The ego has created a world in which it is possible to take without giving back. The ego sees separation from each other and from Source, which is Oneness Itself, as reality. It is not.

Today's practice sessions (there should be three) should be familiar by now. Take a seat and close your eyes. Relax. Take three deep, cleansing breaths. Let go of all tension. With eyes closed, say in your mind, "A meaningless world engenders fear." Then, gently open your eyes and slowly look about for no more than a minute or so. As you look, without focusing on anything in particular, say in your mind, "I am looking at a meaningless world." End the practice by closing your eyes again and saying to yourself, "A meaningless world engenders fear because I think I am in competition with God."

You may find this last sentence challenging. "I am not in competition with God! I love God!" you might respond. But consider this: if God is changeless, all knowing, Oneness, then why do we constantly question and resist what has been placed in front of us? "My neighbor is a fool." "My sister is jealous of me." "Those politicians are idiots." "Those foreigners shouldn't be here." If you are in disagreement about an aspect of your life, or your reality, you are in competition with what is and see yourself separate from it.

Why do we see ourselves as separate from God? Why do we not treat our neighbor as our self? Why do we value things that are valueless? Why do we live in fear?

We are asked not to overthink this lesson, but rather to notice the feelings that come up. In thinking about today's lesson, it may be helpful to consider the following quote from Dr. David Hawkins:

> In a completely integrated universe, on all levels, nothing accidental is possible.

If Source is everything then it follows logically that nothing can be outside It. If nothing is outside Source, nothing cannot have any meaning. Put another way, everything has meaning. No exceptions.

Lesson 14

God did not create a meaningless world.

In the past two weeks you have been told your thoughts and your world are both meaningless. The rug has been pulled out from under your feet. But you are still standing, are you not? Today's lesson tells you that while we may have created a meaningless world God did not and that is all that matters.

Everything begins and ends in the mind. Our mind sees one kind of world. God's Mind is a different matter. Now, hold onto your hat for you about to be given the keys to the kingdom. What God did not create DOES NOT EXIST. The world we see has nothing to do with Reality. It is of our own making and it is not real.

To consider this world unreal is a challenge, to say the least. We look, we see, we feel its reality. It appears solid. But the mind is a powerful thing, especially the mind that has forgotten its own creative ability. There is a great freedom in this lesson, a freedom beyond anything we can imagine right now.

Quantum physicist Fred Alan Wolf writes, "According to the tenets of the complementarity principle, there is no reality until that reality is perceived..." In other words, reality does not exist until we perceive it. But our perception is limited, so we do not see all there is. For example, we do not see all possible colors with our eyes, yet we know they exist. We do not hear all possible sounds with our ears, yet we know there are sounds all around us. We live in a three-dimensional world, but we know there are more dimensions. There are so many realities we do not perceive!

Nothing is outside of God. Yet we must acknowledge we do

not see it all. Therefore, we are not seeing all of God, and God IS Reality. In this lesson, you will begin to open to new worlds.

The practice periods today ask you to do two things. First, you will consider your own disturbing creations. Then you will replace them with peace. There are three, one-minute practice periods required. Can you give yourself three minutes today?

Take your seat and close your eyes. Take three, deep, cleansing breaths and relax. Feel your feet on the floor. Let your tummy be soft. Let your shoulders relax. Now, allow your mind to bring up the world. Stay relaxed, but allow its "horrors" to arise. There are many to choose from, are there not? Name each one specifically. Consider it briefly. Then say in your mind, *"God did not create that (war, cancer, airplane crash, villain) and so it is not real."*

When you have spent no more than one minute on your personal list of horrors, and acknowledged God did not create them, conclude the practice by saying in your mind, *"God did not create a meaningless world."*

This is your lesson. What God did not create can only be in your mind, apart from the Mind of God. Nothing apart from the Mind of God exists. Therefore, it has no meaning. It is all our own creation, and our own illusion. This Course will not leave you stuck here. It will take you far beyond your own mind. These exercises are preparing your mind for the journey.

If there is anything that disturbs you today, you should feel free to apply this lesson to it. Be very specific while saying in your mind, *"God did not create a meaningless world. God did not create (specify what it is that is disturbing you) and so it is not real."*

This is not a lesson in wishful thinking! Heisenberg's "uncertainty principle" proves that the mere act of conscious observation changes "reality." The mere observation of a photon of light alters its perceived state from that of a wave to a particle. The human eye perceives only in three dimensions, but physics tells us with certainty that there are more than three! We see only what we expect to see. As we enlarge our expectations, more becomes apparent. God did not create a meaningless world.

Lesson 15

My thoughts are images that I have made.

We were created to be creators. This world is our creation to the very last detail. Does that feel like too much responsibility? It most certainly is for the personal mind. Yet for the Self, it is simply part the Creator's gift.

What an amazing universe we have created! It is truly an astonishing feat of Mind! But we have become lost in our creation. We believe the ego's perception that we are merely our form rather than the Mind that created it. It is time to wake up.

Today's lesson introduces a phrase that is one of my personal favorites. ACIM says, "It is because the thoughts you think you think appear as images that you do not recognize them as nothing." There are two major points in this sentence and both rest on the idea of creating and then forgetting. First, the images we think we "see" externally are the product of consciousness that is accessed internally. The bodies and eyes with which we "see" and experience the world are "out-pictures" or "projections." They appear very real, but like pictures on a screen, they are the creation of something greater than the image itself.

The second point is, we have forgotten we are creating the images. In other words, the world we see on the outside is being projected from within. We are not IN this world. This world is IN us. We have it all backwards. It is thought that creates form. Mind is the builder. "Thoughts are images that we have made."

Once again, take your seat. Close your eyes and take three, deep, cleansing breaths. Relax your shoulders and your tummy. Relax your neck and your eyes. Just allow yourself this moment of quiet awareness. When you are ready, say in your mind, "My thoughts are images I have made." Then, gently open your eyes and look around the room and apply the idea to whatever you see. You might say, "This pencil is an image I have made." Or, "The snow is an image I have made." Or, "My cat is an image I have made." Go slowly here. Look softly. Take your time. Repeat this lesson three times today, for no more than a minute each time. If the words of the lesson pop into your mind today, go ahead and apply them to the specific thing in front of you. But be gentle about it.

If you have made it to lesson 15, you probably recognize that ACIM truly is about mind training. And, if you've made it this far, please know that you possess a mind that is perfectly capable of understanding this Course. Stay with it. The best is yet to come.

Lesson 16

I have no neutral thoughts.

Have you ever heard the saying, "If wishes were horses beggars would ride?" I remember feeling great disappointment when I first heard my mother repeat this old adage. It took a bit of life out of me. It wasn't exactly right either.

"Thoughts are things," said American mystic Edgar Cayce. "Thoughts are electric and feelings are magnetic," says energy teacher Jim Self. We may not be able to conjure a horse out of thin air, but thoughts and feelings have a force that has been clearly documented. Stressful thought affects the heart, stomach, nervous system, and brain. Thoughts of peace and loving kindness lower the body's production of stress hormones.

We have ignored the power of thought because we cannot see or measure it. It doesn't fit into the realm of material physics. This is a difficult concept to understand. For now, we are asked only to accept that thoughts have effects and that all thoughts contain an emotional component.

Yesterday we practiced with the idea that thoughts are images. Today we consider that, "I have no neutral thoughts." In other words, nearly every thought I have is qualified in some way. No thought is without some judgment.

Today's lesson should be practiced four or five times. Take your seat and close your eyes. Take three deep, cleansing breaths. Relax your shoulders, the space behind your eyes, your tummy, and your chest.

Now, in your mind, say to yourself, "I have no neutral thoughts." Then sit quietly, with closed eyes, and allow your thoughts to arise naturally. As each thought arises, hold it softly in your mind and say to yourself, "This thought about (_____) is not a neutral thought." Spend about one minute sitting in this manner.

Allow whatever thought arises to be as it is, no matter what its content – large or small. If a thought arouses uneasiness, pay attention to how it feels in your body and repeat, "This thought about (_____) is not a neutral thought, because I have no neutral thoughts."

Why do we not see clearly that thoughts have effects? Because of linear time! Quantum physics tells us that linear time is an illusion, and that all time exists NOW. But for those of us still "stuck" in linear time, the effect of our thoughts is often so drawn out that we do not recognize the link between a thought and its manifestation. To further complicate things, we are so regularly unaware of our thoughts we miss obvious connections when they do present themselves. Yet we have all experienced synchronicity – the almost mystical connection between a thought and an event.

Please do not underestimate the power of lesson 16. It is revolutionary! We are being asked to grow up and take responsibility for our thoughts. Every thought contributes to truth or illusion. Every thought either extends peace or war; love or fear. A neutral effect is impossible because a neutral thought is impossible. To know this is to begin awakening from the dream.

Lesson 17

I see no neutral things.

Yesterday we learned we have no neutral thoughts. And because what we think is reflected in what we see, we also see no neutral things. We see no neutral things because we have no neutral thoughts. Seems simple enough. But this lesson contains the fundamental idea that thought creates "reality." Perception is a mirror.

Thought comes before creation. If this were not so, perception itself would be impossible. This may seem complicated if you've never really considered it. Indeed, it is a reversal of what we have been taught. But all of our previous lessons have been saying this same thing. Our world arises continuously from the mind. We create and then we perceive what we have created. Mind is the creator.

Today's lesson should be practiced three or four times for a minute or so. Take your seat and keep your eyes open. Take three or four deep, cleansing breaths and relax into your body. Now, say in your mind, "I see no neutral things because I have no neutral thoughts." Then look about the room letting your eyes focus softly on things in your view. Spend just enough time on each thing to note it and say in your mind, "I do not see a neutral (_____) because my thoughts about (_____) are not neutral." For example, "I do not see a neutral (body, plant, pencil, computer, rug, calendar...) because my thoughts about (bodies, plants, pencils, computers, rugs, calendars...) are not neutral." After a minute, or even less if this practice makes you uncomfortable, close your eyes and rest for another minute.

There is one more idea to consider in today's lesson. Do not make any distinctions between what you perceive to be "good" or "bad," or what seems "alive" and what appears to be "inanimate." In reality, there is no difference. Everything is "alive" with energy we cannot see with the eyes. For example, physics tells us that all seemingly solid matter is composed of electrons that are continuously pulsating in and out of a wave/particle duality. That we do not perceive this with our eyes makes it no less true. All around us, everything is vibrating, dancing, in and out of "existence." Sounds like science. Sounds like magic. It is all a product of the mind.

This lesson is about cause and effect. Our world is a creation of group thought while each of us has our own experience of it. This is a fundamental lesson. Have fun. Play with it!

Lesson 18

I am not alone in experiencing the effects of my seeing.

This week challenged you to question the way you see the world. You practiced with the idea that "our thoughts are meaningless and they create a meaningless world." But you also learned that "God did not create a meaningless world." So how is it this world appears meaningless to so many?

The truth is we are never, ever, alone in our thoughts no matter how alone we may perceive ourselves to be in the moment.

Most people are familiar with the concept of ESP. Many have had the experience of "knowing" the phone was going to ring and who would be on the other end. While these are intriguing and interesting in themselves, the meaning of lesson 18 goes far beyond ESP or phone calls. We are now asked to deny the denial of our shared humanity. No less than this is possible.

The world we perceive individually is an illusion produced by group thought. Put another way, it is a dream we are having alone together. What does alone together mean? It means oneness having the experience of separation. It is this we must confront to heal the unhealed mind.

Practice today's lesson for a minute or so, three or four times today. Take your seat and close your eyes. Relax into your body. Gently place your awareness on your breath for about ten breaths. When you are ready, open your eyes and gently look around the room. Allow your gaze to rest softly on specific objects and say in your mind, "I am not alone in experiencing the effects of how I see (this paper, this wall, this tree, this snow…)."

Be mindful of any feelings that arise during this practice. It is important now to increase your level of awareness to include the feelings you experience. Conclude the practice by saying in your mind, "I am not alone in experiencing the effects of my seeing." Then close your eyes and rest gently for another minute or so.

Lesson 19

I am not alone in experiencing the effects of my thoughts.

You are not alone in experiencing the effects of your seeing. This was yesterday's lesson and today you receive its logical companion. Minds are joined and thoughts are shared. We see examples of shared thought over and over again but rarely do we consider it "normal." ACIM says this recognition is "rarely a welcome idea at first, since it seems to carry with it an enormous sense of responsibility." It may also feel like an invasion of privacy. Neither of these dilutes the truth. Thoughts are causes, "reality" is the effect, and we share it all.

Imagine a world where there are no private thoughts. At first, people might feel embarrassed, or threatened. There might be much confusion and resentment. "I had no idea I made Joe feel that way!" "She thinks THAT about ME?" You can probably come up with many scenarios.

But think of it this way; if minds could consciously be joined without words, the depth of our understanding would surpass anything we can imagine. Everything would be immediately transparent. No one could lie or deceive. Think of the laws we could get rid of! Think how effortless every business transaction would be. No one would ever pay more than the seller knew it was worth!

In many respects, this kind of transparency is beginning to happen on our planet now. Governments and businesses find it more difficult to hide information. What happens in one part of the world is instantly available to the other half via technology. A single teacher can reach millions of students. Language and borders are no longer the barriers they once were. This dream of separation is slowly being shown for the illusion it is. Our children are growing up in a different world. We are not alone in experiencing the effects of our thoughts.

Today's lesson reflects the idea of cause and effect. Thoughts are causes and their effects are what we perceive. Group thought is reality, as is group perception. This lesson also marks your first attempt at meditation. Do not let that word scare you. Meditation is natural and easy. You are asked to sit for about a minute, three times today.

Begin by taking your seat and closing your eyes. Place your awareness in the body. Relax your shoulders, your neck, and the area behind your eyes. Relax your tummy. Now place gentle awareness on the breath. Breathe naturally and do not force anything. Trust your body to breathe at it should. Your only job is to notice. Sit like this for about ten breaths, or more if you find it comfortable.

When you are relaxed, say in your mind, "I am not alone in experiencing the effects of my thoughts." Then simply allow your thoughts to arise naturally and notice each one. When you have noted a thought, say in your mind, "I am not alone in experiencing the effects of this thought about (the weather, dinner, my boss, the news of the world...)."

Don't overthink this lesson. You may have many thoughts or

no thoughts at all. When you have spent a minute or so watching your thoughts arise, conclude the practice. Say once more, "I am not alone in experiencing the effects of my thoughts," and relax comfortably. When you feel ready, the practice session is complete. Enjoy your day.

Lesson 20

I am determined to see.

This is a commitment you are making to yourself. If you are able to commit only partially now, be okay with it. There will come a time when you will see beyond anything you can imagine.

True seeing is inner vision. It is not difficult but it does require willingness to explore beyond the boundaries of the physical. ACIM calls this "seeing with the eyes of Christ." When you see with the eyes of Christ everything changes. What appears to be calamity now holds opportunity. What appears to be senseless becomes but a thread in the fabric of a weaver beyond time.

Today's practice sessions are different. Every half hour stop whatever you are doing. With eyes closed or open, slowly and positively say to yourself, "I am determined to see." If you are in a sticky situation, or if someone or something is particularly annoying, repeat the lesson in your mind before taking any action. If you forget the lesson, FORGIVE YOURSELF. Again, this is not a marathon! Be gentle with yourself. The last thing ACIM seeks is to promote your guilt or frustration. They will undo your learning. A happy learner is the most able to learn.

Have fun with this lesson. You may set your watch or phone on the half-hour as a reminder. You might also change your ring from one finger to another. But do try to give yourself the gift of this lesson. Its benefits are many.

Lesson 21

I am determined to see things differently.

According to family lore, my sister had a childhood habit of sharing biscuits with our dog, Joe. She would take a bite and then give a bite to him. The folks thought it cute at first, but one morning decided enough was enough, and told her to stop.

With the quick reasoning of a precocious two-year-old my sister decided that if she couldn't see them, they couldn't see her. With one hand she covered her eyes. With the other she continued reaching into the box of biscuits, taking a bite herself and then sharing with Joe.

I love this story for so many reasons: a child's delight in the company of her dog, the gentleness of Joe who patiently waits his turn, the sheer joy of sharing something between two species. But it is also a clear example of the split mind at work. Ego believes in separation, which means separate thoughts, separate seeing, and separate causes and effects.

The ego operates on the level of a two-year-old with its belief that each of us has thoughts, feelings, and experiences that can be hidden from each other. In other words, we still cover our eyes and decide, "If I can't see you, you can't see me. Nor can Source." Not true then, not true now. It is time to lift the veil. When the veil is lifted, this is what I see: God is One so there is nothing that is not God. Nor is there anything you and I can truly hide from each other.

When I lift the veil I see that all viewpoints are true to the viewer. However, unless I also see my Oneness with you, I will be unable to reconcile our different viewpoints. Seeing Oneness does not mean covering my eyes and assuming everyone sees what I see. It means opening my eyes and allowing that what is unique is still joined above the level of self.

It is true that each of us is unique. But we also share an

eternal consciousness in the Self. Seeing this shared eternal consciousness is the next step in our evolution as spiritual beings living in seemingly separate bodies. If we are to have peace this way of seeing is essential. There really is no getting around it.

Today's five practice sessions should last about a minute or so. Begin by taking your seat and closing your eyes. Relax into your body. Gently place awareness on the breath. Breathe naturally for about ten breaths, or until you can feel your whole body soften into centered calmness. Take whatever time you need.

When you are ready, repeat in your mind, "I am determined to see things differently." Then gently allow any person or situation that has caused you to be upset to come to the surface. Even little upsets are suitable. Notice the feeling that comes with the upset.

Hold the specific person or situation in your mind and say to yourself, "I am determined to see (the person or situation) differently." For example, you might say, "I am determined to see Fred differently." Or, "I am determined to see the broken computer differently." Try not to put any effort into seeing the person or situation in a different light. Just be present with the words and allow any shift to occur naturally. All we are doing now is making a statement of determination, not forcing change before its time. Just allow what arises and notice it.

End the session by repeating the lesson, "I am determined to see things differently." Notice how it feels to say these words. Take a minute or so to gently watch your breath before opening your eyes and continuing on with your day.

Again, if you forget a practice session, forgive yourself. You are only giving five minutes of your day to these practices, but the hustle and bustle of life can be a challenge. Remember, a little willingness is all that is needed.

Lesson 22

What I see is a form of vengeance.

My father was a career officer in the U.S. Air Force. Family dinners often focused on politics and world events, especially as my siblings and I got older. As you might imagine, arguments occurred about things like Vietnam, the Soviet Union, and the military budget. My father was emphatically supportive of the military. "The best defense is a good offense," he told us time and again. At the time I saw his point, but even then something seemed amiss. Now I know what it was and it is fully contained in today's lesson.

Before delving deeply into this lesson it will be helpful to share some concepts and terms. This lesson is very short but extremely powerful. To fully grasp its importance requires a foundation. Are you ready?

First: our true nature is spirit, not form. Second: everything in our universe vibrates at a certain frequency. This includes the spirit and the body. Invisible light vibrates at a higher frequency than dense, visible matter. So your invisible spirit vibrates at a higher frequency than your physical body.

Third: the higher frequency of spirit does not fit into the denser, lower frequency of the body. Let me repeat: the totality of your spiritual Self cannot presently be held in physical form. The two are not a match. As a former teacher described it, "The wind cannot all fit into the jar."

When we incarnate into physical form our first response is something like, "Holy Batman! I'm not all here!" A feeling of fear immediately follows. Thus, loss and fear are among the first emotions we have in physical form. Both are always associated with the body. The experience of being in a body is the experience of feeling alone, vulnerable, and capable of loss. The ego's response is, "I must defend."

Fear is a thought system based on defenselessness and attack. This cannot be overstated. It is the thought system of this world.

Rarely does the ego see itself as the attacker. It is always the victim. Hence my father's quote: "The best defense is a good offense." This closed-loop thinking has become our unquestioned reality. We can see it in every single conflict – global and personal. As long as I perceive myself as separate, vulnerable, and destructible, I must need a form of defense because I perceive attack as inevitable. Make no mistake: defense is the first act of warfare. Can you see this?

Would it not be a gift to escape the cycle of fear and attack that is the thought system of this world? Today's lesson offers the only way out. Do not be concerned if you find yourself arguing its validity. That is fine. You are asked only this: look at your thoughts and the experiences that arise from your thoughts. Do not take my word for it. Do not take ACIM's word for it. Have your own experience and come to your own truth. That is all that is required of you.

Today's lesson accurately describes our current thought system. It is the thought system of anyone who thinks he or she *is* his or her body – which describes most of us. What the unconscious, personal mind always sees is a form of vengeance. Vengeance takes a thousand different forms. Learn to recognize them. Fear will be behind them all.

Practice today's lesson for about a minute, five times today. Take your seat and close your eyes. Let your feet rest gently on the floor. Let your shoulders relax, and then your arms and hands. Relax the area behind your eyes and then place your awareness gently on the breath for about ten breaths. Take as much time as feels right to you and then open your eyes and look around. Let your gaze softly focus on specific objects and say calmly in your mind:

I see only the perishable. I see nothing that will last. What I see is not real. What I see is a form of vengeance.

End the practice period by asking gently, "Is this the world I want?"

God is in all in a very literal sense. But we must first see and then refuse to acknowledge fear as the ground of our experience in this world. This is the beginning of real love. Awakening to it is why we are here.

Lesson 23

I can escape from the world I see by giving up attack thoughts.

Today's lesson builds upon yesterday's. You have been told your thought creates your reality. Every image, all people, all things, all places, and all events are of your own making. Mind is the cause and physical reality is the effect. If you still find this difficult to digest do not be concerned. However, understanding this concept is where your true power lies. It is where the human species begins its transition into spiritual adulthood.

The world you see outside is a mirror of what is inside. There is no point asking the world to change. It is incapable of change until you change your own thoughts.

Currently, most human beings see a world of separation, scarcity, mindless competition, and brutality. Just watch any football game and its accompanying commercials. Go into any movie theater and bear witness to the previews. Watch the evening news. The multi-million-dollar salaries we pay those who bring us these images are testament to what we currently believe has value. It is valueless. Yet we watch these images and do not recognize who is behind the camera. It is us.

We are the image-makers, created in the image of God, with God's ability to create. We have created this world and everything in it, down to the last leaf on the last tree.

If you are facing illness or the loss of a loved one, these words are very, very difficult to accept. They should never, ever be used to inflict guilt or blame. In this world, where we have come to remember our divine inheritance, mistakes in thinking are part of the requirement. We are literally re-membering our Oneness. This is why forgiveness is a fundamental aspect of the new thought system ACIM brings with its lessons. Forgiveness is like sacred oil in the machinery of enlightenment. Its value cannot be overstated.

Today's lesson asks you to notice your thoughts more deeply. As you pay more attention to your mind you will notice the quality of its thoughts. When most people start to pay attention to their thoughts they are often taken aback at their degree of negativity.

Exactly what is an "attack thought"? An "attack thought" is any thought that leaves you feeling vulnerable, separate, or alone. If you think for any reason, in any circumstance or relationship, that something can be done TO you, that is an "attack thought."

An "attack thought" is a belief that you are a body only, that others are bodies only, and that we can actually hurt each other at a level that is unrecoverable. None of this is true. The body may be hurt. It can even "die." But your Self can never be attacked. Furthermore, because we are One, any attack you make upon another is an attack upon yourself.

Five practice sessions of a minute or so are asked today. Take your seat and relax. Take three, deep, cleansing breaths and then look softly around the room and repeat in your mind, "I can escape the world I see by giving up attack thoughts."

Now, close your eyes. Place about half of your awareness on your breath and the other half on gently noticing any thoughts that arise. You might recognize discomfort in your body, in your heart or solar plexus. You might see a brief scene from the news or a past experience that creates mental agitation. As you notice the feeling say in your mind, "I can escape the world I see by giving up attack thoughts about (whatever subject arises)."

Hold each attack thought in your mind as you repeat the lesson, and then let it go. Soon, another thought will arise. Say again, "I can escape the world I see by giving up attack thoughts about (my sister's jealousy, my boss's criticism, my partner's selfishness, my lack of patience…)."

It does not matter if you are the attacker or the attacked in this practice. Because we are One, both are the same. When you have practiced for about a minute, clear your mind and relax again. Take three, deep cleansing breaths and, say in your mind, "I can escape the world I see by giving up attack thoughts." Feel this blessing, for that is exactly what it is. Then move on with your day.

As you go about your day apply this thought to any situation that creates discomfort, anger, or even mild resistance. The more you witness your own thoughts, the easier this training becomes. The deepest learning comes through experience. Experience your thoughts! Watch what they tell you about your world. If your car breaks down, if the computer blows up, if someone cuts you off in traffic, if the bank calls to remind you your loan payment is due, remember you are One with your Self and Source. You are invulnerable.

Lesson 24

I do not perceive my own best interests.

Have you ever had the experience of being disappointed about something that has not gone the way you'd hoped, only to discover in retrospect that it was actually in your favor? If so, you have had a direct experience with today's lesson.

For the past three weeks, ACIM has emphasized two ideas that appear to be opposites: first, we create our own separate reality, and second, we are One. Here is how they are related: if I perceive only separateness that is what I will see. If I perceive myself without direct connection to my Source, then I will not perceive my experiences as part of a whole.

Imagine the universe as an immensely complicated piece of woven cloth. This planet and everything on it is but a strand in a single thread. The personal self is completely unequipped to perceive the whole cloth. In fact, it thinks its little place in the thread is all there is. So it travels blindly along confused, hurt, and angry when it bumps into things, unravels itself, or gets all tangled up. Its limited information, which it is convinced is all the information there is, makes self-guidance risky at best. There is another way, but it requires admitting the ego knows nothing.

There are five practice periods today, each two minutes long. Your eyes will be closed for this practice, as it is a form of meditation.

Take your seat and close your eyes. Take a few deep, cleansing breaths. Now place half of your awareness on the breath and half on feeling within your body. Watch your breath and sense your internal state of being. Relax into it. Give yourself a minute or so to just sit like this, noticing and feeling.

When you are ready, repeat in your mind, "I do not perceive my own best interests," and then allow a conflict in your life to arise. Look at the conflict and consider how you would like it to be resolved in a way that most benefits you. Perhaps you want a new contract to be signed this week, or need a check to come by Monday. Perhaps you are arguing with someone and want your ideas to prevail. Be clear about your goals for each unresolved issue. There may be more than one goal for each situation. For example, you might say in your mind, "In the situation involving (_____), I would like (_____) to happen, and (_____) to happen." Play with this as much as you like. Enjoy it.

If you are practicing sincerely, you may realize there are lots of things you want to happen. Some of those things might even be in conflict with each other. It may come to you that your goals are not really clear and that, regardless of what happens, you may not be totally satisfied. That's okay. Don't get attached to any outcome. This is just an experience.

When you have created your list of goals or outcomes for a situation, say in your mind, "I do not perceive my own best interests in this situation," and then move on to the next situation that arises.

After a couple of minutes, end the practice by placing your awareness again on the breath. Feel within your body for any stress or tension and breathe it out. Sit for a minute or so and then gently open your eyes and continue your day.

Here are a few quotes from the 2011 movie, *The Best Exotic Marigold Hotel*. They illustrate this lesson perfectly!

Evelyn: *"Nothing here has worked out quite as I expected."*

Muriel: *"Most things don't. But sometimes what happens instead is the good stuff."*

Sonny: *"Everything will be all right in the end... if it's not all right then it's not yet the end."*

Lesson 25

I do not know what anything is for.

Today is one of the last lessons in which you will be asked to experience the confusion of the ego. It is very difficult to admit that we are confused because it can leave us feeling open and vulnerable. We will not stay in this place very long, but it is crucial that you see the personal mind for what it is.

ACIM defines the ego as the entire self we think we are: a separate entity, a separate mind, a separate physical body, with its own separate will, its own personal past, present, and future. If we are to know the Self, the mistaken identity of the ego's thought system must be exposed.

Who we are is an eternal part of the Whole, forever linked with each other and with our Creator. Awakening to your Self is why you are here. Who in their right mind would choose to remain asleep in this illusion? Or, as a former teacher once asked of us, "How's it working for you?"

When your true nature goes unrecognized, the illusion is confirmed and treated as reality. If you believe the illusion is reality, you will never see the purpose of anything. If you cannot see the purpose of anything, you cannot know what anything is for. It's that simple. When you see only with the ego you see only the personal, the separate, and the most superficial. You see only the stone skipping across the pond.

A total of twelve minutes is asked today, in six sessions of two minutes each. This is how mind training effects true change. You are literally rewiring your thought system.

Take a seat and keep your eyes open. Relax into your breathing. When you are ready, say in your mind, "I do not know what anything is for." Then slowly, gently look around the room. Let your eyes rest on whatever catches your attention within the room or outside of it, human or nonhuman, "important" or "unimportant," and apply the lesson to it. For example, you might say, "I do not know what that tree is for." Or, "I do not know what this rug is for." Or, "I do not know what this pencil is for."

When you have spent a couple of minutes looking, and repeating the lesson, close your eyes and place your awareness on the breath for about five to ten breaths. Relax and savor the moment of respite. You have just opened your mind. Let the fresh air in.

Lesson 26

My attack thoughts are attacking my invulnerability.

About 25 years ago I went to a conference on aging. The keynote speaker was Deepak Chopra, who told us of an amazing experiment. A group of elderly nursing home residents were given mental aptitude tests. Their scores were recorded and then instead of returning to the nursing home, they were moved to a new residence. The new residence had been reconstructed to resemble a home in the time when the residents were in their prime, physically, mentally, and emotionally. After about a month in their prime environment the residents were tested again for mental aptitude. The results were astounding. Every single new test score was significantly higher than the original taken in the nursing home.

Dr. Chopra explained that the experiment offered concrete evidence of brain plasticity: mental acuity was not a fixed thing. The brain is affected by the thoughts we think. If we think we will age in a certain way, we do. This knowledge applies directly to today's lesson. Attack thoughts have effects that reach far and wide.

What is an "attack" thought? It is any thought of guilt, fear, or judgment. Attack thoughts are a fundamental expression of the ego, which sees itself as alone, vulnerable, and limited in time.

Who is it we attack most? It is our selves, of course. I am the origin of every attack thought I have about myself. I must first think myself vulnerable or attack would be impossible.

In truth, we are not vulnerable, but because we believe we are, a false image now seems real. The cycle of victim, perpetrator, and savior is born within the personal mind. It is a cycle that can be cured only at the level of its cause. "Nothing except your own thoughts can attack you. Nothing except your own thoughts can make you think you are vulnerable. And nothing except your own thoughts can prove to you that this is not so."

Practice this lesson six times today, for about two minutes each.

Take your seat and say in your mind or out loud, "My attack thoughts are attacking my invulnerability." Then close your eyes and relax. Now place half your focus on the breath and the other half on watching whatever mental thoughts arise. Breathe normally and don't force anything. After a time you will notice areas of concern that may feel like worry, irritation or even outright fear or anger. You may feel a sense of depression or heaviness. Let it come up. It is there to inform you of something.

If you can, name the thought or feeling. For example, you might say, "I feel a sense of irritation. I am concerned about (_____)." Then consider every possible outcome of the concern. Be specific. You might say, "I am afraid (_____) will happen if (_____) happens." You should come up with several specific concerns and fears. Focus carefully on each one. After you have listed the outcomes of which you are afraid, say in your mind, "That thought is an attack upon myself."

This practice might bring up all kinds of discomfort. That's okay. After about two minutes spent with your thoughts, conclude by saying in your mind, "My attack thoughts are attacking my invulnerability."

End this session by going back into awareness of the breath. Relax the body. Breathe into any areas of tension and let them go. When you are ready, continue with your day.

During the day today, pay attention to any feelings of tension, irritation, or fear, however trivial. Use this as an opportunity to repeat in your mind, "My attack thoughts are attacking my invulnerability." Notice how this feels each time.

Lesson 27

Above all else I want to see.

When I first practiced this lesson we were experiencing a blinding snowstorm. It seemed a wonderful metaphor.

The body's eyes cannot be relied upon for true sight, for it is the heart that sees truly. Quiet, peace, and calmness enhance true seeing. The jarring loudness of this world draws attention away from true sight and we are suffering for it.

To see truly, we must remember our invulnerability because sometimes the moment feels uncomfortable and we may want to flee from it into mental thinking. So true seeing also means being patient and sometimes courageous.

Today's practice is very simple. You are asked to remember to repeat the lesson in your mind throughout the day. But you are asked to repeat it often – every 15 minutes. In a way, this is like spending the day in prayer or mindfulness meditation. Today's practice takes mind training to a new level. You will experience an inner retreat, even though your body may be moving in the outer world.

Don't worry if you don't believe the words, "Above all else, I want to see." It doesn't matter. The words will do their job. Just go about your day and try to remember the lesson. As you repeat it, relax and be present in the moment. Look around and take a breath. Try to experience the words inside yourself.

True learning means knowing, and knowing is a product of experience. Play with this lesson. Say the words and see where they take you. There is no "right" way to do it, except to practice it and see what comes up in the moment! If you forget (and you will) do not make yourself suffer! Guilt is an impediment to learning and has no value. Just try to remember the next time.

Have fun. Be at peace. Enjoy yourself today.

Lesson 28

Above all else I want to see things differently.

Today's lesson is a more specific application than the one practiced yesterday. You are asked to apply the words to objects in your view.

You are making a series of "definite commitments" in these lessons, but whether you keep the commitment is not of primary concern now. If you are willing to make the commitment for today, you are on the path. All journeys begin with one step and you are at the beginning.

Why does it matter how you see a table, a chair, or a rug? In itself, it is not important. The point is, you see lots of separate things, which means you are not seeing deeply. There is a light, literally and figuratively, in everything around you. It is the same light that is in all things, in this world and, indeed, in the entire universe. The light is a vibration, a frequency that lifts all things. You can feel it in your body. Most of us cannot see it yet but feeling it is just fine.

Here is the point: When I say, "Above all else I want to see things differently," I am making a commitment to withdraw my preconceived ideas about the world. I am opening my mind to the possibility of a deeper experience of reality. I am decoupling my vision from the physical as the sole arbiter of reality. I am not using the past to define the present. I am allowing the thing to present itself to me now, rather than telling it what it is based on my past experience or future expectation.

Seeing a table differently "is not an exclusive commitment." My willingness to see a table differently applies to all other things I see, as all things are joined in Oneness. The table, seen in its Oneness, literally shows me the purpose of the universe, which is a shared joy in the creation of all things. Nothing is excluded from this joy – not the table, not the rug, not the plant, not the pencil, not the person.

As you practice today, play with what you see. Be committed but do not force anything. Allow what you look upon to reveal its purpose to you. Even if it is just for a moment, lift your judgment. Pretend you have never seen that table, that chair, that plant. What comes to mind? What do you see or feel in the table, the chair or plant that you haven't noticed before?

To practice today, take your seat and relax. Take a few deep, cleansing breaths. Let all tension go in your body. When you are ready, say in your mind, "Above all else I want to see things differently." Then look around with gentle eyes and allow your gaze to focus on specific objects.

Rest your gaze on the object and say, in your mind, "Above all else I want to see this (_____) differently." Be slow and thoughtful. Do not hurry. This whole practice takes only 12 minutes of your day. Surely you have the time.

Enjoy. Be happy. Be very pleased with yourself.

Lesson 29

God is in everything I see.

The last two lessons asked you to make "seeing" a priority among your desires. In this lesson, we learn that true seeing is the recognition that the light of God shines in every single thing.

You might consider it silly to think of a table as having God in it. You might believe God does not exist in a glass of water. Yet, if you think of God as pure energy, then God is in everything. And if you think of thought as energy, you can begin to see creation in its most fundamental sense. The mind creates through thought, and God is in your mind.

The application of today's lesson opens the door to appreciation, love, and open-mindedness. We begin to see the unlimited Oneness that is our world. There is a light in every single thing that surrounds us, both animate and inanimate. Everything is connected. Nothing is as it appears. For many, this is difficult to absorb. It certainly goes beyond the way most people see the world. We have a hard enough time seeing God in our neighbor, much less in the tree in the back yard.

And yet, we are learning that nothing exists outside the Mind of God. This is an entirely logical thought. There can be only one First Cause. Everything that exists contains It, and nothing exists apart from It. We are inseparable and completely free all at once. What a wonderful thing to know!

Today's practice follows a now familiar pattern. Take your seat and place your awareness inside. Let go of the world and allow the body to relax. Place your attention on the breath for about ten breaths. Don't force anything. Allow the breath to be as it wants to be. It will settle itself into its own relaxed pattern – just watch it.

Now, with eyes open, say in your mind, "God is in everything I see." With soft eyes, look around the room, out the window. Without judgment, let your gaze fall on specific objects, people or things, and slowly repeat the lesson. For example, you might say, "God is in this printer. God is in this lamp. God is in this piece of paper. God is in the asphalt. God is in the tree. God is in my hand. God is in the air. God is in my breath."

Try to practice for two minutes, six times today. At least once an hour, take a minute and look around as you say the words unhurriedly. Give yourself these brief moments of restfulness and contentment today. Notice how it makes you feel to practice the lesson. It should bring peace and certainty, both are which your right.

Lesson 30

God is in everything I see because God is in my mind.

For a month now you have been hearing over and over that this world is a projection of your own mind. You have also been learning that it is possible to "see" and that true seeing is what you really want. Seeing truly means seeing through the eyes of God. Because God is in your mind, you are unlimited in your capacity to see.

Think of it this way: if we are in God's Mind, and God is in ours, then we must share a mind. Indeed, our creative power comes through God's Mind. This is how we created this world and it is why we cannot be separate from our own creation. True vision sees that we are not in the world, but the world is in us, or more correctly, our mind.

Our experience is always the effect of where we choose to focus the attention of our consciousness. And we have chosen to be preoccupied with separation. We spend all our efforts in support of it. This simple choice has had enormous consequences. But it can be undone. Indeed, it will be undone because it isn't real. Wholeness is reality in each and every moment.

Today you will practice mindfulness again. Try to sit with this thought on the hour if you can. Simply take your seat or stand where you are and look about. In your mind, say to yourself, "God is in everything I see because God is in my mind." Feel the words resonate within your body. As you look about the room, at other people around you, at the trees outside, or whatever is in your view, understand the words apply to things beyond your present range of seeing. Real vision is unlimited by time or space. It does not depend on the body's eyes. You are connected to all things, in all places, right now.

In addition to the hourly practice, give yourself about five to ten minutes in the morning and evening to sit with this lesson. Close your eyes, relax your body, and place your awareness on the breath. When you are ready, say in your mind, "God is in everything I see because God is in my mind." Simply watch what thoughts come up. When a thought arises, make a note of it. Then repeat the lesson and go back to the breath. Thoughts will arise. Repeat the lesson and place your awareness on the breath. You should feel a sense of calmness and clarity in these longer practices. Enjoy them.

Lesson 31

When a good friend first presented this idea to me I was aghast. If I had not trusted her wisdom and learning I would have dismissed it out of hand. Instead, I thought about it, explored it, studied it, and found that indeed her words made sense. Today's lesson is:

I am not a victim of the world I see.

This lesson is very difficult to believe if you are mired in a world of duality – a world in which everything can be separated into good or bad, right or wrong. The idea of eternal Innocence is nearly inconceivable to most.

ACIM says we can imagine many things, for we have the power to do so in a spectacular way. We can imagine we can be hurt. We can imagine we are upset. We can imagine we know all about justice and injustice. We can imagine we are bodies limited by form and subject to all manner of disease. That is fine if we wish it so.

However, "Ideas leave not their source." We are an idea in the Mind of God, and we cannot escape our Innocence no matter how powerful our preoccupation with separation might be.

You cannot be a victim of the world you see because all that you experience is your creation. You have used your power to directly and deliberately call it to you. Now, you are free to say, "I do not like what I have called to me." You are free to ask yourself, "Is this an energy I wish to continue with or would I like to create something else?" You are also free to decide, "I will remain confused about my creation by judging it unworthy of me." But if you choose to judge you will never free yourself. You will remain in the cycle of powerlessness.

Today's lesson is a major step toward freedom. It is an undoing of the lie humanity has been taught for eons. It is time for us to take on your true power of creation.

Today's practice consists of two, three to five minute meditations in the morning and evening. Mindfulness of the lesson should also be practiced throughout the day.

For the morning and evening sessions, take your seat and relax. Place your awareness on the breath. Look around slowly, and repeat in your mind, "I am not a victim of the world I see." You may repeat the lesson two or three times, and then close your eyes. Allow your thoughts to arise, as they will. Keep part of your attention on the breath, while watching dispassionately what comes up in your inner world. You might notice certain feelings are attached to your thoughts. Watch these feelings come and go. As you watch the thoughts and feelings, say slowly in your mind, "I am not a victim of the world I see." You may wish to use the lesson as a mantra along with your breath, but do whatever feels natural. There is no hurry.

Take this lesson with you today. Remind yourself often that you are not a victim of the world you see. This is a declaration of independence for yourself and for the world. While you may not see it yet, it is also a declaration of forgiveness and safety. This lesson says you are bound by nothing. You are completely free. This is no small thing – it is the beginning of the end of illusion.

Lesson 32

Most people have heard of the terms "cause" and "effect." For example, the heat from the sun causes surface water to evaporate. When the temperature sinks below freezing ice is formed. The idea of cause and effect has been a central theme of the past few lessons. However, it is critical to your development that you understand your current understanding of cause and effect is limited and limiting. It is limited because it views the material world as cause and mind as its effect. This is completely backward. It is why you cannot be a victim of the world you see. You are the cause of your world, not its effect. You cannot be the victim of your own invention.

I have invented the world I see.

The lesson today is literal. Let me repeat: today's lesson is literal. It applies to both your inner and outer worlds – which are exactly the same. The truth is simply this: mind is the cause and this world is the effect. As I said, most of humanity today is in agreement that the opposite is true.

We have been taught that the physical brain and the body are the source of our experience. And indeed, those who seem to do "best" in this world appear quite adept at manipulating its external manifestations. For this reason, it is easy to understand why so many people continue to value and trust the external more than the internal.

There is nothing wrong with doing well and enjoying the things of this world. But to value this world above the mind is to seek comfort in an illusion rather than its source. It is time to reconsider cause and effect.

Today's lesson asks only that you pay more attention to what is going inside your mind. Focus your efforts on awareness of the content and quality of your thoughts.

Many people are not willing to accept responsibility for their thoughts until they have exhausted all other options, and the choice to see differently is forced upon them. This is completely avoidable if cause and effect are understood. We have invented the world we see. Everything outside is a mirror of what is inside, and because we share a Mind we share in this creation.

Practice today's lesson as you did yesterday. Twice a day, in the morning and evening, take a seat and place your awareness on the breath. Look around at the outside world and say in your mind, "I have invented the world I see." Allow yourself to relax as you repeat the lesson two or three times. Then close your eyes and settle even more deeply, keeping part of your awareness on the breath.

As you sit for three to five minutes, allow and notice your

thoughts. Do not judge or dwell on any in particular. Part of your mind should watch the breath, part of your mind should watch your thoughts, and part of your mind should slowly, calmly, repeat the lesson. Breathe. Watch. Say in your mind, "I have invented the world I see." Do not strain yourself in any way about this. Just try it and allow the lesson to unfold. It will be perfect.

Hold this lesson in your mind throughout the day. If any situation arises that causes the least amount of discomfort, repeat the lesson. Feel the lesson in your body. There is nothing that is not a part of you. You are perfectly safe because of this.

Last, please know that because we share one Mind, a change in one mind affects us all. Your healed mind heals mine.

Lesson 33

When I am conscious of it I recognize that my perception can shift from being "out there" to being "in here." When I am inside looking out, the world is different. It's almost as though I'm in a bubble, safe and sound, while watching a play going on in front of me. I'm with the play but I'm not in the play.

There is another way of looking at the world.

Today you will practice shifting your perception from being "out there" in the play, to being "inside" and watching it. You will watch from a place of silence and peace. Today's practice aids in the cultivation of inner knowing. Two practice periods of five minutes are requested.

Take your seat in the morning and again in the evening. Place your awareness gently on the breath. Relax your body. When you are ready, with open eyes, unhurriedly glance around the room. Gently notice what you perceive as outside yourself, and then close your eyes and place the same awareness on how you feel inside. Just notice. Be casual and don't hurry.

Approach this exercise as you would any break in your day. The only difference is your intention. Sit and look around your world without attaching to anything, then close your eyes and survey your inner kingdom. Be aware of the outside and how you feel inside. This is preparation for future work.

When you have spent five minutes in peaceful awareness, say to yourself, "There is another way of looking at the world." Notice how it feels inside to say the words. Just notice. When you are ready, open your eyes.

As you go about your day, take as many moments as you can to look around and say in your mind, "There is another way of looking at the world." You may do so with eyes open or closed. Play with how this feels. If you experience any discomfort, anger, or irritation with what is in front of you at the moment, close your eyes and repeat the lesson. Relax. Don't take yourself too seriously. You are giving yourself permission to experience your world in another way.

Have fun. Be gentle with yourself today. Enjoy this lesson.

Lesson 34

I could see peace instead of this.

At some point in life all of us reach a place where we have had enough. We have gone as far as we can with a job, a relationship, a living situation, an illness, or a belief system. It doesn't matter what the specific issue is, we just know that what we have been doing with it isn't working anymore.

This is called suffering. It may seem ironic or unfair, but it is one of the best forms of spiritual teaching. For many, it is their only spiritual teacher. We avoid, we substitute, we divert, and finally the suffering become inescapable. It forces itself into our mind and will not leave without being recognized. It is often at this point we say to ourselves, "There must be another way," and when we do something opens up.

Suffering is mental. Even bodily suffering is largely in the mind. In its most fundamental form, suffering is resistance to the moment. We resist, and resist, and resist, until we wear ourselves out. Then we "give in" and a sense of peace often follows. We realize the futility of arguing with what is, we allow it to be, and immediately a burden is lifted. This can often take years.

Being unfamiliar with our own minds, most of us don't even recognize our resistance. We go along with a chronic sense of unease and discomfort until the energy of our disquiet builds to a point that we cannot ignore it. At that point, we find a way to release the energy either by lashing out, getting physically ill, or manifesting a "situation," and the cycle starts again.

Peace of mind requires consciously allowing the present moment to be as it is. Please do not confuse this with passivity: it is an active choice. It can involve hard work, searching, and radical acceptance. It is not for the weak of heart. Today's lesson, "I could see peace instead of this," is for those who have had enough of suffering as their spiritual teacher and are ready for a change.

Today's practice asks for a total of fifteen minutes of your day. Practice is composed of three five-minute meditations. Try to do one in the morning, one in the afternoon, and just before bedtime. These practices will improve your mental state.

Take your seat and close your eyes. Relax the body and place your awareness gently on the breath. When you feel ready, begin to watch all thoughts that arise in your mind. Pay attention to any fearful thought or situation that makes you feel anxious, unloved, or unloving. These may appear unexceptional at first. For example, thoughts such as "I may be late for work if I do this practice now" would apply. Any thought that is not peaceful is fair game.

As each thought emerges into your awareness, note it. Note also the feeling it arouses in the body. Then slowly say in your mind, "I could see peace instead of this." Stay with your breath as another fearful or negative thought arises. Note the thought or situation and slowly repeat the lesson again.

Let the feeling of the lesson sink in. Do you notice any difference in the body when you say the lesson? Does it relax just a bit? Often the body recognizes suffering before the mind does. The body is an important internal messenger for spirit so tuning into it can be a powerful tool.

If you cannot think of any fearful or unloving situations, simply say the lesson slowly in your mind, like a mantra. Don't hurry or force anything. Sit in peace, watch your breath, and repeat the lesson slowly.

During the day today repeat the lesson any time your sense of peace is threatened in any way. You may notice this first in your body. Your stomach may feel tense or your jaw may tighten. Use the body as the messenger it was meant to be. Simply take a breath and place your attention inside yourself. Then say the lesson in your mind, and move into your next moment of experience.

If you notice your lack of peace, and repeat the lesson today, you are well on the path. This does not mean stressful situations will not come up. It means you have opened the door to a new way of responding. This is the beginning of real change.

The world that you perceive can add nothing to Source or to your Oneness with It. But your belief in its reality can blind you. You cannot perceive this world as Reality and know Source as real because only Source is Real. The choice of what is Truth is not yours to make.
– *The Message of* A Course in Miracles, E. Cronkhite

Lesson 35

My mind is part of God's. I am very holy.

The personal self is obsessed with the idea of lack because it was made by your perceived separation from God – which IS lack. It perceives other personal selves as real only to validate its own reality.

– *The Message of* A Course in Miracles, E. Cronkhite

The lessons now change as you learn more specifically about the truth of what you are. It is as if you are on the shores of a great ocean and you are saying, "Yes. I am worthy of knowing myself. I accept the new identity which has always been mine, but which until now has been hidden from me."

Your true nature, joined with mine, is timeless and immortal. Together, we are the Mind that underlies the entire manifested world. Seeing this takes practice. It is as though we have lived in a land that rarely sees the sun, and have gotten so accustomed to the monotony of gray that we cannot imagine there might be another place that contains a whole variety of color and light. The lesson for today tells you where you come from and what you are beyond the dullness of this world.

What is true is true and must always be true. Is it ever true that the sun is not there, even if it has been hidden by the clouds?

The personal self believes it is its own source. This idea is meaningless and frightening so it tries to join with other personal selves in special relationships to validate its own existence. But it also insanely attacks other personal selves to make itself appear strong. It cannot, however, question its own origins because the belief that it is independent is the very foundation of its existence. But your mind is part of God and you are One with the Whole of It. This is the one thing you cannot choose for your Self.

Practice three times today, for about five minutes each. Try to remain mindful in between practice times. Every mind, no matter how seemingly separate, is part of your mind and God's. This includes the guy who cuts you off in traffic or the gal who speaks rudely to you on the phone. They are part of the "Whole

I" too, even if they don't know it in the moment. Believe it or not, your practice today will reach their mind because all minds are One. This IS how you serve.

Today's practices are a bit different. Again, there are three. Begin as usual by taking your seat. Place your awareness on your breath and relax your body. When you are ready, with eyes open, repeat the lesson slowly. Say to yourself, "My mind is part of God's. I am very holy." Then close your eyes, keeping part of your awareness on the breath and begin to think of various ways to describe yourself. For example, you might say, "I see myself as a straight shooter," or "I see myself as impatient," or "I see myself as successful," or "I see myself as unfulfilled," or "I see myself as overweight." Be creative and truthful.

Feel the feeling that arises as you define yourself. It doesn't matter if your descriptive words are "positive" or "negative"; they are all equally unreal because you are not seeing yourself through the eyes of holiness.

After you have named yourself each time, say in your mind, "But my mind is part of God's. I am very holy." For example you might say, "I see myself as fearful, but my mind is part of God's. I am very holy." Feel these words! Notice the difference between the two ways of seeing yourself – first as a personal mind, and then as part of something completely inclusive, eternal, and loving.

As you practice the seated meditation, you may find that no descriptive words arise in your mind. Don't strain to come up with anything. Just go back to watching your breath and repeat the lesson gently in your mind. When a new thought arises, as it will, watch it for what it says about your personal self. For example, a thought might arise about a recent time you disagreed with someone. Say in your mind, "I see myself as thoughtless." Feel this feeling. Then say to yourself, "But my mind is part of God's. I am very holy." Now feel this feeling too. It points to your real Self.

As often as possible today, become of aware how you might describe yourself in the moment. Repeat the attribute and then repeat the lesson. If you cannot think of anything, just repeat the lesson, letting its truth sink in.

Lesson 36

My holiness envelops everything I see.

ACIM has only a few "rules." One of them regards the concept of "Truth." What is True must always be True or it is not True. There cannot be a little Truth; it must be wholly True, or it is false. So when a lesson tells me, "My mind is part of God's. I am very holy," there can be no halfway Whole. My mind is forever part of God's Mind or it isn't. There is no negotiation on this point.

The world "we think we think" we see is a completely made-up story. It is a world in which conflict is normal, pain to be expected, and loneliness constant. This is not the world God created. Remember, what is true must always be true. Source is either all loving or not. It cannot be only partially loving or loving only under certain conditions. All of Source's creations are created in Love. If Love is not present, you can be sure illusion is.

The personal mind created and sustains this three-dimensional "reality." This world is a frightening and insecure place. Fortunately, there is a greater Reality that is more significant than this one. It has more dimensions than this one. When Jesus said, "My father's house has many rooms," he was referring to the idea of multidimensional reality.

Today's lesson shows us True Vision. It challenges the personal mind's mistaken projection of separation. If my mind is part of God's and I am Whole I, then everything I see with True Vision must also be Whole and part of me. What is Whole cannot be separated from Source or from anything created by Source.

Traditional Christian teachings use the concept of sin and guilt. ACIM denies the reality of both. "Sin" is merely the perception of separation from Source, and because I am never separated (except in illusion), I cannot "sin." Illusions are not sins. I can make the mistake of thinking and behaving as if I am separated, but such actions are not real. How can they be real when reality is Whole? What is True is always True.

Today you will practice seeing with Whole vision. The idea of sin and guilt serve no useful purpose for you or anyone else. They obscure the Reality of Source. If your mind is part of God's, you must be sinless, or a part of God would be sinful.

Try to practice four times today, for three to five minutes each. This practice is enjoyable and will make you feel at peace. Take your seat and place your awareness on the breath. Just relax and close your eyes. With eyes closed, repeat the lesson in your mind and then open your eyes and look around slowly. Let your gaze fall gently upon objects around you and say in your mind or out loud, "My holiness envelops... everything I see." For example, you might say, "My holiness envelops that rug," or "My holiness envelops that chair, that body, these fingers, that tree."

Several times during the longer practices, close your eyes, place your awareness on the breath, and repeat the lesson in your mind. Let it sink in and feel the truth of its words. Give yourself permission to feel your own holiness. Remember, you cannot make the choice not to be Whole because that is how you were created. Source's Mind does not know separation.

Be mindful of these words today. As often as you can, close your eyes and repeat the lesson. Then open your eyes and look about, applying it to whatever falls within your field of vision. Be slow and effortless in this. Let the peace of the words become you, even if only for a moment.

There is only one way out of the world's thinking, just as there was only one way into it. Understanding totally by understanding totality.
– ACIM

Lesson 37

The family, environment, the communities, the nations, the world can only be saved through spiritual consciousness – not through verbal persuasion, religious conversion, theological decrees, political aggrandizement, or any other human endeavor.
– John Randolph Price

ACIM is very, very clear on this point: we are here for one purpose and it is not to make a fortune, to invent the latest microchip, or even discover a cure for cancer. None of these compare to the simple understanding and application of today's lesson, which is this:

My holiness blesses the world.

Your single most important purpose in this life is to know, to express, and to be in service to your own Wholeness, your Oneness with All That Is. No matter what your past has been or what your future might hold, nothing is more important than to accept yourself as you truly are, always will be, and always have been: eternally loved without exception, part of the One.

This lesson is about the end of sacrifice. You may see yourself as guilty, shameful, petty, jealous, fearful, failed, or even murderous. None of this is your true nature and none of it is really true. The first month of lessons explained clearly that nothing in this world is real except the unending Love of Source, which extended Itself to create us. Our view of "reality" is limited. We perceive only a small fraction of what is all around us. Today's lesson restores and extends True Vision, which is your birthright, my birthright, and the birthright of the Whole.

Today's idea offers everyone her/his full measure of guiltlessness. There is no sacrifice ever required of any Child of God. If I am required to sacrifice to obtain guiltlessness, then God is not perfect and has not created in perfection.

It is we who demand sacrifice. It is we who demand a payment of something from someone. Everyone who projects the idea of sacrifice must already see herself/himself as having lost. Why else would sacrifice be required? What we have lost is our own Holiness, our own Wholeness. We see ourselves as lost and project our loss onto everything else. You cannot project a sick world and not feel sick yourself.

Those who see themselves Whole know all they need will be provided. It cannot be otherwise, for in Oneness all that is required is given freely. Your purpose in this world of dreams is to remember who you are. Through your remembering, you awaken and so awaken the world.

The practice today is joyful. Sit with the lesson four times today for about three to five minutes. Never feel guilty if you find you cannot do a practice. Just do the next one and be at peace. And if the lesson feels uncomfortable – as if you do not deserve to say the words – please say them anyway.

Take your seat and place your awareness on the breath. With eyes open, slowly repeat in your mind, "My holiness blesses the world." Now look about with gentle eyes and apply the lesson to whatever you see. You might say in your mind, "My holiness blesses the table (the glass, the dog, the bird, the photograph...)."

Now close your eyes and place awareness on the breath. Allow people in your life to come into your awareness and say in your mind, "My holiness blesses you (Natalie, Don, Jane...)." If this feels awkward it is an indication that your personal mind is still unwilling to know Itself. That's okay. We have been well trained to see ourselves as unworthy. Spend about five minutes with this lesson. Let the statement of your holiness be enough.

Conclude the practice period with a repetition of the idea with your eyes closed and then open them and repeat the idea once again. Breathe. Relax into the words. Feel the depths of your holiness, your Wholeness within All That Is.

Throughout the day, practice mindfulness by repeating the idea as often as possible. Apply the idea to whatever is in front of you, animate or inanimate. Please do try to repeat the idea any time anything or anyone causes you any discomfort. The more you keep the idea in your awareness the deeper the lesson penetrates your mind.

Lesson 38

There is nothing my holiness cannot do.

"Your holiness reverses all the laws of the world. It is beyond every restriction of time and space, distance and limits of any kind."

Your holiness is unlimited because it establishes you at one with the Mind of the Creator.

This idea may seem audacious at first. I am not suggesting anyone take off running down the streets proclaiming, "I am the Lord of Light!" But the truth is, the idea that we are as God has been actively discouraged, in part because its awareness would remove the need for an outside entity to "interpret" God's word for us. But it is also true that we have been content to deny our identity because we do not want to accept the responsibility for our own power.

The power of God is expressing Itself now through you. It expresses Itself with every thought, every feeling, and every relationship that is experienced. My holiness envelops yours because we are Whole with Source. So, both of us, recognizing our holiness, is a blessing to the world. And make no mistake, the world cannot help but acknowledge our recognition because it is One with all. Oneness is not a half-truth. It means all the time, everywhere, now.

Our limited perception denies this lesson. If I used my power to acquire an earthly fortune for myself, while I watched others suffer, I would be denying my Oneness with you. If I believed my body was the sole arbiter of my reality, I would be denying my eternal nature.

Yet who has not heard of bodies that experience spontaneous remission from disease? Who has not heard of near death experiences in which people return with overwhelming love and acceptance? Scientists have studied such experiences and can offer no rationale for them. They transcend our current thinking. But those who have had such experiences say they are real, more real than anything else. They have a sense of knowing beyond the thinking mind.

Today's lesson offers release from limitation. Even if you cannot accept the words with your thinking brain, try to experience them in your feeling heart.

Practice four times today, for five minutes each time. Can you give 20 minutes to yourself today?

Take your seat and close your eyes. Gently place your awareness on the breath. You may notice that with each out-breath, the body relaxes a little more. Let any stress you are holding flow out with the out-breath. When you are ready, allow your thoughts to arise. Notice any thought that brings unhappiness, loss, or fear. Then, say in your mind, "In this situation involving (the car, my job, my partner, my health…) in which I see myself, there is nothing my holiness cannot do."

Some of your thoughts may be about other people. For example, you might be worried about your brother, your husband, your dog, or your cat. Apply the lesson to them as well. Say in your mind, "In the situation involving (John), in which (John) sees himself, there is nothing my holiness cannot do."

If this practice makes you feel uncomfortable or even fearful it may be helpful to include the thought, "There is nothing my holiness cannot do because the power of God lies in it."

Why would one feel fearful about this lesson? Because the personal mind benefits from your helplessness. If you are helpless your connection to Source must be limited. The ego wants you to feel limited because it wants to be in control of your mind.

The purpose of today's exercise is to instill a sense of your own unlimited power. You cannot know this power if you do not believe in it. Remember, ACIM wakes us gently. You are not required to have a near death experience, or become deathly ill. You are asked to try, to trust, and to have your own experience of the truth.

Feel good about yourself today. You are not overstepping any bounds here. You are merely recognizing your inheritance. You are Love in form. You are sovereign. You are very, very capable.

Lesson 39

My holiness is my salvation.

Did you know the force of Love has predictable consequences? Indeed, there is a Law of Love that functions in a multidimensional reality above three dimensions. Being unfamiliar with any laws except those of three dimensions, we are unfamiliar with the Law of Love at best, and at worst deny its very existence.

The purpose of studying these lessons is to give you a jump-start in this life, about laws that apply above three dimensions. While they may seem unknowable to us here, or even unworthy of trying to understand, they influence every facet of three-dimensional life. Learn the Law of Love in this world, and your happiness will increase exponentially.

The Law of Love, which recognizes the Holiness of everything, is like white light that contains all colors, some of which we cannot even see. When I look at the color blue, I do not see its white light. The same is true for the colors green, red, yellow, purple, and so on. But the white is there in each color. Love is like white light. It holds everything within it, and it is contained in everything.

Each one of us is her own, his own, unique color of light yet all of us are contained within the whole white light of Source. When we look beyond the differences in gender, color, size, personality, indeed any attribute in this three-dimensional world, we can see the wholeness within each person. This is seeing with the eyes of God. Make no mistake: Source sees above three dimensions and knows the Law of Love. Source IS the Law of Love.

My salvation – your salvation – the whole planet's salvation, is born from the Law of Love. In this three-dimensional world, the Law of Love is expressed through forgiveness, which comes from seeing the light that is held within each person, each living thing. The recognition of the holiness of each and every thing is the foundation for forgiveness.

Consider the words "for" and "give." Forgiveness is an eternal payment forward, given before it is even perceived as necessary. Forgiveness is the key to perception above three dimensions and it must begin with yourself. This lesson is the beginning of the end of guilt, for how can you to whom holiness belongs be excluded from it? The lesson for today is your own healing.

Today, four five-minute meditations on the lesson are requested. Try practicing before you get up, mid-morning, mid-afternoon, and in the evening before bedtime. Take a seat and close your eyes. Relax into the body and gently place your awareness on the breath. Notice how relaxation seems to deepen on the out-breath.

When you are ready, repeat in your mind, "My holiness is my salvation." Now allow any thoughts to arise, as they will. Notice any thought or feeling that contains uneasiness, depression, anger, fear, worry, attack, insecurity, etc. Any unloving thought about yourself or others is suitable. Make note of the thought. Feel the thought in your body.

When you have felt the thought fully, say in your mind, "My unloving thoughts about (_____) hold me apart from my Self. My holiness is my salvation."

If no thoughts come to you, that is fine! Just watch your breath and slowly repeat the lesson in your mind. For example, on a long in-breath you might say in your mind, "My holiness..." Then, on the out-breath say, "... is my salvation." Do whatever works for you. Play with it. End your five-minute practice period by repeating the lesson in your mind.

Stay mindful during the day today. Several times an hour, repeat the lesson in your mind. During your day, stop often and notice how you feel. If there is even the slightest discomfort, guilt, anger or even boredom, say to yourself, "My holiness is my salvation. If guilt denies the Law of Love (and it does) then what is its opposite? Its opposite is holiness."

Remember, what is true must always be true or it is not true. You can never be sort of guilty or sort of whole. You are always holiness. So is the person next to you.

Lesson 40

I am blessed as a Son of God.

The "Son" is neither human nor limited to humanity. It is the true identity of everything and it is, ultimately, without form at all. It is nothing less than the extension of Source Itself. As an extension of Source, the "Sonship" contains Its original perfection, and Its eternal nature. The "Sonship" completes Source and is a treasure to It. I sometimes think of it as the "Sunship."

Today's lesson is the assertion of your right to know your own true identity. Anyone who knows she is united in eternal consciousness cannot help but feel peace, contentment, and safety. Most of us do not spend much time contemplating our eternal nature.

There are no longer practice periods required today. Instead, you are asked to practice mindfulness throughout the waking hours. This is your introduction to what will eventually become a daily practice of remaining mindful throughout the day. But remember, each time you forget becomes an opportunity to forgive yourself. Take each opportunity as it comes, in whatever form it comes.

Today, as often as you can (every ten minutes is preferable) repeat the idea in your mind. You may choose to keep your eyes open or closed. Say the lesson in your mind and then add several attributes you associate with being a Son of God. For example, you might say, "I am blessed as a Son of God. I am happy, peaceful, loving and contented." Or, "I am certain of myself. I know what I am. I am safe, complete, and perfect as I am. Nothing more is required of me."

If you want to take five or ten minutes to meditate upon this lesson, by all means do so. Take your seat and close your eyes. Relax your body and place your awareness on the breath. Slowly repeat the lesson in your mind, and allow thoughts to arise, as they will. Note each thought and then repeat the lesson, returning always to the breath. If you wish to use the lesson as a mantra, that is fine. Just place your awareness on the breath and slowly say the lesson. For example, on the inhale you might say, "I am blessed." On the exhale, say, "As a Son of God." Use whatever works for you.

As always, if you forget to repeat the lesson today, don't punish yourself. Just be glad you remembered, repeat the lesson, and make a commitment to remember next time.

Lesson 41

God goes with me wherever I go.

When I was about twelve, I got separated from my family at Disneyland. I turned around in the crowd and realized they were nowhere in sight. All adolescent confidence evaporated and I came close to panic. Luckily I discovered my parents a short distance away, but the experience left me feeling raw and vulnerable.

As spiritual children, we have lost sight of Source. We feel abandoned and without protection. Fear, greed, aggression, and depression are the inevitable consequences of separation and abandonment. That is why so many of us experience anxiety, a deep sense of helplessness, and fear of scarcity. To "cure" these feelings we have devised a great number of protections and diversions. We work ourselves to exhaustion, leaving no time to think. We change partners, jobs, exercise, go shopping, and dull our senses watching movies or endless news.

When it gets really bad we seek the help of professionals. The American Psychiatric Association regularly publishes a *Diagnostic and Statistical Manual* that classifies nearly 300 mental illnesses. Mental health professionals cannot be reimbursed unless they classify their patient with a definable disease. Drugs to cure depression and anxiety are so common they are now considered a source of water pollution. Our treatment systems cannot filter them out.

The foundation of most mental illness is spiritual dis-ease. As one famous psychotherapist said, "An instant of spiritual healing does more than a decade of psychotherapy." Yet we resist bringing God into the healing process because it requires an acceptance that we, ourselves, can do nothing alone. We must surrender into something that seems beyond us. We must entertain the insane thought that we can trust the invisible, unknowable. The paradox is that when we do surrender we become more sane.

Today's five-minute practice is your first real attempt to go more deeply into the experience of connection. There is only one practice period today. Try to do it earlier in the day, but if that is not possible, do it when you can.

Take your seat and close your eyes. Relax your shoulders, your tummy, and your feet. Just settle in. When you are ready, place your awareness gently on the breath. Be happy watching the breath for as long as you like, and then say in your mind, "God goes with me wherever I go." If you want to use a word like Source, or Universe, that is okay, just make sure the feeling of the word is all-encompassing because the feeling is what you are attending to.

As you repeat the lesson, feel the words in your body. Let it reflect the feeling of the words. Imagine what it is to never be alone, for that is the truth. If thoughts arise, as they will, repeat the lesson in your mind, feeling each and every word as deeply as you can. End the five-minute practice peacefully watching the breath, with one last repetition.

What you are looking for in this meditation is a feeling/ knowing that Presence is always within you. This is not intellectual. Don't try to "get" to the feeling – allow it to come to you. Reaching Source is natural. It is not about trying: rather it is about letting go of the barriers to what is already there, waiting for you.

If your mind is too cluttered to find peace today, don't feel you've failed. Release all attempts to succeed for they are barriers in themselves. Give up and feel what you feel. How often does giving up actually open up to peace?

Be mindful today. From time to time, repeat the lesson. You are never alone. Peace is alive within the center of your being, no matter what is going on around you.

Enjoy your day. Peace be within you.

Lesson 42

God is my strength. Vision is God's Gift.

We are powerful beyond measure. It is our light, not our darkness, that most frightens us. We ask ourselves, "Who am I to be brilliant, gorgeous, talented, fabulous?" Actually, who are you not to be? You are a child of God.
– Marianne Williamson, *A Return to Love*

This lesson describes a logical relationship of cause and effect: Source created us, and Source has given us all of Itself. We are free to deny it. We are free to fear it. We are free to imagine that we can relinquish our strength and vision to something outside our self. But the truth is, we are all made of the same stuff as our Source.

Today's practice is to allow the truth of these words to permeate your mind and body. It is about allowing their frequency to vibrate through the whole field of your being, so that even the cells of your body awaken to the truth of Strength.

The Gift of Vision is not precognition or clairvoyance – it is right-mindedness looking upon the world. It is willingness to say, "I have created this mess. I must undo it. I have no idea how to undo it. Therefore, I must ask outside myself and accept a greater wisdom." True vision forgives all things, trusting they are part of a perfect flow of events in a perfect universe. This is "loving what is" and it is not passive. It is very, very active and very, very intelligent. Nothing else is worthy of a child of God.

Two, three-to-five-minute practices are required today – one in the morning and one before bedtime. Take your seat, keeping your eyes open. Repeat the lesson and look around the room. Then close your eyes, relax your body, and repeat the lesson again. "God is my strength. Vision is God's Gift to me." Allow each word to sink in as deeply as possible. Feel the words resonate in your body.

Now, place part of your awareness on the breath and allow your mind to search for feelings and thoughts that support today's idea. For example you might feel and say, "I am strong," or "I have everything I need," or "I am certain. I am certain I can tie my shoe." Don't laugh… this is the level of certainty you are looking for in this practice!

Allow your mind free rein in these thoughts of strength and vision. Be creative. Allow yourself to feel good about yourself! If your mind wanders, come back to the breath and repeat the lesson in your mind. If no thoughts come at all, simply watch the breath and repeat the lesson like a mantra. Do not stress.

Be mindful today. The more often you repeat the lesson in your mind, the more often you will be reminded of who you really are.

No one created by God can find joy in anything except the eternal; not because they are deprived of anything else, but because nothing else is worthy of them.
– ACIM

Lesson 43

God is my Source. I cannot see apart from God.

ACIM makes a fundamental distinction between the real and the unreal. Reality is total, limitless, eternal, and unambiguous. The unreal is an illusion of limitation, a projection of separation made by a mind that believes it can and has become its own creator.

The illusory world of form is a world of bodies and things that have beginnings and endings, birth and death, loss and decline, scarcity and fear. What thinks itself separate fears attack and defends against anything it perceives as a threat –

and eventually everything is a threat. Even those you think you love the most eventually become threats to the ego. Has this not been your experience?

We have made a mess of our creation. We have created a labyrinth and are lost in it. We cannot find our way out of our creation using the same thoughts that brought us here.

Truly, there is only one way out. Suffering is one form of learning and most of us choose it over many lifetimes. Suffering is a limited curriculum but we must experience it to understand its limitations. Eventually, we will all take up another curriculum. This is the curriculum of forgiveness based on the reality of Oneness. Only forgiveness reverses the ego's creation of separation and loss.

Today's practice sessions continue your training in true perception. You are learning to see past the ego's projection. True seeing is accomplished in the heart and mind, not with the body's eyes. These exercises might seem very simple and even silly, but they are powerful. Their effects are a form of miracle which might not be recognized until later, when it is least expected.

There are three, five-minute practices for today. Each practice has an opening statement and then a short meditation. Try to space them out in the morning, afternoon and evening if possible.

Take your seat and keep your eyes open. Relax into your body. When you are ready, say in your mind, "God is my Source. I cannot see apart from God." Now simply glance around the room and apply the idea specifically to what you see. For example, you might say in your mind, "God is my Source. I cannot see this table apart from God." Please don't discriminate in your choice of objects. Let your sight be directed casually, without exclusion.

After this short external practice, close your eyes and relax more deeply. When you are ready, repeat the lesson again in your mind. Feel the words in your body. When you are ready, allow yourself to imagine the world perceived through the eyes of Oneness. Let go of this world and feel your way past your body, past thoughts and memories, to a place of peace. Feel what it would be like to see things as Holy, Whole, One.

Can you feel the table as part of your own energy? Can you feel the space around your body as part of your own body? Can you go inward and feel your body vibrate with the frequency of unseen energy that lies within your cells and the space between them?

As you travel inward, feel your way into the center of your being. It will be quiet and peaceful. Say in your mind, "God is my Source. I see the world with forgiveness," or "God is my Source. I feel the gentleness of my own connectedness," or "God is my Source. I know who I am. I sense the boundlessness of all things." As you say these words, notice the vibration they create within the center of your being.

Practice mindfulness today. Apply today's lesson as often as possible: when standing in line at the store, when stopped in traffic, when meeting a stranger on the street, or having a meeting at the office. If you have read this far, you know you have come here to learn this curriculum and you are on your way Home.

Lesson 44

God is the light in which I see.

Today's lesson asks you to make an inner journey. It may seem strange that traveling inward to a place that feels dark and void can lead to fullness and light, but it can.

A couple of years ago I had a dream experience about this particular lesson. In the dream I saw myself as a ball of light, floating in a void. I was perfectly clear and aware of my own identity as a light. As I looked around in the distance, I saw another enormous ball of light, composed of innumerable smaller lights. Drawn to the big ball of light I felt myself merge with it. As I merged I knew that each smaller light was as different and perfect as myself, and yet we were all one. It felt like seeing both sides of a coin at the same time, or like having a 360-degree view while standing in one place. There are no words to describe the feeling of the dream but I awoke with a deep understanding that uniqueness and oneness are not self-contradictory. This feeling continues to inform me today.

Who knows that God is light? I knew in my dream. But the transition from dream light to the light of day can feel very challenging. Which is real, the dream light or the light of day?

ACIM tells us that if we believe only in the light of day we are not seeing; we are only perceiving. In order to see the light, we need to look within because that is where Source placed it. We did not make the light – Source made it and we must find it where Source determined it should be.

Today you will practice with in-sight. You will apply in-sight to the outer world by opening your mind to it and letting it float lightly upon all it touches. There are three practices, each about five minutes long. The practice begins with saying the lesson in your mind, and then doing nothing more than watching the breath and watching the thoughts that come and go. In a very real sense, you are becoming the inner witness of the outer dream.

Take your seat. Relax the shoulders and the arms. Feel your feet connect with the earth. Relax the tummy and let the area behind the eyes relax. Now place your awareness on the breath. Breathe naturally and watch the breath do what it always does so effortlessly.

Now, in your mind, say, "God is the light in which I see." Then go back to watching the breath. On each out-breath, release a little more tension. Let the out-breath carry away all that is not peace.

As you breathe allow thoughts to arise. Do nothing with the

thought or feeling. Simply recognize it and then say in your mind, "God is the light in which I see." Feel the words as you say them, and trust that whatever comes up is perfect for you. If no thoughts come, slowly with intention, repeat the lesson and watch the breath.

Are you certain you can tie your shoe? Be just as certain you can see in the light of God.

This mind training is giving you the tools you need to begin to see the light in all things by focusing on your inner experience, rather than what is happening in front of you. Several times today stop and look around. Go inside yourself, even if only for the time it takes to repeat the lesson in your mind. Notice how this makes you feel and how it changes your perception.

Lesson 45

God is the Mind with which I think.

Every mind that lives now, has ever lived, or will ever live, resides in timeless Mind. When you join with Mind of God, access to all information in all time is available to you.

Do you believe it is possible to join with Mind of God? Do you feel you deserve it? You don't have to be special. In fact, once you open to the possibility and begin to pay attention to your thoughts, you will be surprised by how much more information becomes available.

Because we are born in God's Mind, we have within us the Wholeness that is our Source. Thoughts do not leave the Source that created them. We are a Thought of God, and therefore we are with God. Its Mind is our birthright, our inheritance.

Today's practice asks you to go beyond "the thoughts you think you think." Put another way, you are asked to deny the denial of your true nature.

We think thoughts of separation, scarcity, and fear. Our small mind is filled with attack thoughts about ourselves and others. But a Mind that knows its Oneness does not even have a name for fear.

Imagine that you are part of a magnificent dance, a symphony of cooperation. Imagine the dance involves every aspect of creation. You are the Self you see as the atom and the nucleus with it. You are the self you see as the plant kingdom. You are the Self you see as the world of water. You are the Self you see as humankind. You are the Self you see as the stars and the space between the stars. You are the Self you see as new universes birthing out of antimatter. You breathe in and entire universes contract. You breathe out and they expand into infinity. The whole entirety of this dance is taking place within your Self. Welcome to Mind of God.

Today's practice is an attempt to go beyond the personal mind and reach the peace of God. This feeling of peace is no flimsy thing, although the ego may laugh at its apparent temporariness. Do not allow the ego to dismiss what peace you find today. It is your true nature, beyond the illusions that your personal mind accepts as reality, and for which the small laws of this world seem to be paramount.

There are three five-minute practices today. Try to space each practice in the morning, midday and evening. If you miss a practice, do not let your ego convince you of failure! You cannot fail in these practices! Your mind is part of God's Mind.

Take your seat and close your eyes. Relax into your body. Mentally survey your body and breathe out any place that feels tight or dense. When you are ready, place your awareness on the breath. Calmly, without effort, watch the breath for about ten breaths.

When you are ready, repeat in your mind, "God is the Mind with which I think." Feel these words resonate in your body. Allow your whole self to relax. It is in peace that we connect to the Mind of Source. You get there not by force, but by allowing, accepting, and doing nothing. Never dismiss the miraculous power of doing nothing.

After you have imagined this peaceful connection for a bit, deepen the focus of your intention by saying in your mind, "My real thoughts are in my mind. I would like to find them." And now, simply watch the breath and go deeper into the peace of God. Force nothing. Let peace come to you. It will come because it has never left. It has been covered up, but it is impossible for it to remain out of reach. Sink into the peace of the breath.

When thoughts arise, as they will, watch them come and then go. If it helps to repeat the lesson as a mantra, please do so. Say the words slowly and purposefully in your mind. The words have the frequency of thought. Get to know the feeling of this frequency.

The foundation of peace you find today is the foundation of creation. When your mind is joined with Source, there can only be a sense of quiet satisfaction, contentment, or even joy. Doing this lesson should leave you feeling happy with yourself.

Practice mindfulness today. Frequently stop whatever you are doing to repeat the lesson in your mind. Stand aside, however briefly, from all thoughts that are unworthy of the peace that is your birthright. If you find yourself feeling gratitude as well as peace, you most certainly have found what you are looking for. Enjoy.

Lesson 46

God is the Love in which I forgive.

Today's lesson on forgiveness is a foundation for nearly all the teachings of ACIM. ACIM does not use the term forgiveness in the traditional sense – it goes far beyond to ask, "What God would condemn Its own creation? In fact, what God would knowingly even create a situation that requires forgiveness?"

Most religious traditions hold to the idea that God is both wrathful and forgiving. A sin is committed and God is petitioned for forgiveness. We are told someone died for us and we need only accept Him to be forgiven. But consider this: if forgiveness is required, someone first has to be condemned for bad behavior. Who is condemned, and who is doing the condemning? If God is One, is God not condemning an aspect of Itself? Does God need to forgive Its own creation – a creation which is Itself? If so, then God is in conflict.

There is no conflict in Source. Source sees all things as Itself, and Source does not hurt Itself. That would be insanity and God is not insane. It is we who are in conflict. We have hurt each other and ourselves.

You have learned your thoughts are images you have made. This includes everything down to the last leaf on the last tree. The catch is this: the personal mind now completely identifies with what it has created. Some images it judges good, others it judges unworthy. That which it judges unworthy, it denies creating at all. This is the conflict of separation. It is called projection, and it occurs on a group scale far beyond the conscious awareness of the personal mind. The personal mind has literally walled itself off from remembrance of its own creation and its own Divinity. Helplessness, despair, guilt, revenge, and blame are the logical consequences.

Helplessness, despair, guilt, revenge, and blame are not in alignment with Mind of Source. It is Source's will that we be happy forever, creating without any judgment or fear at all. It takes great courage to admit you do not like your creation. But as long as you choose to remain a victim of the world you see, you will be out of alignment with Source. This is why the miracle of forgiveness was given to our mind. This is why we are asked to "become again as a little child." We were created Innocence. Forgiveness returns the mind to alignment with its Source. It is required in every single circumstance the personal mind judges anything at all.

Today's three practice periods are the beginning of soul growth in a form this world rarely experiences. This practice asks you to remember your invulnerability and extend this knowing to others through forgiveness. Each practice should be a full five minutes.

Take your seat and relax. Close your eyes and sink into the body. Place your awareness on the breath for about ten breaths. Allow all tension to flow out of the body on the out-breath. Now, allow your mind to search for anyone in your life you have not yet forgiven. Even small grudges will do. We forgive entirely or not at all.

See the person who needs your forgiveness and say in your mind, "God is the love in which I forgive you, (name)." If you feel resistance to these words, that is fine. Just notice it. Relax with it. Do the best you can, and whatever you cannot forgive, hand over to Source. Then move to the next person.

You should be able to find a few people for this lesson. Repeat the process with each person until you feel satisfied and then apply the idea to yourself. Say in your mind, "God is the love in which I forgive myself." Allow these words to penetrate your heart. You might also say, "I am as love made me," or "There is nothing for me to fear," or "I am an eternal being. I cannot truly be attacked." End the practice by repeating the lesson to yourself.

Be mindful today. As often as you can, even every half hour, repeat the lesson to yourself. If you find yourself feeling irritated, annoyed or "attacked" in any way, repeat the lesson. Each irritant or "attack" offers an opportunity to connect with your Self. Each offering of forgiveness is its own blessing upon the entire world.

Lesson 47

God is the strength in which I trust.

The belief in separation from Source comes with a deep sense of vulnerability. Yet the personal mind's fear of its own death appears even worse to it. ACIM is very clear about this: the recognition of Oneness does mean the death of the personal mind. A house divided cannot stand. A personal mind that sees itself separated from its Source will never know the strength that lies beyond it.

Remember, the personal mind has become attached to its creations, even though they are painful. It is so attached it feels it will die without them. "I am my pain." "I am the one who lost his house in a fire." "I am the one who stole from my brother." "I am the mother whose children do not appreciate her." "I am the body that gets sick and suffers." The personal mind is willing to have you suffer and die so long as it achieves its goal of remaining a victim.

We want joy, safety, and freedom. But to achieve them we have to trust, allow, witness our creations, and let them go. We have to cultivate the willingness to enjoy and accept all that arises, seeing it as nothing more than an experience we are having in the moment. This requires courage and strength beyond the personal mind. This requires alignment with the strength of Source.

Today's practices will total twenty minutes: five minutes each, four times today. Can you give your Self twenty minutes today?

Take your seat, close your eyes, and relax the body. You should be able to do this on your own now. When your body is relaxed, place your awareness gently on the breath. When you are ready, say in your mind, "God is the strength in which I trust."

Then gently search your mind for a situation that makes you fearful. You must have many to choose from in today's world. Notice the feeling in your body when you think of the fearful situation. Fear is an energy form. It has a specific expression or frequency. Learn to notice this feeling and it will serve you well.

Stay present with each feeling and use the breath as your anchor. For example, you might say, "I am afraid my life is out of control. I am afraid the world is out of control." Then repeat to yourself, "This fear is only a feeling. God is the strength in which I trust."

When you are finished with one situation, move on to another. Pay attention. Notice the feeling of fear rise, peak, and then subside like a wave. Remain anchored to the breath. End each fearful situation with the words of the lesson.

Today, as often as you can, remember: "There is a strength above my own. It is mine to trust and I choose to trust."

Lesson 48

There is nothing to fear.

Let us speak a moment about fear. It is one of the first emotions we feel. It arises from a sense of vulnerability and it is almost always bodily based. Why do we get up in the morning and go to jobs that do not make us happy? Why do we bear the burden of a mortgage? Why do we allot thousands of dollars for insurance against sickness? Why do we wage war for resources? All of it is to ensure the safety and protection of the body.

Our complete identification with the physical body creates a chronic low-level dis-ease. The money we spend to protect and heal the body says it all. Besides being a major national and global industry, health care is among the top items in most people's personal budgets. It isn't that we don't have fun in the body, it's just that we believe it is all we are.

But take a moment and imagine that you exist without a body, as pure consciousness that never dies. Think of having the freedom to shift from one form to another just by desiring it. Imagine it is possible to join with another and wordlessly share experience. Take a moment to consider how it would be if you could exist in a state with no fear at all. What would that be like?

Today's practice is very short, very simple, and very frequent. Simply repeat the idea to yourself as often as possible throughout the day. Use this lesson as the foundation for all things you experience today. If you have any moment of upset, say in your mind, "There is nothing to fear in this." If you are stuck in traffic, hear of someone's illness, see something disturbing on the news – repeat the lesson to yourself. If you wake up anxious in the middle of night, remember the lesson. There is no limit to the number of times this lesson can be remembered.

If you wish to take a few minutes, sitting in peace with eyes closed, do so. Watch your breath and slowly repeat the lesson in your mind for as long as you wish. Watch your thoughts as they arise. How do your thoughts benefit from the words of this lesson? What does the heart feel when the mind accepts this wisdom?

Fear is the result of trusting only your own mind, your own perception, and your own strength. A greater strength is always available but it does require giving up separation from Source. A house divided cannot stand. You are not a house divided. You are creation itself, flowing from Mind of God. You will go on forever and forever and forever. "Nothing real can be threatened. Nothing unreal exists." There is nothing to fear.

Lesson 49

God's Voice speaks to me all through the day.

Remember yesterday's lesson, "There is nothing to fear"? Please apply this to the lesson for today. Today's lesson was among those I found most challenging at first. "What if I don't hear a Voice? What if I fail?" The answer is really simple: I was trying too hard. You cannot fail at today's lesson. You cannot *not* hear the Voice for God.

The Voice of God may be experienced differently. Some may perceive words. Some may have a feeling. I have known teachers who smelled fields of flowers. That was their version of God speaking. If you can sit and quietly say to yourself, "I like myself. I am happy with myself. I am good," if you feel the certainty of these words, you are hearing the Voice of God.

Part of your mind is in constant communication with Source, whether you are aware of it or not. The part that is not aware is absorbed by the functions of the world and obeys its laws. This part of the mind is constantly distracted, uncertain of itself, and disorganized. Why? Because the world is disorganized.

The mind that is in touch with its Source is calm, always at rest, and wholly certain. It is content to ask and then listen. Often, the feeling is simple satisfaction. Rest assured you are in the frequency of Source any time you feel peace. The Voice for God needs no work or effort to "hear." Indeed, trying too hard gets in the way. Be still and allow. You have never left your Source and you cannot be apart from it.

Today's practice consists of four five-minute periods. Take your seat, close your eyes, and relax the body. When you are ready, place your awareness on the breath. Rest in about ten deep, relaxing breaths, and then say in your mind, "God's Voice speaks to me all through the day." Then watch the breath and be still. Thoughts will arise. Notice each and how it feels in the body. Thoughts will cycle through as you sit in stillness. Do not be discouraged if you have an active mind! Just say to yourself, "The mind is active now," and go back to the breath. Don't resist resistance – accept it and watch it.

Sink deeply into the stillness of these practice sessions. You are trying to reach your real home. It is a place where you are truly welcome. If you experience only a moment of deep stillness, you are well on your way. You are building a path to the Voice of Source but it isn't created in one day.

Be mindful. Repeat the lesson frequently throughout the day. Stop. Listen. Play.

Lesson 50

I am sustained by the Love of my Creator.

Spirit, which vibrates at the highest multidimensional frequency, cannot be fully contained in your physical form. You may remember the quote, "All the wind cannot fit into the jar." That about sums up this lesson.

We are always looking for ways to get more "wind into the jar." We do this by exchanging energy with other people. You know how this goes. You give me your energy when I'm depleted, and I share mine with you later. I complement you. I defend you. I pay attention to you. Money, influence, prestige, wearing the right clothes, or knowing the "right" people – all are attempts to obtain and maintain "wind in the jar."

All of these energy sources have one thing in common – they feed the ego rather than spirit. The ego can never be completely satisfied by these exchanges, so it is constantly looking to be refilled.

Choosing the ego's method to fill the jar cannot make you happy. On this basis alone, the ego's value should be questioned. There is only one Source that offers complete, never-ending energy – energy that requires no bartering and no exchange. This energy is a perfect match for spirit and it fulfills completely.

Source is the energy from which we create. It is the Wind Itself. Do not rely on the energy of those who do not yet know their own Source of energy for your own! You cannot fill yourself with illusions of love, faith, or commitment based on the ego's gratification, or conditions of exchange. Only Source sustains.

Today's practice sessions take you fully into meditation. Practice twice today, for ten minutes each – preferably in the morning and evening. Choose a time and place when you can remain peaceful and undisturbed.

Take your seat and close your eyes. Let your shoulders relax. Let the heart center relax. Soften the tummy. Feel your feet on the floor and let the legs relax. Soften the whole body. When you are ready, place your awareness gently on the breath. Watch the effortless inhalation and exhalation of the breath. When you are ready, slowly say in your mind, "I am sustained by the love of my Creator."

There should be no effort here. Spend ten minutes watching the breath. If it helps, slowly repeat the lesson in your mind. Use the words to pace your breath. Embody the words. Feel their safety and protection. Nothing can disturb or threaten you. Your connection with Source is eternal. You are protected in all circumstances, forever.

Review I

Lesson 51: Review

We will undertake periodic reviews of the lessons. This is not a waste of time or a diversion – quite the opposite. Reviews reinforce the ideas behind individual lessons, allowing you to deepen the connection between them. Reviews offer the opportunity to integrate the core teachings into a logical, cohesive, thought system that will sustain you in this world.

Here is how to practice these reviews:

Begin in the morning by reading each of the five ideas, along with the brief commentary on each idea. This should be done sitting in a quiet place. Once you have read all of the ideas for the day, choose a couple that most appeal. Then close your eyes and repeat the ones you've chosen in your mind. Don't worry about the commentary unless it's helpful. Place your awareness on the breath and allow the central concepts of each idea to resonate in your mind and body. Allow. Don't expend effort. Spend about two minutes doing this.

As often as possible during the day, take two minutes for reflection. You may choose one or two ideas but do make sure that by day's end you've had the chance to reflect upon each of them. During this reflection, try to empty your mind of the outside world's concerns and pressures. Use the words to create a pathway to peace.

Again, the purpose of these practices is integration. The ideas need to be integrated in your mind, and the practice sessions need to be integrated into your day. At some point, you will carry the ideas with you all the time. I've been practicing these lessons for years now, and I can say from experience it becomes natural. It will change your day if you practice. I promise, it will save you from many uncomfortable experiences and disturbances.

Today's ideas are:

1. Nothing I see means anything.
Commentary: What I see is my own projection. I perceive only what my physical eyes tell me I see and what my limited mind says is real. This is not true seeing. True seeing looks beyond the physical illusion of this world and feels its way into knowing. I must let go of my limited perception so that true vision can take its place.

2. I have given what I see all the meaning it has for me.
Commentary: What I see is my own projection. I have done all of this and given it all the meaning it has for me. I project, forget I am a creator being, and then judge my projection. My projection is an idea of separation: separate bodies, separate minds, and

separate interests. I am willing to question my perception.

3. I do not understand anything I see.

Commentary: I cannot hope to understand what I have judged incorrectly because my understanding is based on limited perception. Unless I see from the perspective of the Whole, I am seeing only a miniscule portion of Reality. I can exchange my limited sight if I wish to do so.

4. These thoughts do not mean anything.

Commentary: My ego does most of my "thinking." This isn't really thinking – it is planning, responding, resisting, and rarely, reflecting. Thinking blocks my awareness of peace, which is the Voice for God. The knowing that arises from peace is the truth because I am thinking with my Source.

5. I am never upset for the reason I think.

Commentary: What I see is my own projection. I see what I want to see, what I expect to see, and then try to justify it in my mind. I think defensively, making nearly everything my enemy so that my anger is justified and my attacks are warranted. I think myself blameless, or a victim, when in reality I have created it all. I am willing to let go of my defense system in return for the freedom of truth.

Lesson 52: Review

Today we continue the review sessions as a way to integrate the lessons. You will undoubtedly notice that these lessons are about letting go of the ego's way of perceiving reality. These lessons can be a bit challenging but the personal mind needs to be seen for what it is – a creator of illusion. When we let go of illusion, the truth of our Reality becomes apparent.

Here is how to practice these reviews:

Begin in the morning by reading each of the five ideas, along with the brief commentary on each idea. This should be done sitting down in a quiet place. Once you have read all of the ideas for the day, choose a couple of them, close your eyes, and repeat the ones you've chosen. Use the commentary if it is helpful. Place your awareness on the breath and feel the central concepts of each idea in your mind. Spend about two minutes reflecting upon the ideas in peace and quiet.

As often as possible during the day, take two minutes for reflection. You may choose one or two of the five ideas at a time. Just make sure that by day's end you've had the chance to reflect upon each of them.

1. I am upset because I see what is not there.
Commentary: We exist in a multidimensional Reality of which we see but a tiny part. Reality is eternal and peaceful because It is One with Itself. We have replaced true vision with illusion and it is upsetting. It is frightening! My upset does not change Reality one bit. I am always upset by nothing because my perception is partial.

2. I see only the past.
Commentary: My understanding of the world is based on past experience. I may think I learn from the past, but it holds me in a grip of illusion. I hold the past against everyone and everything. When the past is forgiven (meaning seen as it truly is, which is not there), I see more clearly. Letting go of the past helps me forgive myself and see myself as I truly am, Innocence having experience.

3. My mind is preoccupied with past thoughts.
Commentary: My preoccupation with the past is more than just illusory – it actually prevents me from being present in the moment. When I am preoccupied by the past I am literally using time against myself. When I allow the moment to be as it is I am

giving up nothing.

4. I see nothing as it is now.
Commentary: If I see nothing as it is now, then I see nothing. The choice is not to see the past or the present; the choice is whether to see or not. True vision sees clearly now. Being fully present with what I see creates space, allowing the true nature of what I see to show me itself.

5. My thoughts do not mean anything.
Commentary: If I spend 90% of my time in thoughts of the past or the future, then do my thoughts have meaning? I can only be here now. Thoughts that take me out of now are meaningless and only hold me back from awakening.

Lesson 53: Review
Here is how to practice these reviews:

In the morning, choose a quiet place and take a seat. Read each of the five ideas, along with the brief commentary. Choose a couple of the ideas and close your eyes. Repeat the ideas you've chosen in your mind. Use the commentary if it is helpful. Place your awareness on the breath and feel the central concepts of each idea in your body. Spend about two minutes reflecting upon the ideas in peace and quiet.

As often as possible, take time to sit in quiet and reflect upon one or two of these ideas. Make sure that by day's end you've had the chance to reflect upon each of them.

Today's ideas are:

1. My meaningless thoughts are showing me a meaningless world.
Commentary: The personal mind sees only separate images. It thrives on specialness, which comes from the idea of being set apart. Source sees only Oneness and Oneness is the more

significant Reality.

2. I am upset because I see a meaningless world.
Commentary: The thought I am separated from Source is upsetting, even frightening. The ideas of scarcity, failure, loss, fear, and chaos come directly from the thought of separation. I cannot live in peace in such a world – even if it is punctuated by moments of happiness. I am grateful this world is not real and that I can look past it to Reality with my mind. I have free will to choose what I value. I do not choose to value what has no meaning.

3. A meaningless world engenders fear.
Commentary: Nothing in this world can be trusted to last. Even the moments of peace and joy I find here are quickly replaced by judgment and loss. This leaves me living with the pain of the past, and fear of the future. True peace is not temporary. I have given this world its illusions of chaos, loss of safety and loss of hope. Now I choose to withdraw from this illusion and seek what lies behind it.

4. God did not create a meaningless world.
Commentary: Love did not create a world that values separation as reality and Oneness as fantasy. This world is my doing through a mind that believes it has separated itself from its Creator. Let me remember this: the power of my decision to create a world of separation can also be used to undo it. I use the power of my mind to choose meaning.

5. My thoughts are images I have made.
Commentary: Thoughts become things; such is the power of my creative ability, given me in Love by my Creator. What I see is a reflection of my mind. But the Thought that created me has never left my mind. I have access to this original Thought in

peace and stillness. It is my will to return to it.

Lesson 54: Review

Today's review is founded on the fact that thought has energy. Thought and emotion appear to be formless. Because we cannot measure them directly they have been ignored as creative forces.

This belief is slowly disassembling. The medical world recognizes formless mental and emotional stress as a prime component in a wide range of physical ailments from cardiac disease and stroke to Alzheimer's and gastrointestinal problems. Other areas of scientific inquiry have confirmed evidence of mental and emotional connections between people that defy space, time and distance.

Non-locality, which Einstein called "spooky action at a distance," has now been proven beyond all reasonable doubt. Non-locality describes the faster-than-light relationship between light particles. It defies the normal laws of physics. We seem to be on the cusp of a deeper understanding about the energetic connectivity of all things – an understanding ACIM described over 50 years ago. This review takes us deep into a timeless terrain of truth.

Here is how to practice these reviews:

Begin in the morning by reading each of the five ideas, along with the brief commentary on each. Once you have read all of the ideas for the day, choose a couple of them and, with eyes closed, repeat the ideas you've chosen in your mind. Don't worry about remembering the commentary unless it is helpful. Place your awareness on the breath and feel the central concepts of each idea. Spend about two minutes reflecting in peace and quiet.

As often as possible during the day, take two minutes for reflection. You may choose one or two of the five ideas at a time. Just make sure that by day's end you've had the chance to reflect upon each.

Today's ideas are:

1. I have no neutral thoughts.
Commentary: All thought has effect. My thoughts directly affect my reality. What I see in my world shows me what thoughts I have. My thoughts reflect either truth or illusion.

2. I see no neutral things.
Commentary: What I see is a direct reflection of my mind. If I look on the world as separate, that is what I will see. I know my state of mind can change and with it the world I see.

3. I am not alone in experiencing the effects of my seeing.
Commentary: There are no private thoughts in Oneness. Even the idea of separation had to be shared before it could become the basis of the world I see. We live now in a collective illusion. I can call upon my real thoughts, which are also shared. As my thoughts of separation call to the separation of others, so my real thoughts awaken the real thoughts in them. When I awaken, I awaken those around me. This single truth realized will change the world.

4. I am not alone in experiencing the effects of my thoughts.
Commentary: I have the creative powers of my Source. I am alone in nothing and everything I do or say reaches far beyond my current recognition. When I change my thoughts, the effects are felt beyond the stars. Such are the powers I have as an aspect of my Source. Again, this truth understood will change the world.

5. I am determined to see.
Commentary: My will is unlimited. What I do here and now has ramification beyond space and time. I am determined to extend my thought beyond the limitations of this self-imposed illusion, for that is the only way I can see what is Real. All experience is shared. Love extends Itself endlessly. I am joined with all minds in the shared experience with my Source. I am determined to see

this. In seeing it, I know it. In knowing it, I am it.

Lesson 55: Review

Nothing beyond you can make you fearful or loving because nothing IS beyond you. You cannot understand that Time and Eternity are in your mind as long as you believe that anything that happens to you is caused by forces outside you.
– ACIM

Here is how to practice these reviews:

Begin in the morning by reading each of the five ideas, along with the brief commentary on each idea. Once you have read all of the ideas for the day, choose a couple of them and, with eyes closed, repeat the ideas you've chosen in your mind. Don't worry about remembering the commentary unless it is helpful. Place your awareness on the breath and feel the central concepts of each idea. Spend about two minutes in reflection.

As often as possible during the day, take two minutes for reflection. You may choose one or two of the five ideas at a time. Just make sure that by day's end you've had the chance to reflect upon each one.

Today's ideas are:

1. I am determined to see things differently.
Commentary: This idea is quite simply a statement of independence. Am I satisfied with imagining myself a victim of the world I see, or is it time to see things differently? Am I ready to look with an open mind, or do I wish to continue along a path that says I cannot know myself?

2. What I see is a form of vengeance.
Commentary: When I see separation between myself, and the rest of the world, I distort Reality. Only fear can be the result.

When I see myself separate from my Source and others around me, I will constantly feel under threat of attack. I am creating this threat myself, with my visions of separation. Yet Love knows only Oneness with Its creation. I am willing to see beyond my fear and the vengeance it creates.

3. I can escape from this world by giving up attack thoughts.
Commentary: Forgiveness returns love to my awareness. Forgiveness is the recognition of my own invulnerability and wholeness. It requires no sacrifice on my part. I cannot attack my Self nor can I my Self be attacked.

4. I do not perceive my own best interests.
Commentary: How can I perceive my best interests if I see myself alone and separate from my Source? If I do not understand that giving and receiving are the same, I will never forgive because I will see it as sacrifice. Forgiveness is awakening to my own best interests.

5. I do not know what anything is for.
Commentary: The purpose I have given this world is simple – to reinforce my thoughts that there can be separate interests, separate bodies, separate minds, and separation from my Source. I have learned this lesson well and therefore do not recognize the real purpose of the world. Let me open my mind and withdraw the purpose I have given the world. Let me see my mistaken perceptions and choose another way.

Lesson 56: Review

It is one thing for a student to read, "I want to see," but another to understand how to do so. Today's review covers the critical question of how to see truly. Seeing truly takes persistence, but it is inevitable.

Free will is paramount, so we are free to determine for

ourselves when we want to see. If suffering is your chosen teacher, seeing will take longer. But each of us will see because it is the will of Source that illusion must end.

Here is how to practice these reviews:

Begin in the morning by reading each of the five ideas, along with the brief commentary on each idea. This should be done sitting down in a quiet place. Once you have read all of the ideas for the day, choose a couple of them. Close your eyes and repeat the ones you've chosen. Don't worry about remembering the commentary unless it is helpful. Place your awareness on the breath and feel the central concepts of each idea. Spend about two minutes reflecting upon the ideas in peace and quiet.

As often as possible during the day, take two minutes for reflection. You may choose one or two of the five ideas at a time. Just make sure that by day's end you've had the chance to reflect upon each.

Today's ideas are:

1. My attack thoughts are attacking my invulnerability.
Commentary: When I choose the personal mind as my teacher, I see myself under constant attack. All of life is threatening and my hopes and dreams appear to be at the mercy of a world I cannot control. But I can choose other thoughts! I can choose to know invulnerability is my inheritance. I am free to see this now, in this moment, and in every moment.

2. Above all else I want to see.
Commentary: The greatest lesson I can learn is that what I "see" is a reflection of my own mind. Here is Truth, and there are no exceptions to this ever: even the worst visions that seem to be "outside" of me are my creations. The world is an image I have made – it is temporary, full of opposites, unreliable, and only rarely at peace. Vision sees the illusion and looks deeply into it. There is Truth in this world, but it is not seen with the physical

eyes – it is known in the courageous heart and mind that look at separation and see its false facade.

3. Above all else I want to see differently.
Commentary: While I see through the ego's fearful eyes, Truth cannot enter my awareness. I would let the door behind this world be open for me so I can look past it to one that reflects the dimensions of Light, Wholeness, and Love. The simple act of deciding I want to see differently sets me upon a whole new path. I am at the foot of the mountain now.

4. God is in everything I see.
Commentary: How do I see beyond this world? By recognizing that nothing leaves its Source. God's presence is here – even in my illusion. How can it be otherwise? I have not left my Source and neither have my creations however strange and unhappy they may seem. I am part of my Source and I am fully capable of looking past all appearances of separation and recognizing the truth of Oneness beyond them all.

5. God is in everything I see because God is in my mind.
Commentary: Do I think myself so unique that God cannot be in my mind? It is only my ego, which thrives in the illusion of separation, that tells me I am so special I cannot see. I cannot lose the knowledge that all is One forever! I did not create Source; Source created me and Its Mind is my inheritance kept, for me always.

Lesson 57: Review
The ideas for today are not hyperbole, embellishment, or new age jingoism. They concern "perceptual physics." Do you think such a thing does not exist? Consider this:

Nothing is real unless we look at it, and it ceases to be real as soon as we stop looking.
– Physicist John Gribbin

A thing ceases to be real as soon as we stop looking. Forget about changing the world today. Be happy just to change your own mind.

Here is how to practice these reviews:

Begin in the morning by reading each of the five ideas, along with the brief commentary. Once you have read all of the ideas for the day, choose a couple of them and close your eyes. Repeat the ideas you've chosen in your mind, using the commentary if it is helpful. Place awareness on the breath and feel the central concepts of each idea in your body. Spend about two minutes reflecting upon the ideas in peace and quiet.

As often as possible during the day, take two minutes for reflection. You may choose one or two ideas at a time. Just make sure that by day's end you've had the chance to reflect upon each.

Today's ideas are:

1. I am not a victim of the world I see.
Commentary: My mind is the means by which I determine my own condition. I choose to open my mind. I am free because I see, not with the eyes of the body, but with the eyes of a healed heart.

2. I have invented the world I see.
Commentary: I was given all the creative powers of my Source and it was with these powers I made this illusion. I have lost myself in it. I have deluded myself into believing it was possible to imprison a Child of God. I can choose to see differently and it is with this choice I open the door. I am as God created me, not as I created myself.

3. *There is another way of looking at the world.*
Commentary: The laws of this world are upside down. What we value here is form, when the truth is only formlessness is eternal. I am free to look beyond form if I use my heart and open my mind.

4. *I could see peace instead of this.*
Commentary: The laws of this world are changeable, illusory, shifting, and completely limited by rational, linear thinking. The laws of this world try only to contain separation so that a modicum of peace can temporarily exist. The law of Source is multidimensional. It is one of unending unity and therefore unending peace. I choose what I "see." Today I see my own eternal nature and my own unending union with everything and everyone.

5. *My mind is part of God's. I am very holy.*
Commentary: God's mind contains all things. Nothing lies outside of Source. When I use my conscious mind in alignment with Source, I am invincible. I am not a body. I am spirit. I am free.

Lesson 58: Review

Self-love is not showy, indulgent, self-important, or arrogant. It does not announce itself "special." Self-love is secure, calm, patient, generous, and gentle. In order for love to be shared, self-love must be already present. How can I extend to you that which I do not have? Source has extended Its Self-Love to you and all your creations. Walk in certainty with It today. It is not arrogant to love yourself but it is arrogant to deny it.

The ideas for today are:

1. *My holiness envelops everything I see.*
Commentary: Today I will be in my own authority. I will not

pretend I am powerless, because I know otherwise. I am never alone or powerless because Love is what created me, and I am forever joined with It.

2. My holiness blesses the world.
Commentary: Love is the energy of creation. Only Love lasts and only Love is real. My recognition of my wholeness does not go unfelt in the entire universe. Oneness calls to Itself through me. Seeing Its light within brings joy to all things, because all things share in my wholeness.

3. There is nothing my holiness cannot do.
Commentary: I do not give my power up to something outside myself, nor do I claim abilities I do not have. Love creates with Love, for Love is the only creative force that is Real. I decide whether to create with Love or fear today. I can do nothing with fear because its premises are illusion. When I create with Love, I create in union with my Source and I cannot fail.

4. My holiness is my salvation.
Commentary: What is salvation but a mind healed of false limitations? I am not a body, I am spirit, unlimited and united with all creation. Recognition of my true nature, my wholeness, changes everything. It transforms my internal being and my physical body. It changes my relationships with everything around me. When I act from wholeness, I act without fear. I am free and share my freedom with the world.

5. I am blessed as a Being of God.
Commentary: Everything blessed is of God. I am no exception. I have played in this world for lifetimes. Now I awaken to claim my goodness and forgive my mistakes – past, present and future. All goodness is always mine because Source directs that it be so.

Here is how to practice the ideas for today:

Begin in the morning by reading each of the five ideas, along with the brief commentary on each idea. Once you have read all of the ideas for the day, choose a couple of them and, with eyes closed, repeat those you've chosen. Use the commentary if it is helpful. Place your awareness on the breath and feel the central concepts of each idea in your mind. Spend about two minutes reflecting upon the ideas in peace and quiet.

As often as possible during the day, take two minutes for reflection. You may choose one or two of the ideas at a time. Just make sure that by day's end you've had the chance to reflect upon each.

Enjoy your day!

Lesson 59: Review

To be true, something must always be true. God cannot be partially true. We are either of Source or we aren't.

ACIM seems radical because it seeks nothing less than an end to the ancient human cycle of vendetta and counter-vendetta. Is it radical to ask that you recognize your invulnerability? Is it radical to suggest you end the attack you make against yourself?

Today's lessons speak to your invulnerability. As you read and practice with them, allow the meaning behind the words to penetrate your being. The more you love yourself and trust in Source, the more you think and act with Source. The more you think and act with Source, the more you ARE Source. Today's review lessons are:

1. *God goes with me wherever I go.*
Commentary: Do you think this wishful thinking? It is either true or it is not. If it is true, then we need to act like it. If not, then we must be willing to accept that we are lost. God has led you to this place. You are awakening to Love's presence now.

2. God is my strength. Vision is God's gift.
Commentary: I need not ask for this gift. I need not earn it. It is given freely. I need only be willing to perceive it and trust in it with the knowingness that is within my being.

3. God is my Source. I cannot see apart from God.
Commentary: This world is as I perceive it to be. If I see alone, without Source, I misperceive. I am free to see apart from my Source if I choose. But only when I see all things as One, and myself as invulnerable, am I seeing truly.

4. God is the light in which I see.
Commentary: The true nature of Source speaks in my mind, where Its light remains unchanged. The more I practice seeing with the light of Source, the greater my connection with It is. I am reconnecting with a path I left long ago, but the path is still there and I can find it.

5. God is the Mind with which I think.
Commentary: I cannot see without the light of God, nor can I truly think without allowing my mind to connect with Source. What a joy to know that God is in my mind! Today, I will allow myself to feel this connection. I will take the time to listen for the voice that tells me I am eternal, wholly connected with all around me, created by Love, and forever safe.

Here is how to practice the ideas for today:

Begin in the morning by reading each of the five ideas, along with the brief commentary on each. Choose a couple of them and, with eyes closed, repeat them in your mind. Use the commentary if it is helpful. Place your awareness on the breath and spend about two minutes reflecting upon the ideas in peace and quiet.

As often as possible during the day, take two minutes for

reflection. You may choose one or two of the ideas at a time. Just make sure that by day's end you've had the chance to reflect upon each.

Lesson 60: Review

Here is how to practice the ideas for today:

Begin in the morning by reading each of the five ideas, along with the brief commentary. Once you have read all of the ideas, choose a couple and repeat them in your mind. Use the commentary if it's helpful. Place your awareness on the breath and spend about two minutes reflecting upon the ideas in peace and quiet.

As often as possible during the day, take two minutes for reflection. You may choose one or two of the five ideas at a time. Just make sure that by day's end you've had the chance to reflect upon each.

1. God is the love in which I forgive.
Commentary: Source has no need to forgive because It has never condemned. The blameless do not blame. I accept myself as blameless, for that is the perfect truth. My innocence is reflected also in everyone I encounter. Only through forgiveness will I recognize my Self.

2. God is the strength in which I trust.
Commentary: I am not expected to do all of this myself. I am never alone and can call upon the strength of my Source at any time for anything. I am part of the Oneness and have all Its attributes because that which created me gave them to me. When I find forgiveness difficult, I have Source to help, but I need to remember to ask. Then I let go.

3. There is nothing to fear.
Commentary: Fear of loss, fear of death, fear of scarcity, fear

of punishment – all of these have guided my days. My fear has been like a prison without walls. When I remember I am eternal consciousness the whole world is seen in a new light. Source created me fearless and that is what I am.

4. God's Voice speaks to me all through the day.
Commentary: In stillness I hear the Voice of peace. All throughout my busy day It is speaking. I need only decide to stop and listen. The Voice of Source has directed me since my creation and It directs me still. Today, I listen in peace and trust. There is nothing to fear. I am without blame or guilt. I am perfect consciousness having a human experience. I forgive myself for my mistakes and I forgive all those around me for theirs.

5. I am sustained by the Love of God.
Commentary: Love created me like Itself. What holds the atoms and molecules of this world together except the Love of God? Everything is light. Even the densest form is simply light slowed down enough for me to perceive it with the body's eyes. I am of the Light, and I am sustained by the Light that holds all time and space within Its Mind.

Lesson 61

I am the light of the world.

To the personal mind this idea is the epitome of self-aggrandizement. But I urge you to think again. The denial of your divinity in favor of limitation is its own form of arrogance. It is not humility that says, "I cannot be the light of the world." It is not humility that says, "I am not masterful. I am not certain of myself. I am not capable of recognizing my own glory." It is not humility that denies the light within, but it IS fear.

The denial of your divinity is a form of perversion. Do you

think Source sat on Its throne and thought, "I wonder if I'm worthy to create today? I wonder if I am worthy to share my divinity with my children? Is beauty beyond my capability?" Source has no fear of Its abilities and no judgment of Its creations. It looks at Its creations and says, "This is most excellent. I shall extend Myself further still!"

Created by Light, you are Light. Know yourself of It. Today's practice is mindfulness. As often as possible throughout the day, take two minutes to sit quietly and say in your mind, "I am the light of the world. My only function is to remember it. This is why I am here."

Think about these statements with your eyes closed and allow the feeling of the words to sink into your very being. You may hesitate at first. Your mind may tell you, "I am not capable. I cannot be certain. I do not really know." Watch these feelings. But be open to the possibility that you do not know what you do not know. The rational mind cannot conceive of all that you are.

Here is a short story that might help with today's idea. It is taken from Robert Brumet's *Birthing a Greater Reality*.

Imagine the human personality is like a block of ice. We identify completely with the block of ice and live in constant fear of melting or being damaged in some way. As a block of ice we cannot merge easily with other pieces of ice because our edges are jagged and pointy. We are alone and always vulnerable.

But let's imagine the block of ice has a spiritual experience and discovers its true nature is H2O. Knowing now it is H2O, it is no longer afraid of melting or being damaged. It can melt into water, or become invisible vapor, but it is still its essential self. It can merge with other blocks of ice as water, or become unlimited and invisible as steam. If it wishes to become solid, it can freeze back into ice. None of these changes affect its true nature, so it is free from its former fear. It is free to be whatever it needs to be at any given time. It knows what it is.

So it is with the individual self that knows its essential nature as spirit. She or he is free to function in this world without fear of intimacy or even death. She has faced her fear and transformed. She is now free to bless others who do not yet know about H2O. And in so doing, she or he has become the light of the world.

Enjoy two minutes remembering your light as often as you can today.

Lesson 62

Forgiveness is my function as the light of the world.

Nothing I am aware of in another is not also in myself. The very fact that I can judge another requires me to know that which I judge. If I am honest with myself, I see that I judge constantly and harbor hundreds of unkind thoughts each and every day. I may not act out my thoughts. I may dwell on them for only a split second, but the energy has come into my field and I recognize it. Who, then, is less than I am? Who, then, is worthy of my condemnation? Who, then, is unequal to me? Who, then, is worthy of my forgiveness? Everyone. But I must know forgiveness for myself before I am able to extend it to another because forgiveness is my bridge to Mind of God.

So, I forgive myself for my rage. I forgive myself for not being enlightened yet. I forgive myself for choosing pain. I forgive myself for feeling frustrated. I forgive myself for wanting more than I have, and I forgive myself for feeling guilty about it.

I forgive myself for being sick, for holding grudges, for being afraid. I forgive myself for not liking my body. I forgive myself for holding onto the past. I forgive myself for being angry about the state of the world. I forgive myself for waking up this morning and finding myself tired with it all. I forgive myself for forgetting to forgive.

When I forgive, I feel an inner alignment with peace. When I am in alignment, I become a conduit for a higher power that knows how to use my energies in exactly the right way. Aligned and unburdened by guilt, forgiving miraculously becomes easier and more frequent. My perception shifts. Things I did not see before become apparent. There is no limit to the gifts of forgiveness, or the number of times I can forgive the same thing. It is, after all, MY PURPOSE HERE.

And so you are asked to forgive yourself. And when you do so, know that I receive your forgiveness because we have inherited Wholeness together. Let us hear the truth about ourselves. We are ONE, eternal and blameless consciousness incarnated in a body, reawakening to our Self.

In this world, forgiveness is the foundation of awakening. When I forgive, I am liberated. Once liberated, doors open to multiple realities as yet unknown. It is our *right* to choose forgiveness. It is our right to be liberated to know who we truly are.

Begin and end your day by taking a seat, closing your eyes, and saying in your mind, "Forgiveness is my function as the light of the world." Then sit quietly for two minutes in peace. Thoughts will arise. Some will be thoughts of guilt or attack. Let each one go saying, "Forgiveness is my function." As you say the words, notice the change in your body. It will relax. It will settle in. Your breathing will slow and deepen. Be happy with yourself. Like yourself. This is who you really are.

As often as you can, repeat the lesson in your mind today. Feel the words in your body. Know what you are. Know how you serve as the light of the world. Give yourself this gift.

Lesson 63

The light of the world brings peace to every mind through my forgiveness.

We are conduits of energy. To the degree that our minds are in perfect working order, energy flows so freely, so radiantly, that we are transparent. Yet for most, this energy is blocked and the flow is limited. Thus, our sight and knowing are also limited.

We are like a traveler in a wood who sees only separate trees above ground. Below, an interconnected world thrives underfoot. Fungi extend for miles, sharing light and nutrients with every tree root. The tree roots entwine and support each other when the winds are high above. The consciousness of each tree knows its interdependent nature but also acts for and with the whole forest, above and below.

Forgiveness is a choice that unblocks the conduit. The act of forgiving activates a universal frequency code that opens doors we do not yet see. Each of us has access to the code. There is no need to earn anything, or do anything to give it, or to receive it.

Forgiveness is the choice to release another from your own projections of darkness. It is, therefore, an act of forgiving one's self. Understand this: forgiveness is forgiving yourself for not being aware of your own projections. When you truly forgive yourself, you access the universal frequency. When you access the universal frequency, you shine light; you become light.

Today you will again practice mindfulness. As often as possible, sit with eyes closed, and repeat the lesson in your mind. Feel the vibration of the words in your body as you say to yourself, "The light of the world brings peace to every mind through my forgiveness." Then rest for two minutes or so, and allow related thoughts to arise. Notice them. Some of your thoughts will be peaceful. Some will be uncomfortable, irritating, or fearful. Be aware of the body's response to each thought. As you notice, repeat the lesson quietly, in your mind.

As someone said the other day, "We do not have an economic problem. We do not have an education problem. We do not have an environmental problem, or a political problem. We have a consciousness problem." You are not being asked to solve the world's problems here. Just do your own work and let Source do Its. Relax and trust. You have full access to the Key Code.

Enjoy the day in peace.

Lesson 64

Let me not forget my function.

ACIM teaches the way to peace is through the fulfillment of your function. Because your function was given by Source, its fulfillment is inevitable. It is logical, and ultimately, totally obvious. But it is still a choice.

Your function is to forgive yourself for projecting guilt onto a world that is not real and that you do not understand. Your function is to admit you cannot see the infinite number of patterns in the whole cloth, and therefore do not know what anything is for. Your function is to see it is the arrogance of the ego that leads you to question the function Source has given you.

When I forgive, I open a space in my mind. When I remember my function, I let go of needing to be right about my judgments. I do not need to discover a star, create the next billion-dollar company, or find the perfect mate. I need only remember who I am. Every time I choose whether or not to fulfill my function, I am also choosing whether or not I want to be happy.

My function is so simple. But its application appears complex. My ego loves complexity. It tells me, "Your function applies to him, but not her. There are exceptions after all." This is how, little by little, the personal mind undermines truth.

Forgiveness should be practiced diligently. But Love is Whole and It will help. Once you proclaim your function Source will send you everything you need to practice. You need not travel far. You need not go on retreat. You have declared your desire and it will be fulfilled with Perfection. Love has powers beyond your imagination.

Today you practice only remembering. There are only two teachers to listen to: the personal mind or the Voice for God. Which do you remember most regularly? Which do you listen to?

At least once today take your seat and close your eyes. Relax the body and place awareness on the breath. Notice the breath but do not try to control it or manage it in any way. You may notice that on the out-breath the body relaxes more deeply. This is natural because you are releasing old energy and the release feels good. Let yourself feel good about feeling good. When you are ready, say in your mind, "Let me not forget my function. Let me not try to substitute my will for God's. Let me forgive and be happy." Feel these words in your body as you say them in the mind.

Sit for about ten or fifteen minutes in quiet. Watch your thoughts. If your mind begins to wander, repeat the lesson as often as necessary. Do so slowly, with intention. Let each word sink in, feeling its vibration in your body. What is the vibration of the word "forgive"? What is the vibration of the word "happy"? Just notice. Play with it.

Practice mindfulness throughout the day today. As often as possible, take a moment to sit in quiet as you repeat the lesson. Keep your eyes closed and relax into the words. Or keep your eyes open, look about at your surroundings, and say in your mind, "This is the world it is my function to save. I forgive all that I see before me and I am happy for it."

You will experience this world as you perceive it. Let love be the foundation of your perception today.

Lesson 65

My only function is the one Source gave me.

The rational mind is incapable of seeing beyond the function it has given itself. It has built a box, climbed in, and called itself complete. Projection is the function of the rational mind. It occurs when I deny what I cannot stand to see in myself, so I throw it onto whatever is nearby. What I judge despicable within, I cast out. Thus, what appears to be outside is really inside.

Our universe, this world, is a projection. It is our creation. This is why nothing I experience is not of my own creation. There is only one way out of our creation. It is the way given by Source. It is forgiveness.

Forgiveness is a quantum catalyst. It ends the denial of truth. It corrects perception and allows the light to appear as it truly is – in everything. The rational mind cannot understand this process because it is incapable of seeing beyond the function it has given itself. Fire it as your teacher today.

Our practice periods now become daily meditations. Try to find ten to fifteen minutes to sit at about the same time each day. The purpose of this practice is to train yourself to set apart regular time to open the conduit between your Self and Source. This time is not trivial. The mind needs training to correct misperception. Ten or fifteen minutes are only a little time in relation to all the other things you give yourself to do. But make no mistake, these minutes are the most important thing you will do for yourself all day.

Take your seat and close your eyes. Begin to notice your breathing. Relax into the body. Feel your feet on the floor. Relax the feet, the legs, the hips, and the belly. Relax the chest, the neck, and the shoulders. Relax the area behind your eyes. Now place your awareness gently on the breath. There is no need to control or manage it. You may notice that on the out-breath your body sinks more deeply into relaxation. This is good. Release any tension on the out-breath.

When you are ready, say in your mind, "My only function is the one Source gave me." Try to feel the vibration of these words in your body. Let them become your focus. You give up nothing by giving your function to Source. Instead, you are taking your rightful place in the world with this thought. You did not create yourself, nor did you establish your function. Be grateful for this. It is not freedom from responsibility but it is the end of doubt about your purpose.

Spend the next ten to fifteen minutes watching thoughts that arise. Note each one as it comes up, but do not be overly concerned about it. If your mind wanders too much, simply repeat the lesson slowly, feeling each word.

End the practice period by repeating the lesson once more.

Practice mindfulness today. You are cultivating a way of living. Knowing your function creates certainty. That you are capable of fulfilling your function is beyond doubt. Creation is not mistaken in what It has bestowed upon you.

Lesson 66

My happiness and my function are one.

When safety is not an issue, creativity is effortless. Nothing gets in the way. To make a meal for friends, awaken from a good dream and give it permission to infuse the whole day, listen to another with your whole being – these are all creative acts. Our truest nature is to be open and creative. That is why it feels good.

Creation links me to the Will of God Which shares the joy of my creation. Because all minds are joined, no creative thought is separated from any other thought. The music is heard, the play seen, the dance enjoyed. Even the act of creation itself is shared as unseen partners inform us: "Pick that color!" "Draw that line!" "Take the photo from another angle!" "Lift the note an octave." How many artists say, "I don't know where this came from. I heard the music in my mind. The book wrote itself."

We have learned that forgiveness is our function. But if forgiveness is our function, then so is happiness. It is our function to be happy in this world. Happiness is achieved and sustained through the act of forgiving, allowing, and willing. Our joy is in sharing our treasure with the world.

Today's practice period should be at as regular a time as possible, preferably in the morning before the mind is clouded with a day's worth of activity. We are actively practicing meditation at this point and you should be very comfortable with it by now. The time devoted to these meditations will bring rewards greater than you may know now.

Take your seat and close your eyes. Relax into your body. Feel your feet on the floor, or your hips and pelvis if you are sitting. Relax the legs and the belly. Relax the chest, the neck, and the shoulders. Soften the area behind your eyes. Now place your awareness gently on the breath. There is no need to control or manage the breath. You may notice that on the out-breath your body sinks more deeply into relaxation. It feels good to release tension because goodness is our natural state.

Now, say in your mind, "My happiness and my function are one. My Source has given my function to me. Therefore, my function must be happiness." Give yourself permission to accept that happiness is your function.

If you experience resistance to this idea, know it is the voice of the personal mind. The personal mind will try to convince you that you do not deserve your function. But know this: when you block happiness you block access to Source. The ego is incapable of knowing what you really are or what makes you happy. Source created happiness Itself. That is why it feels good. Take heart in this.

As you sit for ten or fifteen minutes in practice, allow

thoughts to arise. Watch each thought. What kind of thought is it? Does it speak of separation or fear? Is it a thought of mistrust in the future or betrayal in the past? Allow these thoughts to be. Watch them without judgment. They are just thoughts. Do you have to believe every thought you have, or do you get to choose? Where does happiness come from? If your mind wanders, repeat in your mind, "My happiness and my function are one because Source has given me both." Use this as a mantra if you like.

Practice mindfulness today. Try to stop every half an hour and repeat the lesson with eyes closed. Feel the frequency of these words resonate in your body. Give yourself permission to know your creator wants you to feel good about yourself.

The personal mind has no power to distract unless you give it the power to do so. The personal mind is not who you are but do not expect it to say, "I am not real." It won't. However, you are free to evaluate your thoughts in terms of their results to you. Which thoughts bring peace? Which promote discomfort? Your thoughts create reality. Which do you choose?

Lesson 67

Love created me like Itself.

The idea for today is a complete and accurate description of what you are. It is why you are the light of the world. It is why you are one with all Creation. It is why you can never be alone or abandoned at any time for anything whatsoever. Love is Awareness being aware of Itself. It does not abandon Itself or any of Its creations which are Itself.

Love extends Itself and is perfectly replicated in everything that exists. Like a holographic fractal, the complete original is contained in every single extension. There is simply no getting away from Love at all.

Today you reach for this truth. You want to feel it, to accept it within yourself, and to know it with the wisdom of your heart and mind. Even if you feel it only for a moment, that is enough.

Today's practice includes a single ten-to-fifteen-minute meditation as well as mindfulness throughout the day.

Take your seat and relax your body. Let your tummy soften. Let your shoulders go. Soften the area in your chest, your neck, behind your eyes. Feel your feet resting on the floor. Place your awareness gently on the breath. Notice how you sink more deeply into relaxation on the out-breath. On the out-breath let all tension be released into space.

When you are ready say in your mind, "Love created me like Itself." Then allow associated thoughts to form. For example, you might say to yourself: "Kindness created me kind." "Wisdom created me wise." "Compassion created me compassionate." "Grace created me gracious." "Happiness created me happy." "Playfulness created me playful." "Sovereignty created me sovereign." You might also simply say, "I am certain about myself." "I like myself." "I am good." You will know the thoughts by how they make you feel – which should be good, whole, happy, certain about yourself, capable, and pleased with yourself.

You cannot know the presence of God unless you feel it. Feel the words resonate in your body. They have a frequency that is a match for spirit. You are literally raising your mental and emotional frequency with this lesson.

After you have spent a few moments with these thoughts, bring your attention back to the breath, and spend the next five or ten minutes in peace. Watch your breath and repeat the lesson when your mind wanders. Love created you like Itself. This Self must be in you. It is there, somewhere in your mind, waiting for you to find It. You will "know" it through the feeling of satisfaction.

Practice mindfulness today. In fact, repeat this lesson four or five times an hour if you can. You need to hear the truth about yourself as often as possible. You deserve it. This is not some tiny voice: it is the Voice for God. It is your prime directive. It is what you came here to know about yourself.

Lesson 68

Love holds no grievances.

What is a grievance but a complaint about something I do not like? I may have a grievance against my boss, or the fact I must pay taxes. I may have a grievance about drug companies or politicians. Many of us hold grievances about the state of the world today.

When I hold a grievance, I have entered a test of wills with reality. I am saying, "No. I do not like this. I will it to be different." A grievance is a judgment against what is and I will never win in this test of wills. What is, IS, and I have called it to me only to show me Love.

Suppose someone runs into my car and I suffer a broken leg. My personal mind would interpret this event as cause for a grievance. It would portray me as a victim and justify my projection of blame onto the other driver. My friends would sympathize with my projection. My insurance company would sue the other driver for negligence. They would receive financial benefit from my projection.

But I might also open my eyes to see the event through the eyes of the other driver. What was his morning like? Was he unable to afford those new tires? Did she anticipate being fired that morning? Had she argued with her husband? And how many times have I narrowly escaped being in his shoes? Have I not been guilty of driving mindlessly?

When I open my eyes to the other I might see the accident as an opportunity to learn. Who exactly is the other driver? What were the circumstances? Perhaps instead of blaming, I could see this differently. Perhaps I could remember my function and help him remember his?

Seen through the eyes of Love, there is no contradiction in helping myself and the other driver. Seen through the eyes of Love, my accident becomes my opportunity to develop my own power; power from within to create my own reality. In choosing to focus on my power instead of my victimhood, I heal myself and I offer healing to the other person. Now we are joined where before we were separate. This is why Love has no grievances – it never separates, it only joins.

Reactivity is always a sign I am holding a grievance. It shows me I am projecting outward what I refuse to see within. Every grievance is an opportunity for healing. It brings forward an energy, a thought, a feeling that needs forgiveness. A grievance is a blessing often disguised as trouble.

Sit in contemplation for about 15 minutes today. Take your seat and relax the body. Close your eyes and place your awareness gently on the breath. Watch the breath for a minute or so. You may notice your body relaxes more deeply on the out-breath. Enjoy this letting go.

When you are ready say in your mind, "Love holds no grievances." Then allow your mind to search for anyone or anything against which you hold a grievance – no matter how large or small. Perhaps it will become apparent that there is no one or no thing against which you do not cherish a grievance of some sort.

Notice the feeling of each grievance. Take time to wallow in it a bit. Turn it over and look closely at it. Where did it come from? What part did you play in it? See the grievance from all sides. Don't work too hard at this, but be very honest. After you have looked at the situation as clearly as you can, from as many angles as you can, say in your mind: "I would see you as my friend, that I may remember you are part of me and come to know myself."

Your grievance holds an aspect of yourself within it. Forgive yourself. Forgive the person or situation. You are safe in a Source that holds and protects you; that loves you, and that you love in return. Try to feel the safety. Try to believe, however briefly, that nothing can harm you in any way. At the end of the practice period, say in your mind, "Love holds no grievances. When I let all my grievances go, I will know I am perfectly safe."

Practice mindfulness often today, especially when any feeling of discomfort arises for any reason. Remind yourself every half hour that, "Love holds no grievances. Let me not betray my Self." If you forget, don't hold a grievance against yourself! For in forgetting, and then remembering without guilt, you are allowing the opportunity to learn the lesson even more deeply.

Lesson 69

My grievances hide the light of the world in me.

In truth, it is impossible to be separated from the Light. However, in this world it is certainly possible to hide Light's presence behind grievances, just as the sun can be hidden behind clouds. A grievance is my unwillingness to accept my moment of attraction. It says, "I know better than Source what is in my best interest."

The vast majority of this world perceives only the veil of grievances. What lies beyond the veil seems impossible to see. How profoundly tragic it would be if this were true. Be thankful it is not. It takes only a single person to see the Light. When she or he sees, the growth in seeing becomes exponential. This is why the end of separation from Source is guaranteed. It takes far fewer minds to see the Light and end the darkness than it took for darkness to take over. Minds are waking to the light now, even as darkness appears to loom large.

The light is our inheritance. Recognize and affirm this truth within yourself and you are halfway there. Faith is often the first step. The rest is simply practice. It is as though we are laying a path in our mind to the light. Once well worn, the path has become overgrown. It will take some time to lay a new one.

Your practice today is a guided meditation. Read through the meditation at least once before you begin to practice. It's a simple visualization so be at ease with it. If you are not good at visualizing, just read the words.

When you're ready, take your seat and relax the body. Feel your feet resting on the floor. Connect with the earth through your feet. How kind is Mother Earth to support us all! Allow the peace of Mother Earth to flow up your feet and into the legs. Let the ease flow into the hips and release any tightness there. Let your tummy soften and let your heart open. Relax your shoulders and feel the area behind the eyes relax. Let your arms and hands be soft.

Now place your awareness gently on the breath. You may notice that on the out-breath you sink a bit more deeply into a state of peace. This is good. When you are ready, imagine in your mind that you are sitting within a vast circle of clouds. Keep your awareness partly on the breath and partly on this vision. Watch yourself among the clouds. Perhaps you believe the clouds are all there is to this reality in your mind. Take a moment to look around at the vast grayness.

When you are ready, allow yourself to imagine you want to see more. Is there anything beyond the clouds? Reach out and touch them. They are damp and cool. Sweep your hand through the mist and watch it curl like smoke around your fingers. Now, allow the clouds to be brushed away. See them move aside. Watch your breath. Stay with the breath as the mists swirl around your hands.

As the clouds drift away, sense the warmth behind them. This warmth grows stronger until it begins to disperse all the clouds. You need do nothing at all but watch it. Feel the growing warmth on your face. A soft breeze gently moves in your hair.

You are standing now wholly in the light of a warm sun. You see that it was behind the clouds all along. How good to know it was always there!

Allow the warm light to envelop your body. Bask in it. Stay with the breath as you experience the peace of being bathed in the gentle, soaking heat. There is Love in it. Feel that. Give yourself permission to rest in the warm, loving kindness of this place for as long as you like, at least ten minutes.

At the end of the practice say to yourself, "Love holds no grievances. When I let my grievances go, I know I am perfectly safe." Then come back to the present moment and continue with your day.

Practice mindfulness today. Remind yourself that you are not searching for the light by yourself or for yourself alone. When you experience any disquiet, no matter how small, repeat the lesson saying, "My grievances hide the light of the world in me." Notice the peace that returns when mindfulness is practiced. Mindfulness is like an anchor in a storm. If you forget, please remember not to punish yourself! A grievance against yourself will hide the light of the world in you.

Lesson 70

My salvation comes from me.

I recall a former priest's description of his church's view of humanity. "It's a hamburger universe," he said. "Heaven is the top bun. Hell is the bottom bun. The poor human is stuck between the two buns, and the church is constantly vying for their soul."

For those who still believe in a "hamburger universe" today's lesson might verge on blasphemous. But for those ready to step into spiritual adulthood the lesson is freedom in its most fundamental form.

Salvation is freedom from the perception of separation from Source, and the willingness to take responsibility for your creations. ACIM says, "Salvation seems to come from anywhere except from you. So, too, does the source of guilt. When you realize that all guilt is solely an invention of your mind, you also realize that guilt and salvation must be in the same place."

Nothing outside yourself can save you; nothing outside yourself can harm you or cause you loss of peace. Today's idea "places you in charge of the universe, where you belong because of what you are." What an idea!

The personal mind, which relies on separation for its very existence, would have you believe you are powerless to choose. It would deny you your divinity and trap you in an endless cycle of guilt and projection. But like all illusions, the ego is powerless. The Will of Source is salvation and Its Will is yours.

Do you will to be happy? If so, recognize first that you are invulnerable. Recognize that everything vibrates with the Love of Source. Recognize that you are free. We do not live in a hamburger universe, and you are not asked to accept anything on the faith of anyone else but yourself! Become a student of your own mind. Explore its contents fully, as often as possible. Ask, "When does guilt arise?" Ask, "What is it I am afraid of?" Ask, "Is this thought true?" And ask, "What do I wish to teach, love or fear?" Notice when you feel content. Can you see into the source of your contentment?

Today you should practice twice, in the morning and evening if possible. Each practice period should last about 10 to 15 minutes. It would be a good idea to begin now to establish set practice times and places, if you have not already done so.

When you are ready, take your seat and relax the body. Feel your feet resting on the floor. Connect with the earth through your feet. How kind is Mother Earth to support us all! Let your legs relax and then your hips. Let your tummy soften and let your heart open. Relax your shoulders, and the area behind the eyes. Let your arms and hands relax. Now place your awareness gently on the breath. You may notice that on the out-breath you sink a bit more deeply into a state of peace. This is good.

When you are ready, say in your mind, "My salvation comes from me. It cannot come from anywhere else." With awareness on the breath, allow your mind to gently focus on external places where you have looked for salvation in the past – in other people, in possessions, in various situations and events, and in self-concepts you sought to make real. How do these solutions feel in your body as you review them? Did they offer what you sought? Perhaps temporarily so, but none in any way that lasts. As you review them each, say in your mind, "My salvation cannot come from any of these things. My salvation comes from me, and only from me. It comes from my knowing I am already perfect and One with my Source."

Now relax more deeply and place your attention fully on the breath. Allow thoughts to arise, as they will. If your thoughts become too chaotic, repeat the lesson slowly to yourself. Feel each word in your body, then go back to the breath and the peace of sitting in quiet. At the end of your meditation, repeat the lesson in your mind, and gently come back to the day.

Practice mindfulness. If you experience any moment of tension, apprehension, depression, or irritation, say to yourself, "My salvation comes from me. Nothing outside of me can hold me back from my desire."

Lesson 71

Only God's plan for salvation will work.

The lesson for today is about learning itself. There are only two "curriculums" available for learning: that of the personal mind, and that of Source or the Holy Spirit. Only one curriculum teaches Truth and only one leads Home. The other teaches, "Seek but do not find."

Perhaps you remember yesterday's description of the "hamburger universe." This was a view of the human condition offered by a former priest. Humanity is like the meat of the burger, eternally caught between the top bun (heaven) and the bottom bun (hell) – both of which are vying for the heart of the soul.

ACIM finds this image ludicrous for two reasons. There is no hell except that which we create in our mind and there is nothing to save because we cannot be separated from Source.

However, there is one part of the image that warrants discussion – the dual nature of a "split mind." The hamburger image is a visual of our own split mind. We perceive either with the personal mind or through the Holy Spirit. Each offers a radically different "curriculum."

The curriculum of the personal mind is separation. It teaches that if only someone or something was different than it is, all would be well. Something must be altered for me to be happy. My day must change. The weather must change. My body must change. My bank account must change. You must change. Each demand is a declaration of denial. The ego's curriculum demands that everything or everyone must change... except itself.

But this insane curriculum goes even further. Not only does the ego demand that its grievance against reality be corrected, it also ensures, at the same time, that the correction will never be enough. There will always need to be another correction, and then another, and then another after that.

The personal mind is literally at war with reality and this war is itself what sustains it. The ego's curriculum is, "Seek but do not find." It guarantees that you will never find peace because it channels all your efforts into a search for that perfect something else. The perfect something else is not Mind of God – which is already perfect.

To fight reality is to split your mind in two. It is insane to argue with what is. It is! Peace lies in the curriculum of the Holy Spirit, which is of Source. There is no alternative. There is no other "plan." You need no other, and there is nothing else that will save you from yourself. Personal mind fears what it cannot control. Source would have you let go, and trust in your eternal nature – the nature It endowed you with and which cannot be altered in any way.

What Source has endowed us with is far beyond the ego's tiny, fearful curriculum. Be glad it isn't the one that's real. Source's curriculum is Reality and Source will never abandon what It has created Real. That would be YOU.

Today we have two periods of practice, each about 10 to 15 minutes long. Try to sit in the a.m. and the p.m. hours, in a comfortable place where you will not be disturbed. We are trying to establish a schedule here, a time in which you devote yourself to your Self.

Take your seat and relax the body. Feel your feet resting on the floor. Let your legs relax, then your hips and tummy. Let your heart relax. Release the shoulders, arms, and hands. Let the neck relax, and the area behind the eyes. Let your whole body sink into your seat and then gently place your awareness on the breath. Notice how, on the out-breath, you release a little more.

When you are ready, say in your mind, "Only God's plan for salvation will work." You may find yourself resisting these words. Notice the resistance, but do not judge it. Source's plan is union with Itself. You are already there. Don't worry about it.

After you have repeated the lesson in your mind, simply sit and watch the breath. Center yourself with it. The breath is your own personal centering device. When you are ready, ask these questions one by one, very slowly: "What would You have me do? Where would You have me go? What would You have me say, and to whom?" Do not worry about these questions. Just ask each one slowly, then go back to watching the breath. Wait and allow an answer to arise. Don't force a thing. Just watch.

The answer will be in the form of a feeling or a knowing. It may be fleeting. It may feel like emptiness. It may simply be peaceful silence. Give your practice period over to Source and allow whatever arises to arise. If you are truly willing to ask, you WILL be answered. Do not judge anything, including your own willingness. The very fact that you are sitting is all the evidence you need of your own willingness. The rest of what follows is enough. You have, in your very willingness to sit in meditation, established your claim to Source's answer.

Practice mindfulness today. If you can, it would be helpful to repeat today's lesson every ten minutes. Be alert to any moments of distress, irritation, or annoyance. When you notice them, say in your mind something like: "Arguing with what is, is the opposite of God's plan for me. Let me allow this. Let me watch this moment be what it is without being personally attached to it. Let me be curious. Let things unfold."

Lesson 72

Holding grievances is an attack on God's plan for salvation.

All attack is fear based. The source of all resistance to what is, is fear. Resistance says, "No!" to reality. When I resist, I am holding a grievance for what I have called to myself through my power to create.

> Source is very quiet because there is no conflict in It. Our conflict is at the root of all perceived "evil" because it attacks blindly and does not see what it attacks. But it always attacks you in your Oneness with God.
> – E. Cronkhite, *The Message of* A Course in Miracles

Your goal in today's practice is to become aware of two things. First, you exist in the Mind of God and have never left It. Second, resistance to "what is" is like trying to walk upstream. If you put all your effort into walking upstream, you will never get to the river. Today, notice your resistance, let it go, and see what happens. Lie down in the stream and float with the current.

Continue with two practice periods today, each lasting 10 to 15 minutes. One in the a.m. and one in the p.m. would be best. Take your seat and relax the body. Place your awareness gently on the breath. Sit in peace like this for a bit and then, when you are ready, ask in your mind, "What is salvation? What is my Oneness? I ask Source to show me." Spend your meditation in contemplation of this question. Use the breath as your foundation. Allow thoughts to arise. Feel your way through. Source is very quiet because there is no conflict in It. Ask, "What does Oneness feel like?"

Be mindful today. Once or twice an hour, ask yourself, "Am I in resistance? If so, to what?" Then listen within. If you have any moment of discomfort, know it is because you are resisting something. Notice and relax, then move on. You may say to yourself, "Holding grievances is an attack on God's plan for salvation. Let me accept this moment. What would Oneness with the moment feel like?"

Lesson 73

I will there be light.

The personal mind cannot undo the deeper aspect of your will that is joined with Source. This is why you cannot fail in today's lesson. Only the whole can ever extend from Wholeness and your light is whole. Today's lesson is a reflection of both your light and your will to know the light within yourself.

The will toward light is the will we share with Source. Your desire to experience the light is a decision against the curriculum of the personal mind, and a decision for the curriculum of Source.

There is limitless power in the will to change your mind. My mind changed about this lesson only when I experimented with it. I allowed myself to ask, "What does it feel like to experience the thought that my mind is joined with Mind of Source?" I encourage you to play with this lesson.

For example, what does it feel like to hear God is Love? That you are Love? What do you notice inside when you say these words? What does it feel like to hear that Love is freedom? And freedom is forgiveness? What does it feel like to hear that forgiveness is your only function in this experience you call your life? And how does it feel to know your function and your happiness are one?

If you feel any sense of joy and peace in these words, know it is because in the moment you are reading them, your will is joined with God's. The feeling of peace is an emotional frequency. Feel it and you and God are in direct sharing.

The ego would have you dismiss feelings of joy and peace as a temporary illusion. It will encourage you to remember your grievances and your guilt, calling them reality. Forgive your ego and its arguments for limitation. For in this forgiveness you are asserting your will to light. The more you practice forgiveness, the more you become aware that every choice is between a miracle and a grievance. This is your rise to the awareness of Love's Presence.

Today we practice getting closer to joy. Perhaps it will appear as a small contentment. Perhaps it will appear as a moment free of fear. Perhaps it will grow into a warm light of peace. This is enough. We are laying a path down in a pasture grown wild by an untrained mind.

You have two practice periods again today, each one 10 to 15 minutes in length. Begin by taking your seat and relaxing the body. Take a few deep breaths and sink into yourself. Let your tummy relax. Let your shoulders loosen. Relax the area behind your eyes. Place your awareness gently on the breath. When you are ready, say in your mind, "I will there be light." Know that your will is fully supported by the Will of Source.

Now gently watch the breath and come to a place of silence. Do not worry about thoughts that arise. Watch them come and go like clouds passing through your awareness. Use the breath as your anchor. Allow yourself to imagine that joy surrounds you and is within you. Breathe in serenity and freedom. If you feel even a thread of peace, hold on to it. Allow it to move within you. You are entitled to it.

Do not strive in these meditations. Just be still and watch your breath. Be open to anything as you listen without effort to what presents itself. Listen for the feelings of joy, for this is the will of God, and it is your will, joined with God's. Thoughts will rise up that threaten this feeling of peace. Don't worry about it. Watch the thought, feel any feeling that accompanies it, and return to the breath. Another feeling of joy will arise, then a thought. Forgive all that arises, and joy will follow your forgiveness.

End your practice by repeating the lesson. You are beginning to realize that your will is light. When you find it, even for an instant, it will begin to magnify and grow.

Practice mindfulness today. Close your eyes each hour and go into the silence where light lives. Cherish these little moments of mindfulness. If you feel any grievances today (and you will) use the grievance as a reminder that you will the light, not the grievance. Forgive yourself if the grievance seems to hold more power. The act of forgiveness is more powerful than any grievance. The more you practice forgiveness, the more your mind remembers. This is the miracle behind the grievance!

Lesson 74

There is no will but God's.

This lesson is entirely logical. If God is everything then it is impossible that anything could exist outside It. It follows, then, that nothing accidental is possible. I repeat: nothing accidental is possible or it would occur outside Mind and Will of God. All dimensions, all universes, all time, all events, all beings, all consciousness, are Mind of God. What we perceive as chaos is merely our inability to perceive the Whole.

This logical thinking may feel confusing and threatening, but it can also bring great peace. It tells me that as an expression of the Will of God, I can have no goal that is not in alignment with It. This means every error I believe I have ever made must eventually lead back to Source. Free will says I can take as long as I want with this game. Source is endlessly patient because It rests in the Knowledge that all things lead back to It.

You should now be in the practice of twice-daily meditations of 10 to 15 minutes each. Try to enjoy this quiet time. You deserve it.

Take your seat and relax your body. Close your eyes and place awareness on the breath. On the out-breath, notice how the whole body sinks into a deeper state. It feels good because it is good. When you are ready, say in your mind, "There is no will but God's. I cannot be in conflict because nothing exists outside Mind of God."

If thoughts of conflict arise, or if you feel any bodily discomfort, say in your mind, "There is no will but God's. Thoughts of conflict have no power." Then return to the breath and feel the peace that comes from letting go. All will be well because there is no other option but God's will.

Try to repeat the lesson in your mind every half hour or so today. You might say, "There is no will but God's. I seek the peace of Source." There is nothing you can do to undermine Source. You can only temporarily undermine your relationship with It by resisting forgiveness. But you exist within It and are Its effect.

Lesson 75

The Light has come.

"The light is here now." This statement is the truth. We are all already healed. We have never left our Source. End your need for sacrifice and know the light.

Forgiveness is the key that opens the door to the light that has never, not always been here. Every time you experience a feeling of peace, joy, or even quiet acceptance, you have opened to what is always there behind the noise of the world.

Source's language is inner light known in gentle stillness. You are not a body. Form and matter cannot hold or define you. Illness and suffering cannot limit you. Forgive your mistaken notions about what you are. Lay aside your identification with the body today, even if it is only for a short while.

Two practice periods of 10 to 15 minutes are asked today, one in the morning and another in the evening as close to bedtime as possible. Take your seat and relax. Center your mind with the breath. Allow your body and your mind to find a place of stillness. When you are ready, say in your mind, "The light has come. I have forgiven myself and the world." As you repeat these words, try to feel them in the body. The words have frequency. This is mindfulness working on the physical body. It is powerful and real.

For the duration of this meditation hold your attention on the breath. When you find your mind wandering, return to the lesson and say, "The light has come. I have forgiven myself and the world." Repeat the words gently, without rushing. Let them sink in. After about 10 or 15 minutes, gently return to the present moment.

Throughout the day, every 15 minutes or so, say in your mind, "The light has come. I have forgiven myself and the world." You can do this without disturbing anything else that is going on around you. If you experience a stressful thought or situation, repeat the lesson in your mind. In fact, stressful situations are a perfect reminder for this lesson. There will be many reminders in your day! If you forget to repeat the lesson, see it as a way to apply it. Say to yourself, "The light has come. I forgive myself."

Lesson 76

I am under no laws but God's.

Consider the laws under which we live. We believe that little plastic cards and numbers in a bank account show us our value. We believe a faceless institution like a bank can tell us what we are worth. We believe that because you were born in a certain part of the world, you can be excluded from access to another part. We believe it is okay to lie if you are powerful, but if you are powerless and get caught you should be punished. We believe it is wrong to commit murder, but it is forgivable to take the life of an enemy, even if that enemy is a child. We believe we can judge another as less worthy. We believe we know what beauty is and what it is not.

We like to think our laws are consistent and that they have universal application. But most of our laws do not hold true in different places, for different people, in different times. The laws of this world are ours. Some are highly complex, such as the laws of mathematics and physics. Yet even these have changed with times and with new discoveries. How creative is our unlimited genius!

Unlike human law, the Law of All That Is is simple and has universal application. It always has been and will never change. The Law of Source is contained in the Law of Oneness and it supersedes every law we have ever made.

What is the Law of One? It is fundamentally a Law of Love. Yet because we know nothing of Love here, we do not comprehend

It. The Law of Love is simple. It is this: Nothing I do to you is not also done to myself. The Law of Love is perfectly consistent and perfectly sane. It extends everywhere to everything.

The Law of Love is in complete contradiction to the laws of this world. For example, it says, "I must give what I want to keep." It says, "If I believe in scarcity that is what I shall have." The Law of Love denies nothing. Give only Love because that is what you are.

Practice contemplation in the morning and evening today, for 10 to 15 minutes each. Take your seat and relax. Close your eyes and place your awareness on the breath. Relax and let go deeply on the out-breath. When you are ready, gently direct your mind to the "laws" under which you think you must live.

For example, you might consider the "laws" of finance in which you "must" maintain good credit or lose your house. It may be the "laws" of medicine that offer defense against sickness and disease. You might also review the "laws" of relationship, which demand reciprocity as well as being "good" and "selfless." You might consider the religious "laws" you have been taught about God's damnation and punishment if you "sin." Just about every rule you have been taught is probably up for grabs.

Notice each of the "laws" which you have accepted as true. Then allow yourself to be free of them all as you repeat in your mind, "I am under no laws but God's." If you feel any discomfort from these words, you might add, "There is nothing to fear." As you sit with this lesson, notice your feelings. This may be the first time you have ever felt really free. Allow this feeling of freedom, for it is your natural state.

Do not get up immediately after your contemplation. Give yourself permission to sit in peace, with eyes open and look around. Every single thing you see is part of God's Law.

Try to remind yourself of today's lesson as often as possible today. It is your ticket to true freedom. At least four or five times an hour (yes, every 15 minutes or so!) remind yourself you are free. You are, of course, free not to do this at all. The decision is always yours to make. Go ahead. You can't fail no matter which you choose.

Lesson 77

I am entitled to miracles.

The conventional definition of a miracle is a divine and very rare occurrence that happens only to special people or in special circumstances. It may be an event or a physical healing of some kind. It may be a vision or an angelic visitation. But almost always, miracles come from the outside. They are blessings randomly bestowed for reasons often unknown.

ACIM defines a miracle differently. They happen all the time. We just don't notice. We don't notice because we perceive through the framework of a personal mind that doesn't pay attention to events outside its scope of reference. ACIM teaches that a miracle always involves a healing of inner perception. For a brief moment, the veils of the personal mind are lifted and we see truly, with the heart.

Miracles come in many forms. One might arise in a flash of insight about a problem or a person. One might arrive in a dream. Physical events can bring forth miracles. A synchronicity is a miracle arriving through time.

All miracles involve Love in some form. Even if one appears complicated, it is just as powerful as one that seems simple. In other words, there are no small or big miracles because all expressions of Love are maximal. Miracles occur naturally, as an outgrowth of Love, which is the basic building block of the universe.

Do not think of miracles as magic. It is more apt to call them a learning device. They offer a sudden change of perception – one that is closer to the Truth. Miracles help us learn to see that things are not always what the personal mind believes. A miracle is a bridge to Mind of God.

Miracles are involuntary. In other words, we don't work for them and they cost nothing. They are a kind of exchange that reverses the rules of scarcity, which say, "To give something, I must lose something." No one loses with miracles. A miracle always releases fear and restores the mind to its fullness.

Today's practice proclaims what is rightfully yours and is always available to you. Practice the lesson in the morning and evening for 10 to 15 minutes.

Take your seat and close your eyes. Relax the body and place your awareness on the breath. Relax deeply into the out-breath. When you are ready, say in your mind, "I am entitled to miracles." You ask for no more than what belongs to you. Now just wait in peace.

Whatever thoughts come up are perfect. Trust. Notice the thought and repeat the lesson. Center your awareness in the breath. Breathe the lesson in. Breathe the lesson out. This is meditation with a holy purpose. It is meditation on the only entitlement program that matters. But remember this: You do not provide the miracle for yourself. You ask, and it is given. Be mindful of this! Allow the miracle to present itself in the form of its own choosing. Your role is to ask, then step back, and allow the unfolding.

Be mindful of this lesson as you live your day. If you pay attention to the small things you will recognize the bigger pattern. Notice! Remain aware of yourself being aware and you will see synchronicities abound.

If you can, repeat the lesson to yourself every 15 minutes, but do not feel badly if you forget. Just try to remember next time. If you have any moment of upset, ask for the miracle to which you are entitled. You do not create miracles but Source has established them as your right. You want only what belongs to you – true perception, true peace, and true forgiveness – all for free.

Lesson 78

Let miracles replace all grievances.

My limited vision makes it impossible to see the threads that form the pattern of my life: how one decision leads to a whole series of occurrences I could never have foretold.

I take the left-hand turn out of my driveway. Immediately I find myself stuck behind an elderly driver going 30 in a 45mph zone. Just as I am about to curse her for the third time, another driver makes an unsafe turn right in front of us. If I'd been going my usual speed, I might very well have hit him. The person I was cursing seconds before now becomes my friend.

Knowing my vision is limited doesn't always make things easier. I still suffer much unnecessary confusion, pain, and fear. ACIM teaches that "seeing behind the grievances" is critical to advanced understanding. But I am not always able to see beyond the grievance. This is where I relearn the art of forgiveness.

It has been my experience that when I habitually refuse to look truthfully at what is going on within myself, I will attract another person, or event, that mirrors my inner reality. This is not a punishment but it is a wake-up call. What other choice than awakening do I really have, or want? As James Baldwin said, "Not everything that is faced can be changed, but nothing can be changed until it is faced."

Every thought I have is based on my choice. It is true I sometimes willingly choose against my own best interests. That's okay. The point isn't which choice I make as much as the knowing I am free to choose, and I am always choosing. A major part of the job is to pay attention to what happens when I choose one way or another.

No matter what choice I make, I am still eternal spirit, at one with All. This is the miracle. Knowing what I truly am makes it easier to accept the limited vision that is available to me now.

Today's lesson is a statement of willingness to expand your vision. It should be practiced for 10 to 15 minutes, in the morning and evening.

Take your seat and relax the body. Place your attention on the breath. When you are ready, say in your mind, "Let miracles replace all grievances." Now choose someone to be a "target" for your grievances. Bring up all their faults. Have fun with this! Perhaps the person instills fear or hatred in you. Perhaps they are demanding, judgmental, or ungrateful. They may be a new acquaintance or an old enemy. Go ahead and wallow in it.

After you have thoroughly explored all the pain, the neglect, the little hurts, and the larger hurts this person has inflicted upon you, repeat the lesson in your mind. You may wish to say in your mind, "Let miracles replace all grievances I have about (_____)."

At this point, you may consider asking for help with this contemplation. You are not asked to complete the task of forgiveness on your own. Ask for help from the part of you that is connected forever with Source – your Holy Spirit. Ask and know your request will never be denied. The Holy Spirit is like a wireless router – it connects you to the main power source from any location.

The help you seek today lies in seeing your enemy in light of his or her true being. He or she is a child of God joined with you – past the confusion, fear, and separation of being in a body, in a form that cannot last. The help you seek is in seeing how their presence in your life has served you in some way. They might never be aware of how they've served your learning. Their service to you might seem to be a very small thing. If you can't find it or feel it, just allow peace. There is no demand for forgiveness before you are ready.

When you have spent as much time with your person as feels right, let him or her go from your mind. If your pain has been replaced with even a small sense of gratitude, know your enemy has also received the miracle. Minds are joined.

If you have someone or something else you would like to forgive, repeat this process within the ten or fifteen minutes you have for this lesson today.

Continue your mindfulness today by repeating the lesson often, especially when you notice any thought that contains even the smallest grievance, or resistance to your moment. Make no mistake, this is no small thing you are doing. The entire Universe is changed as a result of your willingness.

Lesson 79

Let me recognize the problem so it can be solved.

A problem cannot be solved if you do not know what it is. Even if it is already solved you will still have the problem, because you will not recognize it has been solved. This is the situation of the world. The problem of separation, which is really the only problem, has already been solved.
– ACIM

Can you remember a nightmare from which you awoke instantly knowing it was just a dream? How happy you were to awaken knowing it wasn't real!

In dreams, we imagine many things. While in the dream these things seem real. This is the state of our world: it is a waking dream we believe to be true. In this group dream we are alone, vulnerable, and locked in a human body. Few people ask if this dream is real or not. Everyone appears to believe it. Death seems to be the only release.

But what if it isn't true? What might happen if we began to awaken from the waking dream? What if we began to understand that the single, underlying cause of every problem in this world is the belief that we are separate, for this is the same belief that says, "I can lie to you, steal from you, wage war against you, shame and judge you, watch you suffer in pain, die from hunger, and it will not have any impact on me." What a dream of misery.

We live in a dream of separation at the level of group consciousness. However, awakening from it occurs at the level of the individual mind. This is because the solution to the problem must occur at the same level it appears. We think we are separate body/minds, so we seem to awaken separately. But here's the miracle: your awakening helps me, and my awakening helps you. It cannot be otherwise because the problem of separation has already been solved.

Today's lesson begins a reversal of a thought system that has been in place for eons. To see through it we must see where its malformations begin. This is why it is so important for you to see unity. Once seen, the change begins, even if it feels like you shoulder the burden by yourself at first.

Today ask not that your problems be solved, but that you recognize the common theme behind them all.

Practice in the morning and evening. Your practice will consist of asking a question, and then feeling your way into the answer. Try not to think this through. Knowing comes from feeling beyond thinking. The rational mind cannot see beyond itself and this IS BEYOND IT. Experience your knowing.

Take your seat and close your eyes. Become aware of the breath. When you are at ease, ask yourself, "What is the problem?"

Be curious about this. Above all, be confident in yourself. Be certain about yourself. Like yourself. You are fully capable of understanding what the problem is. Feel your way deeply into the question. In a way, you are daydreaming the answer.

If you find your mind wandering during this practice, it is probably because of fear. The personal mind does not want you to perceive the problem. It thrives on complexity. It will tell you there can be no end to all the problems of the world. It will tell you there is no way they can all be solved. It does not want you to recognize that every problem stems from your perception of separation from Source.

Simply go back to the breath and ask the question in your mind again. But remember: you are not trying to solve any problems in this meditation! You are trying to recognize that you have been given the answer by recognizing the truth about what the problem really is – a belief in the illusion of separation.

The answer to your question, "What is the problem?" will be known by a feeling. You will succeed to the extent you let go of the personal mind's perception. You will realize that you have only one problem, which until now you have failed to recognize. Stay the course. Let your journey be guided by your own Oneness with Source. You will be told what your problem is and what the solution to it is.

End your meditation by returning attention to the breath. When you are ready, open your eyes and continue your day.

Practice mindfulness today. Remember, the personal mind will perceive each problem as a separate issue because it hides behind complexity. If you experience even the slightest irritation ask for clarification about it. Say in your mind, "Let me recognize this problem so it can be solved." Wait for the answer through feeling, not thinking. The answer will always come to you. It cannot be otherwise for Minds are joined.

Lesson 80

Let me recognize my problems have been solved.

Every single thing we perceive to be outside of us is inside of us. All those we perceive to be separate bodies, separate objects, separate nations, separate seasons, separate moments in time, are One in the Mind of Source. Do you imagine yourself to be so special as to be excluded from this Oneness?

We are master creators because Source created us creators. We have all the creative powers of the One. It would be very helpful to this world if we could do two things: first, allow ourselves credit for our own mastery; and second, take responsibility for what we have created.

There are many variations of Oneness to be sure. And often, I seem to not enjoy what I have created. But every problem I have comes from my perception of separation. It is why I hate my day. It is why I hate my neighbor. It is why I hate politicians, corporations, rich people, poor people, sick people, old people, and myself. Most of all, I hate my separation from Source.

But I am not separated from Source. In truth, I have no choice about it. It's a "what is." Only in a dream can we believe it to be true. The sooner we recognize the false "specialness" of the ego, the sooner we will leave the confusion of spiritual adolescence behind. Freedom from conflict has been given. But we must allow ourselves to see it. That is exactly what these lessons will do, if you will allow it.

There are three five-minute meditation periods today. Can you give yourself fifteen minutes of peace? Take your seat and close your eyes. Allow your body to sink into the chair and relax. When you are relaxed and comfortable in the body, place your attention gently on the breath. On the out-breath, release any remaining tension. When you are ready, in your mind, say to yourself, "Let me recognize my problems have been solved."

And now relax. Watch the breath. Allow thoughts to arise, as they will. When they do, just notice, and say the lesson again in your mind. Notice how the words resonate in the body and go back to the breath. Stay with the breath and the words of the lesson. You should enter a state of peacefulness. Enjoy it.

Be mindful throughout the day today. Repeat the lesson as often as you can, especially when you encounter a "problem." Use your body as an indicator of your own peacefulness. If you feel your tummy tightening or your heart area constricting, you are unconsciously having a "problem." The body always knows what the mind refuses to recognize. Repeat the lesson and feel its warmth infuse the body. You have a right to peace. Take what is offered to you today.

Review II

Lesson 81: Review

You are now ready for another review period. If you've come this far, you are well on your way. Remember, the purpose of these reviews is to integrate key concepts. Linking core ideas together deepens and reinforces your knowing.

This week we cover two ideas per day – one idea in the morning and the second idea in the evening. Each idea is followed by a brief commentary to help frame the idea. You may, at this point, begin to use your own thoughts and experiences to add to the commentary. Contemplation of the idea should take about fifteen minutes. Enjoy the quiet time.

Here is how to practice:

Take your seat and relax. Slowly and quietly, read the two ideas for the day along with the commentary. Don't rush this reading. Then choose one of the ideas. With your eyes open, say the idea slowly out loud, or in your mind. Feel the words. Then close your eyes, repeat the idea, and place awareness on the breath.

Allow thoughts to arise, as they will. If your mind wanders, repeat the idea in your mind and go back to the breath. Don't worry if you have to repeat the idea like a mantra.

Sink deeply into relaxation with each out-breath. Trust in the words of the idea and trust in your breath. Don't worry if your mind is restless. It's all okay, just stay with it. You may have moments of intense thinking, or you may have no thoughts at all. The breath should be the foundation upon which all of this practice rests, but there may also be times when even awareness of the breath falls away. Just have your experience and allow it to be as it is. Do not judge yourself in any way.

Today's ideas are:

1. I am the light of the world.

Commentary: Your presence here is no accident. When you know what your true purpose is, you can be at peace because everything you do has meaning. Your light is part of the Great Light of Being. You did not create the Light and nothing you do can alter It. Source created you as you are, and It has given you your purpose.

2. Forgiveness is my function as the light of the world.

Commentary: It is your function to learn the gentle art of forgiveness. You may not understand it completely now, but do accept it. Ask for deeper understanding and then pay attention to what is offered. Forgiveness is yours. Receive it by giving it. There is no sacrifice in forgiveness and its power is beyond your comprehension. Its effects are felt throughout time and space.

Practice mindfulness throughout the day. In the morning hours, repeat the first idea often in your mind. In the afternoon, repeat the second idea of the lesson. Feel these words! They offer you your birthright and your purpose in this lifetime. Be determined not to leave your function unfulfilled. This is your service to your Self.

Lesson 82: Review

The personal mind analyzes. The Mind at One with Source allows. To analyze means to break down, to separate out. But Wholeness can only be appreciated through acceptance because only acceptance allows the multiple variations of Source's extensions to be experienced in every moment.

Today's ideas continue the unveiling of our true nature, what we are, and how we serve.

1. *The light of the world brings peace to every mind through my forgiveness.*
Commentary: Forgiving and allowing are closely related. When I allow you the freedom to be yourself, I also am free. Because I receive exactly what I give, forgiveness is the only means by which I can be healed in this world. What I allow, I am allowed. The power of my forgiveness is such that it extends to the whole world because giving and receiving are one. I share the light of the world with all I forgive.

2. *Let me not forget my function.*
Commentary: Every single question about life's purpose is answered in this idea. Truly, I have no other purpose than to learn forgiveness. There are as many ways to learn forgiveness as there are people, or situations, on this planet. This idea may threaten the personal mind, which sees itself separate, special, and always under attack, but it cannot change my function in any way. I can relax and experience this life without fear.

Here is how to practice these reviews:
Twice a day, in the morning and evening, select one of the ideas and devote fifteen minutes to it in the following manner:
Take your seat and relax. Read the two ideas for the day along with the commentary. Then choose an idea for the morning or evening. Spend about three or four minutes reading about the idea and its commentary. Don't rush. With eyes open, slowly repeat the idea. Allow the feeling behind the words to fill your entire being.
Then close your eyes and repeat the idea again. Place your awareness on the idea and the breath. For the next ten minutes watch the breath and allow thoughts to arise, as they will. Notice the thought and go back to the breath. Repeat the idea often if it helps focus your mind.
Trust whatever happens. Your aim is to reach a place of

stillness and peace. When you get there, even if just for a minute or two, know you have tasted Reality and your true nature.

Be mindful throughout the day by repeating one or both ideas in your mind as often as possible. Twice an hour would be good, but especially remember them if your mind is disturbed by anyone or anything. The time you spend remembering the ideas will greatly increase the happiness of your day.

Lesson 83: Review

Knowledge of Self has been hidden by the personal mind. But it cannot destroy what it did not create. True happiness comes from alignment with Source, not with the illusions of the personal mind.

Today's ideas are:

1. My only function is the one God gave me.

Commentary: We behave as though we either created Creation Itself, or no one did. We think we can understand Creation though thinking, analyzing, and taking apart. Yet, after all our effort, we find ourselves further from the answer. Recognize your Source and be released from conflict. Source has no conflict with Itself. It is not insane. Source is what you are. It knows your function.

2. My happiness and my function are one.

Commentary: When I resist my moment, I cannot be happy. Resistance is judgment. Resistance is contraction. But forgiveness expands, loosens, and allows. I am happiest when I refrain from judgment because it frees me from self-condemnation. Source gave me my function because Source wills my happiness.

Here is how to practice these reviews:

Twice a day, in the morning and evening, select one of the ideas and devote fifteen minutes to it in the following manner:

Take your seat and relax. Read the two ideas for the day along with the commentary. Then choose an idea for the morning or evening. Spend a few minutes reading about the idea and its commentary. Don't rush. With eyes open, slowly repeat the idea. Then close your eyes and place awareness on the idea, and on the breath. Repeat the idea often if it helps focus your mind. For the next ten minutes watch the breath and allow thoughts to arise, as they will. Notice the thought and go back to the breath.

Trust whatever happens. Your aim is to reach a place of stillness and peace. When you get there, even if just for a minute or two, know you have done what you came to do. You cannot fail at this.

Be mindful throughout the day by repeating one or both ideas in your mind twice an hour, if possible. Remember them if your mind is disturbed by anyone or anything. The time you spend remembering the ideas will greatly increase the happiness of your day.

Lesson 84: Review

How much do I want peace? I will know the answer by observing what I treasure.

1. Love created me like Itself.
Commentary: Few of us experience the unconditional depths of Love. Yet its memory remains alive in the heart. The more we share love, the more we feel it. Love did not create me only to see me imprisoned.

2. Love holds no grievances.
Commentary: Grievances are a form of denial. What is denied can only be my eternal light, which no earthly situation can ever obscure. Love does not deny anything except guilt, and this it denies everywhere. I am released from all lack when I release myself from grievances and the guilt they create.

Here is how to practice these reviews:

Twice a day, in the morning and evening, select one of the ideas and devote fifteen minutes to it in the following manner:

Take a seat and relax. Read the two ideas for the day along with the commentary. Then choose an idea for the morning or evening. Spend about three minutes reading the idea and its commentary. Don't rush. With eyes open, slowly repeat the idea. Allow the feeling behind the words to sink into your entire being. Then close your eyes and repeat the idea again. Place your awareness on the idea and the breath. Repeat the idea often if it helps focus your mind. For the next ten minutes watch the breath and allow thoughts to arise, as they will. Notice the thought and go back to the breath.

Trust whatever happens. Your aim is to reach a place of stillness and peace. When you get there, even if just for a minute or two, know you have tasted Reality and your true nature.

Be mindful throughout the day. Repeat one or both ideas in your mind as often as possible. Twice an hour would be good, but especially remember them if your mind is disturbed by anyone or anything. The time you spend remembering the ideas will greatly increase the happiness of your day.

Lesson 85: Review

What is a grievance but a perceived wrong against which one has the right to complain, to protest as unfair, or to resent? Grievances may be slight or murderous; it doesn't matter. When I keep hold of my grievances I am hiding my own power from myself. Even when I believe my grievance is held against another person, it is always me, and only me, who suffers. It is always me, and only me, who withholds power from myself.

Today's ideas are:

1. My grievances hide the light of the world in me.
Commentary: Grievances tell me only one thing – that I can be hurt

and hurt another in return. Neither of these is true. Grievances hide the light within, and true vision and light must go together. Laying aside a grievance does not mean I "lose" and the other "wins." Nor does it expose me to manipulation by others. It simply means I am free to see the light of the world in myself.

2. My salvation comes from me.

Commentary: Salvation is the end of the ego's illusion. Salvation does not come from anyone outside myself: not from a religious leader, not from a government, not from a bank, not from earning yet another degree, not from more or less money, but only from myself. I have never separated from my Source. I am in God and God is in me. I need look no further than my own mind as the means to perceive my Oneness, which is the only salvation that is required of me.

Here is how to practice today's review:

Twice a day, in the morning and evening, select one of the ideas and devote fifteen minutes to it in the following manner.

Take your seat and relax. Read the two ideas for the day along with the commentary. Then choose an idea for the morning or evening. Spend about three minutes reading the idea and its commentary. Don't rush. As much as possible, allow the feeling of the idea to sink into your entire being. Then close your eyes and repeat the idea again. Place your awareness on the idea and the breath. Repeat the idea often if it helps focus your mind. For the next ten minutes watch the breath and allow thoughts to arise, as they will. Notice the thought and go back to the breath.

Trust whatever happens. Your aim is to reach a place of stillness and peace. When you get there, even if just for a minute or two, know you have tasted Reality and your true nature.

Be mindful throughout the day by repeating one or both ideas in your mind as often as possible. Twice an hour would be good, but especially remember them if your mind is disturbed by anyone or anything. The time you spend remembering the ideas will greatly increase the happiness of your day.

Lesson 86: Review

The personal mind is obsessed with differences. It has convinced itself that it can only understand a thing if it determines how it is different from another thing. Differences are named and given an identity. With the logic of circular reasoning, the personal mind's focus on differences morphs into a perception of chaos. This is our world today.

The personal mind cannot teach what it denies. It will never see beyond its own perception because all its witnesses attest to separation. If you want to remember what you truly are, you must look beyond the personal mind. The only Mind that knows yours is the One that created it in the first place. Only Source knows what you are and how to bring you back.

Today's ideas for review are:

1. Only God's plan for salvation will work.
Commentary: Salvation is the undoing of illusion. It is recognition of the Law of Oneness. What I give, I must receive. Only when I forgive can I perceive myself forgiven. There is no other way to transmute this world.

2. Holding grievances is an attack on God's plan for salvation.
Commentary: I am not my own creator. I did not make the Law of Oneness. I can choose to resist because I am free to do so. But if I choose to resist, to hold grievances, then I am choosing to go it alone, which is not my natural state, and which must produce anxiety, an acute sense of aloneness, isolation, and fear. Accepting what is, is not laziness. It is not the relinquishment of power. It is taking back my power to be free. I do not have to like my experience but I do have to accept it is mine. That is where all change begins.

155

Here is how to practice today's review:

Twice a day, in the morning and evening, select one of the ideas and devote fifteen minutes to it in the following manner:

Take your seat and relax. Read the two ideas for the day along with the commentary. Then choose an idea for the morning or evening. Spend about three minutes reading the idea and its commentary. Don't rush. With eyes open, slowly repeat the idea. As much as possible, allow the feeling of the idea to sink into your entire being.

Then close your eyes and repeat the idea again. Place your awareness on the idea and the breath. Repeat the idea often if it helps focus your mind. For the next ten minutes watch the breath and allow thoughts to arise, as they will. Notice the thought and go back to the breath.

Trust whatever happens. Your aim is to reach a place of stillness and peace. When you get there, even if just for a minute or two, know you have tasted Reality and your true nature.

Be mindful throughout the day by repeating one or both ideas in your mind as often as possible. Twice an hour would be good, but especially remember them if your mind is disturbed by anyone or anything. The time you spend remembering the ideas will greatly increase the happiness of your day.

Lesson 87: Review

The truth is you are always united with the Lord. But you must know this. Nothing further is there to know.
– Upanishads

The laws of the universe do not permit contradiction. What holds for God holds for you. If you believe you are absent from All That Is, then you will believe that It is absent from you.
– ACIM

Today's ideas for review are:

1. I will there be light.

Commentary: I am in command of my own mind. I intend to know myself. In the end, nothing else is worth knowing except who I am. My will to find my inner light is a form of spiritual instinct. My will has all the power given me by Source so there is no possibility of failure. Nothing can hide the light I will to see.

2. There is no will but God's.

Commentary: All That Is cannot, and does not, desire my suffering. Source has no concept of loss. Source wills me to remember my Oneness with It. I cannot die and need not perceive suffering as a requirement. The question I must ask myself is, "Do I want the problem, or do I want the Answer?"

Here is how to practice today's review:

Twice a day, in the morning and evening, select one of the ideas and devote fifteen minutes to it in the following manner:

Take your seat and relax. Read the two ideas for the day along with the commentary. Then choose an idea for the morning or evening. Spend about three minutes reading the idea and its commentary. Don't rush. With eyes open, slowly repeat the idea. As much as possible, allow the feeling of the idea to sink into your entire being.

Then close your eyes and repeat the idea again. Place your awareness on the idea and the breath. Repeat it often if it helps focus your mind. For the next ten minutes watch the breath and allow thoughts to arise, as they will. Notice the thought and go back to the breath.

If your mind wanders, repeat the idea slowly. Realize that whatever form your thoughts take, they have no meaning or power beyond what you give them. Trust whatever happens. Your aim is to reach a place of stillness and peace. When you get there, even if just for a minute or two, know you have tasted Reality and your true nature.

Be mindful throughout the day by repeating one or both ideas in your mind as often as possible. Twice an hour would be good, but especially remember them if your mind is disturbed by anyone or anything. The time you spend remembering the ideas will greatly increase the happiness of your day.

Lesson 88: Review

You may have noted the inherent logic of ACIM. It stems from the premise, "What is true must always be true, or it is not truth." So, if $(a + 1) = (b + 1)$, then "a" must equal "b" and must always equal "b."

So it follows that if Source created us Whole, we must always be Whole. If it appears otherwise, it is illusion. This is the spirit in which today's review should be read.

1. The light has come.

Commentary: The light has never left. I am Whole, even if I do not yet perceive it so. But why would I continue to see what makes me feel alone and unhappy? The light is in me and in everything I see around me. It is my will to see it.

2. I am under no laws but God's.

Commentary: This is the perfect statement of my freedom. I am constantly tempted to make up other laws and believe they have power over me. I suffer only because of my belief in them. But if truth is total, then untruth cannot exist. I can wear myself out if I want to. I have lived many lives believing the ego's laws reign supreme, but time is of no meaning to Oneness! Knowledge is total, even if the ego does not believe in totality. But I am not my ego and its illusions are not mine. Today, I recognize I am under no law but God's and the light has come – it has never left.

Here is how to practice today's review:

Twice a day, in the morning and evening, select one of the ideas and devote fifteen minutes to it in the following manner:

Take your seat and relax. Read the two ideas for the day along with the commentary. Then choose an idea for the morning or evening. Spend about three minutes reading the idea and its commentary. Don't rush.

Then close your eyes and relax even further by placing your awareness on the breath. In your mind, slowly repeat the idea. As much as possible, allow the feeling of the idea to sink into your entire being. For the next ten minutes watch the breath and allow thoughts to arise, as they will. Notice the thought and go back to the breath.

If your mind wanders (and it will), repeat the idea slowly in your mind. Realize that whatever form your thoughts take, they have no meaning or power beyond what you give them. Trust whatever happens. Your aim is to reach a place of stillness and peace. When you get there, even if just for a minute or two, know you have tasted Reality and your true nature.

Be mindful throughout the day by repeating one or both ideas as often as possible. Twice an hour would be good, but especially remember them if your mind is disturbed by anyone or anything. Is it not true that the time spent remembering the ideas increases the happiness of your day?

May your day be full of light.

Lesson 89: Review

So nothing new is given by the teacher. The question contains the answer. In fact it arises out of the true answer. If this were not the case, if we did not already know the answer, how would we recognize it when we hear it?

– Rupert Spira

Miracles are answers to the unasked question: "Who am I?" They point to our divinity. They may last an instant, but their answer is timeless. We are the Divinity. We live within It. We are Its expression. We are our own question and we are our own answer. We bring miracles to ourselves because Source is within us.

Our two review ideas for today are:

1. I am entitled to miracles.

Commentary: Miracles are not earned or awarded selectively; they are always there for everyone. I am entitled to miracles because I am under no law but the Law of Source.

2. Let miracles replace all grievances.

Commentary: I am a divine thread in the tapestry of the Whole. When I understand that I cannot see the Whole from the perspective of separation, a doorway opens in my mind. This is the beginning of true perception. Let me see that every grievance is a reminder that I am not truly seeing. This recognition is itself a miracle. Oneness has no opposite, no exceptions, and no substitutes.

Here is how to practice today's review:

Twice a day, in the morning and evening, select one of the ideas and devote fifteen minutes to it in the following manner:

Take your seat and relax. Read the two ideas for the day along with the commentary. Then choose an idea for the morning or evening. Spend about three minutes reading the idea and its commentary. Don't rush.

Then close your eyes and relax even further by placing your awareness on the breath. In your mind, slowly repeat the idea. As much as possible, allow the feeling of the idea to sink into your entire being. For the next ten minutes watch the breath and allow thoughts to arise, as they will. Notice the thought and go back to the breath.

If your mind wanders, repeat the idea slowly in your mind. Realize that whatever form your thoughts take, they have no meaning or power beyond what you give them. Trust whatever happens. Your aim is to reach a place of stillness and peace. When you get there, even if just for a minute or two, know you have tasted Reality and your true nature.

Be mindful throughout the day by repeating one or both ideas in your mind as often as possible. Twice an hour would be good, but especially remember them if your mind is disturbed by anyone or anything. Is it not true that the time you spend remembering the ideas has increased the happiness of your day?

May your day be full of miracles.

Lesson 90: Review

There can be no problem that does contain its own solution. Do you see the logic of this statement? All things exist in Mind of God and God's Mind is complete, whole, and unified. Therefore, it is a logical impossibility that any problem could arise that does not also contain its solution.

How radical is ACIM to tell us there are no problems! I can hear your response to this and understand it well. "Of course there are problems. Only the naïve believe there are no problems!" Yes indeed. Problems seem to abound in this world of time, space, politics, violence, turmoil, and fear.

The solution to a problem cannot be found unless the problem itself is understood. To understand a problem, we must see where it originates, for only there will its solution be found as well. Today's review ideas challenge our concept of problems.

1. Let me recognize this problem so it can be solved.
Commentary: Without exception, every problem originates in the mind. And the truth is, there is really only one problem and only one solution. The origin of every problem is a grievance

against what is. The solution is the miracle of forgiveness, or allowing the moment to be what it is, and not spending a second resisting it. When I release my fear, I step away from my own ego and dance with the moment, allowing the universe to show me what happens next. This decision is an energetic invitation to Source, and Source will always respond in the positive.

2. *Let me recognize my problems have been solved.*
Commentary: I want to believe that my problem comes first, and then a solution is found. Yet, in the Mind of God, the problem and the answer arise simultaneously. It is impossible to have a problem that has not already been solved. Even the illusion of time cannot separate my problem from its solution.

Here is how to practice today:

Take your seat and relax. Slowly and quietly, read the two ideas for the day along with the commentary. Don't rush this reading. Then choose the morning or evening idea as appropriate. Say the idea slowly in your mind and let it sink in. Then close your eyes and place your awareness on the breath.

Allow thoughts to arise, as they will. If your mind begins to wander, repeat the idea and go back to the breath. Sink into relaxation more deeply with each out-breath. There is no other requirement. Trust in the words of the idea and trust in your breath. Don't worry if your mind is restless. It's all okay, just stay with it.

You may have moments of intense thinking, or you may have no thoughts at all. The breath should be the foundation upon which all of this practice rests, but there may also be times when even awareness of the breath falls away. Just have your experience and allow it to be as it is. Remember not to judge yourself in any way.

Time and Space are where you chase things you pretend you

don't have – love, friends, abundance – while worrying about things you pretend you do have – problems, challenges, and issues. Then one day, you happen to notice the prophetic powers of pretending...
– TUT

Lesson 91

Miracles are seen in light.

We do not believe winter is over simply because the calendar says it is, but because we experience the effects of spring. We trust that winter is over because we see it in the lengthening days and the touch of warmth on our skin. We experience the coming of spring each year – so we have faith in it. Seeing is believing.

It is important to remember that miracles and vision necessarily go together. This needs repeating, and frequent repeating. It is a central idea in your new thought system, and the perception that it produces. The miracle is always there. Its presence is not caused by your vision; its absence is not the result of your failure to see. It is only your awareness of miracles that is affected. You will see them in the light; you will not see them in the dark.
– ACIM

Miracles must be experienced to know their truth. They are not a subject to study or master. They are known through your experience of the effects of forgiveness.

The dance with Oneness has a major requirement: we must leave behind the thought that we are a separate body, and only a body. It is almost impossible to overstate the degree of fixation we have upon the body. Everything in this world speaks to physical form. Almost all our thoughts are concerned with protecting the body, ensuring its survival, its freedom from pain, or attack by another body. To experience miracles, we must see and release the limitations of bodily attachment because that is where all fear resides. Fear obscures the light! Let go of being a body, even if only for a little while.

The light of our physical world is the densest form light can take. Indeed, the light of the physical world is so dense it is almost imprisoned. The light of miracles is beyond any of our physical laws. And yet, it is not beyond being experienced. It is not beyond our experience because Source has placed it within our minds.

How do you experience the light of miracles? You feel it. You feel it in freedom, in a sense of total safety and peace. You feel it in your desire for peace. You feel it in forgiveness.

If I am not a body, what am I? If I am not a mother, a father, a daughter, a citizen, a worker, a professional, what am I? If I am not human, what am I? Know this: you are none of these things. Your identification with them is a limitation no matter how much prestige or financial worth they might seem to impart. You are far, far beyond any of these identifications. This is your meditation today. Today you practice telling yourself the truth about what you are.

Begin by taking your seat and closing your eyes. Relax your body. You know how to do this now. When you are ready, place your awareness gently on the breath. Allow your mind to focus on the breath for a bit. When your mind is calm and focused, say in your mind, "Miracles are seen in light. The body's eyes do not perceive the light. But I am not a body. What am I?"

Ask this question calmly and peacefully. "If I am not a body, what am I?" Now answer the question in your mind by saying the following, placing your full awareness on how it feels to say these words:

"I am not weak, but I am strong." How does it feel to be

strong? If you are fully in the moment, saying these words, you will feel a shift in energy. The words, "I am strong," produce a distinctly different bodily response than the words, "I am weak." Experience this energetic quality to know it!

Now say in your mind: "I am not doubtful. I am certain." Place your attention on the sensation of being certain. How does it feel in the body to say, "I am certain of myself? I am certain I can tie my shoes." Sure, we can all tie our shoes. This is not the point. It is the feeling of being certain that is key here because feeling certain is your right. You want to get to know this feeling.

Now continue slowly and purposefully to feel your way through thoughts such as:

"I am capable." "I am sovereign." "I am gracious." "I am presence." "I am gentleness." "I am goodness."

If you are paying attention, you will notice that just reading these words shifts something in your heart and solar plexus. It feels good because it is good. And it is who you are. Spend the rest of the practice period, which should last 20 minutes, watching the breath in peace. If your mind wanders, repeat a phrase such as "I am certain" or "I am good" and go back to the breath.

Be mindful today. As often as four or five times per hour take a minute to feel your way into thoughts such as: "I am strong." "I am certain of myself." "I am capable." "I am sovereign." Experience the feeling of knowing these words are the truth about yourself.

Lesson 92

Miracles are seen in light, and light and strength are one.

Source created both light and strength. To know them in their fullness, I must join with It.

Truth calls for faith and faith makes room for Truth.
– ACIM

Today, you are asked to meditate upon strength again. You will seek connection with that which knows no conflict, no uncertainty, and no weakness. This is where the light lives and it is also the home of strength. You do not need to work at it or earn it. It is your birthright. But you must allow it.

Your meditation will be for 20 minutes in the morning and evening. Take your seat and relax. Place your awareness gently on the breath. And when you are ready, say to yourself, "Miracles are seen in light, and light and strength are one." Then wait without worry or expectation. Accept whatever comes up and watch the breath. You will find yourself move gently into a deepening quiet. Continue to watch the breath. Anchor your mind with it. Feel your body. Allow thoughts to arise as they will. Watch them come and go like clouds moving across the sky. Place your trust in your connection with Source.

If your mind begins to wander, say to yourself, "I am certain." Or say, "I am sovereign." Or, "I am good." Play with these statements! Feel the vibration of each one in the body. Choose the phrase that makes you feel best – for that is certainty. If you find another phrase of your own choosing – go for it! Just make sure it feels good, strong, certain, and whole. Watch your breath and repeat the statement as you need to in order to remain calm and focused.

Be mindful today. If possible, stop every ten minutes or so and remember, you are One Self. You are noble, you are bright, you are a miracle, and so is the person next to you – all these things and more.

Lesson 93

Light and joy and peace abide in me.

The first few lessons of this course required you to question your perception of reality with statements such as, "Nothing I see means anything," and "I am upset because I see a meaningless world." You needed to tear down the false defenses of the ego. The lessons now are about building on the truth of who you really are.

A major goal of ACIM is freedom from fear. Fear is the continuous state of existence for the ego and you cannot learn from it. Subdued panic is not conducive to understanding anything.

The fear of God is one of the oldest beliefs in all of humanity. Fear of the God arises directly from the personal mind. Why? Because the personal mind is convinced it created itself and is capable of judgment. In order to sustain its illusion of control, the personal mind supplanted Source's Will for its own. Only fear can be the result. The ego is fear itself.

It is not God's Will that we live in fear. Therefore, fear must be unreal. This is a profound and logical truth. Fear is the creation of a mind that believes in the illusion of death, separation, guilt, and powerlessness. Fear is a lie.

Oneness is guaranteed. Creation is unalterable and eternal. Despite its insistence otherwise, the personal mind has no control over this. Take heart in this today and acknowledge the reality of what you are. Light and joy and peace abide in you. What do you think holds the atoms of your body together? Love. What do you think created you? Love.

Today you will deepen the practice of accepting the truth about yourself. Whatever mistaken thoughts you've held about yourself can be let go now. You will practice twice today, in the morning and evening, for about 20 minutes each. Please take this time to experience the light of what you are.

Take your seat and close your eyes. Relax the body. You know how to do this by now. When you are relaxed in the body, gently place your awareness on the breath. Allow the breath to be as it is. It knows what to do all by itself. Just watch it peacefully. Take a moment to enjoy the peace of the breath, and when you are ready, say in your mind, "Light and joy and peace abide in me. My sinlessness is guaranteed by God."

Now simply go into the quietness. Watch your breath and feel the words of this lesson. You are Innocence created by Innocence. You are light and you are peace. Try to let go of anything other than the feeling of knowing you are wholly One and wholly without guilt, shame or fear. You need do nothing but accept this truth about yourself. Truth is experienced first as faith and then as Truth Itself.

If your mind wanders, go back to the words of the lesson. Say in your mind, "Light and joy and peace abide in me." Say the words very slowly. Savor each word as you watch the breath. Breathe in light. Breathe out fear. Breathe in peace. Breathe out fear. Breathe in love. Breathe out fear or any discomfort you might have. Establish your own rhythm. Do what feels best for you.

Be mindful today. If you can, take five minutes every hour and sit with this lesson. Close your eyes, repeat the lesson, and breathe. Watch your breath and try to feel your way into the peace.

May love follow you and may you know Its presence all day long.

Lesson 94

I am as God created me.

This is the only truth about yourself you will ever need. If you accept this single statement about yourself, you will know salvation. Please do not mistake the simplicity of this lesson. Its depth is beyond your present experience.

We are as God created us. We have been given the full creative powers of our Creator – hence our creation of this illusory world. Still, there is one thing we did not do and cannot do – we did not create our Creator and we did not create ourselves.

We cannot choose to escape the care of God. We cannot choose to escape the love of God. We cannot choose to escape our union with God and with all of God's creations.

We are as God created us. We are our brother and our sister. We are the dog that barks down the street. We are the acorn and the soil it roots in. We are the wind in the trees. We are the sun and rain. We are the molecules of air we breathe. We are the stars and the space between the stars. We are matter and antimatter. All of this we are.

The vastness of what we are instills fear in the little mind. The apparent complexity of our relations seems too great. But it is our little self that is false and all things of the little self will pass away.

God does not know death and certainly did not create it. Nor does God know "sin." Indeed, there is no place for guilt or shame of any kind in God's creation. We are not being tested or measured here, but we are free to test and measure ourselves. God has no need to test or measure! Who would say God knows not what She has created?

We have not been asked to work out the plan for our return to Love because that is beyond us. We can, however, recognize it and thereby ourselves. We are as God created us. How simple and profound.

Today you are asked to sit in meditation, morning and evening, for about 20 minutes. Your goal is simple – to feel your way to knowing what you are.

Take your seat and relax. You know how to do this by now. As your body relaxes, place your awareness gently on the breath. Simply watch the breath for a moment or two, and when you are ready, say in your mind, "I am as God created me."

Now feel, or imagine, what it means to be of God. How do you do this? Don't think. Feel. Feel your way to a sense of absolute certainty. Imagine within your mind, within your being, what it would be like to have no conflict of any kind. Imagine a joy that cannot be threatened. Imagine putting aside your body and becoming the light being you are.

You have experienced a taste of the certainty and peace of God in your dreams, whether you remember them or not. Try now to feel, if even for a moment, a place where you cannot be threatened by anything ever at all. Try to feel within your being that you are One Self. You are One with God, One with all your brothers and sisters. Try to imagine within your being that you are One with all life – the earth, all of the shining Milky Way, and then beyond to all the star systems, the black holes, the light bodies of the universe. Allow yourself to accept this is your rightful state. This is how God created you.

If you can imagine peace, you can imagine freedom. If you can imagine freedom you can imagine safety. Know that if you can imagine any of these it must be real. You cannot imagine anything you do not already know. Imagining is nothing more than remembering!

If your mind begins to wander during the rest of the meditation, go back to the breath and repeat the lesson slowly to yourself. Savor every word! Take time to feel the vibration of each word: I am. As God. Created Me. Repeat the lesson as often as necessary, anchoring your attention with the breath. You cannot fail at this lesson. Allow whatever experience you have with it to be as it is. Just do it.

Be mindful today. If it is possible, take five minutes every hour to stop what you are doing, close your eyes and breathe the words of this lesson.

We are here only to remember who we are. This is our purpose above all others. This is salvation. Forgiveness is merely the remembrance that we are but One Self; that duality and conflict cannot exist because they are not of Source. You are of Source.

Lesson 95

I am one Self, united with my Creator.

How often have you asked yourself, "Who am I, really?" Is it possible you believe you cannot really know?

Why do we not dig more deeply? It isn't because we're lazy. It isn't because we're uninterested. It isn't because we don't care. Could it be, at least in part, because we behold the world we have created and feel only its loss and grief? To behold this world is to identify with suffering.

The lesson for today uses strong language because the goal of ACIM is nothing less than a complete return to love, which is the underlying truth of what you are. Furthermore, we must all return together, or not at all. We cannot return unless we know who we are.

The personal mind is completely unequipped to tell you what you are. It will dismiss this lesson as naïve, unproven, and even useless. It has worn deep grooves in the path away from Source. It takes willingness and persistence to find the path Home. This is why you have been asked to stop every five minutes to remember! Has this been a burden to you? Do you feel guilty about not stopping every five minutes? Do you see how deep are the old grooves? Waste no time in guilt. I repeat, waste no time in guilt! It is nothing but an impediment to learning.

Today you will begin to practice in a new way. Every hour you are asked to stop, repeat the lesson in your mind, and feel its truth.

You have undoubtedly noticed the challenges of mental focus. Here, I would urge you to replace guilt with desire. Ask yourself, "What is my true desire?" Desire is everything, for without desire, no thing can arise. So, be very clear about what you want. Be very clear that your greatest desire is to know yourself, for nothing of any importance will manifest until you do.

Your mind is untrained and needs the structure of these repetitions. You are literally creating new neural pathways in your brain. Desire to remember the lesson. But if you forget, forgive yourself completely. You cannot lose here, for you will either remember the lesson, or receive the benefit of forgiveness.

Practice today for five minutes each hour. Rest in the moment. Place awareness on the breath and calmly say in your mind, "I am one Self, united with my Creator, at one with every aspect of creation, and limitless in my power and in peace."

Repeat again, "I am one Self." Allow the words to sink in. Feel them in your body. You are perfectly whole, perfectly protected, perfectly connected in perfect meaning and harmony with all things now – past, present and future. This moment is yours. You know who you are. Let all doubt go. You cannot do this exercise incorrectly.

This is no idle work you are doing. You are calling to the entire world in your mind. It will recognize your call and meet you in oneness. You may not feel it in the moment. But your call will be heard and answered. You will know its answer.

To everyone and everything you experience today, offer the promise of the one Self. Remember as you look upon the world, "You are one Self with me, united with our Creator in this Self. I honor you because of What I am, and what Source is, Who loves us both as One."

Lesson 96

Salvation comes from my one Self.

Am I a body or am I spirit? Can I be both? Is it possible to not decide? Can I just alternate my identification with each idea and call it good?

You do not come from this world, nor can your salvation come from it. Give up on the expectation that a world which holds guilt as truth can ever become the heaven you seek. Heaven does not exist in duality. Heaven cannot be held within the personal mind.

This world is the creation of a split mind. One half believes it is separated from Source. The other half knows Oneness with All. We are free to play in this world as deeply and as long as we desire. But today's lesson asks that we now also play with being whole.

How real separation appears! I wake up every morning still here, in this aging container, with all its aches and pains. Certainly this body is not my salvation but it seems to be all I know. No one questions whether the body is real. The body just is and the debate, if there ever was one, is over.

But to fulfill your purpose, one must make a choice. One must either identify with the body, or with the one Self. Trying to be both simply continues conflict and confusion. Illusions cannot be reconciled with the truth. If I am only physical, then my spirit must be unreal. If I am spirit, then my body is ultimately meaningless.

You are not being asked to deny your body here. Active denial only reinforces its reality. Let the body be! It is neutral. Pay attention to it gently, but do not focus on it and do not treat it as overly special. Do not fear it, and do not worship it. Do not worry about it too much.

Here is the truth: Your body is your creation. Spirit informs the mind and mind creates the body. To believe otherwise is to let the tail wag the dog. How long has the tail been wagging the dog!

Today you will practice joining mind with spirit. Doubt and fear will be gently laid aside. You will imagine how perfect harmony might feel. You have access to your one Self because it is part of who you are. It is your bridge to Source. You will know your Self because it will feel peaceful, good, and whole.

No effort is required to reach the bridge and cross over it.

Your practice today is without effort. Every hour, for five minutes, take a break from the day and seek the quietness within. Wait patiently. Allow. Do not judge anything. Just stop what you are doing, close your eyes, and focus on the breath. Take a few deep, calming breaths and then say in your mind, "Salvation comes from my one Self. Its thoughts are mine to use." Then imagine a place beyond thinking. Imagine a place that feels at peace, safe, whole, and expansive. Imagine a place of total acceptance, where there is no need to do anything, or be anything. Imagine a place of absolute certainty that all is well, that conflict of any kind simply does not exist. This is your bridge to Self. Begin to know it. Create a path to it in your mind.

If you forget to practice (and you will!) do not feel guilty! Guilt is an impediment to learning. Just pick up where you left off, and begin again. Enjoy this practice. You are entitled to it.

Lesson 97

I am spirit.

Imagine you live in a tar pit. It has been your home for as long as you can remember. The tar is sticky and thick. It covers your feet as you walk, dragging you down and making every step a chore. The smell of the tar permeates everything – your clothes, your skin, your hair. Even the faint, cool breezes that find their way to the bottom of the pit offer only a whisper of the fields and flowers that lie above.

Today's lesson offers a ladder down into the tar pit. Its message is unequivocal. "You are spirit." It is time to climb the ladder out of the tar pit.

You have lived long in the tar. It has weighed you down almost to the point of death. You have trusted before and been disappointed. But now is the time to allow trust, not in anyone or anything else, but in your own experience.

Trust does not come naturally to most of us and that is why I use the word "allow." We must allow, and allow, and allow, all the things of this world. We must allow while looking at each and every one of them through the lens of our one, eternal, unimpeachable, and untainted Self. We must ask continuously, "Am I okay in this moment?" And then, "Am I okay in THIS moment?" We must ask until slowly, but surely, we realize our lives are one, continuous, "YES. I am okay, in this moment." We must ask this even into death for the tar pit is nothing but fear.

Each moment of conscious questioning raises me up the ladder. I climb with every five minutes of practice. I climb with every minute I spend in meditation upon, "The light has come." I climb with each confirmation that, "I am entitled to miracles," and with every "aha" moment I have. I climb, thought-by-thought, experience-by-experience, until the sun begins to penetrate the depths of my unconsciousness.

This is all it takes – one moment after the next. I forgive myself for forgetting to ask, "Am I okay in this moment?" I remember to remember that I am free of all limits, safe, and healed, and whole. And each moment that I remember to remember frees me to forgive my sister, my brother, and myself. Remembering leaves me free to help them out of the pit.

Today you are asked to pause for five minutes each hour. Relax your body and place awareness on the breath. Ask yourself, "Am I okay in this moment?" Feel the answer, "Yes, for I am spirit. I am free of all limits. I am safe and healed. I am free to forgive all things, all persons, and all events. I am free to be myself, to allow everything and everyone to be its Self, and together we save the world."

This is a happy practice. Sink deeply into the peace of forgiveness, which is the recognition that everything is spirit, regardless of the tar that seems to cover it.

Give yourself this gift today as often as you can. Be assured that you will practice in exactly the right way. Try to spend five minutes each hour. Do your best. That is all you can do, and it is enough.

Lesson 98

I will accept my part in God's plan for salvation.

I have only two choices in every moment. Do I allow things to unfold, or do I fight against what is? Do I condemn this moment and what is contained within it, or do I forgive? No one can make this choice for me. However, my choice will either be a blessing or a curse for all who share it with me.

Today you are asked to make the choice to dedicate yourself to salvation from guilt, as Source planned it. There is no other plan.

The law of Oneness shares forgiveness with everyone and everything, everywhere. Forgiveness is the Cosmic Alchemy of Source. Its effects are not limited by time or space.

The choice to forgive signals my acceptance of God's plan for salvation. It is a discipline. With practice it becomes a full release from the personal mind.

Today you are asked to practice every hour for five minutes. Is it not worth five minutes of your time to accept the happiness that Source has given you? Is it not worth five minutes hourly to become your function? Make no mistake: your acceptance changes everything. Offer your acceptance and Source will do the rest.

Every hour, take a break. Close your eyes if possible. Say in your mind, "I will accept my part in God's plan for salvation." Then place your awareness gently on the breath and feel the release this acceptance brings. Your part is to forgive. All the rest is done for you. You need do nothing! Allow yourself to experience the relief of letting go. A major source of your power in this world lies in the recognition that you can choose to let go and allow.

Be mindful today but do not feel guilty if you miss a practice. Simply make the correction and move on. Your acceptance is your freedom but you must experience freedom to know it. Play with this lesson. Acceptance is not a contract or a requirement. You are free to choose whatever you wish. Experience for yourself.

Lesson 99

Salvation is my only function here.

Accept your brother in this world. Accept nothing else, for in him you will find your creations because he created them with you. You will never know that you are co-creator with God until you learn that your brother is co-creator with you.

Wholeness is indivisible, but you cannot learn of your wholeness until you see it everywhere.

Eternity is one time, its only dimension being "always."
– ACIM

The truth of wholeness cannot be known until you see it everywhere. The full potential of our all-knowingness will not become accessible until we end the myth of separation.

So long as you are in this world your only function is to rise above its limitation of separation. And there is only one way for you to rise above separation: forgiveness. Forgiveness is the realization that nothing is wrong. It is impossible to fail. To forgive is to look beyond error and see that while another may mistakenly still believe in the illusion of separation, she or he is never, not your own perfect Self.

You are not yet asked to understand the entirety of Oneness. You are asked to practice and trust that with experience, you will. We learn through experience that we are co-creators, but we cannot learn until we practice seeing beyond error!

We have co-created this world together and we re-create it over and over again each time we agree to judge and separate. We do not trust easily and we do not forgive easily. Forgive yourself for not trusting and for not forgiving.

Use your time today to undo illusions. Take a break each hour. Close your eyes and gently lay aside fear and worry. Take a few relaxing breaths, and then say in your mind, "Salvation is my only function here." Feel the certainty of this statement you have made about yourself. Allow yourself to trust and accept your function. It has been given to you by your Creator. For five minutes, watch your breath and relax. You know without any doubt why you are here, in this world, at this time. You have been born in this lifetime to learn this lesson.

Try to see the wholeness of things today. On the hour, gently put aside all accusations of unfairness. Make room in your mind for peace and joining. If everything is a part of you, will you not accept everything?

Lesson 100

My part is essential to God's plan for salvation.

Is it possible to argue with God? We can't but the personal mind does anyway, making itself unhappy in the process. Knowing only happiness Itself, Source wishes us only perfect happiness too – even as we argue with It.

The One whose Will is happiness cannot fail, but forced happiness is not God's Will. So we are free to hold to a vision of separate thoughts and separate forms. We have the right, at least for a while, to close off from Love. We can experience lack of joy, lack of abundance, lack of respect, lack of surety and safety, and lack of time.

Source knows eternal patience in the eternal Now, but it is

also true that each of us must wake up to Reality at some point. None of us will be left behind because each of us is essential to the Whole.

Our part in God's plan is to remember how to be happy. Happiness requires trust because it means facing the fear with which we have blocked Love's presence. We must walk through fear to find the light on the other side. We pass through fear to regain the wisdom of our true nature – eternal, unafraid, certain of itself, gracious, sovereign, and in union with everything.

Practice trust again today. On the hour, take a break and place awareness on the breath. Repeat the lesson in your mind and allow happiness to arise within. Your part in God's plan is to be happy. No sacrifice is required at all. If you cannot reach happiness, then seek contentment. If you cannot find contentment, look for peace. If you cannot find peace, rest in silence.

I have included a longer meditation for you in this lesson. It comes from *Journey Beyond Words* by Brent Haskell. Read through it slowly first.

Meditation on Oneness

Take your seat and close your eyes. Relax your body and place gentle awareness on the breath. When you are ready say in your mind, "My part is essential to God's plan for salvation." Hold awareness on the breath and repeat the lesson slowly. Feel the words. You will come to a place within yourself that is peaceful.

When you feel this peace, venture a bit deeper. Say the word "unity" to yourself. Feel the word in your body. Try to imagine that everything you have ever experienced, or will experience, is part of a unified, timeless, whole. All of it is in perfect harmony. Extend the thought of harmony to everything and everyone around you. Everything is part of everything else.

Now go a bit further. Try to imagine there is nothing outside your Self. There is no "outside." No separate worlds, no separate personalities, no separate moments in time. If nothing is outside of you, then you are part of everything that is now, has been, or ever will be. Allow yourself to become aware of just how safe you really are in this unity. In fact, you are absolutely free to experience anything you can imagine in complete safety. You are beyond the body. Nothing can harm you at all. Everything that exists in Oneness must, by its very nature, be in harmony with everything and this includes you, your spirit, and any form you might wish to play with.

Allow yourself to feel the happiness of Source as an unshakeable, unchangeable Freedom. Nothing can take it away from you. Nothing can alter this Freedom or threaten it. All your imaginings otherwise are truly nothing. They are the most minor setback along a path that is known by your inner heart. A path guaranteed by Source. A path you did not create, but was created for you in Love. Sit for five minutes in the certainty of your unity. Breathe. Feel. Repeat the words of the lesson. Then arise and continue your day in peace.

Lesson 101

God's Will for me is perfect happiness.

The key word in this lesson is "perfect." Can you see that by its very nature, perfection is all-inclusive? Perfection implies total harmony in complete wholeness.

Can you see that perfect happiness means I do not get to be happy at your expense? Can you see that I cannot treat happiness as a scarce resource, to be guarded at all times?

In the unity consciousness that is Source, my perfect happiness must grow in proportion to yours, which becomes mine also. Perfection is Oneness and I cannot be happy alone. This understanding would turn our world upside down.

My perfect happiness is an inner contentment that cannot be

threatened. My perfect happiness comes from understanding that lack cannot exist because I am One with infinite Source. "My" perfect happiness is not really personal at all.

Perfect happiness is both freeing and freely available. It does not require payment. One does not earn it. It is not withheld as punishment for "sin." It does not require amends for misbehavior through suffering. Perfect happiness is not purchased from penance.

What sort of God would knowingly create a world in which "sin" was real only to punish us for the "sin" It knowingly created? Does Source delight in testing us and then punishing our failure? Only the God of a sick, conflicted mind could do such a thing. Source is not insane. If Source had not desired to extend Love, we would never have come into existence. Our very sense of self arises from Love.

We need to practice loving ourselves. We need to practice feeling the inner happiness we were created with. Today, at the beginning of every hour, for five minutes, stop what you are doing and connect with your own inner peace. Take a break from self-denial, self-criticism, and the soul loneliness of it all.

Sit with eyes closed. Relax your body and place gentle awareness on the breath. When you are ready, say in your mind, "God's Will for me is perfect happiness. There is no sin; it has no consequence." Now make it your will to imagine what it must be like to know you are eternal, that nothing can hurt you, and you can never really hurt another. It is only a mistake to believe otherwise. Watch the breath. Soften your heart. Soften the area behind your eyes. Soften your shoulders. Soften your brain. Soften your breath. Feel peace, for you are the extension of Love in form.

Try to stop every hour for five minutes today. Gift yourself, if only for a moment, the feeling of happiness. Forgive if you forget.

Lesson 102

I share God's Will for happiness for me.

Even the Christ felt anger. So long as we are in a body, we will experience it too. The response to anger varies. Sometimes we bottle it up. Sometimes we lash out thoughtlessly.

Many spiritual seekers repress anger. They see it as "bad." But the truth is, anger is nothing but energy. All emotions have energetic vibration. Anger itself isn't the problem. It's a signal something is out of balance. It is what we do with anger that becomes a problem. This is why forgiveness is your function.

When I recognize my anger and consciously allow it to move through me, I make room for something else to come in. I do not unconsciously attack anyone. I do not feel guilty about it. I sit with it. Feel it. Watch it arise, peak, and subside. I do not repress what seeks only acknowledgement and release. Most of us have years of anger in our energy field. This is especially true for those whose families discouraged its healthy expression.

ACIM is very explicit when it says, "Accept only the function of healing in time, because that is what time is for." Time is for healing. That is its main purpose. Use time to understand the vibratory quality of anger. Do not bottle it up or throw it onto the person in front of you. Time supports the lesson of forgiveness, and with forgiveness, also happiness.

Today, practice awareness of anger energy. Ask for help if you need it. This earth is a tough school and we are not meant to sit in class alone. There are beings surrounding you whose only job is to assist you any time, any place. Let them perform their function and enlist their aid.

On the hour today, close your eyes and relax the body. Place your awareness on the breath. When you are ready, say in your mind, "I share God's Will for happiness for me."

Say the words, and then notice your feelings. You may have

just left an argument. The news might be on, leaving a feeling of agitation. Perhaps you are bored or frustrated. Watch the feeling rise like a wave, crest, and then subside, and move out. It may take several minutes for heavy feelings to move. Feelings that are fully moved will be replaced by a sense of peace. This peace may grow into a small, fluttering happiness.

Do not force happiness and do not feel a bit of guilt if you resist. Instead, ask where the source of your resistance is. Go deeply into it without fear. Happiness lies there, in what you have buried. Bring it out into the light and place it on the altar of forgiveness. This simple act of integrity and forgiveness is your gift to yourself and it will make you happy. Take it today. Sit for five minutes on the hour, close your eyes, watch your breath, and share in the Will of Source for your own happiness.

Lesson 103

God, being Love, is also happiness.

The next few lessons take us further on the search for truth. And the truth is, happiness and Love are entwined. When Love is present, happiness is always the result. Yet, in our experience of this earth, this place of limited vision, it is not always easy to perceive Love. It seems to be available only in certain times or under certain conditions. Love is a rare commodity that shows itself intermittently and never lasts.

Most of us believe in both love and fear. But we focus on fear. We seek to avoid all situations that might add to it. We even associate love with fear, for we fear love's withdrawal! Our predominant focus on fear makes it seem more real than love. This is a "basic error, which must be brought to truth." The truth is: Source did not create fear, so it is not real. All fear is based on illusion. What is the illusion? The body.

All fear is bodily based. It requires constant protection from what it perceives as threats to its safety. We must transcend the fear of our own survival in the body to be released to Love.

Only Love is real. Its opposite is an illusion born of a mind that has lost its connection to Self, seeing only vulnerability and meaninglessness. Fear is mental and bodily pain. Fear creates a distance between everything that is Truth. It makes Love seem unreal and happiness a temporary thing. It is ironic that in order to go beyond fear, fear itself must be faced. But it is critical to learn it isn't real. We learn through daily awareness and experience that it cannot kill. Fear is an emotion that must be moved through, for that is where freedom and happiness are found. Fear is illusion. Only Love is Truth and Truth has no opposite.

Today you will seek no less than to uncover the happiness that is your underlying Reality. On the hour, take a seat and close your eyes. If you cannot sit, or are in the middle of a meeting or activity, keep your eyes open and simply go into a quiet space in your mind. Actually, it is time you learn to do this now because the world will always seek to insert itself into your peace. Take your peace inside. Use the breath as your personal, portable centering device.

Enter the quiet place with a few centering breaths. Then anchor awareness in the body. Feel your feet on the floor as you breathe consciously. After a few breaths, when you feel a sense of calm presence, say in your mind, "God, being Love, is also happiness. It is happiness I seek. I cannot fail, because I seek the Truth." Allow yourself to feel these words as you say them slowly and consciously in your mind.

If you can, go more deeply into the words. Try to sense that only illusions can prevent your peace. There is nothing "out there" that can take away your freedom. Your home is in the Mind of God – always accessible through the stillness within. This is where your One Self exists.

ACIM teaches, "Real vision is not only unlimited by space or distance, but does not depend on the body's eyes at all. The mind is its only source." Look for happiness in the only place it is truly constant – your mind. The mind that is joined with its Source cannot help but know the happiness that comes with complete, unlimited safety. This is your inheritance, and because Source gave it to you, nothing can take it from you.

Lesson 104

I seek but what belongs to me in Truth.

What we seek is perfect happiness, which is our right. If it is our right, why does it seem we do not have it? We do not have it because we refuse to see it, and it is right in front of us.

The mind must be ready to receive the happiness that is offered. Peace is a package deal and we don't get to decide what the package is. Happiness begins and ends in a mind that is at peace with the world. This doesn't mean the world must be at peace. Stop looking for the external world to offer you something it can never give.

Happiness is relearned as you accept each moment, perfect as it is. Every moment you experience has one common denominator: it is given to you as a living, moving part of the eternal Mind of God. Learn to accept the perfection of the moment whatever it is, without resistance, and happiness will follow. Make no mistake – it takes practice to do this. This is why we do the daily lessons. But don't take this lesson on faith. Have your experience with it, and then decide if it is true or not.

Practice today for five minutes each hour. Take your seat and close your eyes. If you cannot sit, or if you are in the middle of an activity, you may keep your eyes open and simply go into the quiet space of your mind. Use the breath as your personal, portable centering device.

Enter the quiet place with a few centering breaths. Then

anchor your awareness in the body. Feel your feet on the floor as you breathe consciously. After a few breaths, when you feel a sense of calm presence, say in your mind, "I seek what belongs to me in truth. Joy and peace are my inheritance." Then lay aside the conflicts of this world, a world whose gifts are shallow, transitory, and nothing more than a projection of a group mind that awaits your awakening to inner connection with Source.

Seek the depths of this lesson. Try to sense what is rightfully yours. Nothing can prevent your peace without your permission. There is nothing "out there" that can take away your inheritance. It is Creator's Will that you be happy. It is Creator's Will that you be at peace and Source has given you everything you need to fulfill Its Will. Source is not asking you to do something that is impossible, for that would be unloving and that is not what Source Is.

Practice mindfulness today. If you find yourself in a moment of disquiet, irritation, or even slight depression, repeat the lesson in your mind. Remember:

> *Real vision is not only unlimited by space or distance,*
> *but does not depend on the body's eyes at all.*
> *The mind is its only source.*
> *– ACIM*

Look today for happiness in the only place it is truly constant – the mind that is joined with Source. It is always present, always waiting silently, patiently, for you to notice it is there. Peace is one thing you CAN seek and you WILL find. Believe in yourself. Be happy with yourself. Like yourself.

Lesson 105

God's peace and joy are mine.

Today's lesson asks you to be a "happy learner." Source recognizes learning is best when happiness is present. You cannot be forced to learn the peace and joy of Source, nor can you fake it.

Your practice today is a bit different. You are asked to consider those to whom you have denied the right of peace and joy – a right that is theirs under the equal Law of Love. In denying them, you have denied yourself. It cannot be otherwise. Today you claim peace as your own, first by offering it, and then by feeling it received.

On the hour, take your seat and close your eyes. If you cannot sit in quiet, simply do this practice wherever you are, in your mind. Relax your body and place your attention on the breath. Watch your breath gently until you feel grounded in your body. Now, allow someone to arise in your mind – someone from whom you have withheld thoughts of peace and joy. You should have no trouble finding someone.

When you have this person in mind, say to them "(Jane, John, etc.), peace and joy I offer you, that I may have the peace and joy of Source as mine." Don't rush, and avoid feeling you've failed if at first you feel nothing. If you need help, ask for it. The act of asking for help often shifts your emotional frequency into a higher gear. There are beings all around whose only job is to assist. Invite them in to do their job!

If you cannot offer peace and joy at first, then offer neutrality. Sit with it and the neutrality will begin to feel like peace. Extend your own peace to the person you have chosen. You may feel lightness in the chest area. Left to itself, the lightness will grow into joy because joy is the natural outgrowth of peace.

Spend a few minutes sending peace and joy to each of your "enemies." In doing this you are preparing yourself to receive the gifts you've given. When you have extended the feelings of peace and joy to a few people, relax. Stay aware of the breath and place your attention on your own heart. Now allow yourself to receive all that you have given. Watch your breath gently. Notice what you receive.

> *I give you Love that is part of myself. I know that you will be released unless I want to use you to imprison myself. In the name of my freedom, I choose your release because I recognize that we will be released together.*
> – ACIM

Lesson 106

Let me be still and listen to the Truth.

Like most simple truths, today's lesson is one that hides nothing yet is understood by few. The personal mind, which loves complexity, has a tough time with simple truth.

The simplicity of happiness does not sit well with the personal mind because it is convinced that all interests are competitive. The personal mind functions in a very limited range of low-frequency emotion: fear, anger, and judgment. It is suspiciousness at best and vicious at worst. It is incapable of feeling beyond a limited range because it is incapable of allowing. Allowance is a cultivation of looking at events not as competing interests but as learning devices.

You hold two conflicting interpretations in your mind, and both cannot be true. You are either a personal mind or the Self. The personal mind is at war with everything. It is at war because it views itself small and weak. The Self perceives sovereignty and unity without contradiction. It sees all events as experiences only, orchestrated by Source.

We did not establish our value to Source. Our value needs no defense because it was created all powerful by the All Powerful. Nothing can attack it or prevail over it. We are not a body. We are not limited to form. The personal mind cannot and does not define us. We are beyond its illusions because we are free in spirit. This is the simple truth, unknowable by a personal mind that believes death is supreme, sickness is reality, time is linear and limited, the physical constitutes all we are, and separation from Wholeness is possible.

Today's practice, which should be done each hour, for five minutes, is to receive the Truth of what you are. Your goal is to allow the peace of Truth.

There should be no straining here. Your mind is already joined with Source! You do not have to work at it but need only recognize it. Simply take five minutes to sit in quiet and allow what is already joined to rise out of the quietness and make itself known. If you have any fear or hesitation about your ability to do this, acknowledge the fear and ask for assistance. That is all you need to do. Relax in the unseen Peace that surrounds you entirely.

Sit quietly. When you are ready, say in your mind, "I will be still and listen to the truth." Then ask, "What does it mean to give and to receive?" Now sit in silence and feel. What is it like to know that all you give in peace is received and then returned to you completely? Imagine for an instant what it would feel like to receive the peace you give away. What does it feel like to know the loving kindness you extend is returned to you a thousand-fold?

This practice will add peace to your day. Receive the peace and give it away. This is where salvations starts and this is where it ends. When everything is yours, and everything is given away, it will remain with you forever. This is the lesson: to have love, be love, and give it away.

Lesson 107

Truth will correct all errors in my mind.

The personal mind is incapable of distinguishing between what is True and what is not because it insists on complication. Truth is uncomplicated. It follows a simple rule: What is True is always True or it is not the Truth. Truth cannot be partly true. Oneness is both always true and all-inclusive. Do you see this?

The greatest struggle of our human experience lies in understanding the simple truth that separation is untrue. Separation is a perceptual illusion of the personal mind. It seems real only because the personal mind accepts the body as its home. In a very real sense, the body is an attack upon the Truth.

The personal mind is the major stumbling block to Knowing. The error of separation is possible only in an unhealed mind that remains unaware of its inherent Source. Oneness is the Truth. It is always true. It is never not true, and it is all-inclusive.

Can you imagine what a state of mind without illusions is? How would it feel? Try to remember when there was a time – perhaps a minute or two, maybe even less when nothing came to interrupt your peace; when you were certain you were loved and safe. Then try to picture what it would be like to have that moment be extended to the end of time and to eternity. Then let the sense of quiet that you felt be multiplied a hundred times and then be multiplied a hundred times more.
– ACIM

This is what Truth feels like and our Self knows it. Like spiritual homing pigeons we are drawn to its experience.

Today you will practice letting go of the personal mind with all its thoughts of separated needs, separate truths, of attack and defense. Remember, you do not ask for what you do not already have. You ask only for what belongs to you in Truth. It is impossible not to succeed.

Practice every hour today for five minutes. Take your seat

and close your eyes. If you cannot stop to sit in silence, then take a minute to go into your mind silently and repeat the lesson, "Truth will correct all errors in my mind." Then relax into the breath and let go of this world. Receive the peace that is yours by right. Breathe in peace and breathe out any cares or worries you feel at the moment. Spend about five minutes breathing in and out like this. Then continue with your next hour.

If you miss a practice, do not worry. This lesson is an exercise in forgiveness, which is also the truth. If you are in the middle of something and cannot sit, then say the lesson silently in your mind. Try to feel the words as you say them. Use your breath to anchor the words in your body. Silently breathe in peace and breathe out worry.

Be mindful today and have confidence in yourself. Let go of your littleness today. It does not serve you and it never will. Source is peace and Source is Truth.

Lesson 108

To give and to receive are One in Truth.

I think you will find today's practice to be a joy. It is a foundation of ACIM's thought system. You may wish to take two ten-minute practices today, instead of the recommended five minutes each hour. Either way, have fun. And remember, failure is impossible.

The central idea for today is harmony. You cannot be one with God and leave anything out. Source includes everything. So it follows that everything that Is must be in harmony with everything Else because It all exists in Mind of God. In other words, It all balances. Where the personal mind perceives chaos, Source see meaningful pattern.

A mind in harmony experiences giving and receiving as different halves of a single Whole. One translates into the other seamlessly. A mind in harmony knows this truth because it

191

knows loss is illusion. Here is a short story that summarizes today's lesson.

One day my washing machine broke. I was in an early morning online chat with a guy named Joe about scheduling repairs. When we ended our chat, Joe kindly asked if he could help with anything else. I had heard about an online coupon for 10% off the cost of the repair, which was $500, so I asked him about it. He immediately replied he would send the coupon and it was for 20% off, not 10%! So when we ended the online chat I expressed my gratitude. And then I was moved to add, "And may the force be with you today!" His reply was immediate. "You have a WONDERFUL day!" he replied. This simple little extension of giving and receiving online just filled me with joy. And I clearly sensed his joy too. My giving was received and then returned to me with delight. Harmonious!

A couple minutes later I was on the phone with a different service representative about something else. This person was also very helpful. Just before our call, I'd been reading that day's lesson, which was: "I offer peace and joy to you that I may have God's peace and joy as mine." When we had finished our conversation she asked if there was anything more she could do for me. Taking what felt like a bit of a risk I answered, "Yes. You can take a few quiet moments for yourself today and find peace." Her response was immediate. She extended my warmth right back with a lovely laugh and confirmation that she would indeed. Again, what I gave was received and given back to me. Now both of us were enriched. Harmonious!

These might seem small soon-to-be-forgotten exchanges. But they colored my whole day. And I bet if you asked, they'd colored the day of the two other people as well, because giving and receiving are one in truth. But there is more. Giving and receiving are not simply linear exchanges; they grow exponentially. The two folks I'd spoken with may well have passed their peace to the next caller or to their colleague. This is the whole idea of paying forward and it is real. True vision sees this and knows it for the light it holds.

Today's practice will make you feel good; so do not deny it to yourself. Take your seat and close your eyes. Place your awareness on the breath as you relax your body. Breathe in peace and breathe out all physical and mental tension. Take as long as you want in this breathing. Enjoy it.

When you are ready, say in your mind, "To give and to receive are One in Truth. I will receive what I am giving now." Then go into your mind, and find what you would give to everyone so that it might be yours. For instance, you might say, "To everyone I offer loving kindness." Or, "To everyone I offer freedom from pain." Or, "To everyone I offer peace of mind." Or, "To everyone I offer gentleness." Come up with your own offerings. Try them each and experience how they resonate within you.

Say each phrase slowly and then pause. Notice. You will feel the gift you gave. It will return in the amount you gave it. You will find that as you offer more and more, the return increases. This lesson is not about reading the words, but it is about experience. Give yourself this experience to know it.

Today you understand more deeply the effects of your thoughts. Think of this practice as a quick advance in your learning, made still faster and surer each time you repeat the lesson: To give and to receive are One in Truth. Know this, and you know the key to your happiness here, in this world and beyond.

Lesson 109

I rest in God.

Rest in God. Allow all things. To allow is to be humble only in that it signals the recognition that you must submit to something beyond your intellect, beyond your personal mind. You have relied upon them for survival but they offer no lasting peace because they are incapable of the task.

Today you are asked only to rest five minutes each hour and sit in stillness to receive what Source offers. Just sit. Whatever arises is as it is. Do nothing but notice and watch without attachment. Be conscious of being conscious.

If it is easier to sit twice today for about 20 minutes in the morning and evening, then do so. Take your seat and relax your body. Feel your feet resting on the floor. Allow your hips to relax, then your lower back and tummy. Relax your heart area. Let your arms and shoulders go. Loosen your neck, the jaw, the muscles of the mouth. Relax the area behind your eyes. Soften the top of your head. With your awareness on the breath, say in your mind, "I rest in God (or Source, All That Is)."

Allow thoughts to come and go. Remain focused on the breath as you watch each thought rise up and pass away, bringing with it emotions or feelings that also rise and fall away. If your mind wanders use the lesson like a mantra. Repeat it slowly in your mind, savoring each word. Let the idea of resting in perfect safety fill your being. "I rest. In Source." After all, where else could you be?

Practice mindfulness today. Lasting happiness requires consciousness and curiosity about the contents of one's own mind. These hourly practices are steps toward this consciousness and their value can only be known through experience. Experience your mind but do not trouble yourself about your thoughts. They will come and go. It is no matter. All rests in Mind of Source.

Lesson 110

I am as God created me.

Surrender yourself to the fact you did not create yourself. Nor do you know how you were created. You cannot create even a leaf on a tree. You do not even create the movement of your hand to the teacup. You certainly cannot create a solar system or even a single star.

What created you? Truly, this question is the only one that matters. Until I have a sense of who I really am, nothing I do or think has any contextual foundation. This question is the basis of all my decisions, all my desires, and all the choices I make. It determines whether I plan for the long run. It determines how I treat my enemy. It informs me continuously about everything.

This is the only question that matters. Yet rarely is it asked with any depth at all. This is because the answer would bring down the artificial powers of this world. The answer would end the banking system that thrives on profits at the expense of life. It would end kingships and religious hierarchies. It would end the rule of the wealthy over the poor. It would expose the cynicism and lies of politicians. War would no longer be seen as a legitimate activity. It would abolish the current system of education. For-profit health care would end. Science would have to include vastly new information. It would expose all injustices, but it would require something too. It would ask us to be responsible for our creations.

It is not a waste of time to consider that I am as God created me. It is a revolution. What is justice? How do we punish? What is useful knowledge? What does illness mean? Why is there violence? Can I imagine never being alone with my thoughts? Does this make me feel comforted or is it an intrusion that engenders guilt?

Is it even possible to fully consider you are still as God created you? Are you able to comprehend your inherited Divinity? I understand. Trying to think of it is impossible.

Imagine conceiving all the events in the world happening in the past, now, and in the future. Imagine assigning roles to the billions of characters with innumerable options for events in such a way they would all fit together and be blended into a unified, harmonious whole. It would soon dawn on you that even the biggest computer and the smartest minds in the world could not begin to accomplish the task. The personal mind cannot fathom it at all. It calls it chaos.

Yet, we have done so. Not the small we; the big WE. At play in the fields of God's Mind, we have given our selves form and experienced aloneness to know what Wholeness is. We seem to have denied our own freedom when it is freedom itself that has allowed this illusion of denial. We have created guilt and limitation – knowing both are impossible. We call this chaos because it seems beyond our comprehension. In fact, it is all occurring within our one, harmonious, joined Mind.

Every aspect of our creation is in perfect, invulnerable harmony. We are free to remain asleep, or to awaken from the dream. Awakening begins with asking, "Who am I?" And in answering this question, we become awake. And in our awakening, we become as Source created us.

Today's practice asks for five minutes each hour to sit in silent contemplation. Find a quiet moment and remember, "I am as God created me. I can suffer nothing. I am God's creation." Then allow yourself to imagine what this means.

Imagine all you call chaos is actually a perfect harmony beyond your ability to comprehend. Imagine your spirit is part of the Unlimited extending Itself into eternity. You are completely free of all worry about error or judgment. Nothing you can possibly do can take you out of harmony for the world is in you. You are not in it.

Explore your world today in freedom and love. This is where the Mind of God connects with you. There can be no guilt here. There can be no pain here. There can be only yourself, which is also me, and everything else around us.

This world is within your Self. It is your creation, for you are as God created you. And for this, practice being pleased with yourself today.

Review III

Lesson 111: Review

Your next review begins today. There will be two lessons every day for ten days. Reviews allow you to see the interrelatedness of each lesson and deepen your understanding of the ideas behind them.

To practice, simply read each lesson and sit with its message for about five minutes. Do this twice a day, in the morning and before bedtime. Read over the ideas and comments. Let your mind relate them to your needs, your concerns, and any problems that seem to be present in your life. Know that you are not alone while you read and contemplate. Your mind is connected to the One Mind, and indeed, to all minds.

If you can, on the half hour, bring at least one particular lesson to mind. It will most certainly bring peace to you. You must decide for yourself if you want this peace. No one can make the decision for you. But don't make it a rigid ritual and don't feel guilty if you cannot achieve your goal. The goal is peace, not guilt! Learn to feel the difference between the unavoidable presses of life and your own unwillingness or avoidance.

Here are the lessons for the day. Enjoy them. Be with them. Feel them within your being as you read.

1. Miracles are seen in light.
Commentary: The light we are speaking of here is the light of an unclouded mind that is present in the moment. Fear of the future and regrets about the past obscure the moment. The truth is, we do not know enough to judge. Allow the moment to present its light.

2. Miracles are seen in light, and light and strength are one.
Commentary: Incapable of true connection, the ego is isolated, and helplessness seems real. But Mind of God holds your mind

and shares Its strength with you. What created you in Oneness extends Its attributes, if you will but allow it.

On the hour remember: Miracles are seen in light.

On the half-hour remember: Miracles are seen in light, and light and strength are one.

Lesson 112: Review

For morning and evening review:

1. Light and joy and peace abide in me.

Commentary: I am as God created me, so Light and joy and peace must be within my mind. I cannot perceive the Light when my mind is in denial of Source. Let my mind open to the Light so I can know my Innocence.

2. I am as God created me.

Commentary: God created me Whole and so I am. There is no defect in me whatsoever. I desire to know my Self.

On the hour remember: Light and joy and peace abide in me.
On the half-hour remember: I am as God created me.

Lesson 113: Review

For morning and evening review:

1. I am one Self, united with my Creator.

Commentary: What a thought! I am one Self, united with everything, animate and inanimate. Where am I united? In my mind. My mind is shared with everything and everyone. I am never not connected, which means my open mind has access to all the knowledge I need, all the answers to my questions, and all the peace I seek. I ask for help opening my mind today.

2. Salvation comes from my one Self.
Commentary: The memory of my Self remains within, where Source placed It. In my Self is the Knowledge of my Source and Its perfect plan for my Salvation.

On the hour remember: I am one Self, united with my Creator.
On the half-hour remember: Salvation comes from my one Self.

Lesson 114: Review
For morning and evening review:

1. I am spirit.
Commentary: A while back we had to buy a new washing machine. The sales guy and I were joking around, and I half seriously posed the question, "Who am I, really?" He stopped for a minute to consider and answered, "Mostly I just want to know, 'Where are my pants?'" But the truth is I am not a body. Those who live and move around me are not bodies. We are all spirit. No body can contain my spirit or impose any limitation on me that Source Itself has not imposed. And Source has imposed none of the limits I think I think I live with now.

2. I will accept my part in God's plan for Salvation.
Commentary: I am free to play at being human. But the highest and best role I have in this life is to remember my true nature, which comes from Source. The role Source has given me is far greater than the one I believe I've given to myself. I acknowledge that I am unable to understand the Whole from the perspective of my limited ego. I accept that the Plan of Source is for me to remember what I am in Truth.

On the hour remember: I am spirit.
On the half-hour remember: I will accept my part in God's plan for salvation.

Lesson 115: Review

Harmony might be described as a combination of separate notes, or parts, that form a pleasing whole. Today's review asks that you open yourself to the experience of harmony by awakening to Wholeness, which is also called salvation.

For morning and evening review:

1. Salvation is my only function here.

Commentary: This world tells me I have many duties and obligations. Most of them are merely distractions. My function here is to forgive all the "errors" I seem to have committed and that seem to have been committed against me. This is the only way I am released from them.

2. My part is essential to God's plan for salvation.

Commentary: I am essential to God's plan to save the part of my mind that perceives this world as reality. I need not strive. I need to listen. I need to allow.

On the hour remember: Salvation is my only function here.
On half-hour remember: My part is essential to God's plan for salvation.

Lesson 116: Review

Be kind to yourself about this business of awakening. Your kindness to yourself is the first step in learning real kindness to others. We all fall down. We all drift back into dreamland. The simple act of reading the lesson reverberates in ways that you may not know in the moment you are reading. Hours, days, or even weeks later, the words of the lesson may come into your awareness. In this moment, a miracle occurs, as a distant memory awakens.

Awakening from the dreams of illusion requires us to pass through layers of guilt and shame. "Enlightened neurosis" is the way one teacher described the process. Become aware of the perfection in your process. Every single highly charged emotion that comes up for you is powerful wisdom. Stay with it. Sit and stay open. Be a friend to yourself. This is perfect happiness. Even what feels imperfect contains perfection.

For morning and evening review:

1. God's Will for me is perfect happiness.
Commentary: The key word here is "perfect." Perfection is harmony. Harmony involves a multiplicity. What I give, I also receive equally, in perfect harmony.

2. I share God's Will for happiness for me.
Commentary: Even as I fall down, or go back to sleep, my willingness remains alive within. I share God's Will for me because I am One with It. I want only It because that is All there is.

On the hour remember: God's Will for me is perfect happiness. On the half-hour remember: I share God's Will for happiness for me.

Lesson 117: Review
Nothing in form comes from form. All arises in the mind. Where we place our attention determines what we see. Today, place your attention on what you seek from spirit, which can only be perfect happiness.

For morning and evening review:

1. Source being Love is also happiness.
Commentary: All That Is, is Love. Love loves Itself without condition. Nothing created from Love can be threatened. Nothing not created from Love is real. I will not choose illusion over Love.

2. I seek but what belongs to me in Truth.
Commentary: Love is my heritage, and with it joy. I accept all that is mine in Truth.

On the hour remember: Source being Love is also happiness.
On the half-hour remember: I seek but what belongs to me in truth.

Lesson 118: Review

> *Your condemnation of yourself is the root of all your attack.*
> *You project away from you your condemnation of yourself by*
> *judging another as unworthy and deserving of punishment.*
> *Here lies the split in your mind. Your mind perceives itself as*
> *separate from the mind that it is judging, believing that by*
> *punishing another, it escapes punishment.*
> *– ACIM*

For morning and evening review:

1. God's peace and joy are mine.
Commentary: I assure my own peace and joy when I extend it to others. Today I end self-condemnation and attack. I claim my Innocence and receive the peace of Oneness.

2. Let me be still and listen to the Truth.
Commentary: I will be still today and put aside the chaos of the world that distracts me from the truth about myself. I need not fear the world or anything of the world. All else may shift around me, but the Love of Source is the foundation upon which I stand. As I look around my world today, I will do so from a place of internal peace. I am loved, I am safe, I am protected. As I see this truth for myself, I gift it to others. As I gift it to others, I experience it even more deeply in myself.

On the hour remember: God's peace and joy are mine.
On the half-hour remember: Let me be still and listen to the Truth.

Lesson 119: Review

For morning and evening review:

1. Truth will correct all errors in my mind.
Commentary: I am in error when I judge myself or anyone else as unworthy in any way. I have never sinned and guilt is without any merit at all. I am eternal. I am Love. My True Self rests safely in Its Source.

2. To give and to receive are one in truth.
Commentary: One of the great illusions of this world is that giving requires loss of any kind. In truth, giving confirms my own abundance and adds to it. The real gift I give is not a physical thing, but the love of sharing, which itself lies behind the gift. To know this truth, I must experience it. I can recognize what I have received today by giving it – for my gift is the proof of having.

On the hour remember: Truth will correct all errors in my mind.
On the half-hour remember: To give and to receive are one in truth.

Today, try to have at least one conscious experience of receiving through giving. You will know you've succeeded because you will feel good. Truth always feels good because it reconnects us to our Source, which is Love. Be free to be kind to yourself and others today.

Lesson 120: Review

For morning and evening review:

1. I rest in God.

Commentary: Know your own safety in this moment. You are not your body and whatever happens to the body is, in Reality, of little concern. Rest your mind in this moment, in certainty about your Self and Source.

2. I am as God created me.

Commentary: I am either a body or I am Spirit. I cannot be both. God created me Spirit so that is what I truly am. Nothing can alter this – not even lifetimes of illusion can change what God has shared – Himself, Herself, Itself. No physical form can ever contain all that I am. When it is gone and I have woken from the dream, my Spirit will remain. It is forever and forever.

On the hour: I rest in God.
On the half-hour: I am as God created me.
Be mindful of your feelings and emotions today. When you experience even the slightest sense of disquiet, notice it, and say to yourself, "I rest in God today."
It will give you time to choose another way.

Lesson 121

Forgiveness is the key to happiness.

We leave behind review lessons today and move into new territory. Today's lesson will give you an experience of forgiveness, if you will allow it.

How easy it is to deny my responsibility for creation. How difficult it is to accept that every falling leaf, every breath of wind, each drop of rain, all sunsets that ever were, every moment that appears to pass before me takes place in my own mind – and it is a mind I share with you.

If I am not creating all that is before me, then what is? God? Source? Nothing? This is exactly where even the most intelligent minds get lost. Where they get lost lies in the argument about "good" and "evil." What is "good"? What is its counterpoint? The truth is simple, but it requires acceptance of the idea and logic of Oneness.

Oneness requires that when I forgive you, it is always also myself I am forgiving. When you forgive me, you are always, without fail, forgiving yourself. There is no "good" or "evil" in Oneness. There is only Oneness experiencing Itself from a variety of positions. All events are neutral. It requires a certain maturity to accept the truth of this, but it is also the key to happiness.

A child wants protection from her parent. A teenager blames her parent. An adult sees herself as the parent, remembers she was once a child and a teenager, and appreciates what it is to be responsible. Are you the child, the teenager, or the parent?

What I leave unforgiven in another remains unforgiven in myself. What is forgiven in another is forgiven in myself. Giving and receiving are One in truth. If you learn nothing else in all these lessons but this, you will know the path of peace.

Today, you are asked to devote two, ten-minute practice periods to giving and receiving forgiveness. You will do this by forming a trinity, the holy number of completion. Read through this contemplation, then practice with it in the morning and evening.

Take your seat and close your eyes. Relax your body and place your awareness gently on the breath. Sit in stillness a moment, then allow your mind to bring up a person who has wronged you, a person you do not like, or wish to avoid. It could be a lifelong enemy, a colleague, or a relative. Be sure it is someone you know well enough. See this person in your mind's eye and allow yourself to clearly feel what it is you do not like about him or her. You may feel the dislike in your body or heart area. It may be unpleasant. Stay with the feeling a bit. Sit with its flavor and texture.

Now, shift your attention and try to find something about the person that is positive. Find some little thing that shines in them. There will always something. It may be a trait you've chosen to ignore. It may be some little thing you saw and passed over. Place your focus on this quality of goodness, however small, and try to let it extend until it covers your mental image of the person. You have now replaced the feeling of dislike with something you can like. Sit with this image until you feel it soften the tightness in your heart.

Now bring to mind someone you call a friend. Allow the feeling of your friend to rise and settle comfortably within your heart. This will feel good. It is always a good feeling to be open because it's your natural state. Now for the tricky part. When you are ready, take the same light you found in your "enemy" and place it on your friend. See this friend now as even more dear to you than before. He or she now has all their original qualities, plus the new ones from your "enemy."

Now comes part two of the trinity. Look upon your friend and imagine her or him offering you all the light you've just given – the light you found in your "enemy" as well as the friend's original light. Feel this blessing. Take all of the light into your heart.

Here comes the trinity. Now, let the image of your "enemy" join with your friend and let them both offer you a blessing of light. Now you are one with them and they are one with you. A holy trinity has been formed: you, your "enemy," and your friend – all one self together. You have now been forgiven by yourself.

Do not discount the level of healing you have just accomplished. It transcends space and time. This is where your true power lies. You have opened doors you may not have known even existed. Be very happy with yourself.

Every hour today tell yourself, "Forgiveness is the key to happiness. I will awaken from the dream that we are all anything but perfect in the Mind of God."

Know this: forgiveness begins and ends with the self. Forgiveness, given to the self, extends to the other. Forgiveness, given to the other, extends to the self. Learn this and you will know the Peace of Source.

Lesson 122

Forgiveness offers everything I want.

Play easily today. Place no obstacles in your own path. Let go of your thoughts. Let go of your feelings. Let go of expectations about what should or should not be. None of it means anything at all. Do not value the valueless.

Today is your movie and you are seated safely in the theater. Many things will pass in front of you today. Make no demands on them or on yourself in relation to them. Just sit comfortably in your seat. Be willing to align with the flow of each moment as it arises to greet you. Stay awake as the movie plays. Be in your moment. When you find yourself sleeping (and you will) forgive yourself and be happy to awaken again.

This is forgiveness. It is nothing more than allowing the moment. Accept what the universe is offering, knowing that you are always in the care and safety of Source. Allow yourself to be a happy learner. Consider this, from ACIM:

The happy learner cannot feel guilty about learning. This is so essential to learning that it should never be forgotten. The guiltless learner learns easily because her thoughts are free. This entails the recognition that guilt is interference, not salvation, and serves no useful function at all.

You are whole only in your guiltlessness, and only in your guiltlessness can you be happy. To wish for guilt in any way, in any form, will lose appreciation of the value of your guiltlessness, and push it from your sight.

The power of decision is all that is yours. What you can decide between is fixed, because there are no alternatives except truth and illusion. And there is no overlap between them, because they are opposites which cannot be reconciled and cannot both be true. You are guilty or guiltless, bound or free, unhappy or happy.

Practice twice today, morning and evening, for 15 minutes. Take your seat and relax. Close your eyes and place your attention gently on the breath. Sink into peace as you say in your mind, "Forgiveness offers everything I want. Today I have accepted this as true. Today I receive the gifts of God." Then watch your breath and allow thoughts to arise as they will. If your mind becomes too active (and it will), simply repeat slowly in your mind, "Forgiveness offers everything I want." Savor each word. Feel it in your body.

Forgiveness is your purpose here. My purpose is the same as yours. We are joined in our purpose here. Play easily today. Place no obstacles of guilt in your own path.

Lesson 123

I thank my Creator for Its gifts to me.

Today's lesson asks you to be thankful. But what if you don't really feel so thankful today? What if you've woken up late after a not-so-great sleep, or a dream that has left a vague sense of discomfort? What if you've had an argument with someone yesterday that was left unresolved, or if the morning news makes thankfulness seem like a bad joke?

If you feel like this, know you are not alone. Don't force the feeling of being thankful, or feel "less than" because it isn't there. Why resist what you feel? Allow your not-so-great feelings to rise up in your mind, in your heart, and your body, and be recognized. Say hello to them. Wallow knowingly in them if you want. They are there to be seen in the light. Only then can they be released.

But do yourself a favor, a big favor, and try to know that your feelings are not who you are. The very fact that you are able to watch them or say to yourself, "I'm wallowing in these feelings," is enough. For if you allow all feelings and just keep watching, eventually you will sense beneath the discomfort something gentle, sustained and connected. It won't punish you for your feelings but it will reward you for having the courage to sit with them until they've had their say, and then softly, perhaps slowly, disappear into something else.

For nearly six months you have been learning this world is illusion. It is difficult to be told, "I tell you this world is not real." Do not make yourself wrong for having chosen this illusion. Do not punish yourself for being here. Do have unconditional friendship with yourself. Do try to watch the contents of your own mind, for only then will you see that nothing lasts. Seeing that nothing lasts opens the door to the question, "What am I, then? What am I truly?"

The answer is, "I am a being who is able to question my own thinking. I am a being who is able to see that my own thoughts are fleeting; that my own feelings change like quicksilver. I see that within each day my heart experiences lots of openings and also lots of closings. I am a being who is curious. I am capable. I am powerful. I am here. I am willing."

Practice contemplation in the morning and evening today for 15 minutes. Take your seat and close your eyes. Place your awareness gently on the breath. Relax your body. Feel the breath, as it rises and falls all by itself. Do nothing. Expect nothing of yourself. As you exhale, let all stress go. As you inhale, breathe in peace. As you exhale, imagine the breath carrying away all that is not of benefit to you. It leaves your body and extends to the ends of the universe. Take as long as you want breathing in peace and breathing out all that does not serve you.

When you are at rest, when you feel ready, say in your mind, "I thank my Creator for Its gifts to me." As you breathe in, try to imagine peace. As you breathe out, know that all you do not need is being taken away effortlessly. As you breathe in, know that Source is with you and is thankful to you for sharing your mind. Source holds you and cares for you without limit forever. Stay in peace for as long as you can. Watch your breath. If thoughts arise, and they will, go back to the lesson. Can you give yourself half an hour of peace today? It will not be wasted time.

You belong to the First Cause. It created you like Itself. You are spirit. You are free. Today, accept your freedom and be thankful you are not what you have been taught you are. Cultivate unconditional friendship with yourself. Like yourself. Someone has to. It might as well be you.

Lesson 124

Let me remember I am One with God.

This world would have you believe in the absolute value of your unique identity. In fact, it tells you that our uniqueness is all you are – that without it, you are nothing. This special self is the ego's identity and believing in it leaves you all alone with your preciousness.

The personal mind's desire to be singular and special is upside down. It is not the Most of What We Are. Indeed, the Most of What We Are is unified with that which created us in the first place. Our identity as special and singular comes at a great, great cost. It leaves us feeling vulnerable, alone, afraid, isolated, and meaningless.

We are a Unified Self, expressed as fragments of Self. There is no harm in enjoying your small self but there is harm in the perception that it is the full extent of "you." Here, in this world, we have traveled far afield. We have forgotten our true identity. And we can only remember our identity when we give up the insane desire to control reality. We cannot even control our personal self, our ego, yet we try again and again to make this world something it can never be and wasn't intended for.

I did not create myself, nor did you! Even the most delusional personal mind can see the truth of this statement. We did not create ourselves and it is not up to us to decide what reality is! Source is Reality and the Laws of Love are the Laws of Source. Our obsession with the separate, personal self obscures love, its laws, and the Wholeness that is What We Are.

Yet, Source has placed Wholeness in our mind. We can deny Source, but we cannot forget what It has placed within us. What we have made invisible to the small self is still there, within. We are holograms of Wholeness and our attraction to Love remains because Love's attraction to Love is irresistible.

Do not resist this truth today. Behold your role within the universe! Do not be afraid to leave the ego's little self behind, for no miracle can be denied to those who know they are One with Source.

Today's practice takes you into a deeper form of meditation. Find a quiet place, at a time of your choosing, and sit for thirty minutes in contemplation of the thought you are One with God. If you need additional guidance please refer to the chapter on meditation and contemplation.

Take your seat and place your awareness gently on the breath. Repeat in your mind, "Let me remember I am One with God." Use the breath as your anchor and watch whatever thoughts and feelings come up. Trust yourself. Ask for help. Use the lesson as a mantra if you like. Breathe in and notice. Breathe out and notice. You cannot fail. Even if you sit with a wild mind, and rise from your seat believing there has been no benefit – do not worry. You have gained something and it will come to you. Just begin to notice. It is inevitable. You are deepening your practice now.

Be mindful today. Remember you are totally safe, unbound, and wholly loved. Your function here is to awaken. You awaken through forgiveness. Forgive yourself for still believing the illusion is real. Don't take anything too seriously and just enjoy the ride.

Lesson 125

In quiet I receive God's Word today.

Amidst the chaos let this be a day of rest in your mind. This is a choice you are free to make and only you can make it for yourself. No one can hear with a mind full of noise. You need do nothing for all has already been done for you. Nothing has an effect upon you unless you choose to allow it. Give up your heavy burden of control.

The world will change through you. Your work today, if it can be called work, is to find peace, to cultivate it in yourself, and quietly share it with all those Source has placed in your path. No more is asked, but do not take this task lightly. What you will find in peace and quiet is the only thing that is real in this world. Look upon your sister and brother. Remember, all you give to them is given to yourself. There is no sacrifice.

Three times today, in the morning, midday, and evening, take ten minutes and sit in quiet. Leave behind this world that measures achievement through strain and effort. Leave behind the voices that judge this and that as worthy or not. Just for a little while, give yourself freedom from limitation. Seek the vast quiet peace that waits in silence beneath the chaos.

Take your seat in a place you will not be disturbed. Close

your eyes. Let the body relax, and place your awareness on the breath. Be gentle with yourself as you say in your mind, "In quiet I receive God's Word today." Now do nothing but watch the breath. Thoughts will arise. Allow them. Feel them in the body but do not be taken away too much by them. On each out-breath, let go of tension. On each in-breath, allow the light to enter. Allow, allow, and allow. Sit. Stay. Be still and listen with a soft heart.

Be mindful today. If you can stop each hour and be still a moment, do so. Remind yourself each hour that no one can listen for you. Only you can hear, and you can only hear in silence. It is your own voice you will recognize.

Lesson 126

All that I give is given to myself.

Twenty years ago, when I first began my spiritual journey in earnest, I was instructed to do a breathing practice. In this practice I was asked to breathe in light and breathe out fear, guilt, shame – basically any feeling that was a burden. I was to imagine the light streaming in from all parts of the universe and infusing every cell of my body. Light to my feet. Light to my back and sides. Light into my chest and neck. Light into the top of my head. On the exhale, anything that did not serve me was to be let go in a cloud of blue smoke, streaming out of each cell to the ends of the universe.

This exercise was deeply satisfying because of the exhalation. My burdens streamed out of my entire body. But breathing in light was a challenge. I could find little room in myself for the light. Luckily, for some reason, I didn't see this as a problem I needed to fix. I just figured it would take time to make room for the light. And it did – after about five years of daily practice. Does that seem like a long time?

It's hard to stay with highly charged emotions. It requires courage to stay with discomfort. Self-judgment could have made me rush into "accepting" the light before I was ready. But I wouldn't have emptied myself completely and the end result would have been less room for light. Now, when I breathe in, I am empty of all barriers to light. I can fill myself with it so completely it seeps out into the space that surrounds me. But I had to wait for it.

"All that I give is given to myself." How does this relate to breathing in light? When I breathe in, I am breathing in you. When I breathe out, I breathe out to you. You receive me and I receive you without boundaries or barriers of any kind. Breathing in and out is a literal experience that giving and receiving are the same. And if giving and receiving are the same, then all that I give is given to myself.

Only the heart that can give forgiveness can receive it. Only the heart that can receive forgiveness can give it. Forgiveness is not charity but self-interest. It is our right because we were created out of Love and that is still what we are. If you don't see this, if you don't feel it or believe it, don't give up.

How radical it is to say forgiveness is self-interest! It's even more radical to say no one is guilty. Is Oneness radical? At the present time, it is for many. But the truth is that forgiveness heals the mind that gives it, for giving is receiving. What remains ungiven cannot be received, but what has been given must be received. All that we give is given to our self. The out-breath is given to myself. The in-breath is given to myself.

Today you will practice understanding the lesson that giving and receiving are the same. Your practice will take place in the morning and evening for fifteen minutes each.

Take your seat and close your eyes. Gently place awareness on your breath. Ask for help understanding today's idea and trust you will receive what you have asked for. When you are ready, say in your mind, "All that I give is given to myself." Breathe in forgiveness. Breathe out all your fear and shame. Relax and breathe in light. Breathe out the blue smoke that holds you back from receiving. Watch your thoughts, repeat the lesson in your mind, and relax. If you hold this focus, you will begin to sense an inner cleanse. There will be more space inside you.

Watch your thoughts today. If you feel any moment of disquiet, annoyance, anger, or frustration (and you will) say to yourself, "All that I give is given to myself." Breathe in peace and breathe out discomfort. Send it all away to the end of the universe. Create space for light.

Lesson 127

There is no Love but God's.

There are many names for what we are, but the truest one is Love.

ACIM says this lesson is "the largest single step this course requests in your advance towards its established goal." Only the Love of Source is Real. It is what we are, and it is without limits of any kind.

This world teaches only a limited and malformed translation of Love. It does not know Love's unlimited nature because illusion can only simulate Reality. A reflection of a tree in water is not the tree itself. The reflection lacks the wholeness of the real thing, just as this world lacks the Wholeness of Reality.

Do not look for Love in this world. It cannot show it to you. You will search endlessly for it and never find it. Love in this world is conditional and does not last because everything in this world is conditional and does not last.

This world refuses to extend Love unless circumstances are "right." In our ignorance of Wholeness, we see giving as sacrifice. But Love, as an extension of endless, unlimited Source, knows nothing of sacrifice. It is safe to say that most of us have never, ever experienced the unlimited depths of unconditional Love. We experience only its imperfect reflection.

Love is not hierarchical. It does not judge. It does not punish. It does not measure. Love does not fear and love does not end. It does not value one thing over another. It sees no specialness or level of degree. Love does not contain, or limit. It does not work or strive. It knows no resistance to anything because It is at ease and comfortable with all things, knowing It is never vulnerable at all. Love is never, ever, not all-encompassing forever. You can see how Love is not of this world, but remember: Love exists. This world does not.

The return to Love will be your healing. But the "return" itself is only a perception because you cannot return to what you have never left. Separation is the illusion of your split mind. You have never been separated from Love because Love has no end. Who could be beyond what is everywhere?

This is how we will know Love – when we honor everything our mind perceives. This is how we will know our own Perfection – when we see everything is a reflection of Perfect Love. Do you believe this is impossible? Do you believe you must wait a while before experiencing Love? Consider this: waiting to find your place is possible only in time, but time has no meaning in infinity. Your place in the Mind of Love awaits you now. If you find even the faintest glimmer of it today, you have advanced immeasurably toward your release from the personal mind's "laws" of this world. This is the truth: *you have already succeeded in your goal to know Love.*

Twice today, take fifteen minutes to escape from the "laws" of this world and find peace in Love. Take your seat and rest easily. Relax your body. Close your eyes and place your awareness gently on the breath. In your mind, ask All That Is, God, Source, the Mother, the Father – whatever appeals to you – to help you. How can God not hear your request when your mind lives in the Mind of God? Ask Source to guide your thoughts. You wish to know Love's meaning and your will cannot be denied. When you are ready, say in your mind, "There is no Love but God's."

Now place your awareness on the heart. Let it soften. Feel its warmth and breathe into it. Soften your belly, then your throat. Soften the back of the neck. Soften your brain. Soften the forehead and the area behind the eyes. Soften the soles of your feet. Soften your hands. Soften the heart again and feel it relax even more. Let your whole body soften.

Gently watch your breath, and feel your way into a quiet space. Love is there, in the quiet. Do not strive to know. Allow Love to come to you. It will. Forgive all thoughts. Allow all thoughts. Let them arise, repeat the words of the lesson, and go back to the breath. Feel your way into peace. You will know when you've arrived and Love will be there to greet you. It will not say a word but you will feel a smile begin to form. This may take all of your fifteen minutes. Allow yourself this gift. Breathe. Repeat the words of the lesson. Soften. Go inward to the silence.

Be mindful today. As you look about your world today, see beyond it. Beneath the seeming ignorance, the guilt, the impatience, the fear, is Love. All of it is having the experience of being seemingly separated from something that cannot ever be separate! Forgive the ignorance. Forgive the blindness. Forgive your own loneliness and desperation. Your knowing is their salvation. Save them and save yourself.

Lesson 128

The world I see holds nothing that I want.

Today's lesson is nothing if not blunt. The world you "see" offers nothing you want. Believe this now and you will be saved from years of fruitless searching, false leads, futility, and despair.

Understand this: what you value is what you perceive as part of the self you think you are. All you seek from this world to enhance your small self does nothing but limit you. It satisfies only temporarily. Indeed, what you perceive of value in this world hides your True Worth from you. This world cannot and will not offer you salvation ever.

Your True Worth is not understandable to the world you see. How can a world created from the illusion of separation ever reflect your True Worth? Stop expecting it! Escape the limitations it places upon your mind. There is nothing to hold on to here that is worth one instant of pain, diminishment, or doubt. Does this mean you ignore the world? No! Have your experience but do not become your experience. End your practice of using its value system as a measure of your worth.

Today, your practice is to let go of the value you have given to the world you perceive. Leave it free of purpose for you, for its only purpose is to prove that you are free.

Three times today, allow your mind to rest for ten minutes. Take your seat and relax. Place your awareness gently on the breath and close your eyes. Ask for help if you require it. Then repeat in your mind, "This world holds nothing that I want." Now, let go of all thoughts and concerns this world holds for you. It does not define you. It can never contain you. All its glitter is false. All its promises are but obstacles in your path.

Then spend ten minutes in silence. Allow peace to guide you inward. If thoughts arise, and they will, go back to the breath and repeat the lesson in your mind. Watch your feelings. Allow them to rise, move through you, and then fall away. Let breath be your anchor. Thoughts and feelings are but waves upon the shore. Hold firmly to the breath and let them wash over you. Go beyond this world. Reality is not "out there" but inside your heart/mind.

Be mindful today. If you feel discomfort, anger, disappointment, or frustration (and you will) just notice it.

Powerful wisdom is often found in the most highly charged emotions. Ask yourself, "How does this feeling serve me?" Ask yourself, "How is this of value to me?" Then listen gently for the answer. Forgive yourself as often as you need. Ask for help as often as you need. There are no limitations in eternity. The Unlimited has never limited Itself or Its Creation.

Lesson 129

Beyond this world there is a world I want.

The cause of this world, its engendering if you will, arises out of thoughts in your mind. At this point in your training you perceive illusion to be true, pain to be real, and suffering to be expected. You are free to continue with your perception. But you are also free to use your mind to see Truly. ACIM calls this True Perception.

True Perception does not require you to hate this world. It does not require you to ignore it or move to a cave in the desert. It does require that you quit your unquestioned belief in its value. True Perception does not leave you with a worthless world. This would only be depressing and end your progress. True Perception is given by Source as a means to see beyond this world – not as in some dream, but as a means of getting closer to the truth of what lies within it – unseen by the personal mind. Look at this comparison between the personal mind (p) perception and True Perception (TP).

p: We are all separated beings.
TP: We are all One.

p: We are separated from Source.
TP: We are One with Source.

p: We can only perceive three-dimensional space and time.
TP: We are multidimensional beings capable of perceiving the All.

p: We are subject to fate.
TP: We are creators of reality.

p: Matter is the primary substance of the universe.
TP: Feeling/Thought is the primary substance of the universe.

p: Death of the body is the end of life.
TP: Death is a transition to an expanded reality.

P: We are judged in life and after death.
TP: Source judges nothing. Only we judge out of ignorance.

p: Scarcity is real; only the fittest, smartest, most deserving survive.
TP: Reality is Limitless and without hierarchy.

p: Humans are the masters of the earth.
TP: Earth has a consciousness we share.

Beyond this world is a world you want. True Perception can show up as a physical world transformed by Love, or as an inner Kingdom beyond form. For as long as you experience yourself in form, both experiences will be available to you. Your Self knows its True Home is not in form at all, although it may still use form for a while.

Practice today consists of three ten-minute contemplations: morning, afternoon, and evening. Use your practice to play with True Perception. See how far your mind can rise above this world when you release it from its limitations. Do not strive for release but allow the mind its natural leaning. Guidance is all around and it will assist you.

Take your seat and close your eyes upon the world you see. Relax your body and gently place your awareness on the breath. When you are ready, say in your mind, "Beyond this world there is a world I want. I choose to see that world instead of this, for here is nothing that I really want."

Then feel the light that is not of this world. Soften your heart and mind with its warmth. Feel beyond the body into the pure energy of your being. Know you are safe. The only fear was fear of loss, and there is no loss at all. Let go of loss for the opposite is true. There is only wholeness, felt directly by the knowing of your heart. Watch your breath. Feel the peace. Let thoughts arise. Go back to the breath. Say the lesson in your mind and go back to peace. Rest your mind here a while.

Lesson 130

It is impossible to see two worlds.

The day science begins to study non-physical phenomena, it will make more progress in one decade than in all the previous centuries of its existence.
– Nikola Tesla

The other day a friend and I were walking along the shore beyond our house. As we stood on the shore she pointed to the great expanse of water and sky and exclaimed, "But the universe is so big! And I am so small! It's overwhelming to contemplate it all."

Who has not had this ancient feeling? Who has not imagined the world, the solar system, the galaxies, and the universe – and not felt small and insignificant? But what if all of this, every boson, electron, atom, rock, organism, planet, galaxy, solar system, and indeed the whole universe was your creation? Can you imagine the possibility?

You are either the tiniest fleeting speck of dust in an endless universe or you are the universe itself. If you are only a speck, then you can go merrily on your way, knowing nothing you do has any real consequence. If you are the universe itself, then all of it is contained within you, and you within all of it. You are either on your own or connected. If you're on your own, you are truly meaningless. If you're connected, what you do has consequence.

ACIM teaches there is no middle ground and only one of these explanations is true. Perception is consistent. What you see reflects your thoughts and your thoughts reflect your desire. Source has made us capable of discerning between the two, and ultimately we must decide which one we desire. We are either tiny specks or we are Creator Beings. It is impossible to be both at once.

The power to decide is yours. There is no punishment for either choice. But it is impossible to see both Oneness and separation for only one is true, ever. Forgiveness, allowing, acceptance... these form the bridge between the worlds. This is the architecture that crosses the gap. Fear is the gap.

Be fearless! Let go of your nothingness. What loss can there be in choosing not to value nothingness? You are here for a short time, playing in form. That is all it is. You play in the reflection of your own mind, which is joined forever and always with Mind of Source. See your mind reflected in Source and let go of littleness.

Your practice today is to let go of littleness. Six times today, give yourself five minutes to the one thought that is true. End your compromise with nothingness.

Begin by taking your seat and relaxing the body. Close your eyes to the world of perception and go inward. Ask for help from All That Is, God, the Father, the Mother, or from whatever feels right for you. Your goal is to open your mind to True Perception. You do not want illusion or its values.

When you are ready, say in your mind, "It is impossible to

see two worlds. Let me accept the strength Source has placed in me and see no value in this world, that I may find my freedom and deliverance."

Source is there. You have called to your Self, as Love calls to Love. Sit in quiet and peace. Forgive this world. See through it and beyond to your One Self. You have come to this world to find your Self, but you will not find it in this world. This world and this universe will pass away but you will not. You are spirit. You are free, as God created you.

Be at peace today. If you miss a practice (and you probably will) use it as an opportunity to learn more deeply the lesson of forgiveness. You will undoubtedly experience things that will challenge your peace. Use these challenges as opportunities to dismiss the temptation to believe this world is real. Remember, your choice either limits you or expands the power of your True Perception.

Lesson 131

No one can fail who seeks to reach the truth.

Yesterday you learned it is impossible to see two worlds. Today you learn you cannot fail in your effort to see with True Perception.

We recognize from our own experience that what happens in dreaming seems real while we are asleep. But upon awaking we realize everything that seemed to happen in the dream did not happen at all! Rarely do we think it strange or silly that the laws of this world do not apply in sleep.

We dream of flying. We dream of being chased by monsters. We dream of playing music effortlessly. We dream of singing before a vast audience in a strong, clear voice. We communicate without words. Want to be somewhere else? It happens instantly. We create through desire in dreams. Sometimes we know we're dreaming in the dream and still continue to dream. What mind can do all of this!

The dreaming mind is closer to Reality. But would you bother to reconcile the dreaming life with waking life if you knew Reality is neither? We dream we are awake as well as asleep. It is time to awaken from both. We are a Mind that is Awake to Its Self and is telling us now to awaken. We awaken slowly, for the Truth of our Wholeness would be too much to bear all at once. So we dream ourselves awake until we dream no more. The truth is: You are already Home, dreaming of exile.

We came here to search and find. The goal we seek is peace without end. But peace will not be found in this world, where nothing lasts, everything is destroyed, and we dream of darkness and loss. What is here is meaningless. It was born in the fear of forgetfulness. This was your first lesson, "Nothing I see means anything." It was true then, and it is true now. Lesson one began your awakening to Reality.

Your mind is capable of making a world and calling it real. But it can also awaken from the world it made because it is free. You have denied yourself so much and Source, in Its love for you, does not want it thus. Source knows you only as free. But if Source intervened, it would be an attack on your sovereignty and this Source will not do. Source does not attack Itself, which you are. Seek the door and it will open, but before you reach, remember you cannot fail.
– ACIM

Sit three times today for ten minutes, in the morning, at midday, and before bed. Your goal is to feel the way into your true nature – which is eternal. End the dream you are a beggar! If you believe you are only your body, you have beggared yourself. Go beyond its limitations into the quiet beyond thought. You awaken to another world when you let go of this one. Let go and allow

Source to guide your mind.

Take your seat and relax. Close your eyes and place your awareness gently on the breath. When you are ready, say in your mind, "I ask to know the peace of Source. I ask to join my mind with Source." You might add, "I am awareness becoming aware of Itself. I am at peace, expecting nothing but open to anything."

Now watch the breath and allow thoughts to arise as they will. Notice them. Some will feel peaceful. These are a mirror of Source's Mind. Some will feel compulsive, distracting, even disgusting. These are not real. They are of the dream. This is true: all thoughts and feelings of peace are real. Anything that is not peace is unreal. However, be at peace even with thoughts that are not of peace. You are the awareness behind the thought. You must be, or you would not be aware of the thought itself. Peace is real. Unease is not.

Watch your breath and do nothing. Just allow, even if it is only for a moment. Behind all thought is a place of light and gentle silence. Walk through its open door. Slip effortlessly into it, simply by not resisting anything. Breathe in the light and breathe out all that is not needed. This is all. Enjoy what you find, even if it is only for a moment. This is awakening from the dream. We will all awaken. It is inevitable because it is the Will of Source. Remember, you are already Home, dreaming of exile.

Be mindful today. Look for grace. It is all around. It lives between moments in time, the words we hear, the shifting winds and demands of the dream state perceived as reality. Seek grace in silence, for there is its Home, and yours. No one can fail who seeks to reach it.

Many blessings.

Lesson 132

I loose the world from all I thought it was.

Some loosen their grip only at the moment of death. Others find release in art, extreme sports, or meditation. And for a few, the loosening comes in dreams, synchronicities, or even near death experiences. Whatever the form, the effect is like rebooting a computer; a fresh start, a new perspective, is created. The effect of loosening your grip upon this world is a feeling of spaciousness.

We hold this world in a constant grip of low-level fear, expressed as control. We seek to be prepared for all possible events. This is a defensive posture at best and an offensive stance at worst.

Your practice today is to release your hold on what you think the world should be. Look around, find silence, and be content. Place yourself in the flow of life. End your defensive resistance to it! Stop the contraction of control. Be present in the moment, for the present is the only time available for salvation to enter your mind.

Free the world from all you think it should be, or could be, and accept your moment as it is. This moment is yours. It belongs to no one else. Take it. Live in it. Free yourself of expectation about it. Notice the beauty, not the strain. There is nothing in your moment that will harm you – so be at peace with it.

Practice twice today, for fifteen minutes. Take your seat and close your eyes. Place awareness gently on the breath. Relax your body. When you are ready, say in your mind, "I remain as Source created me. I free the world from all I thought it was. I am real. This world is not, and I would know my own reality."

Now do nothing but watch the breath and your thoughts. Simply be present with them. Use the breath as an anchor and let thoughts and feelings rise up like waves and wash right over you – right through you. Keep your feet firmly planted in the sand of now.

Throughout the day, be mindful. Take every moment you can to be in the now. You may say to yourself, "I loose the world from all I thought it was," if that is helpful to you in the moment.

You will be freer today than you were yesterday if you practice this lesson. This is what it feels like to waken from the dream.

Be happy with yourself. Be certain you are a Child of God.

Lesson 133

I will not value what is valueless.

Imagine you are a container of spirit. For so long as you perceive yourself to be in this world, separated from Source, your container can only be filled halfway. Instinctively knowing this, you seek to energize your spirit through special relationships with others. When you meet that special someone and resonate with them, energy is shared and both of your containers feel more full.

This is all well and good. But one day, your partner is feeling low. You offer them a little extra energy as a boost, knowing they will return the favor. (This is called giving to receive.) The problem is, when you pour your energy into their container, a little spills out. So, when your special partner later repays the loan, you don't get filled up to your original level. Still, you both go on sharing until neither of you is able to fill the other sufficiently, and the relationship ends. Oh, the futility of "love!"

How many of you have sought Love in a special relationship, in a special job, or through possession of a special thing? How many of you have looked upon your partner, your children, your parents, your house or your job hoping they would fill you up, sustain you, and support you? Hear this: no one, and nothing, in this world will ever, ever, fill your container. There is only one relationship that offers an unwavering, unchanging Source of Energy, and that is the one between you as a soul, and your Creator.

This lesson is not telling you to abandon your relationships or quit your job. Quite the opposite. But as a creator being, you must know what it is you are creating with. You must know the source of the energy that sustains your creations and your relationships. Indeed, if you value your creations you would do well to understand how to determine what has lasting value and what will wither on the vine. All things are either valuable or not. All things are either worthy or not worthy of your effort, your desire, and your willingness. Choosing is easy. But the ego loves complexity. It will offer you an array of deceptive choices that drain your container and offer nothing in return. If you learn this lesson it will help you understand clearly what has value and what is valueless.

The first criteria of value is permanence. If you choose something that does not last forever, you are choosing the valueless. If time or conditions can change what you value, it is not valuable. What fades and dies is not really here. It is a deception in a form you think you like.

Second, value does not require loss. If someone needs to lose in order for me to get what I want, it is valueless. The valuable is not gained through taking or giving only to get. In other words, if my gain is achieved only by getting you to give up something, then what I've gained is really loss. Remember, the law of the One is a universal law. Your loss must also be my loss, just as your gain is also mine. What has real value is Everywhere and costs nothing.

Third, ask yourself, why does something have value for me? What purpose does it serve? What is my goal in getting it? If you get what you thought had value, yet later feel only emptiness by it, then it had no ability to fulfill you in the first place. If you think you cannot live without that special something or someone, then know it has no real value.

Last, what is valuable is egoless. It should bring no guilt, remorse, or be cause to puff yourself up in any way. Selling high and buying low is valueless. Getting a "deal" has no real value. Giving the past or future more value than the present moment is always valueless. What is of value should bring only peace because only peace is what you want. You will come to peace with nothing only to find it holds everything because you have given up the valueless.

Practice today in the morning and evening by contemplating what is valuable to you. Lay aside all self-deception and ask yourself what you really want. What would make you happy and why? Will it last? Can you share it without fear of loss? Does it fill your container fully? Is it always available in the exact amount you need?

Take your seat and relax the body. Place your awareness gently on the breath. Take time breathing in and out. Just be. When you are ready, say in your mind, "I will not value what is valueless, and only what has value do I seek, for only that do I desire to find." Then relax into quiet.

Watch your breath and seek a place that knows the value of lasting peace. If thoughts arise, ask gently, "What does this thought say to me about what I value?" Answer briefly but truthfully in your mind, and then go back to the breath. If your mind wanders too much, repeat the lesson in your mind: "I will not value what is valueless." How does this thought feel?

What is valuable belongs to you already. No one can take it away without your permission. Do you value anger, pessimism, time, special relationships, or other things? Just notice today. There is no need to do anything about it. Simply be with the awareness of what is valuable to you in the moment. Notice and repeat the lesson to yourself, then move on. Finally, nothing, nothing, nothing holds any real or lasting value except your relationship with Source. It is the only thing that can fill your container to the brim.

Lesson 134

Let me perceive forgiveness as it is.

Take a moment and imagine that before your birth you got together with all your dearest friends and decided to write a play. In this play, some of you would take the role of villain, some the poor fool, others the wealthy magnate, the harried mother, the inventor, and so on. Each role would not only be fun but would offer the actor wonderful information about herself that would enhance the whole group when it got back together again. Last, to make things even more fantastic, exciting, and valuable, you would all become your roles, forgetting the whole thing was a play.

As silly or merely imaginative as the above may sound, it is a metaphorical representation of our true condition here. We have become lost in our play. We have forgotten the part about it not being real. We believe in what seems to be causing all our pain and suffering. But there is a way back to remembering our true nature and the true nature of our friends, and it is in today's lesson.

In the boldest of terms, what this lesson says is, "You are in your own play. Every wrong done to you or by you is a part of the play. Don't take it seriously and make it real. And by the way, you make it real when you don't forgive your fellow actor for playing his or her role well."

Of all life's lessons, the hardest to learn is true forgiveness. This is why ACIM teaches that our function – our only function – is forgiveness. Forgiveness is the lubricant in the gears of enlightenment.

The only perception of forgiveness that is true is the realization that there is nothing to forgive, for nothing has been done, or can be done, to harm you. The withholding of forgiveness is an attack upon your own invulnerability.
– ACIM

If I forgive only because I think it is the "right" thing to do, then I am making "sin" real. "It is impossible to think of 'sin' or 'error' as real and not believe forgiveness is a lie." Only if I forgive because I perceive the illusion as it is (a little play in which you and I have a role), am I being an honest participant in my own salvation.

I am bound to my attacker with the guilt I lay upon her. If I want freedom for myself, I must accept my part in the illusion and free us both. I cannot leave the play alone. I must take my fellow actor with me for my fellow actor is me.

There is a very simple way to understand forgiveness. When you are tempted to judge or condemn, ask yourself, "Would I accuse myself of doing this?" Don't dwell on the specifics of the wrongdoing, but ask instead if you can truly know that you would never, ever, make the same mistake for any reason whatsoever. The answer will always be, "No, I cannot." And there forgiveness rests its case.

Forgiveness stands between illusions and truth, between this little play and the world that is the true Home for yourself and your fellow actors. It is the bridge across the gap. It is quantum in nature, for it is the only bridge that crosses between worlds.

Practice twice today for fifteen minutes, preferably in the morning and evening. Your work today is imaginative, but very powerful. Take your seat and relax the body. Place your awareness gently on the breath. Close your eyes, and when you are ready, say in your mind, "Let me perceive forgiveness as it is." This honest request will open a doorway, for if you have asked in earnest, you cannot be denied.

Now allow someone to come to mind that has caused you suffering. You will know the right person. One by one, catalogue the wrongs they have done to you but do not dwell on any one for too long. After each wrong, ask yourself, "Would I condemn myself for this?" Be honest. Can you truly know you would never, ever do what she or he has done? What has been done? Has anything really been done?

If you are practicing with honesty you will feel a shift in your perception. There will be a weight lifted as you answer honestly and free the person from certain judgment. This freedom is for yourself. You will know it by its lightness. When you feel the shift, notice the feeling, and allow it to inform you. Relax for the rest of the practice. Watch your breath and repeat the lesson as needed to focus the mind. Allow whatever thoughts arise to come. Feel them in the body. Stay open.

Be mindful today. There will be many times you will need to remember what forgiveness is. It is required for even the smallest irritation, for there is no difference in illusions – they are all alike. When the need arises, say in your mind, "Let me perceive forgiveness as it is. Would I accuse myself of doing this? I will not lay this burden upon myself." Then loosen the hold of judgment and free yourself.

Give. Forgive. Receive. Enjoy. Like yourself.

Lesson 135

If I defend myself I am attacked.

In this world it seems I must defend myself. It's instinctive. But defense is much more than just reaction to attack; it is a way of life. Defense is a form of fear. Purchasing insurance is a form of defense against fear of a future moment, is it not?

Most of us would agree that it is wise to protect ourselves now from future harm. But is this not also a projection? The future is not here. What is it we are protecting? It can only be the past. Projection is carrying the past forward into the future. Most of us live this way all the time.

The personal mind invests heavily in the past because it believes it is the only aspect of time that is meaningful. The personal mind exists for you only in the past. We pay for the

"sins" of the personal self's past in the future, so the personal self's past determines your future, which makes the past continuous and leaves you without any present moment.
– E. Cronkhite

The unhealed mind believes separation from Source has occurred, so defense is justified. It initiates all manner of plans as defenses against a past brought forward into the future. It never allows, and never trusts enough to simply witness the unfolding of a Plan created by a Mind that far exceeds its own.

An unhealed mind resists change because past experience is relied upon as the foundation of present and future realities. An unhealed mind must anticipate and plan, because it has no confidence in a connection to its Creator. It blocks the present moment and therefore also blocks the truth that is revealed only in the moment. An unhealed mind attacks what has already happened and tries to prevent what it can never control.

A healed mind relies on Source. It is relieved of the belief it must plan, even when it does not know what the outcome will be. What if we stopped planning? Is there really anything you would not accept if you knew that everything that happens – all events, past, present, and to come – are already planned by One Whose only purpose is your good? What could you not accept if you knew this was true?

Who of you by worrying can add a single hour to this lifespan? Consider the lilies of the field; they do not labor or spin.
– Mathew 6:28

Do not defend yourself against the future or the past today. Allow it to unfold. Time is not what you have been taught to think it is. All that is, has already been. Linear time is an illusion of this dimension. The closest you can get to eternity in this dimension is now. Now is zero-point and it is the only point in which you have any power at all.

Today, anticipate only that all you need will be provided. Be confident that things will unfold exactly as they should. As much as possible, be present in the moment with no defenses. Allow all things. Trust all things.

Practice twice today, in the morning and evening, for fifteen minutes. Sit and rest from senseless planning. Let go of fear and experience what lies beneath it. Fear of the future is a veil against the power of the present moment. It hides the keys to the Kingdom.

Take your seat and relax your body. Gently place your awareness on the breath. When you are ready, say in your mind, "If I defend myself, I am attacking myself. But in defenselessness I am strong, because I learn what my defenses hide."

Now do nothing but watch the breath and allow your mind to open and receive. If there are plans to be made, you will be told them. If there are problems to be solved, the answers will come, but they may not be what you expect. What you receive will be what you need now. All that is asked is that you live fully in the moment for fifteen minutes.

Today, live without fear from one moment to the next. You cannot conceive of what is truly most beneficial because your mind cannot see All That Is. How could it possibly to do so alone? Join your mind with Source. It is connected already by a quantum thread that cannot be broken. Eternal spirit needs no defense. The body is not real. The past is gone. The future will arrive in this moment, and then this moment, and this moment.

You will undoubtedly need to plan some things today, but do so quickly, and then let go of the outcome. See what happens.

Lesson 136

Sickness is a defense against the Truth.

Yesterday you learned the unhealed mind projects a guilt-filled past into a fearful future.

Today's lesson tells us the unhealed mind is also the source of all sickness in the body. Remember, it is the nonphysical mind that projects or "creates" the physical body.

Let me say before we begin that every master teacher I have known has experienced bodily illness. Cancer has taken several of the best, including Ken Wapnick and Sri Nisargadatta Maharaj. Several others are cancer survivors. What I am trying to say here is, do not under any circumstance feel guilty about any bodily illness you have now or have ever had. Now, may we continue?

Imagine your liver telling the rest of the body it no longer wanted to be associated with it. "I want to stand on my own!" the liver tells the heart. Imagine an eye or a hand saying the same thing. "I yearn to be free!" it announces to the rest of the body.

Sounds silly doesn't it? Yet, this is exactly what we have done on the metaphysical level. The unhealed mind announced its separation from God and all other parts of the Whole. And Source, in its infinite wisdom, responded lovingly, "Knock yourself out. I'll be here if you need me," knowing full well we could never be separate from It.

Only an unhealed mind considers separation from Source even possible. Only an unhealed mind disagrees and blames, judges and justifies. Only an unhealed mind creates sickness in a body that was created to be a neutral experience. The body itself is wholly neutral because it has no "self" or identity apart from the mind. A mind apart from its Source has lost its true identity as well.

And so it follows that sickness in the body is a form of denial. Denial of what? Denial of the Truth about what we are. We are not a body. We are spirit. But the personal mind remains unconvinced of its connection to Source. It believes in the sickness it has itself created. Please understand this: the unhealed mind uses the body's illness to reinforce its false identity. Sickness is a form of attack upon the Truth. Sickness is a projection of fear.

To the unhealed mind, sickness appears to be an attack upon the body by something outside itself – a germ, a virus, a bad fall, an accident, or even another body. But make no mistake, all of these are products of an ego that lives in fear of being found that it is not real – that Wholeness rules, not the ego. The ego would have you think it needs to be defended, when in fact it is attacking your Self. The ego would rather you suffer in sickness than discover your unhealed mind is actually part of Mind. The ego wants you asleep in a dream of living, which is not really life at all but a brief, unhappy moment before death.

"If I defend myself, I am attacked." Sickness is an attack hidden in defense. Do you see this? If you do, please congratulate yourself now, for you have discovered a key to your own health. It does not mean you will never be sick again. We awaken from the dream slowly. But it does mean the beginning of the end of ego's domination over your mind. A healed mind creates a healed body. All of us are in the process of healing our mind.

Your practice today is with mind healing. Give yourself this healing for fifteen minutes in the morning, and again in the evening. Do you see that all our practices are really mind healing?

Take your seat and relax your body. Gently place your awareness on the breath. Breathe naturally. Watch the in-breath and the out-breath. Trust that whatever form your breathing takes, it will be just perfect.

Keep your eyes open, and when you are ready, say in your mind, "Sickness is a defense against the Truth. I will accept the Truth of what I am, and let my mind be wholly healed today." Then close your eyes and repeat the lesson in your mind. Now place your awareness on the words of the lesson. Feel the words in your body. Allow their vibration to inform it. These words have a healing power because they are the Truth, and your healed mind recognizes them.

Sit in the feeling/vibration of these words for the rest of the practice. Watch your breath, and repeat the lesson, as you feel necessary. If your mind wanders, practice forgiveness and go back to the lesson. Forgiveness is a cure for the unhealed mind. Forgive, forgive, forgive! Forgive the body. Forgive your unhealed mind.

If you are tempted today to focus on illness, bodily discomfort, or fear, say to yourself, "I have forgotten what I really am by mistaking my body for myself." Or, "Sickness is a defense against my Wholeness. But I am not a body. I remain as God created me. I cannot be Truly sick."

Notice, but do not focus on your bodily discomforts today. Do not fight any pain or call it unreal for that only gives it power. Just forgive yourself for forgetting what you are, accept that in time you will know, and stay present in the moment.

Note: Medicines are a form of "magic" but they are powerful magic. Allow the magic to work for you if it heals your pain or makes you feel better. Take your medicines without guilt. Just remember they are nothing compared to the power of a healed mind.

Lesson 137

When I am healed I am not healed alone.

Yesterday you learned that the body is a smokescreen, or more accurately, a diversion. We can respect the body and we should treat it well, but in the final analysis, it's not what we are. Too much focus upon it diverts attention from seeing what it is, or is not.

Real healing is in the mind. And because minds are shared my healing is not for me alone. This is the central idea of ACIM and it is why your own healing is so important for the world.

"No one is sick alone and no one enters Heaven alone."

Physical health is certainly to be valued over sickness, and there should be no guilt in it. The most advanced spiritual teachers experience all sorts of bodily ailments. But our desire not to be ill only emphasizes the value we place upon the body and makes it more real.

The cure for illness is the same cure required for all the problems of this world: forgiveness that it seems to exist at all. This doesn't mean I don't seek a cure. It does mean my personal bodily illness, and the illnesses of this world, are just experiences that have no lasting effects whatsoever. Knowing this is what allows the freedom to heal. But if illness is illusion, then healing is too. In truth, there is nothing to be healed. What we call healing is, in a very real sense, a counter-dream. It brings one closer to the truth, but it is still within the dream.

The deepest and truest healing you can experience in this world is the release of all your guilt. Guilt is the source of sickness.

Your purpose here is to undo your dream of guilt. The undoing of your guilt is crucial to us all. All guilt stems from the mistaken belief that separation from Source has occurred. Thus, true healing must acknowledge it has not. Our minds are One joined Mind. This is why we never heal alone. When you are healed, you become an instrument of healing.

Today you begin true healing by freeing your mind from its over identification with the physical body. The body is a symbol of separation. It has no real value. It doesn't last because nothing lasts in this world. What is real does last. What is real contains no guilt. The purpose of today's lesson is to teach you the freedom of guiltlessness. You are powerful in your guiltlessness because you are more fully your Self.

Today's practice asks for ten minutes in the morning and evening.

Take your seat and relax the body. Place your awareness

gently on the breath. Let all worries and discomforts be released with each out-breath. With eyes open, say in your mind or out loud if you wish, "When I am healed I am not healed alone. I share my healing with the world so sickness might be banished from all minds, who are my One Self."

Now close your eyes and say the lesson again in your mind. Feel the vibration of the words in your body as you say them. Allow your mind to know it is Whole and healed already. There is no need to struggle for healing. It is already yours and has always been yours. No one and nothing can take your healing from you. Be at peace now and watch your breath. If thoughts arise, repeat to yourself, "When I am healed, I am not healed alone," and go back to the breath.

Your function here is to be healed. Your healing carries itself far beyond your little body. A healed mind is a gift to the entire world. Look upon yourself and your world with kindness. God is present in it because ideas leave not their Source. We are all born from one Idea and that is what we are still. Your healing is contained in the recognition that you are already healed.

On the hour, remember, "When I am healed, I am not healed alone."

Lesson 138

Heaven is a decision I must make.

In this dream world Heaven appears to be a choice you must make for or against. The personal mind loves complexity, and affirms its existence by showing you that all things have an opposite, and you must decide between them. Remember the "hamburger universe" in which humanity is sandwiched between God and the devil?

There is no choice to be made. It is a logical impossibility. First cause has nothing that precedes It for nothing can precede the Beginning. There is no opposite to Source. However, Source cannot take away your free will any more than It can deny Itself, even if that will is to perceive only illusion.

> *In this world Heaven is a choice, because here we believe there are alternatives to choose between. We think that all things have an opposite... if Heaven exists there must be hell as well, for contradiction is the way we make what we perceive. Creation knows no opposite... You need to be reminded that you think a thousand choices are confronting you, when there is really only one to make. And even this but seems to be a choice. Do not confuse yourself with all the doubts that myriad decisions would induce. You make but one. And when that one is made, you will perceive it was no choice at all. For truth is true, and nothing else is true. There is no opposite to choose instead. There is no contradiction to the truth.*
> *– ACIM*

The personal mind makes this world so complicated that the simplicity of heaven is obscured. Think of all the pressing choices you must make! What phone plan should I buy? Should I take this flight or that one? What if I don't choose the right school? Should I take this route to work or the alternative? What if I'm late? Should I say what I really think? Life is burdened with choices and you live in fear the wrong choice will have lasting ramifications.

A healed mind feels compelled to make fewer choices. It is content to allow, seeing that everything is part of All That Is. It is willing to let go of control, trusting all will be well. Basic goodness is a foundation of existence, but this recognition is learned through experience. This is why trial and error are to be forgiven rather than judged. How often have you come to truth only after trying every other option? No one can tell you but you must choose consciously. You cannot make the choice until you have accurately seen and understood its alternatives.

Practice three times today, for five minutes each. In the morning, begin your day with five minutes of contemplation. At noon, take another five minutes. End your day in peace with the lesson.

To practice, close your eyes and rest the body. Place awareness on the breath. When you are relaxed and calm, say in your mind, "Heaven is the decision I must make. I make it now, and will not change my mind, because it is the only thing I want."

Then spend five minutes in contemplation of the idea that basic goodness surrounds you and is, in fact, the Ground of All Being. You may notice resistance to this idea. Allow it. Do not resist your resistance, but do make the conscious choice to be aware of it. Ask yourself, "Am I all right in this moment?" Undoubtedly, the answer will be, "Yes. In this moment I am all right. I am here. I have what I need now." Now is all you need because it is all you have. Now, bring to light all that frightens you, attacks your safety, and justifies your attack against yourself. Watch yourself place it on the altar of forgiveness. Repeat the lesson. Watch your breath. Be sure of yourself and your choice for Source.

On the hour, take a moment and repeat the lesson. Use the breath to calm and center your mind, wherever you may be.

Lesson 139

I will accept Atonement for myself.

Renowned spiritual teacher Eckhart Tolle tells of his experience on the dark night of his awakening. Full of self-loathing and contemplating suicide, he thought over and over, "I cannot live with myself any longer." Suddenly he became aware of what a peculiar thought that was. "If I cannot live with myself, there must be two of me: the 'I' and the 'self' that 'I' cannot live with." "Maybe," he thought, "only one of them is real."

Tolle's question forms the heart of ACIM. Who am I? Which self is real? The answer is stunning, for ACIM teaches:

Uncertainty about what you must be is self-deception on a scale so vast its magnitude can hardly be conceived.
– ACIM

What is this vast self-deception, the magnitude of which can hardly be conceived? It is so simple, and yet so profound it appears impossible at first. The self-deception is that there is a separate self at all. There is no separate self. None. Only the illusion of it.

In this dream world the idea there is no separate self seems insane. The opposite is true. In this dream world we experience a separation from Source that is so profound it is insane. It is insane to destroy the very earth upon which we live. It is insane to establish hierarchies of need so that some thrive while others suffer. It is insane to think external validation can measure self-worth. It is insane to believe I can harm you and remain unharmed myself. It is insane to believe Source could make sacrifice a condition of salvation. Ask no more of this illusion! Waste no more time hoping it will change for you. The purpose of this dream world is to show you what you are not.

What you truly are is beyond doubt. It is beyond doubt because the personal mind did not design it. Your origin is from the One, of the One, and still resides in the One. You may wait for death to know it, or you may begin to experience it now. You may experience it now by acting like it now. Whatever you choose, your Oneness is unchanged by any belief you might not know who you are.

Your practice today is to recall the memory of your True Nature, not just for yourself, but for all. When you remember your Self, you also remember for me. When you accept your Atonement, which is the correction of the perception of separation from Source, all other choices the personal mind places in front of you become moot. Your perception that you even have other possible choices is only a reflection of its uncertainty. There are none. You are One.

Practice today for five minutes in the morning and evening.

Take your seat and relax the body. When you are ready, place awareness gently on the breath. Allow your breath to rise and fall naturally. When you are calm and centered, say in your mind, "I will accept Atonement (at-one-ment) for myself. For I remain as God created me. I am of the One, with the One, and in the One, still."

Now sit with full confidence that you have not lost the knowledge All That Is gave you when It created you like Itself. You remember for everyone, for all minds are joined. If you feel doubt, allow it and ask for help. Do not feel guilty about your doubt – that is the little "I" raising its little voice. Resistance to it only gives it energy. But consider this: even the thought, "What am I," is not really a question; it is Self-denial. What you are is far beyond doubt. The magnitude of what you are can hardly be conceived, yet it remains in your mind.

Sit in peace. You need only accept what you are. Be mindful of your breath and repeat the lesson. Forgive and allow. Peace is Atonement. Happiness is Atonement. Contentment is Atonement. Self-respect is Atonement. Certainty is Atonement.

Throughout the day, on the hour if possible, repeat the lesson. Feel the certainty of your Oneness. Know your Self. Take a moment and look around. The images that appear so real are temporary at best. The body's eyes do not perceive the Truth. Everything is light. And all light is One. Oneness feels good and that is how you know you're on the right track.

Lesson 140

Only salvation can be said to cure.

The word "salvation" is laden with ancient stuff. For me it conjures images of tent revival meetings, and someone getting slapped upside the head. Perhaps you have your own associations.

ACIM often upends the traditional meaning of religious words. For example, the word atonement is reversed from one that implies guilt (what else is one atoning for?) to one that extends oneness to all things and makes guilt impossible.

Today's lesson upends tradition, for "salvation" is defined as the undoing of thought. The thought that needs undoing is the belief in separation from Source along with the guilt it brings. So, salvation is not about saving a soul from wrongdoing, but about correcting a mind that cannot see its own Oneness with everything.

Only the mind needs to be "cured." The idea of bodily cure adds illusion to illusion, for the body is of the mind. Medical cures do not recognize, nor are they concerned with spirit, so they completely miss the origin of all disease. "There is no remedy the world provides that can effect a change in anything. The mind that brings illusions to truth is really changed. There is no change but this."

We are either asleep to the reality of atonement or we are awakened to it. The body is either real or it is not. Salvation, the recognition of Unity Consciousness, is either the only cure or it is no cure at all. The source of all illness is the mind that believes it is only a body. The only lasting cure is Wholeness of Mind.

Do not look outside yourself for mind healing. Medicine is fine – take it if you need it, but do not confuse its temporary magic with true and lasting healing. Lasting healing comes from connection with Source, forgiveness, and the extension of Love to every thing. Peace to you who are cured in Source. There can be no other way.

Today's practice asks you to look inside at what needs curing. Only there can healing can be applied. If you are sick in body as you read this, do not feel guilt about your illness. Never refuse medicine that makes you feel better. Suffering in the body only reinforces its seeming realness. The truth is, you cannot fail to achieve a healed mind. Awakening to a healed mind is as natural as flight is to a bird. Do remember: atonement has already occurred.

Practice today for five minutes in the morning and evening. Stop on the hour and repeat the lesson as well.

Take your seat and place gentle awareness on the breath. When you are calm and centered, repeat in your mind, "Only salvation from guilt can cure my mind." Then sit in silence. You are listening for the Inner Voice, the Holy Spirit, which is in your mind. It is in your mind because you are part of It. You will know It by Its quiet peace. It speaks the truth of what you are and ends all illusions of what you are not. The only goal is to set aside all interfering thoughts. That doesn't mean not having interfering thoughts; it means recognizing them, allowing them, and returning to the breath. Do you see the difference?

Today, you seek to change your mind about the source of sickness. Do not seek cure in illusions. Do not be misled by outer forms of sickness. Go beyond appearances and reach the Source of all healing.

On the hour remember this: your mind holds the healing knowledge Source has placed there. Nothing can disturb it or take it from you. You will succeed to the extent you understand there are no degrees of untruth. All illusions can be cured because they are not true.

Review IV

Lesson 141

Today begins another ten-day review period. The purpose of this review is twofold: first, it integrates prior lessons, and second, it facilitates your readiness for learning new ones. In this review you will be introduced to a central theme that unifies the ideas behind the lessons. This readies your mind for the introduction of a new way to apply the Truth. The central theme of this review period is:

My mind holds only what I think with God.

This is a fact. Only what you think with God remains part of your healed mind. Furthermore, you can only create with the part of your mind that is healed. Source created you a creator being, but It will not allow you to create anything Real that is not in alignment with Love. No thought that is not of Love can dwell in or share Mind of God. Illusions about illusions are simply not real, which is why thoughts of separation are unreal.

Your mind holds many different thoughts at many different times during the day. Often these thoughts are in conflict with one another. "I like Judy, but when she drinks too much I don't want to be around her." "I don't like my job. I need a raise." "I love my partner, but he has this annoying habit." What is happening here?

What is happening is... nothing. Your thoughts come and go, like clouds across the face of the sun. Most of them are purely mental noise. But the thoughts you think with God are more permanent. You can recognize them by the feelings of peace and connection that accompany them. Your very existence is a Thought in Mind of All That Is. Anything that is not in alignment with It is not real. Only the thoughts you think with God are real because only what is of Source is real.

What we are is what our Creator Is, and yet we seem unable to perceive it. Why can't we just know this and be done with all this foolishness? ACIM is very clear about this question: "If you do not see clearly it is because you are interpreting against Love and therefore do not believe it."

The next ten lessons gently teach you to be less willing to interpret against Love. You deny Love by blocking its presence from your perception. Anything you resist, judge, rail against, hate, push away, blame yourself or others for, or consider even the least bit unworthy, is a block. Eternal Mind fears nothing and therefore accepts everything. We limit habitually.

This lesson cannot be thrust upon you. It can only be offered and accepted when the receiver is willing. Because linear time is an illusion, there is no need to hurry or worry about running out of it. Take all the time you want. You've already taken lifetimes.

But, when you have tried all other venues, and you are finally ready – accept unlimited forgiveness and see what happens. I can tell you your experience will change but we all have to have our own experience of it. Experience the change and your belief will change. Change your belief and your mind will change.

Here is how to practice for the next ten days with the next ten lessons.

Begin and end each day by devoting five minutes to the central theme. Then read the two ideas for the day. Hold them in your mind. Feel the reverberation of the words in your body. Let them light your mind. During the day, take a moment of each hour to spend in quiet with the ideas of the lesson. Repeat the two ideas unhurriedly. Allow their gifts to rise into conscious feeling and settle into your mind. In a sense, the next ten days will be spent in retreat, even as you move normally in the world. Get used to the peace of this practice. It will become a way of life if you let it.

To recap: in the morning and evening take your seat, close your eyes, and place your awareness gently on the breath. When you are ready say in your mind, "My mind holds only what I think with God." Now open your mind to these words. Clear all other thoughts away and let this one thought permeate your being for the next five minutes. Feel it. Be it. Trust it. Each thought you have is from Source. Do not judge it. Flow with it.

After five minutes with the central theme, read each of the two ideas for the day that follow. Close your eyes and say the two ideas slowly in your mind. Do not hurry. Let the vibration of the words sink in like a gift, for that is what they are. Take the gift.

The ideas for today are:

1. Forgiveness is the key to happiness.
2. Forgiveness offers everything I want.

Practice mindfulness today. Every hour, take a moment of peace. Remember, "My mind holds only what I think with God. Forgiveness is the key to happiness. Forgiveness offers everything I truly want."

Lesson 142

My mind holds only what I think with God.

1. I thank my Creator for Its gifts to me.
2. Let me remember I am one with All That Is.

Lesson 143

My mind holds only what I think with God.

1. In quiet I receive God's Word today.
2. All that I give is given to myself.

We are born not remembering
How to see.
Fear makes seeing impossible.
Love, allowing all, restores vision.
– ACIM

Lesson 144

My mind holds only what I think with God.

1. There is no love but God's.
2. The world I see holds nothing that I want.

Do you really believe you can make a voice that can drown out God's? Do you really believe you can devise a thought system than can separate you from Source? Do you really believe you can plan for your safety and joy better than Source can?
– ACIM

Lesson 145

My mind holds only what I think with God.

1. Beyond this world there is a world I want.
2. It is impossible to see two worlds.

Lesson 146

My mind holds only what I think with God.

1. No one can fail who seeks to reach the truth.
2. I loose the world from all I thought it was.

All your healing is your release from the personal self's past. The very real difference between the personal mind and Mind of God is obvious if you consider this: There is nothing incomplete about God. Every Part of God is Whole, therefore no Part of God is separate.
– ACIM

Lesson 147

My mind holds only what I think with God.

1. *I will not value what is valueless.*
2. *Let me perceive forgiveness as it is.*

Lesson 148

My mind holds only what I think with God.

1. *If I defend myself, I am attacked.*
2. *Sickness is a defense against the truth.*

Lesson 149

My mind holds only what I think with God.

1. *When I am healed, I am not healed alone.*
2. *Heaven is the decision I must make.*

> *The end of the world is not its destruction, but its translation into heaven. The reinterpretation of the world is the transfer of all perception to knowledge.*
> *– ACIM*

Lesson 150

My mind holds only what I think with God.

1. *I will accept Atonement for myself.*
2. *Only salvation can be said to cure.*

Lesson 151

All things are echoes of the Voice for God.

Today begins a new series of lessons. This lesson, understood and experienced, would end every one of the personal mind's conflicting goals. If nothing exists outside Mind of God how can conflict be?

Every single moment of time, every object, every color, every sound, contains the echo of Source. The stars are echoes. Gravitational waves are echoes. The hummingbird and the wind are echoes. All of our feelings and thoughts are echoes. Nothing is not part of the glorious harmony of All That Is. Each of us is a perfect note in a symphony of unimaginable proportions. It is the sheer unimaginableness of the song that makes it impossible for us to comprehend and, not being able to comprehend, we determined to judge instead.

Our view of this world is confused because it is based on partial evidence. We do not hear the whole symphony. We hear only our own single, plaintive note while the symphony that surrounds us plays on unrecognized. Each of us values her sound above others and so she is lonely in her assumed perfection. But the union that created you connects you also. Its mystery is beyond comprehension and yet it moves in every aspect of your being.

This lesson is very clear: you cannot judge on partial evidence, and the personal mind is incapable of perceiving anything else. It cannot be relied upon to judge correctly ever. But there is a Voice within you that can. It was given to you at the very moment your mind determined to play in the illusion of separation. Do you think Source would not assure your safe return Home, even as you seemed to lock the door against yourself on the way out?

ACIM calls the Voice for God the Holy Spirit, or the Whole-I-Spirit. It is also known as the Universal Translator, and the

Key Code. It is like Spiritual DNA that crosses the boundaries of illusion and leads you back to Reality. It is a note that can be heard in the wilderness. It is your Source Inheritance that you can never, ever lose. The Holy Spirit is the Voice for God. Your job is to learn to listen for It, and to It, rather than the personal mind.

As you practice today do not be content to simply read the words of this lesson. Go more deeply than mental agreement. Rather, attempt to allow the experience of the words, at the level of feeling and awareness beyond your thoughts, to become a part of you. Let the feeling of the message contained in the words permeate your heart. The heart is the listening device you have been given to hear the Holy Spirit. Its message is simple: be kind and do not judge what you cannot understand.

Practice twice today for fifteen minutes in the morning and before bedtime. Take your seat and be comfortable. Let your body relax and place your awareness gently on the breath. When you are ready, slowly and unhurriedly, say in your mind, "All things are echoes of the Voice for God." Then sit in silence and give your thoughts up to Source. Ask the Holy Spirit to direct your mind. Thoughts will come up naturally. Watch them come and go without attachment.

Let each thought and feeling arise, move through, and out. This is the art of listening. Listening and allowing are the stage upon which the music is played. If it is helpful to repeat the lesson, by all means do so. If you spend the entire fifteen minutes slowly, unhurriedly, repeating the lesson and watching for thoughts, it will be time extraordinarily well spent.

As you go about your day today – listen. What may appear to be unnecessary is not for you to judge. You cannot judge fairly without full comprehension. Do you have the patience to wait until your mind becomes silent and the right response arises all by itself? The Voice for God is a song of benevolence and love. It is playing now. It never stopped playing and it never will.

Lesson 152

The power of decision is my own.

There are a few absolutes in this lesson, the first of which is that Truth is unequivocal. To call something true, and then acknowledge it has exceptions, is a contradiction. Truth is whole – it is complete in its entirety. Truth has no wiggle room: it either is or it isn't. Salvation is the recognition that Truth is True always. Here is a fundamental Truth: Source created you a co-creator with all freedom to create. You can create anything you wish, with one exception. You cannot and did not create Source.

Do you believe it is True that Source created you? Do you think it True that Source created us each in perfect equality? Do you believe you were created without sin of any kind? Each idea is either true or not. It makes a world of difference. What do you choose to believe?

The gift of free will is Truth in the most extreme sense because we are free to deny it. We are not free to change it because we did not create it. But we can pretend not to know it. If it is True we have been given the gift of everything, then loss cannot be real. But with the power of decision given us, we can choose to believe in loss. And so we have. And so we do.

If it is True that Source created us eternal, then there is no death. If we were created unchangeable, then all transitory states must be false by definition. The rise and fall of emotions, the changing conditions of the body – all of these are transitory states. To accept the ephemeral as real is to lose the meaning of Truth. Is Eternal true for you?

No one can suffer loss except by his or her own choice. We have made this world and called it true by the power of our own free will.

Source is either Love or It is not. Do you see that it contradicts the Truth to believe Source created chaos? It is we who have invented chaos. It is we who have created opposites to Love. It is arrogant to believe the Oneness of Source is not true, but that suffering is. It is prideful to believe we can create a world where the Laws of Source do not apply. How silly and childish it is.

It is humility that accepts the Truth of Oneness. It is humility that accepts the Truth of Love. It is humility that decides to accept our rightful place as co-creators of the universe. Be humble and accept what you have made as the illusion that it is. It is arrogance to deny it.

Today's practice is one of true humility. Only the ego can be arrogant. The Truth is humble in acknowledging its mightiness, its eternal wholeness, its changelessness, and its all-encompassing connection to its Source. It is humble to perceive your own arrogance and it is powerful to decide against the denial of Truth.

Practice today for at least five minutes in the morning and evening by sitting in silence with the thought, "The power of decision is my own. Today I accept myself as Source created me to be." Take your seat, relax the body, and place gentle awareness on the breath. Without any hurry, when you are ready, say in your mind, "The power of decision is my own. I accept myself as Source created me to be." Then sit in silent meditation on this Truth.

Ask for help understanding this idea. It represents your graduation from the role of victim to that of co-creator with Source. Allow your Self to be revealed to you in whatever creative way happens for you. You cannot know as yet what form this will take, but trust it will come.

Be mindful today. On the hour, silently acknowledge the power in your mind – the place where all things are born. Listen to the Voice for God there. If you will allow it, Source will replace all frantic thoughts with Truth. The decision is yours.

Lesson 153

In my defenselessness my safety lies.

Fear is fundamental in this world because nothing in it is secure. The body is healthy and then it is not. Fortunes rise and fall. Relationships are formed and love is shared only to be withdrawn in anger. Peace is secured but then someone crosses a line and war is justified.

In this world, the best defense is a good offense. Vigilance requires preparation for the next attack. But the need for vigilance induces a chronic form of unconscious, low-grade anger. Anger makes attack seem reasonable, honestly provoked, and necessary in the name of self-defense. Attack, defense; defense, attack, becomes the vicious cycle of a mental state that regards peace as a temporary luxury. Defenselessness seems foolish. Only children are defenseless. That is why we love them so.

What would happen if we let our walls down? What would happen if we stood, with feet firmly planted in the sand, and let the waves of life roll over us, roll right through us? What would happen if we placed all of our efforts not on unconscious defense, but in becoming conscious of the little fear that arises ten thousand times a day? And what if we stopped for a moment to allow that fear, placing our full attention on its discomfort? We would watch it come and go. We would face the little death and we would know the beginning of freedom.

Fear is nothing more than a little death. The ego lives off its limited energy. It is why the very cells in our body contract when we feel it. Here is the truth: defensiveness is weakness because it proclaims your vulnerability. Defensiveness is a denial of the strength Source has given you. You deny the gift and then feel angry at your weakness. You blame Source for your own self-denial. How many times have you been told it is your own illusions that attack you?

How do I become free of fear? I do not resist my moment. I do not mentally defend against that which is in front of me. Does this mean I do not move out of the way of an oncoming train? No, but I am required to become conscious of the fear that lives in my own mind. I get to know it. Each time it rises (and it does arise a hundred times a day) I watch it move through me, fill me up, and I stay with it until it leaves. It always leaves and I always survive. Each time I survive, I am freer of it. I am freer because I have seen through the illusion that I need any defense at all. Source has made me invulnerable.

Safety lies in allowing the moment to be as it is – even in fear. Safety lies in defenselessness. My boss is yelling at me. I am late for a meeting. My child is having a tantrum. My husband is cheating on me. I have my feelings about all of this, but safety lies in conscious presence. I cannot let fear go if I am not aware of it.

There is no substitute for experience. I can only be defensive if the world is real to me. The more I sit with fear, get close to it, and befriend it, the more I realize it is a temporary thing. I can't do this in my mind. I have to do it in this world to realize it. Our fear of fear makes us run away when what we need to do is sit with it. Get to know it. Watch it up close and let it touch us. That's how we know it is only a temporary feeling that has no real power because illusion is powerless.

Freedom and safety are found in defenselessness. Trust in your own ability to face your fear and know that you are not alone. Allow and allow and allow all things. Do not be passive in your allowing. Actively watch your allowing and see what happens from it. Have the experience and then decide if defense is required.

You practice today in a form that you will maintain now for a while. It is time, and you are ready for it. Know now that you do not practice alone. Invite the Holy Spirit into your mind as you sit in meditation and trust It will be there with you. You will practice twice a day, in the morning and evening for about ten minutes. Every hour, pause and direct your mind toward the lesson. Sometimes you will be able to give it a full minute. Sometimes you will forget. Do your best and do not allow guilt to interfere with your peace.

Take your seat and relax the body. Place your awareness gently on the breath. When you are ready, close your eyes and repeat the lesson in your mind. Say in your mind, "In my defenselessness my safety lies." Now spend the next ten minutes in silent contemplation of the lesson. Consider this: if the Mind of God is perfection and I reside in the Mind of God, then what am I resisting when I defend against my moment? What would happen if I just watched it unfold? What would happen if I did nothing more often?

This lesson is a major step toward freedom. You have been told you cannot judge based on partial evidence. Fear arises out of judgment. Stop judging yourself vulnerable. Lay aside defenses today. Have your experiences, knowing your mind resides in a greater Mind, and you are completely safe in It. Practice defenselessness and see what happens. Choose your moment.

Lesson 154

I am among the ministers of God.

I once attended a conference on gratitude. We spent the day defining it, measuring its effects on the body, and looking at it from different viewpoints. But nothing touched the subject like the panel of three women who shared their experience with it. One of the women, an artist, was a breast cancer survivor. Another woman had lost her child to a viciously debilitating disease. Another woman nearly died of alcoholism but found her way back through the generosity of others.

Each of the women understood gratitude through an experience that felt intolerable at the time. The depth of their thankfulness was expressed by sharing their healing with others. True gratitude can be measured by the intensity of one's desire to give back.

Today we remember that giving and receiving are the same: no one can truly receive until she has passed her gifts along. The Law of Oneness requires me to give as my acceptance of what I have been given.

To receive from Source, I must give the gift away. This thought is in direct opposition to what the world believes – which is that the valuable must be held tight or it will be taken.

Today's lesson runs counter to another common belief, which is that of inferiority. We do not know our strength but Source does. It knows our strengths better than we do. Source is not deceived about what we are. We are messengers for It in everything we do and say.

Once again, ACIM chooses a traditional word and gives it another meaning. A minister is one who has received a message and, without changing it, passes it along. The messenger does not write the message she delivers. Neither does she waste time questioning its accuracy, for whom it is intended, or why she was chosen to deliver it. It is enough that she accepts her role and gives the message to the one who is to receive it. And guess what? The message that is delivered is intended first for the messenger – the one who has been chosen to deliver it.

This lesson is a challenge for a few reasons. First, the word "minister" implies some kind of ordination as a religious person. It is not meant that way, but it does rub a bit. Similarly, the term "messenger" feels like a requirement to do something, which is why we are reminded in the beginning of the lesson about Oneness. The messenger is actually the receiver as much as the giver.

And last, many people resist being told they have been given a role to play by someone else – even if that someone else is Mind of God. In response to this, I can ask only that you go deeper into the realm of experience. Our origin is the Mind of God. This Mind seeks union with us who have forgotten Oneness and are wandering in the dark. You are free to reject the role and continue doing what you've been doing. But if you choose to become the messenger you will find yourself.

So, do consider whether you are willing to accept your role. You may ask what the role is exactly. Your role is nothing more nor less than to practice Oneness. Your role is to practice having the experience of giving to receive. Your role is to listen to the Voice for God by giving your inner life the same attention you give your outer life. And last, your role is to open to the awareness of Love's presence, give your awareness away, and then watch what happens. Give Love to receive Love and be mindful of the result. That is your role here – to be a messenger of Love.

Practice today for five to ten minutes in the morning and evening. If you want to sit in contemplation for a longer time, by all means do so. Pause on the hour to reflect upon your role and affirm your decision to accept it or not.

Take your seat and relax. Feel yourself in your body and let go of all tension. Place your awareness gently on the breath. During your contemplation, remember to hold awareness on the breath as the foundation for your mind. If your mind wanders, come back to the breath. When you are ready, say in your mind, "I am among the messengers of God, and I am grateful that I have the means by which to recognize that I am free." How does it feel to try this sentence on? Like a piece of new clothing, sit with this thought. Is it a comfortable role? Does it feel burdensome? There is no right answer. Only you can know for yourself. One thing is certain, however; you have the means by which to recognize that you are free.

Your function is forgiveness. You become a messenger of

forgiveness by giving it away. In giving forgiveness, you are forgiven – not by Source who sees you are perfect already – but within your own mind. Free yourself today. Forgive yourself and give it away.

Lesson 155

Step back and let the Holy Spirit lead the way.

There is a wonderful, simple, piece of advice in ACIM and it is this: "Resign now as your own teacher." This is today's lesson in a single sentence.

Why can I not be my own teacher? Because I know nothing. I don't even know what I don't know. I know nothing because the ego has been my teacher. It knows only its tiny self. Its curriculum is fear. The ego teaches me my goal is to gain the whole world and lose my soul. Source teaches me I cannot lose my soul and there is nothing of value to gain in this world.

The ego is certain that Love is dangerous because it requires giving up its small self to the Whole. It never puts it this way. In fact, the ego seems to be intently searching for love – but always on its own terms. When its terms are not met, it begins yet another search. The ego's rule can be summed up as: "Seek but do not find."

The Love of Source is the only Love. Its rule is: "Seek and you will find." Its rule is: everything is an expression of One. The Love of Source is strong because it is undivided. Undivided, It never sees anything as capable of attacking It. Never fearing attack, It is open to everything. Being open to everything, all It touches knows Love as itself.

The recognition of your invulnerability is so important to the restoration of your sanity that God has not left it in your hands to learn. You cannot be your own teacher and learn the Love of Source until you set aside the curriculum of the ego. To do this, you need a constant, clear-cut curriculum provided by a Teacher who can transcend its limited resources. The ego's goal is not to learn. The Teacher's goal is to teach you of your own limitless nature. Do your Self a favor and resign now as your own teacher.

There is a way of living in this world called "the middle path." The middle path is in the world, but not of the world. When on this path I become the observer of my own life. I do not direct but I do allow. I accept the truth that I am not in control, never have been, and do not really wish for it. The ego's curriculum is control. How has it been working? The curriculum of Source allows the experience and trusts in invulnerability – in the Love of Source. Does this mean I do not make decisions? No! It means I do not attach my happiness to outcomes the ego seeks but never finds.

Walking this path is a new experience for most. We will often try to take the lead as we adapt to the new curriculum. That is part of the learning. We do not know where we are headed, but we are not alone. We are walking toward Love's freedom and away from the frenzied illusions of the ego.

Practice today for ten minutes in the morning and evening. Sit in silent contemplation. Relax your body and gently place awareness on the breath. When you are ready, say in your mind, "I will step back and let the Holy Spirit lead the way, because I want to walk along the road to Source."

Can you allow yourself to sit for the next ten minutes and watch what comes up in your mind? Some of what arises will be of the ego. Some of it will rise from Love to inform you. You will know Love by its feeling of peace and even joy. Just watch the breath, allow thoughts and feelings to arise, and if it helps, repeat the lesson as a mantra. Step back and let Source inform you in this contemplation.

Today, begin to practice deeply with allowing and watching. On the hour, remind yourself to step back and allow. The Mind of God knows the curriculum but you do not. How does it feel to need to be in control? How does it feel to step back, allow, and watch what happens without judgment or fear? Which path makes you happier? Do your feet stumble when you do not trust? Be mindful today and begin to learn the new curriculum.

Many, many, many blessings. You are safely on the road.

Lesson 156

I walk with God in perfect holiness.

There is no attribute of Source we do not share. We are Its Thought. If Source gave up on us, we would cease to be at all. And so, while we may remain asleep to our Oneness, the Truth is still true. We are an idea in Mind of God and ideas cannot separate from their Source.

The Universe is waiting for you to step back and walk with it. You did not create yourself or your path. Your only choice is whether or not to acknowledge this is true. This is the way Oneness works: we can create with it, but we cannot create without it.

To be free is our instinctive desire but we have completely misconstrued what freedom is and how to achieve it. Freedom to extend myself can only be attained through Love, and Love ends the perception of separation. Denial of my separation reinstates my knowledge of true freedom. When I walk with Source, my freedom is boundless. When I walk alone, I am confined and limited by fear.

What will I experience if I step back and let Source lead? This is the ego's greatest fear. It will tell you disaster will strike if you are not in control. It will show you images of free fall if you do not protect yourself always. But think about it. Are you afraid to fall asleep? Is it fearful going into that unprotected state? The state of sleep is restful not only for the body, but because it is one place in our lives that the shrill voice of the ego cannot easily reach. We do not question our safety in the sleep state and yet, even as you read this – you are dreaming.

Wake up and see Who walks with you. Who walks with you is One Mind, within which you can find your own. Who walks with you is One Love, within which you can know Love. "Who walks with me?" is a question to ask all day, every day until the answer reveals itself to you – as it most certainly will. You do not walk alone – ever. It isn't possible.

Practice today in the morning and evening for about ten minutes by sitting in silent contemplation of this idea. Take your seat and relax the body. Place your awareness gently on the breath. Do not force anything but allow peace to slowly show itself to you. When you are ready, say in your mind, "I walk with God in perfect holiness." Then sit in silence, watching the breath, and allow yourself to understand the full depth of what this means.

There is never a moment you are alone. Aloneness is of the ego mind, split from its Source. But the truth is aloneness is a silly dream. All minds are joined and mind is what you are. You are a thought that has never left its Source. Sit in peace as you say to yourself, "I walk with God in perfect holiness. Holiness lights my mind in Oneness with all who walk the path with me." Feel these words resonate within your physical and mental self. Enjoy the way they feel. This is who you are.

Practice mindfulness today. As blocks to peace arise, and they will, remind yourself that aloneness is a dream. It is not real. You do not walk alone, nor does anyone else. Nothing you have ever done, nothing you do now, nor ever will do, can take away your Light.

Shine on today.

Lesson 157

I enter the Presence of Source Now.

Today's lesson is about peace but what I want to write about first is the concept of value. We value what we feel is necessary to be who we think we are. So often in valuing we look outside for a thing, whether it be money, a new car, a special trip, a special person, more time, or a better body, to satisfy what is required. But how often, upon attaining the thing we value, do we discover that we need yet another thing? The first was not enough. We must have been mistaken. Or we simply love the search itself. So off we go looking again. We spend a lifetime climbing up and down the side of a deep hole, gathering and sifting to find the small bit of light that finally sets us free, or that will sustain us for the next descent.

Slowly, I am learning not to climb down that hole. Slowly, I am learning that what is valuable is not found outside myself. When I cease looking outside myself, I know the freedom that comes from not valuing the valueless. There is nothing except the recognition of my Oneness with you and Source that is of value to me. All else is soil to be sifted through.

The lesson of valuing is one of the most important you can learn on this earth. There is nothing in this physical world that has anything to do with what you are. Today's lesson asks that you take ten minutes to sit in peace and allow the experience. This is called the Holy Instant. The Holy Instant is revelatory. Each experience is unique for each person because each of us has a unique connection to Source. This connection is the only thing of value in this world. It cannot be altered or taken away without your consent but you must accept it. You must be willing to allow it in whatever form it shows itself.

To practice, take your seat. Relax the body and place your awareness gently on the breath. When you are ready, say in your mind, "Into the presence of Source would I enter now." Ask for help if you need it. It is there, waiting for you to call upon it. Now simply sit in silence and allow. Thoughts will arise. Feelings will come up. Just watch them come and go. Then go back to the breath. If it is helpful, slowly repeat the lesson in your mind. Hold each word like a vibration. Feel its presence. If you feel even a moment of release from thinking – you have crossed the threshold.

This lesson takes the student further into the curriculum of the Holy Spirit. It begins a deeper form of awareness in meditation. Do not be discouraged if it feels like nothing is happening when you attempt to enter the presence of Source. That is the ego saying, "See. I told you so. There's nothing in there." The Voice for God is soft, so soft. Its gentleness is limitless. Do not try. Allow. Be content with whatever shows itself to you. I assure you this: every ten minutes you spend in meditation will deepen your connection. Some days will be absolutely marvelous. Other days... not so much. Even the most practiced meditators have good days and not-so-good days. But they have learned the value of staying with it. Such is the nature of meditation: the more you do it, but you experience its value.

Spend today in silence and trust. On the hour, stop whatever you are doing and take a breath. Look around at the world. As crazy as it is now, there is still peace and beauty in it. Allow it to be as it is. It is you, but it isn't you.

Many blessings today. Enjoy your meditations.

Lesson 158

Today I learn to give as I receive.

This lesson contains radical metaphysics. It has the potential to shake one's view of reality in such a way that there is temptation to resist the information it contains.

Very simply, the lesson says, we are enveloped by a higher dimension of light – a dimension invisible to our own. This higher dimension of light contains our own within it, and is aware of ours. The only way for us to reach this higher dimension is through the awareness of Oneness because its language is Oneness. The only way to reach awareness of Oneness is through the experience of forgiving.

For. Give. Forgive. The word means paying forward. Yet you cannot pay anything from an empty bank account. You can give only what you already have. Therefore, it is highly important to know what you have so that you can be sure to give it away.

You own the following:

1. *You are a mind that has never, ever, left its Source.* Your mind is fully capable of remembering its Origin. You need not sweat the small stuff.

2. *You have the ability to recognize the absolute illusion of time.* Time is an artificial mental construct and has no connection to Reality whatsoever. Everything you perceive as the "past" is still occurring. Everything you perceive as the "future" has already happened. This entire universe, all its innumerable manifestations, is the product of a single thought that has already played out its illusion of separation and is now back in Oneness. Therefore you are learning nothing "new" here. You are remembering what you already know, and there will come a point "in time" where you will "see" the whole journey you and I have made together as One Mind. In other words, don't sweat the small stuff.

3. *The Mind of God, of which you are a part, contains no contradictions and no mistakes.* Your mind lacks awareness of the big picture. You need not waste time in doubt, but only reconcile your own limited mind through forgiveness, which is the only form of reconciliation available here. In other words, don't sweat the small stuff.

4. *Everything is light.* The body, the world, the trees, the stones,

the waters, and the molecules of air – all are made of light. And the light is all One. There are no separate bits of light floating around on their own. In other words, don't sweat the small stuff.

5. *Light vibrates at a higher frequency than form.* Forgiveness – both giving it and receiving it – raises the inner vibrations of both giver and receiver. Light cannot be seen but it can be Known. Knowing, which is a combination of feeling and thinking, is achieved in this dimension only on the level of experience. Forgiveness is a light switch. The more it is present in your life, the lighter you feel. This is true across the board. When I am forgiven, do I not feel lighter in my body? When I hold a grudge against another, is there not heaviness in my heart? Figure out what feels happy and do it as much as you can. In other words, don't sweat the small stuff.

6. *You have been given the lesson that you must give to receive.* So you know the corollary must also be true: you will receive as you give. Give what you want to get. If you want Love, give It. If you seek comfort and peace, give them. And don't sweat the small stuff.

Today you will practice learning to give as you have received. This means you will attempt to see the light in everything around you. It means you will notice even the smallest grudge and let it go. It means you will try to practice radical trust in your place in this world.

Practice today in the morning and evening for about ten minutes. Take your seat and place awareness gently on the breath. Feel good about yourself. Be happy with yourself. When you are ready, say in your mind, "Today I learn to give as I receive."

Spend the next ten minutes in silent contemplation of the light you hold within. Your light is immortal, as is the Love that created it. You are readying your mind to receive something. But it will not be offered until you are prepared for it. Give yourself forgiveness. Fill your bank account. Then you will be prepared to give it away. Watch thoughts as they arise. Let feelings come and go. Just watch them and do not attach to them. If you find your mind wandering, repeat the lesson in your mind as you watch the breath. You cannot forgive what you do not acknowledge you have judged. Therefore, notice what comes up. Forgive it. Receive what follows from your forgiveness. You cannot force Revelation. You can only prepare your mind to See It.

Be mindful today. On the hour, remind yourself to lighten the load your carry in your heart by practicing forgiveness.

Lesson 159

I give the miracles I have received.

What is your miracle? Do you believe they even exist? Is a miracle just an anachronism – an ancient and outdated fantasy? I've seen many but that's because I'm training my mind to look for them now.

A miracle is a change of mind that shifts my perspective from one of blame, fear, and judgment, to one of forgiveness, allowing, healing, and wholeness. What other miracle could one ask for really? In this crazy world, every mind needs a miracle.

Here is a miracle for you: There is no problem in your life that does not also have a solution. It is a logical impossibility that they do not come as a package deal. Nothing in Mind of God is not Whole. Therefore all "problems" can be "solved." A miracle is seeing that the solution is already present in the problem.

Often, a problem is a conflict that raises the question, do I want to be right or do I want to be happy? Do I want the solution or do I want to perpetuate the problem? My miracle is the instant in which I know that being right is not as important as the relationship. Who has not had a moment like this, taken the miracle, and been glad for it?

Know that the miracle has been given to you already. Let go of the past guilt and accept it. Let go of the future fears too. It's all yours, this miracle. Place your emphasis on pain and that is what you'll get. Place your emphasis on seeing the miracle and you will see that it has been there the whole time. It's up to you to decide to receive what is yours.

"No one can give what she has not received. To give a thing requires first you have it in your own possession. Here the laws of Heaven and the world agree. But here they also separate. The world believes that to possess a thing, it must be kept. Salvation teaches otherwise. To give is how you recognize you have received. It is proof that what you have is yours."

"You understand that you are healed when you give healing. You accept forgiveness as accomplished in yourself when you forgive. You recognize your brother/sister as yourself, and thus do you perceive that you are whole."

When I truly love myself, it doesn't feel like a burden to love back. There is nothing to do with it but share it. Sharing it expands the feeling. Love is not earned, it's simply the miracle of our own creation. Light created light like Itself.

Give yourself the miracle of self-love today. It is your right. In fact, it is your duty to know self-love. Fill yourself up with it and give it away. There is a treasure house of love awaiting your acceptance if only you can let go of the blocks to its awareness. There is no point in anything else. As strange as it may sound, receiving the miracle is what you came here to do.

Twice today, for ten minutes, sit in meditation on the idea of the miracle. Ask if you are worth the gift of it. Can you cross the bridge, even if only for a little while, and allow yourself a happy dream as you consider the possibilities of a world freed from judgment, fear, and doubt? Dream a happy dream, and for an instant you are joined with Truth. Then rise up from your seat and give the gifts away.

On the hour remind yourself to use your Real Perception. It is what notices the miracles around you. Receive its gift of Whole Vision and become the messenger of miracles for others.

Lesson 160

I am at home. Fear is the stranger here.

I am chased in my dreams by something that means to destroy me. Believing it can, I run blindly ahead as fast as I can go. Terrified, I am barely able to turn my head to see how far back it is, much less stop and confront it. Who has told me my dream is true? What put the fear in me?

In some dreams I do manage to turn and confront the thing that chases me, and I always overcome it. But it's rare that I remember, and each time I dream of my pursuer it seems I must learn the lesson all over again.

Fear undermines all that I am when it takes over. My mind is confused. I can't think straight. I really believe my fear. Except when I don't, and then I wonder why I ever believed it at all.

When I trace the source of my fear all the way back to its origins I think at first it is fear of death. But when I go even deeper I know the terror is of being left totally alone. It's the fear of complete and utter aloneness. And there is only one part of my mind that would ever tell me this is even possible – my ego mind.

We live the dream of fear here in this world. Awake and asleep it arrives at our doorstep and we often let it in. When we do, it takes up residence and begins to tell us it owns the house. It makes a mess of everything and often has to be forcefully booted out the door.

But Source has made this house for you and for me. Source gave it to us, not to our fear. Who is the stranger here? Is it fear or our Self? Both cannot coexist in this place. One allows all things, loves all things, Is all things. The other criticizes constantly, doesn't share the chores, and greedily takes all the best for itself. The decision is easy. Fear has to go. But you and I have to make it leave together.

We are at home together. No one gets left outside. We must support each other in telling this fear to go away and not come back. We must remember together that we are one Self, at Home, with our Source.

Today would not be wasted if you spent every moment of it recognizing every person you encounter as your Self. We have to make fear leave together. It cannot coexist with Love, but if one person remains fearful, it will try to take over the house.

Practice today in the morning and evening for ten minutes. Take your seat and relax the body. Place your awareness gently on the breath. When you are ready, say in your mind, "I am at home. Fear is the stranger here." Then sit in contemplation. If any inkling of fear arises ask, "What is the true origin of this thought?" Become more familiar with it. Knowing one's fear gives you power over it. It is the stranger here. Not because you alone say so, but because it is unknown to the One Mind, in which you exist. Fear simply does not exist in God's Mind. That it seems to exist at all is only illusion, born of the ego's ignorance, and the idea that aloneness is even possible.

What does God have to fear? The question itself makes no sense. But my ego mind, believing it can separate from Source, makes aloneness possible and fear arrives soon after, hat in hand. I am not alone, for you are with me. And we are not alone together, for we are all One with each other and our Source. The certainty of Source suffices in this. Ask for Its help any time you hear fear knocking.

Remember hourly, "I am Home. Fear is the stranger here."

Lesson 161

Holy Child of God, give me your blessing.

When you walk down the street, we would like you to realize one thing: that nobody that you're passing knows who they are on a superficial level, but the truth of who they all are as an aspect of God is fully present in them. Underline the word fully.
– Paul Selig, *The Book of Truth*

We've been practicing with the idea that giving and receiving are one. In simple mathematical terms this looks like A = B. Or even this: A = B = C = D = E = F... and so on. Put a body on each letter, and you've got it. Jane = Joe, and Joe = Jill, and Jill = Sally, and Sally = Bob. There is a divine common denominator in each and every person. We are all One Mind, traveling around in seemingly separate containers that are nothing but imagined wisps we cling to like a life raft.

And so it follows that what I do to you, I do to myself. Jesus told us this. The Buddha told us this. Science is showing us this. The earth is now showing us this, very graphically. We can learn it now or later, but learn it we must.

Today's lesson is a very practical experience of Atonement (at-one-ment). Because we see in specificity, we must heal in specificity. I need to see that one person, one body, is joined with me in a Whole. We need to see a little to learn a lot.

The challenge of today's lesson will tell you a lot about your own mind. Today you ask for a blessing from someone you don't like and whom you believe returns the favor. I'm sure you can think of someone you think has wronged you, knowing they believe you are actually the one at fault. Can you see how separation begins in the mind? Just reading these words is a jolt for some. Are you ready?

To practice, take your seat and get comfortable. Relax your

body and place gentle awareness on the breath. The breath is your anchor to the moment. It is a portable centering device you may take with you anywhere. When you are centered, allow your mind to focus on a person who will be a symbol for all the rest.

Picture this person clearly. See their body completely: clothing, hair, hands, and face. Imagine them as you last saw them. See their gestures as they talk. See their smile. Then think of this: "What I am seeing now conceals from me the sight of one who can forgive me of everything. This is the person who can set me free from every imagined 'sin' I've made. This person is my Self. This person is a divine seed, part of the One Mind we share together."

Now, slowly, and with focused intention, say to this person in your mind, "Give me your blessing, Holy Child of God. Real Perception shows me what we both truly are: Innocence and not bodies at all."

Now see this person as they truly are beyond the body, a light joined with your light. Allow their light to merge with yours in a blessing. Don't force it. Sit as long as you need to allow the blessing to come to you. It will come if you allow it. Look where you see physicality and recognize Christ resides eternally within the temporary container. Ask for help if you need it. Indeed, you may even ask your enemy for assistance!

This lesson signals the end of the cycle of defense and attack. Use it any time today you feel compelled to criticize or judge another – both of which are nothing more than attacks upon your Self. On the hour look at all the temporary containers around you. Use your Real Perception to see the light within.

When humankind realizes what it is – which is the manifestation of the Divine in form, we will actually begin to create a relationship with the physical plane that allows for its transformation.
– P. Selig, *The Book of Truth*

Lesson 162

I am as God created me.

These words define you as what you are: the Word of God. Source created you and me, and Source knows what we are. We may have forgotten but our Creator has not. Against all seeming "reality," it is time to remember who we are. Today, make these words your own.

Own your Self. Honor your Self today. Forgive and allow. Allow and forgive. Allow that Love just might be the backdrop for everything. Forgive your misperceptions about yourself. Accept your own invulnerability. Love your Self. Be happy with your Self. Be certain about your Self. Accept God's view of you.

Your practice today consists of two fifteen-minute contemplations in the morning and evening. This will be a simple practice because the words of the lesson are powerful. You will want to fully absorb their meaning.

Take your seat and relax the body. Place your awareness on the breath. When you are ready, say in your mind, "I am as God created me." Feel the words. I am. As Source. Created me. Thoughts do not leave the Mind that Thinks Them. You remain in Mind of God, blessed as a Divine Spark. Here you are! Sit in your chair or wherever you may be and know you have manifested a physical form. You are here! All that surrounds you is your manifestation. Do you hear a bird? You have called it to you! How beautiful. What else will you call? You are completely free. Who can you send Love to without lifting a finger? What can you receive from Source just by allowing it?

Sit. Breathe. Be aware in your creation. Have an experience of your power. Give your thoughts to the One Mind and experience what is returned.

On the hour today, remember you are as God created you. Either death is real or eternal Life is real. Both cannot be true.

Source did not create death but Source did create you and me like Itself. Your day would be well spent remembering this about yourself, and everyone you meet. Remember, what you rightfully claim for yourself is true for all creation.

Lesson 163

There is no death. I am limitless in God.

Death is a touchy subject. We know it's coming but harbor a secret wish it might just skip over us. Unless you've had a brush with death yourself, it's just too hard to imagine. Many people say it's not their actual death that worries them, it's the process of dying.

I've heard folks say, "I'll be ready to die when I can't walk to the bathroom by myself." Then the time comes when they can't walk to the bathroom unaided and they say, "I'll be ready to die when I can't have a steak for dinner." Then the time comes when they can only take liquid food...

The bargains we make with death just prolong the pain of it. The truth is we are in bodies that are dying now. They die a little more each day. Death takes many forms, often unrecognized. Anger, fear, stress, and worry – each of these is a little death. The ego, from which all fear arises, fears its own death above all.

The ego's idea of death is the opposite of Source. It is impossible to say that both God and death are real. Either all things die or they live and cannot die. Truth is true always or it is not Truth. If death is real, then something more powerful than Eternal Life exists and has done away with It. To believe in death is to say that Source created something that isn't It, is stronger than It, and hates It so much it has killed It. Only the ego could devise such a belief system.

Source does not create to kill. It condemns nothing to death. My form may change but my Mind is not form and that is what

I am, along with you. Mind is not illusion but the body is. Take this freedom today and run with it. Sit and contemplate the fact that your consciousness will never die. How does it feel to know your joined Mind will never be extinguished? How does it feel to know that you are glorious? We are all, every single one of us, invulnerable to death.

Practice today in the morning and evening for fifteen minutes. Take your seat and relax the body. Center yourself with the breath. Allow it to ground you naturally in the moment. When you are ready, say in your mind, "There is no death. God has made me free."

Now sit in silent contemplation of this thought. Allow yourself to be. Try not to think or define. Go beyond the words to the experience of knowing. Feel yourself as the substance of the universe. Open yourself to your real One Self, to all life, everywhere, in all time. You are the One Mind and you are free to know your Self. God did not make death so it is illusion in all its various forms.

On the hour, remind yourself you are free. Death awaits you nowhere. If you can know deep down that all is well and will always be well, you've touched it. Give yourself a hug. To know there is no death, to really know it, is freedom.

Can you who see yourself within a body know yourself as an idea? ... The body cannot know. And while you limit your awareness to its tiny senses, you will not see the grandeur that surrounds you. God cannot come into a body, nor can you join him there. Limits on love will always seem to shut him out, and keep you apart from him. The body is a tiny fence around a little part of a glorious and complete idea. It draws a circle, infinitely small, around a very little segment of Heaven, splintered from the whole, proclaiming that within it is your kingdom, where God can enter not.
– ACIM

Lesson 164

Now I am One with Source.

The world you perceive is in your mind, Now. Now is Whole. Now is the only point, in any time, in which time itself is suspended and Truth can be perceived. It is in the Holy Instant of Now that you find the silence upon which nothing can intrude. It is in the Now that you can wait to receive. It is in the Now that judgment is suspended. Source is timeless Now.

Now is the absolute ground of all being. What kind of Mind could hold all of Now within Itself? This concept is beyond our limited perception.

Arguing with Now is junk food for the ego. It gets a quick energy boost when it competes with Source about what the Now contains. "That shouldn't be!" it exclaims. "Do something! Make it different!" The ego urges us to quick and thoughtless action in an effort to divert us from its real intent. What is the real intent of the ego? To be in control. To be the decider. To be the one that knows. Living in the past is an attack on the Now. Living in fear of the future is an attack on the Now.

How can the personal mind ever hope to supplant the Mind that holds all things within Itself? Do you see why the personal mind teaches only seek but do not find? It is insane. The personal mind avoids Now because Now robs it of its power over you. Real Perception, True Knowing, happens only in the Now moment. It can never come to you in the past and will never meet you in the future. It is in the Zero-Point of Now that All Presents Itself to you.

The practice for today is simple. If you practice faithfully, which is to say mindfully, you will notice things you've never noticed before, such as how often you resist the moment in front of you, and how much you value the idea of control. You may also notice the peace it brings to sit back and simply receive what is given to you by the Now. Remember, you are Home Now in the eternal. Fear is the stranger here. There is nothing you can receive that can ever harm your Divine Self.

Practice today for fifteen minutes in the morning and evening. But consider this: it is mindfulness during the day that may be most instructive.

For your morning and evening practice, take your seat and relax the body. Place your awareness gently on the breath. Let all tension be released on the out-breath. When you are ready, say in your mind, "Now I am one in Source." Place all awareness on the breath and let go of thinking.

If thoughts arise, and they will, do nothing except witness them. They will arrive and depart. Try to let yourself be fully with the breath. Allow it to breathe you. This is all that is required, but if your thoughts wander too much, repeat the lesson in your mind. Breathe. Repeat the lesson. Let the breath and the words anchor you to the Now.

Today, live in the moment. You may use the breath as your anchor. Listen before speaking. Wait before acting. Let Now direct you. You need do nothing. You will know when it is time to eat, do the laundry, wash the dishes, get in the car, and start its engine. Live today mindfully. Practice in earnest and you will notice the little things that are the source of all big things.

Like yourself. You are good. Be kind to yourself. Then share your self-kindness with others in your circle. Notice what happens in the Now and let it flow without trying to control. Sit back and watch.

You can only recognize Truth Now. The present is the only time that there is, and so today, this instant Now, you perceive What is Forever here, not with the body's eyes, but with your Real Perception.
– E. Cronkhite

Lesson 165

Let not my mind deny the Thought of God.

The whole is greater than the sum of its parts. Most of you have heard this phrase. Our body has a heart, brain, liver, hands, and feet, but how they all function together in a creative whole is a mystery. Or consider an ant colony. It is composed of thousands of separate ants, each doing their own thing, but the colony can also function as a well-organized unit, acting like an individual entity. Scientists call this behavior "morphic resonance."

Mind of God has morphic resonance. Its inherent joy is to extend itself, creating innumerable, unending connected consciousness. You and I are seemingly separate minds, but we are part of a Whole Mind. Like the ant colony, we go about our daily business as separate individuals, but there is a hidden force field in which we are joined lovingly and seamlessly. We did not create this resonance, but we can deny it. Denying it doesn't make it so.

Love is stronger than fear because it is undivided. Fear separates and is weaker for it. This is why the recognition Atonement is critical to your sanity. The acceptance of fear and guilt into the mind of humanity was the beginning of separation. The acceptance of Atonement is its end.

The Atonement is the only defense that cannot be used destructively because it is not a device you made. The Atonement principle was in effect long before the Atonement began. The principle was Love and the Atonement was an act of Love.
– ACIM

Today's lesson does not require you to perceive Wholeness before you become Whole. You do not even need to be sure your request for Wholeness is the only thing you want. But you do need to ask and be willing to experience what you receive. The only reason you won't ask for it is because you fear disappointment.

Practice for fifteen minutes in the morning and evening. Take your seat and relax the body. Then close your eyes and place gentle awareness on the breath. Sit in peace for a few minutes, in awareness of your natural breath. When you are ready, slowly say in your mind, "Let not my mind deny the Thought of God."

Try not to think the words but rather feel them. "Let." (Allow. It is your choice.) "My mind." (What is your mind? What are you?) "Not deny." (Do not refuse your right to connect.) "The thought of God." (The Thought of God is One Love.) Allow yourself to become the words, going beyond their superficial definitions into experience. Ask for help if you wish, and know it will be there just for the asking.

When you sit in this way, aware of the breath, allowing whatever arises in your mind, know this: You are opening to the substance of the universe. You are opening yourself to the One Self. You are opening yourself to the Thought of God. Even if a bucketful of thought arises, you are still opening and that is the point! Love calls to Love. The very fact you have chosen to sit, watch your breath, and allow thoughts, is a clarion call.

Practice mindfulness today. If you cannot sit for fifteen minutes, but can only repeat the lesson silently to yourself on the hour, that is enough. It is better to practice hourly mindfulness than to sit for a few minutes and then get up and forget.

Lesson 166

I am entrusted with the gifts of God.

Have you ever heard of "plasma tubes"? They're a phenomenon recently discovered in the earth's atmosphere by Cleo Loi, a 23-year-old student of astrophysics at the University of Sydney.

Created as the sun interacts with the earth's magnetic field, plasma tubes are "solar portals" that float 373 miles above the earth. They open and close about every eight minutes like a solar flower.

I just love it when science approaches the door of spirituality and knocks upon it. How long have we "worshipped" the sun, somehow intuiting its influence on us that goes far beyond simple light, gravity, and warmth? At first, Loi's senior colleagues didn't believe her discovery. They even tried to convince her something was wrong with her telescope. Sounds familiar doesn't it?

Like Loi's doubting senior colleagues we often don't see our gifts at first. We need to be convinced they exist. What are our gifts? How do we know them?

All things are given to you. God's Trust in you is Limitless, because God knows you as One with God… Unless your will is One with God's you will not receive God's gifts. This is the paradox that makes the world that you perceive. This world is not God's Will so it is not real. So, if you think this world is real, you must believe there is another will, and one that leads to the opposite of God.
– ACIM

Contrary to all we have been taught, this world is not our home. But we think it is. We believe it is the only place in all our lonely galaxy with life. We are certain it holds the only safety we can find. We cling to it, hating its pain and suffering, yet holding fast in fear that there is nothing else. But like Loi, we can persevere through doubt, and see beyond the limits we have thus far imposed upon our vision. There really is only one Will. How can there be any other?

We are entrusted with the Will of our Source. It is time to deny the denial of our divinity. This world is not all there is. Do not accept its limitations. We have made it. Being divine beings, we can remake it. But we must recognize our gifts or we limit ourselves to playing in the dirt.

Practice for fifteen minutes in the morning and evening. Take your seat and relax your body. Place gentle awareness on the breath. When you are ready, say in your mind, "I am entrusted with the gifts of God." Try not to think the words but rather feel them. Experience them. Ask for help if you wish, and know it will be there just for the asking. God's gifts are yours. Source has not been outwitted by the ego's tiny mad idea to take a road away from your True Self. God's gifts go with you wherever you might imagine yourself wandering. They are a treasure so great that everything of this world you perceive is valueless compared to them.

Open to the Sun of the universe. Open like the solar flower you are. Reach your mind out and play! What you desire is yours. What is it you desire? Imagine all you wish but do desire the one thing that will give you all the gifts you seek. Desire to accept your Divine Oneness.

Enjoy the power of this meditation. Dwell on the gifts you've been given. Don't worry about thoughts or feelings that arise. Watch them come and go. Give them up to your higher Self who will know just what to do with them and then receive the peace that is returned. Sit with your own divinity.

Practice mindfulness today. If you cannot sit for fifteen minutes, but can only silently repeat the lesson to yourself on the hour, that is enough. It is better to practice hourly mindfulness than to sit for a few minutes, and then get up and forget.

Lesson 167

There is one life, and that I share with God.

Once again, this lesson is not a metaphor. We either share a life with Source or we don't. Source is either the Source of all things or the source of nothing. There is no in between to All. The mind of Source creates everything that is, and we cannot create what is not in Mind of God – except in our own illusion.

What is in the Mind of Source is Real. What does Source create with? Love. None of your creations will ever be real unless they, too, are extensions of Love. What you extend can only be of that which was extended to create you. You cannot make attributes Source lacks. Source lacks death. Source lacks hate. Source lacks fear. Source lacks judgment. Source lacks, lack!

What a mind asleep creates is only a dream. Do you see why you are not the body you dream you inhabit? Do you see why this world of fear and lack is not real? All of what we "see" and "experience" is created in a mind asleep. But a mind awakened knows its Source and creates with Source because it shares its Mind.

What seems to be the opposite of life is merely sleeping. Source will not let us sleep forever, but wakes us gently from our dream. When the dreamer knows she is dreaming, awakening begins. When the dreamer acknowledges the dream for what it is, he begins to see differently. His mind changes and his experiences of the dream shift, ever so slightly at first. But with each passing day of awakening, Reality becomes more and more apparent. All of us are awakening now together, for we share One Mind and it is time to awaken. The time to awaken is not set by us, but it is set by Source.

Practice in the morning and evening for about fifteen minutes. Take your seat and be comfortable. Close your eyes. Settle into awareness of your body and the sounds around you. Then turn your attention gently to the breath. Follow the breath as it happens naturally, with no effort at all. Be at peace in the breath. When you are ready, say slowly and purposefully in your mind, "There is one life, and that I share with God."

Now open yourself to the experience of these words. Open to your own holiness. Open to your own perfection. Open to your eternal mind and know that it will never perish. You will never perish. You are One with all your brothers and sisters, a perfect mirror of the Mind of God. This is a meditation to enjoy. Find your bliss in it if you can. You are beginning to awaken, as it should be, as it must be. Sit and allow the Holy Spirit to direct the Mind you share with Source. Anchor your experience with the breath. Repeat the lesson like a mantra if it helps.

Keep this lesson with you throughout the day. There is one life we share. As you look upon the world, its craziness, its harshness, know it is a dream. You are not crazy for realizing this truth, but you will be happier and less insane for it. And because there is nothing we do not share, your awakened mind will awaken others.

Like yourself. Nothing Source has created is not likeable. If it's not likeable, it's not of Source. That's how you know.

Lesson 168

Your grace is given me. I claim it now.

Grace. Graciousness. Say this to yourself now: "I am gracious." Say it again and really take it in. "I am gracious." Notice how it feels to say this about yourself. It's true, you know. If it hasn't registered in your body, you're not paying attention.

Grace: the word conveys elegance, serenity, calm and peace, dignity and beauty. Inner grace is a state beyond words. It is a feeling that can only be known through direct experience. The state of grace is an aspect of God's love.

You are asked in this lesson to begin an earnest conversation with God. Source is not hiding from you. Why should you hide from Source? Source is speaking to you. Why not speak to It? God is leaning in to you. Why not lean in toward All That Is?

The Voice of Source is still and soft. It often arrives seemingly out of nowhere in the form of intuition. The more I pay attention to my intuitive ability, the more the Voice astounds me with its accuracy. Intuition is me, opening to a force beyond myself, saying, "Yes. I am willing." There's nothing magic about it at all. Prescience is usually just paying attention.

The grace of God is freely given. Our inheritance has been kept for us, even as we've traveled, seemingly lost, through space and time. But we have to show a little willingness. We have to step up to the plate and say, "Yes, I can claim what is mine." All that is needed is this small effort. Source will take care of the rest of it for us. Acknowledge the gift of grace within your heart, and God will do the heavy lifting.

Practice in the morning and evening for about fifteen minutes. Take your seat and be comfortable. Close your eyes or soften your gaze. Settle into awareness of your body and the sounds around you. Then turn your attention gently to the breath. Follow the breath as it happens naturally, with no effort at all. Be at peace in the breath. When you are ready, say slowly and purposefully in your mind, "Your grace is given me. I claim it now."

Now imagine the arising of your own holiness. Imagine knowing that your true nature is grace. Can you accept this might be so? Can you trust that your grace, and the grace of all living things, is the Will of Source? If you can crack the door in your mind just a bit, Grace will be waiting. Source is not trying to hide from you. It meets you as you reach to It. Grace is not a big revelation. But it can be the precursor. Knowing your own grace prepares the mind to accept the miracle.

Enjoy the next fifteen minutes of this meditation. It is the beginning of a lasting conversation, if you will allow it. Watch the breath. Thoughts will arise. Feelings will come up and fade away. You will know which thoughts and feelings are the Voice speaking to you by how they make you feel. Know this: there is nothing you can possibly do to make Source stop talking to you.

Practice mindfulness today. Claim your grace as often as possible, especially when moments of conflict or discomfort arise. Grace is your immortal self, your true self. You are nothing less than perfect grace, ever.

Lesson 169

By grace I live. By grace I am released.

Grace is the aspect of the Love of God which is most like the state prevailing in the Unity of Truth. It is the world's most lofty aspiration for it leads beyond the world entirely.
– ACIM

Why do we need all this reminding about love and grace? It's because we're not really in agreement that it's what we are. Make no mistake: guilt is deeply embedded in the idea of what we think we are. In fact, guilt is present within us as much as the idea of love.

Guilt arises from the idea we can split off from our Creator and be whole within our separate selves. Guilt is our projection onto Source. The idea follows along these lines: "If I can leave God, then God can leave me. Leaving the Creator is an attack on the Creator, therefore It is free to attack me back. I am guilty of wanting to leave, therefore attack must be justified and immanent." You can see how the belief in guilt soon becomes fear. If I can split from my Source, will It not come after me and punish me for my "independence"? And in my independence, am I not now alone and utterly vulnerable?

Guilt is an amazing invention with galactic repercussion. Its creation as an idea had to involve the denial of the True Self. Your task now is to end the agreement that guilt is real by reclaiming your right to know your Christ Mind. This is what grace is all about. Grace is a hand from Source to the personal mind. Grace cannot come from the personal mind because it is the same mind that invented guilt. Grace is Truth, offered by a higher Mind to release you from your own chains.

"By grace I live. By grace I am released." Grace is the goal of learning but it cannot be learned. It comes to the mind that is prepared to accept the truth about itself. Grace is the acceptance of the Love of God within a world that seems to thrive on hate and fear. Grace is the acknowledgement that God Is.

Practice for fifteen minutes today, in the morning and evening. Take your seat and get comfortable. Close your eyes and settle into awareness of your body and the sounds around you. Then turn your attention gently to the breath. Follow the breath as it happens naturally, with no effort at all. Be at peace in the breath. When you are ready, say slowly and purposefully in your mind, "By grace I live. By grace I am released."

Now open yourself to the experience of these words. Allow yourself to feel the words, to be the words. Breathe God in. Breathe God out. God is in you. You are in God. Say to yourself, "I am gracious. I am good. I am One with all around me." Feel the words in the body. This feeling should be one of peaceful expansion.

If you cannot get to a feeling of peace, give yourself the grace of acceptance. Suppose you've spent all day at work. Suppose you were looking forward to these fifteen minutes of peace, but now you're sitting down, your mind cannot stop thinking. Notice and say to yourself, "My mind is full of thoughts. I ask the Holy Spirit to direct my mind." Once you've asked, you will be answered. The answer may even come with more thoughts. Watch the thoughts! Say to yourself, "I allow." Keep allowing and keep watching. You will be directed by grace. Allow and receive what is offered.

Enjoy this meditation. Watch the breath. Thoughts will arise. Feelings will come up. If any thoughts of guilt come up, know it is Source's way of helping you to see what needs to be released and let it go.

Practice mindfulness today. On the hour, remember to claim

your grace. Make it your practice to be especially mindful of any guilt and release it. Grace is not achieved through suffering! It belongs to each of us. It is our rightful inheritance and there is no cost for it at all. The only thing we need do is claim it.

Receive today. Give today. Enjoy the beauty around you.

Lesson 170

There is no cruelty in God and none in me.

This lesson contains vitally important information about how the personal mind works. Anyone who believes their goal is happiness needs to understand this lesson.

> *No one attacks without intent to hurt. This can have no exceptions. When you think that you attack in self-defense, you mean that to be cruel is protection; you are safe because of cruelty. You mean that you believe to hurt another brings you freedom. And you mean that to attack is to exchange the state in which you are for something better, safer, more secure from dangerous invasion and from fear.*
> *– ACIM*

If I am Whole, Eternal, and One, then my attack on another must begin first with an attack against my Self. What am I attacking in myself? My own eternal Mind. I am attacking the Truth, which is that I am invulnerable to attack itself.

"Defense is the first act of warfare." The first act of warfare is always against my own invulnerability. My perceived need for defense arises out of my own denial of my perfect Self. No one can attack me unless I attack my Self first. This is always the case and there are no exceptions.

Cruelty can only come from a mind that has forgotten its Self. Cruelty says, "Not only am I justified in doing harm, but the harm

I do to you will not harm me in any way as a result. Therefore, I can harm you with impunity and justify it as defense." This is a lie of such proportion it cannot be fathomed. It has created all the pain of this world.

Love asks that we lay down our arms – first against ourselves and then those we call "enemy." But in a world that knows cruelty such a move is seen as naïve at best and ignorant at worst. "If you're not prepared for war, you get what you deserve." This thinking makes Love the enemy. With love as the enemy, cruelty becomes a god.

Escape from fear comes from facing fear itself. What is our biggest fear? Our biggest fear is of God. Let me repeat, our greatest fear is fear of Source. This fear, which is kept far below the surface of the personal mind, stems from the idea we have attacked Oneness by splitting from It. We have separated from Source and It is coming after us with a vengeance.

This dream world is built on the fear we have offended the very One who created us, and gave us Its power to create. We have invented separation as an idea. Source did not. We have invented a world in which cruelty can be experienced. Source did not. We have invented a world in which one can conceivably murder his neighbor and get away with it. We invented war as a means to "settle" differences. Source invented none of these things. We have invented a world in which the body can trap the Spirit in a seemingly endless cycle of death and rebirth. Source invented none of this. It is all ours. We invented the idea that we can separate from our Source and It can separate from us. Cruelty is our invention.

The return to Love begins with facing the fear of fear itself. Face your fear and name it untrue. It is the ego that tells you fear is real because it wishes to keep the truth from you. The truth is, it is the ego itself that is unreal. Begin to know your Oneness in Source and fear lifts like the mist it is. There is no cruelty in Oneness and there is none in you. God is not coming after us, but God is inviting us to return Home. Unlike the personal mind, God knows we never left.

Today you will practice facing fear and calling it untrue. Love is your Source and Love does not know cruelty. It exists only in a split mind that values fear as a motivator. Cease the attack against yourself today.

Practice in the morning and evening for about fifteen minutes. Take your seat and be comfortable. Close your eyes and settle into awareness of your body and the sounds around you. When you are ready, turn your attention gently to the breath. Follow the breath as it happens naturally, with no effort at all. Be at peace in it. Allow it to serve as your anchor for a little while. When you are ready, say slowly and purposefully in your mind, "There is no cruelty in God and none in me."

Now think upon this: "Source created me One with every living thing. My form may change, but I can never die. I have no need to fear anything whatsoever. Without fear, I am free to bless this world and all who share it with me. I choose again and make the choice for Love. I am thankful. I am forever safe. I am complete."

Spend the rest of the contemplation in silent watchfulness of all thoughts and feelings that arise. Be mindful of the breath, returning to full awareness of it when the mind wanders too much. Repeat the lesson slowly in your mind if it helps. When you feel peace, when you feel safe, when you feel even the smallest hint of joy – know you are connected to Source.

Be mindful today. On the hour, remind yourself there is no cruelty in you. This lesson is a blessing to yourself. Accept your own graciousness. If you are tempted to disregard your peace, just notice it. Pay attention to how it makes you feel. You are the decider here.

Review V

Lesson 171

Now you begin another review period. This review will prepare you for a new level of understanding that paradoxically includes both independence and increased trust in Source. You are ready for it. Perhaps you have wavered in your certainty. Perhaps you have doubted your commitment. But doubt not. Nothing you have accomplished has gone unnoticed. Take this next step with greater certainty of your goal to be happy, to know your Self, and your Source in every hour of every day.

Anyone who practices the daily lessons knows they work. They do not make you mindless, but mindful. They do not encourage passivity, but responsibility. They do not ask you to simply accept, but to question and see for yourself. As you cross the halfway mark in this year of lessons, be willing to ask if this is true or not for you.

You are now asked to make asking for help habitual. Most of the time, most of us forget to ask. We value independence over interconnectedness, or we fear "going to the well" too many times. But remember, Love's purpose is to assist. In assisting us, Love fulfills its function, and in asking, we fulfill ours. Dedicate your meditations to the One whose purpose is to help you find your way to peace and fulfill your function. Make your contemplation a gift to Source. You are not ever a burden.

Below is the foundational idea for this ten-day review period. It should precede the thoughts for each day. Each daily thought will clarify some aspect of the foundational idea.

God is but Love, and therefore so am I.

What a gift this thought is! It is the fundamental answer to the fundamental question. Take this thought into your heart and mind and allow it to set the tone for all you do. Be pleased with yourself in this knowing.

The practice for this review, and all the lessons that follow, is to be done with an attitude that says, "Bring it on. I am willing and ready to open my mind. I am willing because I trust that what You bring to me I can accept, allow, and use toward Your purpose."

Practice for fifteen minutes in the morning and evening in the following manner: begin your meditation by reading the foundation thought. Then read through the entire lesson. Feel the words in your heart/mind. Then take your seat and be comfortable. Close your eyes and settle into awareness of your body and the sounds around you. Notice without attaching to anything. When you are ready, turn your attention gently to the breath. Follow the breath as it happens naturally, with no effort at all. When you are ready, slowly and purposefully repeat the lesson in your mind.

Now, simply sit. Ask Source to join you. Repeat the lesson, or whatever parts of it most resonate for you. Feel each word in each idea and then allow your mind to go beyond them to the Source of their meaning. Use the words to create an experience that truly cannot be described by words alone. Source will show you the way. The knowledge is in you already. You are simply remembering something you forgot long ago. Trust in your experience. Allow it to take you where it will, knowing you have asked Source to guide it, and resting in the surety you will be answered. Each thought you have is in Mind of God. Where else could it be?

Begin and end each day with the thought, "God is but Love and therefore so am I." Every hour, take time to remember what you are. Ask for help often.

The ideas for today's review are:

"God is but Love and therefore so am I."
1. All things are echoes for the Voice of God.

"God is but Love and therefore so am I."
2. The power of decision is my own.
"God is but Love and therefore so am I."

Lesson 172

"God is but Love, and therefore so am I."
1. In my defenselessness, my safety lies.
"God is but Love and therefore so am I."
2. I am among the ministers of God.
"God is but Love and therefore so am I."

Lesson 173

"God is but Love and therefore so am I."
1. I will step back and let God lead the way.
"God is but Love and therefore so am I."
2. I walk with God in perfect holiness.
"God is but Love and therefore so am I."

Lesson 174

"God is but Love and therefore so am I."
1. Into God's presence I will enter now.
"God is but Love and therefore so am I."
2. Today I learn to give as I receive.
"God is but Love and therefore so am I."

Lesson 175

"God is but love, and therefore so am I."
1. I give the miracles I have received.
"God is but love, and therefore so am I."
2. I am at home. Fear is the stranger here.
"God is but love, and therefore so am I."

Lesson 176

For all of the reasons you might draw someone into your life, one would never be to find their faults.
– TUT

"God is but Love and therefore so am I."
1. Holy Child of God, give me your blessing.
"God is but Love, and therefore so am I."
2. I am as God created me.
"God is but Love, and therefore so am I."

Lesson 177

"God is but Love and therefore so am I."
1. There is no death. The Child of God is free.
"God is but Love, and therefore so am I."
2. Now we are one with God Who is our Source.
"God is but Love, and therefore so am I."

Lesson 178

I have a mind that is in constant chatter. Left untended it wanders into places that are none of its business. While it can seem boring or tiresome at times, I have to mind my mind – to be mindful. I've found that being mindful is ultimately much less work. Before I go too far down a thought path, I remember to stop and ask, "Is this really where you want to go?" Often the answer is, "Not so much."

The chattering brain thinks it's doing its job. Mind training doesn't mean stopping thought so much as allowing it and calmly shining the light of awareness upon it. I've found that feeling guilty about thoughts is a waste of time. They want to be heard and will keep coming back if ignored. Resisting a thought just feeds it. Unpleasant thoughts feel unpleasant. Often we don't even realize we've been taken down a thought path until the body begins to squirm. Enjoy your practice today.

"God is but Love, and therefore so am I."
1. Let not my mind deny the Thought of God.
"God is but Love, and therefore so am I."
2. I am entrusted with the gifts of God.
"God is but Love, and therefore so am I."

Lesson 179

I will say again, forgiveness is spiritual alchemy. You never know what you'll get when you make the decision to let go of the anger, the hurt, the resentment. The decision to consider forgiveness opens a door you often don't even remember has been closed. What lies beyond the door?

When I make the choice to forgive, I expand. When I choose not to forgive, I remain tight. When I open the door, I see things I didn't know I didn't know. Grace is the little voice that prompts me to say, "You may not know. Let's explore a little. Open the door and see what's in that room."

"God is but Love, and therefore so am I."
1. There is one life, and that I share with God.
"God is but Love, and therefore so am I."
2. Your grace is given me, I claim it now.
"God is but Love, and therefore so am I."

Lesson 180

"God is but Love, and therefore so am I."
1. By grace I live. By grace I am released.
"God is but Love, and therefore so am I."
2. There is no cruelty in God and none in me.
"God is but Love, and therefore so am I."

Lesson 181

We now leave last week's review and begin a more advanced level of mind training, the point of which is to maintain a focus on the Now moment. But before we begin, there are a few things to consider.

First, it is important to recognize that what you see is consistent only because your focus is consistent; change your focus and your perception begins to shift accordingly. Most of us are focused on the physical body, an unconscious condition that leads to unconscious thoughts of separation and fear. You are now being asked to focus more intently on conditions beyond the physical. You will place your focus much more consistently on the content of your mind.

Second, you are at the point in these lessons where you can see their benefits clearly, but perhaps you have not been transformed to the degree you'd hoped. This is your personal mind talking. It is telling you to be dismayed by the "depressing and restricting thought that, even if you should succeed, you will inevitably lose your way again." Make no mistake about this: your personal mind is not interested in losing its hold on your thoughts. It will use boredom, defiance, inadequacy, and despair against you. This is a critical junction and it is why ACIM now instructs you to be concerned only with the present moment. It does not matter that you have failed in the past. The past does not exist and the future is only imagined. Concerns with the past and worries about the future are defenses against the present moment. Lay these concerns aside. That is all that is asked.

Today's lesson is:

I trust my brothers (my sisters and all others) who are one with me.

We are able to trust another when we first trust our self. Trust and faith are requirements, especially in the beginning, because the personal mind cannot perceive the Truth. What are we trusting in our self? Only the best: our eternal goodness, our unending connection with Love. We are trusting that the personal mind does not define us.

When I perceive an error in another, I proclaim her limitations as well as my own. When I focus on another's faults they become blocks to my awareness of the Self that unites us both. Often, I do not recognize my judgments because they are unconscious – unless I live in the present moment. The act of being present is the key to ascension. It is what faith makes real through experience. If you have been practicing these lessons, you will have had experiences that have confirmed your faith and advanced it to knowing.

Today's practice is twofold: first, to be present in the Now, and second, to transcend judgment in any form. This is kind of like catching the ball while running. Every form of judgment is a block to perception. As you increase your level of present moment awareness you also notice how habitual judgment is. As you recognize and consciously release judgment, your perception becomes increasingly clear. You begin to see things you were unconscious of before. You notice connections and synchronicities on a new level because judgment contracts vision and non-judgment expands it.

To be without sin means to be without separation from Source. "Sinlessness" is not a fantasy. It is our natural state. As I free my sister from focus upon her guilt, I free myself and I free her – even if she may never "recognize" it. It is a contradiction of Oneness to think I can find salvation and leave anyone behind. It is also a contradiction of Oneness to perceive there is any moment that is real but this one moment.

Your practice expands now as you are asked not only to sit in contemplation, but also to maintain presence during the day. Total dedication is not required but willingness to try is. Become mindful about the contents of your mind. Believe me, this will become easier and easier. You will marvel at the conflict you once engaged in that you now easily avoid.

Practice today at least once, for fifteen minutes. Take your seat and get comfortable. Scan your body for any places where tension exists and breathe into the tension, letting it go on the out-breath. When you are ready, close your eyes and place your awareness on the breath. In your mind, repeat to yourself, "I trust my brothers/sisters who are one with me." Now sit in silence.

Be present in this moment with whatever thoughts arise. Can you trust? Whom do you not trust and why? Can you see that while you may not trust their small self, their Self remains within – even if it is unrecognized? Seek no goal here but to perceive your Innocence and that of the other. Watch the thoughts that come up, move through you, and pass away. Practice being in the moment, seeing Innocence, and trusting It is Real.

Mindfulness throughout the day now becomes at least as important as sitting in contemplation. Mindfulness happens in the present moment, now. As often as possible today, stop, breathe, and be aware of your thoughts. Bodily discomfort can be a valuable tool for mindfulness practice. If you feel discomfort in the body, it is often because the mind is in discomfort. Any time you are in a state of fear, judgment, anticipation or anger, your body will register it through a feeling of contraction, heaviness in the heart, the solar plexus, or any number of other "signals." Begin to notice how your body signals you. It is your friend in mindfulness practice.

ACIM is not about instant revelation. Most of us awaken slowly from the dream – we are not jolted into enlightenment. Step by step, moment-by-moment, you are now increasing your level of awareness. As you begin the second half of these lessons, you are well on the path. Love yourself most heartily today. More than anything, this is what is important. Love yourself for trying. This is your journey of waking up to Love.

Lesson 182

I will be still an instant and go Home.

This world we seem to live in is not our true Home. We did not originate here, and somewhere in our minds, we know this is true.

> *A memory of Home keeps haunting you. It is nothing so definite you could say with certainty you are an exile here. It is a persistent feeling, a tiny throb, sometimes actively dismissed, but surely to return to mind again. We try to put aside this feeling. We occupy our time with games, deny our sadness, or call it illusion. Yet, who in simple honesty, without defensiveness and self-deception, would deny she understands the words we speak?*
> **– ACIM**

There is an inner child who lives in each of us. This child is our Innocence and it is this child who knows she is not Home. I'll tell you a story about this child.

For years I had recurring dreams about saving tiny kittens from destruction. I couldn't figure out why I kept having them, but I knew when I understood their message they would stop. When I read this lesson, I knew. My dreams were about trying to protect the Innocence of my own spiritual self. Like a kitten, Innocence would mature into a powerful being, strong, agile, and capable of seeing in the dark. As I practice forgiveness, I strengthen my own Innocence. In Innocence, I see in the dark, walk between worlds, restore my power, and find my way home. When I realized the meaning of this lesson, my dreams of kittens stopped.

How can we protect our Innocent inner child if we do not recognize her? She needs no defense but recognition. She is the

Innocence within each of us, and she asks us to see ourselves in her. This we try to do today by being still an instant and going Home.

Practice for fifteen minutes at least once today. Begin by taking a seat and getting comfortable. Scan your body for any tension and place your awareness on it. Breathe into the tension and let it go on the out-breath. When you are ready, say in your mind or out loud, "I will be still an instant and go Home." Then relax into the breath. Let the breath be itself, without any effort. Allow the meaning behind the words to guide your thoughts. Put aside all defenses and seek a place of Innocence. If your mind wanders too much, repeat the lesson slowly and purposefully in your mind, like a mantra. It is your innocence you yearn for. "This is your heart's desire. This is the call that cannot be denied. The holy Child remains with you. Her Home is yours. Accept it in exchange for all the toys of battle you have made. Be still an instant and go Home."

Lesson 183

I call upon Source and I call upon my Self.

This lesson asks your willingness to re-member Source within yourself. It is vital that you remember Source gave you all Its attributes. There is nothing you lack because of this. There is nothing you are not capable of perceiving within yourself. No strength, no vitality, no joy, no Love is beyond you, for you are the Word of God.

Source's name is Holy because it includes everything. But the name of All That Is is no holier than yours. Know your Name and you know God's. The Whole of God extends Itself to every part of Itself, so Its identity belongs to each of us without exception.

This world is temporary, changeable, and unstable. Source is forever and forever, timeless, endless, all accepting, all-encompassing. Source is Reality. You and I did not create It and we cannot know It if we look for it in the personal mind's creations. Do you understand your Oneness with Source is within you? You will not see what you do not believe exists.

Know God's name is yours, and come into Its Presence in the Now. Extend your perception beyond the personal mind's limited range. Be fearless about this. You cannot fail. Go in silence beyond the boundaries the ego has established for you. In the Now, you are already there in the Beyond. Your Wholeness is within you. Claim it in silence. Be where you are and consider What you Are in Truth.

To call upon Source is not some magical game you play. But it calls into question the split mind. It brings into focus the Truth of Oneness. Look around and know that all you see is Oneness in vibration, alive in light and sound. It is there beyond the capacity of the body's eyes to see it. Feel it with your inner knowing.

Your practice today is to sit in silence and re-member what you are. You need this confidence in your Self. The personal mind will tell you Source is beyond your reach. It wants you to remain a victim. You will be a victim until you remember Source does not speak the language of little prayers. Little prayers are limited to asking for little things. Ask for connection! All your power lies in your connection with Source.

Your connection to Source is through the language of silent peace, kindness, gentleness, patience, forgiveness, unity, willingness, graciousness, certainty, courage, and acceptance. These are the attributes you share with Source and they are your common language.

Practice today for fifteen minutes. Take your seat and relax the body. Scan it for areas of tension. Breathe into the tightness and allow it to soften on the exhale. Relax into the silence. When you are ready, repeat in your mind, "I call upon God's name and therefore on my own." Now, bring to mind your names for Source. Gentleness. Power. Strength. Oneness. Kindness. Peace.

Eternal. Unlimited. Beautiful. Feel the words. Come up with your own! This is calling upon Source and it is calling up your Self. This is getting to know what you are in Truth.

Now extend to yourself the names you've given to Source. "I am Kindness." "I am gentle." "I am patience." "I am certain." "I am pleased with myself." "I am good." "I am beautiful." "I am powerful." It should feel good to say this about yourself. This is connection! This is how Source feels about you, and how you deserve to feel. Sit for as long as you like in this silent connection. Watch the breath. Come back to the words if your mind wanders. Give yourself fifteen minutes to be in Now, with your Self.

On the hour today, take a moment to stop and be silent. Like yourself. Be satisfied with yourself. Hold yourself in high regard.

Lesson 184

The Name of Source is my own.

One of the ways separation from Source is experienced is through the habit of naming. We look at a thing and focus our perception on its uniqueness. We give it a name and call it different from the other things we named. Oh, the power of a name!

We think this naming makes us understand our world, how it functions, and its purpose. You have your name and I have mine. I will not respond if someone calls me by your name because you are not me! Entire books of different names exist so parents can make sure their child gets a really unique, unusual name that no one else has. Think of all the different names we give to different species, different forms of matter, different star systems. It is all the product of a desire to separate.

As we separate things from each other we think we understand more deeply. This separating out – this naming – gives meaning to the small mind. Years, months, hours, minutes, seconds, nanoseconds, all become discrete events. We measure molecules, atoms, electrons, quarks, neutrinos, bosons, in never-ending detail. We believe this separating is essential to learning, understanding, and communicating. We think it is the only way to know about "reality." But is this true, or does it take us further from knowing? Is it possible to perceive things separately but at the same time understand it all as a unified Whole? Are we capable of perceiving the Whole or are we capable only of partial perception?

Today's lesson explains that we may use a million names for a million things, but in the end there is nothing separate from anything else. We are the thing itself. In fact, we are it and the space in which it seems to exist. Everything that seems to exist apart from you, is you and you are it.

If you spend all day today looking at all the different things in your perceptual field and then name them as yourself, it will take years off your learning. "I am the tree. I am Jane. I am the cloud. I am the birdsong. I am the color. I am the street, the car, the stone, the pavement, the desk, the chair." How is this possible? It is possible because you are creating them out of your mind. Every single one. Knowing this is soul evolution.

Practice for fifteen minutes today, in the morning and evening. Take your seat and get comfortable. Place your awareness on the breath and scan your body for any areas of tightness. Breathe into the tight areas and breathe out the stress. Just relax. When you are ready, close your eyes and say in your mind, "The Name of Source is my own." Then think upon these words as you watch the breath:

God's Name defines everything because we all come from It. What we make and call different names is a shadow we have cast across the Reality of Oneness. It is an error in perception. The True Name for all things is One. I can escape from endless division and separateness. I can perceive Wholeness and the peace of Wholeness. God's Name is my inheritance and It has been kept for me, waiting my recognition of Unity.

Now sit in silence and allow the lesson to penetrate your mind. Watch the breath and repeat the words of the lesson to yourself slowly and purposefully. Be the words. Knowing is being, not naming. You might sit and listen to the sounds around your body and think, "I am one with the wind. The rain is me. The sun I feel on my face is me. Oh! I've brought that fly to myself. What an amazing moment! I'll just sit here and extend my awareness in all directions. How far from my body can my awareness go?" Enjoy your exploration of unity! All you perceive is you.

Throughout the day be mindful of this lesson. On the hour, or even half-hour, look about at the seemingly separate things of your world and feel their Oneness with you. Know that all names are superficial only. All form is superficial only. It is all One Light, one amazing creation of your consciousness.

Barbara McClintock, Nobel Prize winner for her studies on the genetics of corn, famously said, "I know my plants intimately, and I find it a great pleasure to know them." McClintock's genius was that she "became" the corn she studied. She understood the science, but only in closing the gap between herself and the corn could she grasp its true nature.

Grasp your own true nature. Speak your own name. You are Source and It is You. You have never been anything else. Everything in your world supports your knowing who and what you are. Nothing is apart from you.

Lesson 185

I want the peace of God.

We all want the peace of God. It is safe to say no one does not desire it. The question is, what are you willing to do for peace?

"To say these words is nothing but to mean these words is everything."

To say I want the peace of God is easy. But to gain Peace I must end my perception of separation in all its forms. Peace requires that I see that nothing, absolutely nothing, is outside the unity of God's Mind. This is a tall order. Yet, the truth of this lesson allows no compromise.

Your mind can join with Source only in Truth, and Oneness is the Truth. To know peace, you must be willing to perceive beyond the illusion of separation. Separation replaces Oneness with compromise. Compromise says, "Oneness is impossible. This is the best you can do. Just accept it." Compromise will tell you very convincingly that unity can only be experienced partially. But here's the deal: no bargain with separation will ever give you the peace of God because compromise, like separation, is a lie.

There is no bargaining with Truth because Mind of Source is not partial. It is not satisfied with half the Truth. Oneness, and the Peace of Oneness, will be lost to you until you, too, are satisfied only with Everything. This entire world takes place in your mind. You are every single unmet desire for peace that exists.

When you truly want the Peace of God, Source will answer your desire. The answer will be in a form you cannot mistake. But you must be open to perceiving it. The answer will expose your partiality. It will challenge your willingness to accept compromise. Remember, compromise is the goal of illusion. To see past illusion and know the Peace of God, illusion must be recognized where it is. In every situation in which compromise seems preferable, you must be willing to ask yourself, "Is this what I want in place of peace?"

Practice at least once today in silent contemplation of the lesson. Take the time you need. You know how to do this. Find a comfortable position in a quiet place. Place your awareness on the body and find any tension or discomfort. Breathe into the discomfort and then let it go on the out-breath. When you are ready, allow your mind to focus on the breath and go deeper into relaxation. When ready, say in your mind or out loud, "I want the peace of God." Feel each word. Who is the "I" that wants peace? How does it relate to all other minds that seek peace? Can you extend peace to them, and feel your own increase? What does peace feel like? Does it reside anywhere in your body? Can you imagine God's peace? Can you imagine the Unlimited? Can you extend your mind into peace so deep it goes on forever?

Breathe in peace. Let all that is not peace be released on the exhale. If your mind wanders too much, repeat the words of the lesson slowly and purposefully to yourself.

Be mindful as you go about this day. If a situation arises with coworkers, family or friends that disturbs your peace in any way – notice it. Only then decide what to do. You will choose peace or illusion. Whatever you decide, don't agonize or waste time in guilt. Do your best and stay awake to what your Source is delivering to you. The road to peace is built moment by moment. It is not an endless road.

Lesson 186

Salvation of the world depends on me.

Does reading this lesson make you feel just a little nervous? How burdensome these words appear to the personal mind. So much responsibility!

The personal mind interprets this statement as arrogant, burdensome, or even fearful. But look more deeply. This lesson is saying that Source remembers you as It created you. You need not be any different than you really are. Source does not ask for anything you cannot do, or indeed have not already done. It is the personal mind that shrinks from the Call of God.

You may remember that your function is forgiveness. It is a function we often forget. It is a function we often fight against. Today's lesson is a reminder of sorts. It takes you to another level of understanding about your function.

The personal mind will assure you that your function is impossible. In reality, this thought contains the real arrogance. Filled with false modesty, it would have you remain forever undeveloped, confused by conflicting goals, trapped and depressed. Your personal mind wholeheartedly supports the denial of your divinity, telling you it is something unachievable or best left for another day. This is the Great Lie. Source judges you as worthy. So know this: You are worthy.

The personal mind wants its function to replace the function Source has given you. It really is this simple. Ego wants its voice to reign supreme. Its voice insists upon your weakness, vulnerability, alienation, judgment, and impermanence. Source has given you the means by which to hear Its Truth, lovingly offered. Ask yourself this: "Which voice is more likely to be right, my personal mind's or Source's?"

Today, do not fight against your function. Your personal mind did not establish it, and it is not its idea. There really is only one way to be released from its limitations – accept the plan the personal mind did not make. Accept your function and trust the means to achieve it will be given to you. You were not created weak, arrogant, or helpless. You were not created guilty or ignorant. You were created a Holy Child of God. Be what you are.

Practice twice today for fifteen minutes in the morning and evening. Take your seat and relax the body. Place your awareness gently on the breath. Notice where any tension is being held in the body. Let it be released on the out-breath. When you are ready, say in your mind, "Salvation of the world depends on me." Then put aside false humility and listen deeply. Stay with the breath. The part of your mind that perceives a world needs to be released now. Feel the meaning behind the words of the lesson and know that you are fully capable of the role that is asked of you. What other role could you want? It is only humility that accepts salvation as its function. It is only arrogance that would deny it. You are worthy and capable. Rest in this knowing for the remainder of your contemplation.

Be mindful today. As situations arise that challenge, and encourage the ego to engage, take a breath before acting. Remember Who gave your function to you. There is no punishment in choosing for the ego, but there is far greater peace in choosing loving kindness.

Lesson 187

I bless the world because I bless myself.

You cannot give what you do not have. In fact, your giving is the proof of your having. You do not doubt that you must first possess what you give; but what you do not yet understand is this – it is only in giving that you increase what you have. This is the Law of Love, and it is unchangeable.
– ACIM

How is it possible that in order to gain something I have to give it away? The laws of this world tell you otherwise. If we give away a finite thing we no longer have it in our possession! But we are not talking about form here. Form is impermanent. It shifts, changes, and decays. What we are talking about here is far beyond form because it is what creates form. We are talking about thought; not the kind of thinking that engages the brain, but that of the heart/mind that creates through idea, vision, and feeling.

You have heard about the Law of Love previously. It is a Law that applies beyond the causal laws of form. It encompasses the laws of physics and supersedes them. The Law of Love does not change, alter, or decay. It is eternal and it was placed in your mind by Love extending Itself. Understand the Law of Love and you will move and work within a Reality that supersedes form.

There are three simple components to the Law of Love. First, you must possess a thing to give it away. Second, only when you share it can you truly have it. And third, you can increase what you have only through sharing. Giving increases the value of that which you possess.

To give Love you must first know you are Loved. To increase your experience of Love, you must share It. If you value Love, you must realize It in yourself and pass It on. Love multiplies through sharing because it is not form. It is an idea, a blessing, a feeling. Love can be expressed through form, but it is not limited by its expression.

Never forget that you give only to yourself. You bless only yourself. When you comprehend this idea, you will never fear sacrifice again. Indeed, you will see that it cannot be true. Sacrifice is the one idea that stands in the way of all sharing, all peace, and all healing. The thought of sacrifice is what gives rise to suffering. What is insane produces insanity. Yet nothing, even the idea of sacrifice, can alter the Law of Love because the idea of Love is in Mind of God and sacrifice is not.

Today, practice the Law of Love. This only requires you to see everything as an aspect of yourself. If you practice, you will have a moment where you understand this is true. When you do, it will be the beginning of a new way of perception. It may not rock your world entirely at first, but it is the beginning. Be aware, there is no sacrifice in seeing "the other" as yourself. The blessing you extend in your perception must return to your own mind.

Practice for fifteen minutes in the morning and evening. Take your seat and relax into the body. Place your awareness on the breath and slowly and purposefully repeat in your mind, "I bless the world because I bless myself." Now take the blessing for yourself. Breathe it in. As you exhale, extend that which you now possess to everything around you. How far out can you extend your blessing? Perhaps to the plant or the tree outside your window? Breathe in again and allow the blessing to be a light that illuminates every cell in your body. On the exhale, share the light again. Can you extend the blessing even further? Notice how this feels. Sit in peace. Relax. You do not have to work to breathe in the blessing. The Law of Love requires no effort to receive or extend. Allow and know you are Loved.

Throughout the day, practice the Law of Love by giving as you would receive. Love as you would be loved. See how this goes. Have the experience: for only in the experience does the knowing come. Even in this world you are in Wholeness.

Receive today. Give today. Enjoy.

Lesson 188

The peace of God is shining in me now.

Everyone has the light within. You do not need to seek for it. It is yours now. You brought it with you as Source extended Itself into you. Not a single one of us would be here without it. But it isn't perceived with the body's eyes, which are confused too often as the only tool of sight.

The Light within your Mind leads you back to where It came from and where you are at Home. In quietness it is acknowledged. If only for this reason we should all demand more time in our day for peace. The light within is difficult to perceive until we unplug from the lights outside.

Employers who promote meditation and yoga in the workplace expound upon its value. They see increases in productivity and creativity among the workforce. This is great and there should be much more of it. In fact, it should be commonplace. But inner peace is not about productivity or financial gain and should not be confused with it.

The development of inner vision can ultimately free us of the value system upon which this world operates: hierarchy, authority, scarcity, comparison, limitation, linear time, separate bodies, separate needs, and separate minds.

The peace of God shines within each one of us, all the time. That we don't see it, or feel it, doesn't mean it isn't there. It's just that we haven't cultivated our perception of it. Does this world not need more cultivation of light? Make no mistake, when you find your light you will extend it to everything in your purview. What you perceive within yourself becomes your perception of everything.

Cultivate your inner vision in quietness today. Practice for fifteen minutes in the morning and evening. Take your seat and get comfortable. Scan your body for areas of tension and breathe into them. On the out-breath, visualize the tension flowing outward and dissolving into harmless energy.

When you are ready, say in your mind, "The peace of God is shining in me now. Let all things shine upon me in God's Peace, and let me bless them in return with the light of peace in me." Stay in the present moment as you feel the meaning behind these words. The peace of God shines now within. It does not shine in the future or the past, but in the timeless present moment. Breathe in peace and breathe it out. Focus your mind on the light that flows into your body with each breath and then flows out again, magnified by joining with your light. Breathe in the light. Let it flow to every cell in your body. On the out-breath, extend your light and the light you have received as far out as you can. Have your experience. This is a metaphysical journey. It will have repercussions beyond anything your personal mind can imagine.

If you experience resistance to this lesson, or if your mind wanders, refocus on the breath and slowly, purposefully, repeat in your mind, "The peace of God. Is shining in me. Now."

Please give yourself time to sit in quiet today. Allow yourself one half hour out of your whole day and connect with your inner light.

On the hour, journey within and feel the peace that resides there in the quiet space – even as everyone around you may be engaged with other things. These small moments are all it takes to form a connection with the light.

Receive today and give today, dear reader. Cultivate your light as only you can.

Lesson 189

The Love of Source resides within me now.

There is a Light within each of us. We did not create It, but we were created by It. We cannot decide whether It is there or not, but we can choose to deny Its presence. If I choose to see this world as all there is, I will not see the Light because the purpose of this world is to hide it. But I can feel It within myself and I can practice knowing It is there in others.

When I do not perceive the Light within myself, I feel lost and often behave badly. When others behave badly toward me, I often choose not to see the Light in them.

Are we not are taught early on that love in this world is largely reserved for the deserving? Did you do well in school? Did you make your parents proud? Were you polite to others? Did you make the right choices about your job? Do you dress well? Do you make enough money? Is your skin the right color? Do you vote the right way? Do you know the right people? Is your body beautiful enough? Do you always think of others first? Do you get angry? Oh my!

Today you are asked to love without condition. For many, this is an unfamiliar feeling. But remember the three components of the Law of Love: first, I can only give that which I already possess; second, I can only receive through giving away what I have; and third, the only way to increase what I have is if I share it. So it follows, conditional love holds a part of itself back and compromises all three components of the Law of Love.

When I'm told to love myself, and I don't, I feel a bit guilty. What is wrong with me that I cannot love myself? This little guilt blocks my awareness of the Light within. When I'm told to love another, and I don't, I feel guilty again. More awareness of the Light is blocked. This is why forgiveness is our prime function in this world. Without forgiveness we cannot receive the Love of God. Guilt blocks awareness of the Love Light inside.

Love sees Love in you and in me. And Love, wishing to extend Itself, must give Itself and be received. But the ego knows only guilt and conditional love. It cannot receive because it trusts only itself. It doesn't even know the Light is there.

The Love of Source is gentleness. The Love of Source is patient and kind. The Love of Source has no requirements. It fulfills Itself in your acceptance of It. It can wait until you are ready because It knows no time. The choice to receive Love is yours alone, and it must be made over and over again. Only the ego will tell you that you are not yet ready to accept it. Whose voice do you value?

The practice for today sets the tone for the remainder of this year of lessons. It is one of letting go to receive. You need do nothing to receive the Love of Source but get out of your own way by moving though the veil of guilt that blocks reception.

Take your seat and get comfortable. Scan your body for any places holding tension and breathe into them. On the out-breath, relax more deeply. Inhale peace. Exhale tension. Watch the breath. Thoughts and feelings will arise. Just watch them without attaching to any of them. When you are ready, say in your mind, "I am capable of feeling the Love of Source. It is within me now."

Now, put your intention on the word, "Allow." On the out-breath, say in your mind, "Allow." Allow the moment. Empty your mind and allow. Let go of "true or false." Let go of "good or bad." Let go of every thought the mind judges worthy, and all the ideas of which it is ashamed. Hold onto nothing. Judge nothing. Expect nothing. Allow everything. Do not bring with you one thought of the past, nor one belief you ever learned before from anything. Forget the world. Forget ACIM, and trust Source.

You do not need to know the way to Source. It knows the way to you. Your part is only to remove the obstacles that block Love's presence. Thus, make no demands on what you receive. The way to reach Source is merely to let Source Be Itself in whatever form it chooses. Allow. Receive. Forgive. Breathe. This is your only responsibility. Oh yes, and play. Do play.

Sit in receptive meditation for at fifteen minutes in the morning and evening. You do not choose the path to Source. It already knows the way to you. Your choice lies in allowing Source to come to you. And with this choice alone, you have done all you need to do.

As you go about your day, maintain a connection with Source. On the hour, remind yourself, "I will not block Love's presence. My mind resides in the Mind of Love and I need only be open to It. I cherish no belief about what I am except that which Source holds – which is my own perfection. Born in Love, sustained by Love, returned to Love." And so it is.

Lesson 190

I choose the joy of God instead of pain.

To say this world is not real is to invite a certain cynical response. If this world isn't real, then what is? There is no plausible answer for anyone who has not questioned the contents of her own mind.

The lesson for today most certainly invites a cynical response for it goes so far as to say that all pain is in the mind, and only in the mind. For anyone who has suffered, or is suffering now from physical pain, I know this lesson can be an affront. If someone had told me my gallstones were all in my mind, even doubled over I probably would have found the strength to smack them.

And yet the world we see must be known for the illusion it is, for the sight of it is costing us another kind of vision. ACIM emphatically says,

You cannot see two worlds. You do not really want the world you see for it has disappointed you since time began. The homes you built have never sheltered you. The roads you made have led you nowhere, and no city that you have ever built has withstood the crumbling assault of time. All you need to give this world away in glad exchange for what you did not make is willingness to learn the one you made is false.

This is the truth: it is thought alone that causes pain; nothing outside the mind can hurt or injure. Consider this: Pain makes time seem real – giving us a past when it did not exist and a future in which we hope it has gone away. Can you see how powerful thought is?

This world was created out of a thought of desire to experience separation from Source. It is always painful to be separated from Source because it is unnatural. Pain is an illusion because separation is an illusion.

What I have created out of pain and fear cannot be displaced by more pain and fear. In order to dispel my pain – and this takes courage – I must face it. I have to go through it and come out on the other side. I have to stay with it. In a sense, I must be brave enough to let my pain cycle through and see what happens. Think about it, has there ever been a time your pain has lasted? No. Like all illusion it is ephemeral.

Today's lesson is about learning you have a choice with pain. You can feel it in the body, yes. But it is mental pain that causes real damage. Pain is first a thought. It is proof your thoughts are deceiving you about what you truly are. Pain proclaims Source wishes cruelty upon you. Pain proclaims suffering is Its Will for you. But Source has only made you unassailable. Pain is not in Its program.

Pain is of this world. It is in your perception only. Don't lay guilt on yourself about it, but do remember this world has no cause. Illusion can produce Reality. Pain is an effect of a mind that believes evil can be real. It is the personal mind's attack against your Self and your Self is invulnerable always. Lay down your guilt and seek the Peace that is yours. Let go all thoughts of fear and suffering. Reach the peace of mind that is the only place Reality can be found. You cannot see two worlds and the world of pain is false.

Practice today for at least fifteen minutes. Twenty would be better, and thirty would be highly beneficial. Take your seat and get comfortable. Relax your body and place your awareness on the breath. Spend some time allowing the breath to rise and fall naturally, with no effort whatsoever. When you are ready, say in your mind, "I choose the joy of God instead of pain."

Now, in your mind, try to imagine yourself beyond your physical being. Take this leap of faith. Try to imagine that you are not a body. You are free. Take your time with this. Breathe the light in. Release all tension on the out-breath. It may be only a whisper of contentment that arises. Do not make yourself wrong if you cannot imagine joy at first. Be happy with neutrality if that is all you get. Be happy with the absence of pain. See what happens.

Stay with the breath and repeat the words of the lesson. Ask for help if you need it. Lay aside all thoughts of the past or the future. Forget this world and allow Source to show you what It will. If you need to repeat the lesson in your mind – do so as often as necessary, but feel the words. If it is helpful, replace the word Joy with Peace, or Ease. Allow Source to show you what words feel right for you.

On the hour today, repeat the lesson in your mind. It will vastly improve your day. Let nothing get in the way of your contentment – for that is the beginning of joy. Find the vibration of contentment at first. Then happiness will show itself; then a bit of bliss will arise. The full orchestra includes all variations of peace and joy.

Lesson 191

I am a perfect extension of Source Itself.

Today's lesson is a clarion call to wake up to who we truly are – each and every one of us. Think superhero, wise master, great scientist, best-selling author, fearless explorer – we are these and even more. But there is a catch – a little thing that keeps us from reaching our true potential, and it is this: none of us can be any of these things alone. Not one of us can approach the true nature of our powerful Self if the little god of separation, the ego, is involved.

> *Deny your own Identity and you assail the universe alone, a*
> *tiny particle of dust against the legions of your enemies.*
> *– ACIM*

Think not that the great masters created alone. Even they would deny it. Ask a Nobel Prize winner if he or she worked alone. Not one could say they achieved a single thing without assistance. We are nothing alone and everything together. Pain and fear are the direct outgrowth of perceived separation. But Oneness knows no fear of Itself.

We are a Mind that has forgotten Itself and fears its selves.

Still powerful, still capable of great things, we have imagined this world and all its seeming complexity. It has beauty and joy but they are temporary. Nothing is born here that does not also die here. This makes loss seem more powerful than Love. But all together, we are the Whole Creation of Source Itself and this recognition is our release. We have no private thoughts because we share One Mind. Does this feel intrusive?

You are not confined to little points of bone and blood, defined by a little body that seems to struggle against the winds of circumstance. You are the wind and still more than the wind. Today you wake up to an old knowledge born again in your mind. Everything you see, everything you experience is nothing less than a reflection of the creative power you possess as a perfect extension of Perfection.

"I am not a body. I am free. I am as God created me." These words are what you are. As you sit in practice today, feel your way into their deeper meaning. The words speak Truth to your mind and it will recognize It on a level of knowing. Allow that you are a perfect extension of Perfection Itself.

Practice for at least fifteen minutes today in silent meditation. Take your seat and get comfortable. Place gentle awareness on the breath, and when you are ready, say in your mind, "My true Identity is a perfect extension of Source Itself. I cannot suffer, be in pain, experience loss, or fail to do all that salvation asks of me." There is power in these words. Let them inform your mind about itself. The strength in the words belongs to you. How would you ever recognize it if it wasn't already there?

Sit in peace and silent contemplation. Mind the breath and watch the thoughts that come and go. Repeat the lesson as often as necessary to anchor the mind, but try to reach a point of no thought, a point of spaciousness and peace. You will reach this point, and then thought will return. Go back to the breath and repeat the lesson again. This is all that is asked.

Be mindful today. Recognize that every single person you

encounter is a perfect extension of Perfection Itself. The world around contains this Perfection only because it was created by an extension of Perfection. The computer you look upon, the pen in your hand, the sounds you hear, the wind, the sun, it is all you, and you are it. The form is you. The space between the forms is you. You are not your body. You are free!

Lesson 192

My only purpose here is to learn forgiveness.

The next few lessons take Truth to a new level of learning. All of them rest on today's lesson, which teaches that forgiveness is your only purpose while you perceive yourself to be in a body. You did not give yourself your purpose but willingly accept the purpose Source has given you. Learn this lesson and you have fulfilled your function. Practice this lesson, and your peace will increase immeasurably. Money, fame, physical comfort – all of these are nothing compared to Peace.

Physical form cannot contain your entire consciousness. But in "life" here, it certainly seems to. The body is a form of energy. Forgiveness is energy as well, but it is alchemy of the highest order. Forgiveness uses formlessness to undo the fear of form. Only through forgiveness can the perception that you are only a body be lifted from your mind so the Light can enter.

Forgiveness asks you to give up nothing in order to receive Everything. But you will not see it until you learn benefits of forgiveness. The illusion of separation must be forgiven to perceive the Oneness it hides. You have learned the personal mind sees forgiveness as a form of loss. It is a form of loss only to a mind that believes it is only a separate body. Go beyond the body!

Forgiveness is a gentle correction for the personal mind. It stills the little voice that seems so loudly to proclaim its victimhood.

In self-defense the personal mind is convinced it has to forfeit something to that which it forgives. But ask yourself, how can Oneness give up anything? Forgive and you step into your own Oneness and see that you have forfeited nothing at all.

In the Reality of Oneness, forgiveness is not required. Heaven has no need for it. Can you imagine that? But what is unnecessary in Oneness is very necessary here, where we are convinced there is only this world of envy, attack, scarcity, lies, and debasement of self and others. In our perception that we are in this world, we must use lessons in terms this world can comprehend. And so Source teaches us forgiveness.

Practice today for at least fifteen minutes. Twenty would be better and thirty even more so. Enjoy the peace of contemplation. Take your seat. Relax and scan your body for areas of tension. The body is a tool of communication. Its discomfort is a message from the mind. Breathe in peace and exhale the tension. Ease the mind, ease the body, release the mind, and release the body.

When you are ready, say in your mind, "My purpose here is to learn forgiveness." Now relax into the breath and watch all thoughts that arise without becoming attached to any of them. You may receive thoughts about something or someone who needs your forgiveness. There is much in this world that asks to be forgiven, is there not? Allow whatever arises about the person, the situation, or the world to come up. Look at it. Accept your thoughts about it. Do not add to your confusion by blaming yourself for any of your thoughts.

Do ask yourself, "Can I know for certain that my view of this person or situation is true? Is it the only truth? Is it possible for me to hold my truth and their truth as well, and blame no one? Can I see it as temporary? Can I allow that it might be part of a greater purpose I cannot now understand?" Be curious about the situation.

If you can release your own guilty thoughts or actions, then you can also release theirs. When you release both, you are complete. You do not have to run down the street shouting, "I have forgiven!" Just sit with the gentle energy of letting go. Notice what it feels like. This is who you really are.

Forgiveness benefits you. Let go and give the other person up to Source. Source understands what their lesson is far better than you do. You are doing your job by giving space to the emotions of anger, resentment, insecurity, or whatever has come up in the meditation. Watch your breath and repeat the lesson slowly and purposefully in your mind. Allow yourself this time.

Hold no one prisoner today and free yourself. The one you cannot forgive is yourself. Please understand that Oneness is not just a concept. It is Reality. Forgiveness is the corrective lens, if you will, for True Seeing.

Lesson 193

All things are lessons in forgiveness that God would have me learn.

This is Great Metaphysics! Today you will learn about the nature of One Mind and how your mind works together with It. This is not unimportant information. It will show you why forgiveness is your function and the key to happiness in this world.

The words of this lesson are a primer for a truth so enormous it will challenge everything you think you think. All experiences are a lesson. Not some things. Not a few. All. Nothing, absolutely nothing, exists outside of God's Mind. You and I do not get to choose what is in God's Mind.

What then is the lesson God would have me learn about all things? Simply this: "Forgive all things and you will see them differently." You will see them differently because your mind will open to the knowledge it is only ourselves we are forgiving. Our reality will transform to the extent that we bring forth a new ideal of awareness of ourselves as the creative force in the world.

ACIM does nothing less than change reality by teaching we are its source. If we create reality the next question must be, what do we use to create with? There are two choices only: fear or love. When I choose to forgive whatever is in front of me, I begin to create with my divinity. When I choose to argue with what is in front of me, I cannot create at all – I can only resist what has been created already.

We are creating together all the time. We use a group consciousness joined at a higher level than our separated minds can perceive. I can create, as can you, by choosing to align with the creations of our Higher Self, the divine aspect of our seemingly separated selves that already knows our highest good. This is why all things are lessons God would have me learn! The lesson has already been created and we are totally safe in it no matter what it looks like from our limited, separate minds. You and I can only learn the lesson by going with it, forgiving it, and having the experience of it without attaching to it. Learn it Now and let it go. Move into the next experience and continue on. Hold onto nothing. Accept everything.

I can choose to learn now, or wait until later, to understand that what I bring forth is my own creation. But I must make the choice because it is Reality. The curriculum is set but I may take it any time.

Forgiveness doesn't mean I say, "It's okay to hurt that child." Forgiveness means I don't react out of fear. I take a second, just a second, to watch my own thoughts. The second I take is a gap that allows my awareness to inform my mind. And in that small, instantaneous gap, I am able to consider whether I wish to create my response out of fear or love. The choice is this fast.

If I choose fear, I will close off doors to opportunity. What opportunity? I do not know. I cannot know from my limited perspective. If I choose love, I will be shown what to do next. If I act from love, the opportunity will present itself in the moment and I get to choose again. It's all the same lesson and the answer is always the same: choose love.

The world that opens to me from a forgiving consciousness exceeds the limitations of my imagination. It cannot be explained – only experienced. As I learn to forgive, I begin to cultivate a new ideal that is only available to me through creation with loving awareness. I must do it to know it. I must practice in form to rise above form.

And so you practice today. Your lessons take on a new urgency now because you are ready. You are asked not only to sit daily in quiet contemplation, but also to remain increasingly conscious of your thoughts and feelings throughout the day.

Practice today in the usual way. Take your seat and get comfortable. Place your awareness gently on the breath. On the inhale, breathe light into your whole body. On the exhale, release any tension you hold. Take all the time you need for this. When you are fully relaxed and alert, say in your mind, "All things are lessons my Creator would have me learn."

Say the words slowly and purposefully: "All things. Are lessons. My Creator. Would have me learn." Feel the meaning behind these words. They have a vibratory quality that will be of great benefit if you go deeply into them. Spend the next fifteen minutes or so in quiet contemplation. Be at peace. Watch the breath and watch your thoughts. As they arise, notice them and give them away to the Holy Spirit who knows exactly what to do with them. Be at peace.

You may wish to contemplate one particular experience and explore what its lessons for you might have been. Touch the experience with your mind; find the lesson without attaching to any thought about it; then let it go. Do not hang on to the experience. Feel the emotions it brings up, watch them peak in your body, and leave like a wave on the ocean. Go back to the breath. Be grateful for awareness.

Throughout this day and the days to come, consciously begin to watch your thoughts. Are you resisting your moment or are you in flow with it? If you resist even the smallest thing, take notice. First forgive your own resistance, and then forgive the person, event, or thing. If it is helpful, say in your mind, "I will forgive, and see this differently." Or, "In forgiving, I will see this differently."

For every apprehension, every care, and every form of suffering, repeat these words. They hold the key that opens the door to other worlds of which you are now unaware. Do not deny yourself the little steps to reach this door. We are all taking them together and there is unseen help all along the way.

Lesson 194

I place the future in the Hands of God.

This morning my husband and I have a discussion. He thinks I stole the sheets last night, but I'm pretty sure I didn't and I have the proof. He doesn't care about my proof. His mind is made up. Come to think of it, so is mine. Whose mind can I change? Only mine. What can I change about my mind? I can open it – right now. When I open it now, I realize (yet again) that I can choose not to believe what I think I think.

I like this feeling that I don't have to believe my thoughts. Not believing my thoughts is conducive to my happiness. I don't have to believe anyone else's thoughts either. They're just thoughts. One thought can never represent the whole truth, so why close my mind and only allow the ones I think are "mine"?

A mind open now is a gentle mind because it's relaxed. Nothing has power over it now because it's not engaged in resistance to anything. It doesn't hold onto the past and it doesn't fear the future. It just looks easily at what is happening in front of it right now. An open mind doesn't carry the burden of time.

Today's idea, about placing the future in the hands of God, is really about having an open mind. When my mind is open I am in alignment with what is happening now. When my mind is open I allow the fullness of the present to reveal itself to me. And the present moment is the only moment there is. Worrying about the future or holding onto the past takes me out of alignment. It burdens me with concerns that may or may not have any relevance whatsoever to what is happening now.

We all need freedom from fear. This is not conjecture. Today we receive what we need by allowing our minds to rest in the hands of Source. Practice today by being conscious of every instant you can. Ask continuously, "What am I experiencing now? How do I feel now, in my body, in my mind?" If you notice a feeling that is not relaxed and open, look at it and ask, "Am I creating out of love or out of fear? If I am creating out of fear, I let it go to Source." It is highly likely that if you are creating out of fear, it is a fear of the future.

In this instant you do not feel depression, experience pain, or perceive loss. In this instant you do not set sorrow on a throne and worship it. In this instant you do not fear the future, carry the past, or even fear death itself. Each instant given to Source, with the next one already given, is the instant of your release.
– ACIM

Take this day and give each moment to Source. What each moment holds is really not your concern. Your purpose is only to experience the now with an open mind. Decide you will not judge the moment, or yourself having it.

Practice for fifteen minutes in quiet contemplation today. Take your seat and relax the body. Place gentle awareness on the breath. Breathe in peace and exhale tension. Relax. When you are ready, repeat the lesson and then place your awareness on the body. Discern the quality of its inner energy. Can you detect a vibration or frequency within your physical form? It might feel like an internal glass of champagne bubbles. This is your life force. It is present in you now. You cannot sense it from the past or anticipate its future state. It is only available in the present moment. Sit in meditation upon your inner energy state. Repeat the lesson in your mind and use the breath to anchor your awareness. Thoughts will arise. Notice how they affect the inner energy body. This is important information. It offers you another sense with which to experience your moment.

Place your future in the hands of God today. Be mindfully in the present and let the rest go. Give to yourself. All will be well in the end. If it is not well, it is not the end.

Lesson 195

Love is the way I walk in gratitude.

When you are grateful, you walk in the way of Love. When you are grateful you look upon the world as safe, pure, whole, and in right balance. How often are you grateful? Are you sure you even know what grateful means?

> *It is hard for you to learn gratitude when you look at this world and conclude it is real. The most you can do then is see yourself as better off than some others and try to be content because you perceive someone else suffering more. How pitiful and deprecating are those thoughts.*
> *– ACIM*

How many of you have driven by a panhandler and felt gratitude that it wasn't you standing on the corner? "At least I'm in my car, safe and warm," you might have thought. Or perhaps you've had a winter cold and said, "At least it's not that terrible disease my neighbor has."

My mother used to say, "There but for the grace of God go I."

Little did I know this was a misunderstanding of God's Grace. To be grateful that I am not the one suffering only emphasizes my separateness and makes me fearful, because what I have now, you may have tomorrow. And what I see as your lack today may be my lack tomorrow. This is not gratitude, this is fear. It isn't gratitude but it is an evocation of guilt. There can be no fear and no guilt at all in gratitude.

Gratitude in the way of Love transcends the idea that some can have while others suffer. Gratitude is known when it is recognized that all suffering – yours, mine, and everyone else's – is a form of temporary insanity. I am grateful when I can see your suffering and be one with you in it, because I don't fear it and I know you needn't fear it either. You've been there in that fear. You've seen it. Now you can help someone else work his way out. This is gratitude. Be grateful you are strong, and good, and wise, and that you know how to walk in the way of Love.

Suffering is of this world. It always has been and it always will be. And it is always a choice. If I choose to suffer, it's okay. It can be my turn today. But tomorrow it may be your turn. That is the way of this world. But nothing in this world can remove the Truth that Source is One and we are not separate from It, or each other. Gratitude in the way of Love rejoices that no exceptions to Wholeness can ever be made. I am grateful to know that I am eternal, One, and that forgiveness is my function.

Today's lesson asks you to love what Is, and find gratitude in it. You can do this much more easily if you don't take yourself too seriously. It's not that you should ignore suffering, but you should be grateful it isn't real – even as it appears to be. You walk in gratitude when you walk lightly. Love is the way you walk in gratitude because Love Is and there is nothing else.

This day, as you sit in your chair, as you walk down the street, take a moment to look around and try to extend your mind into everything you see – even the things that aren't pretty. Let the boundaries of each thing blur as your vision softens briefly. Let yourself enter the tree, the light, the clouds, the pavement, the flock of birds, the person on the street, be they young, old, rich or poor. Rest assured this is possible because all of them are part of you.

Wholeness is your safety and it is also an expression of your Love. Take as many opportunities to "see" in this way as you can today. Enjoy the differences in things, but remember they are only creative expressions of the One and they are all within your Self. The form Oneness takes is truly irrelevant. It may appear as suffering. It may appear as triumphant. All of it is within the Wholeness that we share.

Practice for fifteen minutes in meditation today. Use your contemplative time to consider that comparison is a form of refusal to recognize your own Oneness. Watch your thoughts. Watch your breath. Allow the Holy Spirit to guide your mind as it opens to the Truth of Gratitude. Feel no guilt about what you thought it was before. Feel no shame or sadness that you didn't understand gratitude in the past. Be grateful it is now, and now you know.

Lesson 196

It can be but myself I crucify.

Have you ever noticed that when you throw away empty bottles of hand lotion there is always about an inch left in the bottom? You just can't get to it, and seems like a waste to throw out. The other day my daughter was cleaning her room. She came down with several different bottles of hand cream. Thinking I'd be a thrifty and environmentally conscious citizen, I scooped the contents into one little jar and put it by the kitchen sink. I inwardly congratulated myself for doing this.

When I came down the next morning the container was gone. My husband had made us dinner the night before and he'd thrown it out. Bummer! What right did he have to throw out my hand cream? In a flash I felt the steam rising. I considered that it would be perfectly justifiable to march right upstairs and demand he acknowledge what he'd done. Then he would apologize.

But I was generous. To myself. I decided to give myself a moment to consider that if the hand cream was supposed to be there, it would be. If it wasn't there, it wasn't supposed to be. That's really all there was to it. If I wanted to, I could go into all kinds of victimization scenarios. But one thing I couldn't do was argue with reality. The cream was gone. So I let it go and felt a weight lift from my chest. I'd chosen not to attack myself. The cream did not disappear just to ruin my day, so why should I let it?

I only crucify myself. The word crucify seems harsh doesn't it? But that is just what we do. We give ourselves little paper cuts of guilt, fear, anger and resentment all day long. The real crucifixion is inner, not outer. It is the feeling of fear and guilt that comes with lack of understanding that we are not guilty and have nothing to fear. We crucify ourselves every time we choose to attack the situation or the person Source has sent our way.

When you fully understand this statement and keep it fully in your awareness, you will no longer attempt to harm yourself, nor make the body a slave to vengeance. You will not attack yourself and you will realize that to attack another that you perceive is to attack yourself.
– ACIM

It is only yourself you give to, and only yourself you take from. No matter where you perceive the attack has occurred, it can only originate in the mind that has accepted the lie it can be vulnerable at all. It is you who crucify yourself. This is hell: belief that separation has occurred, that the other is your enemy (including Source Itself), that they are coming back to harm you, and that they can.

You have not hurt this world, nor can this world hurt you. When you realize, once and for all, that it is fear of yourself you fear – that you have directed your fear outward, and now believe attack is coming back for you – it will be a moment of extraordinary release. Thought does not leave the mind of the thinker. But, if you can only crucify yourself, then this is also true: You can redeem your mind as well.

Practice today for twenty minutes. Sit in contemplation of the ideas in this lesson. Take your seat and get comfortable. Place your attention gently on the breath. Allow the natural rhythm of the breath to deepen your relaxation. When you are ready, say slowly and purposefully in your mind, "It can be but myself I crucify." What do the words make you feel like? Notice without any judgment. Perhaps you don't believe them yet. This is an idea that requires some integration. But if you wish to stand in sovereignty, you must take back your power. Fear makes you powerless. Attack thoughts are fearful thoughts. If you can at least consider whether you want to abate fearful thoughts of attack and retaliation, you will begin the shift in perception. Ask for help if you need it. Spend the remainder of the contemplation watching the breath and allowing thoughts to come and go. Be mindful of your thoughts. Once you understand that fear is never caused by anything outside your mind, your awareness of the Love of God will deepen. This is what you want. It is what you have been waiting for.

Lesson 197

It can be but my gratitude I earn.

It can only be myself I crucify so it can only be my own gratitude I earn. This is the Law of Love, which is also known as the Law of One. It is the Ground Reality in which we all seemingly exist as separate beings.

So what do we do with all this Oneness while we are in seemingly separate bodies? ACIM tells us we have to practice living in Oneness to understand it. It is through the experience of being Oneness we begin to know it. Oneness is a being thing, not an intellectual thing.

Yesterday's lesson, "It can be but myself I crucify," is a practice of Oneness: I cannot hurt you without hurting myself. It is an illusion to think otherwise. Today's lesson follows the same Oneness logic.

When I give, I give to myself, or more accurately, to my Self. My Self is the same consciousness as your Self. Our little selves do not see this Oneness, but that doesn't make it untrue. Can you imagine yourself as a part of One Self? Perhaps this seems intellectually doable. But to practice in "real life" – that's another thing!

The practice of Oneness takes practice. For example, when I give, I almost always look for a payback. I give to you and then stand back, waiting to see how you receive it. Are you grateful? If not, I want to take my gift back. In fact, I may crucify myself for giving it in the first place. Rarely, if ever, is giving in the world a free lunch.

We make attempts at kindness and forgiveness but unless they are received as we think they should be, we turn those same gifts into an attack. Furthermore, and most important, we accuse Source of the same thing. We believe Source's wrath is real, that Its gifts are loans at best and deceptions at worst. Unless we do as Source says, we will be punished because Its gifts of love are conditioned upon our good behavior. Does this sound familiar? Free yourself of this idea! Source measures nothing and gives only without condition.

Source is Love forever without any condition whatsoever. Only we give and then ask for what we've given to be returned if it is not received correctly. This thinking arises in a mind that believes everything can be taken from it, when the opposite is true. The practice of Oneness requires me to understand that all giving is to myself and all taking is from myself as well. True giving has no fear or condition attached to it.

Today you are asked to look at the form your giving takes. You are asked to trust that all the gifts you give are honored simply in their giving. The logic of Oneness tells you that even if you don't see it, your gift is received. It doesn't matter if your gift seems lost and ineffectual. Source gives all to all and has no sense of loss at all.

Today you practice knowing that all gifts are universally accepted and thankfully acknowledged by your One Self, in the heart of God. No gift is ever lost or left unopened. If you find joy simply in the giving, you are giving with real Love.

Today, be mindful of the gifts you exchange. Are they conditional? Can you receive as you give? Do you feel guilty about receiving? This is not unimportant for if you cannot receive freely, you cannot give freely either. This is the law of Oneness in practice.

On the hour, or the half-hour, remind yourself of today's lesson. This will be your practice today. Be mindful of how you perceive every exchange, knowing just as only you can crucify yourself, so also it can only be your gratitude you earn.

Give yourself fifteen minutes for quiet contemplation of today's lesson. Take your seat and close your eyes. Watch the breath and relax the body. On the out-breath, relax more deeply. When you are ready, say in your mind, "It can be but my gratitude I earn." Say the words slowly and purposefully. Allow the meaning of each word to sink in. Feel the vibration of this lesson in your mind and your body. Then watch your breath and allow thoughts and feelings to arise. If your mind wanders, go back to the lesson and the breath. Receive your own gratitude for giving your mind the space to contemplate this lesson.

Lesson 198

Only my condemnation injures me.

Between the two of us there is only one who is real. Only one. We are both real only in our Oneness. The recognition of our Oneness is the beginning of True Perception. It is also the end of the ignorance that causes so much pain. In our unity, we are limitless. The lessons this week have consisted of a series of attempts to get you to see your Oneness. Today's lesson is no different.

Injury always begins as a thought. In fact, the first thought that began this world was the first injury we made upon our Self. And in reality – this is the only injury there is. The original injury takes countless forms but beneath each seemingly separate injury lies one thought: the belief there is a you and a me that cannot join; the belief that I can do unto you what I would not want done to me; and that I can get away with it without repercussion to myself.

The first and only injury in the entire universe is the thought of separation. This thought is wrought with so much fear and guilt that the split mind separated itself over and over again trying to distance itself from its original thought. It looks like there is a you and a me. So, now I can project my guilty thoughts onto you and make you the bad gal, or the bad guy. I'm okay, but you need improvement, which is really saying, "I'm okay because you need improvement."

I know it seems complicated. But actually, it's pretty simple, and so is the solution: see no one as not your Self. Or, more simply, recognize your Self in each and every thing. You can begin today by recognizing that every single judgment you make about another being is really directed at yourself. Condemn and you limit yourself.

Judgment is the ego's fuel. Stop feeding it, and peace will be the result. Cease judging the moment as good or bad. Cease judging yourself as good or bad. Cease judging one political party as good or bad. Cease judging money as good or bad. Cease judging one body, one gender, one race, one nation as better than another. Cease calling one stupid and the other enlightened. Do you see how many forms judgment can take? We actually believe we cannot survive in this world without making judgments.

This world of judgment makes you powerless. Awareness, and forgiveness of that which awareness brings to light, restores power. Awareness can be painful, especially at first, which is a disincentive only to those who believe they are powerless.

Watch your thoughts. Injury begins with thought and so does condemnation. Watch your judgments and use each one as a tool of forgiveness. In this way, judgment can actually become your teacher. But it takes a willingness to be present with the contents of your own mind. Your forgiveness ends all illusions. In this world it is the only thing that points to Truth.

Practice today by watching your thoughts. There is no form of suffering that does not begin with an unforgiving thought. And there is no form of pain that cannot be healed with forgiveness. Be kind to yourself today and be kind to those who share this day with you, in whatever form they appear to you. They are all you and you are them, and we are all One Mind experiencing Itself in a billion seemingly different experiences.

Keep this lesson in your mind today. Let the thought of this lesson replace all thoughts of judgment. If you feel any bodily or mental discomfort, know there is a judgment lurking beneath. Remember, there is only one injury but it takes many forms. See how many forms you can discern and free yourself from today.

Give yourself at least fifteen minutes in quiet contemplation today. Take your seat and get comfortable. Close your eyes and gently place awareness on the breath. Allow the breath to rise and fall naturally. On the out-breath, let your body relax more deeply. Let all of your daily concerns fall away on the out-breath until your mind is quiet. In the space of quietness, say to yourself, "Only my condemnation injures me. Only my forgiveness sets me free." Your forgiveness undoes all illusion. In these words your mind is joined in Oneness.

Now sit in silence. Be mindful of the breath. It may be helpful to still the mind by repeating the lesson slowly, and purposefully. Feel the words. They have a vibration that will lift your thoughts toward healing. Always remember to ask for help. There is a Mind waiting just beyond your awareness that will respond instantly. You may be sent images of past injuries or future concerns. These images are teaching moments. They offer the opportunity to let go of guilt and fear. Let them go and go back to the breath. Each time you choose forgiveness, it is a step closer to Truth.

Be kind to yourself today. It will be tempting to condemn yourself or others masquerading as someone separate from your Self. If you find yourself condemning, go inside and feel the effects of the thought. Does it make you feel more free, or less? Be kind to all your selves today. See their Innocence and know your own.

Lesson 199

I am not a body. I am free.

It is essential for your progress in this course that you accept today's idea, and hold it very dear. Be not concerned that to the ego it is quite insane.
– ACIM

Learn this lesson and know one of the most cherished truths about yourself. Believe this lesson and align your mind with the limitless. Know this about yourself and fear will be recognized as the veil of illusion it is.

You cannot feel free and unlimited as long as you perceive the body to be yourself. The body is a limit to you. It was created to limit you. The entire purpose and function of the body is to make you suffer the pain of its slow demise until its eventual death.

The body is not who, or what, you are. It is a confinement. It offers fun and pleasure on good days. But it cannot ever contain you. The wind of your spirit is too big to fit in any physical jar.

Stub your toe and the personal mind tells you, you are hurt. Receive a diagnosis of cancer and the medical system tells you, you have cancer. Skip a meal and the personal mind screams, "I am hungry!" You are none of these things. The body is the personal mind in material form, but you are a frequency in vibration and the frequency is Love.

Source does not reside in a body, nor do you, as Its Extension. The body is nothing more than a temporary expression of separation, vulnerability, and fear in low frequency form. Return your mind to God's Mind and the body is seen for what it is, or isn't. But we are far from this idea today. Today, you are asked only to free your mind of the thought that you are a body only.

So forgive your body. Allow it to be as it is. Treat it gently and compassionately. It is not what you are, but resistance to it only affirms the illusion. Thank the body but do not worship it. Knowing it is not your Self takes the burden off of it. Fear not what the body experiences.

There will come a time when we will end the dream of being in a body. We will gently step out of it, leaving it to evaporate in the mist of which all dreams are made. Until then, today's lesson is the Voice of your Self, urging you to slowly waken from the dream. Do begin your awakening today.

On the hour, or better, on the half-hour, stop whatever you are doing. There is no need to make a show of it or jump out of your chair proclaiming, "I am free!" Just look around the room and say in your mind, "I am not a body. I am free." Allow yourself to feel the truth of these words. If you do just this every half hour, you will learn the lesson well. Indeed, your entire body will appreciate it!

Give yourself another fifteen minutes in quiet meditation to absorb this important lesson. Take your seat and close your eyes. Let the shoulders relax and soften the belly. Place gentle awareness on the breath. When you are ready, say in your mind, "I am not a body. I am free." Feel these words! Know them as your truth.

As you sit, mindful of the breath, thoughts will arise. Allow them to come and go. Repeat the lesson slowly until only the breath remains in your mind. Breathe the light in, for that is what you are. Breathe the light out, sharing it with all other light around you. If you stay with the breath and feel the light, your body will begin to seem weightless, which is its natural state. For you are light, and so am I. You knowing your light increases the light in the room for all of us.

The mind can only be made free when it no longer sees itself as contained in a body, firmly tied to it, and dependent upon it for its existence. If this were true, you would be vulnerable indeed. Be grateful your mind is free to know its freedom from limitation.

Lesson 200

There is no peace except the peace of God.

When I tell myself I know what should or should not happen, it's a sign I'm confused. I'm pleased when things seem to go well for me, but not so much when they don't. My confusion lies in the belief that there is anything that isn't always in my favor.

When I look to the things of this world to make me happy I may or may not find what I want. I often succeed, but I also often fail. It took me years to understand this simple lesson: it's not the purpose of this world to make me happy.

This doesn't mean I shouldn't enjoy myself, my friends, or

the natural world. I love that I love my friends. I totally enjoy the smell of clean clothes. The sight of a night field alit with fireflies fills me with delight. I can get very upset at the stupidity of greed and war. But I have to step back with both the good and the bad and remind myself I'm making it all up. It's all happening in my own mind. Literally.

"The world you perceive is not where you belong; you are a stranger here. But you have been given the means to no longer perceive the world as limitation."

This "reality" is not our home; it is a sojourn, or a soul journey. We're just playing in the sandbox of physicality. Our real home is not a physical place. Our true nature is not physical at all. This is why yesterday's lesson was a reminder that we are not our bodies. We are free.

In the world where you once limited yourself you can find your Freedom, but you must change your mind about the purpose of the world to escape from it.
– ACIM

This is today's lesson: "There is no peace except the peace of Source." The peace of the Creator is unchanging, unwavering, and always present. The bridge from this world to the peace of the Creator is forgiveness.

We spend lifetimes seeking peace. We find it for a moment and then lose it again. Find it – be happy. Lose it – be sad, mad, depressed. We grow so used to its quicksilver nature that we grow to believe peace never lasts. Yet, like a hamster on a treadmill, we keep looking in the same place for the same thing. This is the definition of insanity.

The Peace of Source comes not from this world but from a place that is beyond this world, a place that contains all worlds and all things beyond all worlds. Yet it is immanently reachable. It is a place we contain within our own minds. It is that close.

This lesson should be practiced for at least fifteen minutes, in silent contemplation. Take your seat and get comfortable. Let your shoulders relax. Relax the tummy. Place gentle awareness on the breath. If you can, imagine breathing in and out through the heart area. As the chest expands, breathe in peace. On the exhale, breathe out peace. When you are ready, say in your mind, "There is no peace except the peace of Source."

Feel the words of this lesson. Allow their vibration to infuse your mind and body. These words alter the space within and without your physical container. They ensure all safety in this world because they assure your existence beyond it. Sit in silence, watching the breath. Allow thoughts and feelings to arise. If fear arises, let it come up and watch it. Feel it peak and then ebb. Stay with the breath and repeat the lesson in your mind. Fear is just another form of confusion – it isn't real. Fear is always bodily based. But we are not our bodies. We are spirit. We are free.

You did not make yourself. As you free one part of your mind, you accept the other part as it is.
– ACIM

Practice mindfulness. Repeat the lesson often as you go about the day. Wear it like a piece of jewelry or your favorite belt. Wrap yourself in the peace of God today.

Review VI

Lesson 201

Today begins another review period. There will be one lesson each day, to be practiced as often as possible, on the half-hour or hour at least. In addition, gift yourself with fifteen minutes of quiet contemplation in the morning and evening. It might be helpful to see these review periods as a hidden retreat. You go about your daily business in the world, but within your mind you carry a place of peace that gives shelter from the noise.

Each of the ten review lessons contains the whole lesson plan of this course. One idea, applied consistently, would be enough to awaken you from the dream. Taken as a whole these review lessons are a harmony of thought. Practice with each one. Apply it to everything you seem to experience. There is one more point: permit no idle thought to go uncorrected. When you notice a judgment, a fear, a sense of loss no matter how small, an irritation, a resistance, or sadness, gently forgive it and replace the thought with the idea in the daily lesson. Use your body to help you recognize what your mind is doing unconsciously. Notice any tightness in the belly or shoulders. Watch your breath and use it to center your mind.

As with the other reviews there is a central theme that encapsulates the ideas of each lesson. Begin and end each day with this central theme, or core idea. The central theme for this review is:

I am not a body. I am free. For I am still as God created me.

Are you a body or a spirit? This is a central question of ACIM. The answer will affect the direction of the rest of your life. ACIM asks, "Do you want freedom of the body or the mind? For you cannot have both. Which do you value? Which is your goal?" If the body's freedom is your goal, you will use your mind to gain it. But why dedicate your mind to free something that isn't what you are in truth? Respect your body, but place your mind in service to seeing past illusion.

Today's review lesson is:

I am not a body. I am free. For I am still as God created me.

Everything I see is One with me.

I am not a body. I am free. For I am still as God created me.

Imagine being free from the body. No feeding it. No keeping it clean. No need of housing. No need to buy clothing. No judgments about how I look or how anyone else looks. No fitness regime. No health insurance. No limits on movement. No worries about illness or pain. And how very easy it would be to trust, because behind all mistrust of each other lies the fear of bodily harm.

Do you see how the belief in being a body erodes our freedom and trust in one another? We are not asked here to ignore the body, but we are asked to see the impact of the belief system that we've built around it.

The belief system of the body can be summed up in one word: Fear. Fear of discomfort. Fear of pain. Fear of death. Fear of having my body controlled by yours. This is the world we choose when we choose freedom of the body over freedom of the mind. Free your mind and the body will follow. Free your mind and you will perceive the Oneness of All That Is.

Begin your meditations today by taking your seat and relaxing the body. Place gentle awareness on the breath and close your eyes. When you are ready, repeat in your mind: "I am not a body. I am free. For I am still as God created me. I trust in the Oneness that I perceive."

Now simply forget the lesson and let your mind go. Let no thought arise that is not calmly observed and given up to Source. Keep your awareness on the breath as an anchor.

There is a paradox at work here. As you gently watch thoughts and emotions, letting them arise and letting them go, there will be spaces in between where there is no thought. Notice this space. It is the natural state of mind, this state of no thought. If you don't reach the space of no thought, that's okay too. Just watch the breath and slowly, purposefully, repeat the words of the lesson. Whatever you experience is perfect for you. Trust what you get.

Be mindful today. On the hour, sing the song of the lesson in your mind. These lessons change the frequency of your thought, and it is thought that creates the world. Even if you cannot hear it now, others are singing with you. A chorus has begun.

Lesson 202

I am not a body. I am free. For I am still as God created me.

I will be still an instant and go home.

I am not a body. I am free. For I am still as God created me.

You are frightened at the very core of what you are. And the moment you realize that you are frightened at what you are at your very core, the field will release. What, at the very core, is it we are frightened of? The answer is simple. You are God in form.
– Paul Selig

Lesson 203

I am not a body. I am free. For I am still as God created me.

I call upon God's Name and on my own.

I am not a body. I am free. For I am still as God created me.

Lesson 204

I am not a body. I am free. For I am still as Source created me.

The Name of Source is my inheritance.

I am not a body. I am free. For I am still as Source created me.

Lesson 205

I am not a body. I am free. For I am still as Source created me.

I want the Peace of God.

I am not a body. I am free. For I am still as Source created me.

You cannot know Source unless you are guiltless, and the Will of Source IS that you know It, so you MUST be guiltless. Your only calling, in your perception that you are in a world, is to devote yourself with active willingness to the denial of guilt in all its forms. Deny Innocence anywhere in your mind where you a perceive a world, and you deny It in yourself.
– E. Cronkhite, The Message of A Course in Miracles.

Lesson 206

I am not a body. I am free. For I am still as Source created me.

Salvation of the world depends on me.

I am not a body. I am free. For I am still as Source created me.

If you do nothing else today, greet each person you meet in silent knowing that you are greeting a part of God. Bear witness to the divinity of everyone who crosses your path – the woman on the corner, the child on the bike, the man in the car ahead of you. Your knowing has a frequency that will extend outward and affect theirs. It will elevate them, even if they are not conscious of it. This is the beginning of the new world. It is now. It is you.

Lesson 207

I am not a body. I am free. For I am still as Source created me.

I bless the world because I bless myself.

I am not a body. I am free. For I am still as Source created me.

Imagine you are gathering at a bus station with thousands of other people. As you look around, you see many faces you cannot recall having known and yet you recognize them all, if not by name. It seems everyone has been called to take this trip and everyone gets on the bus. Once everyone has boarded, the bus leaves the station and quickly picks up speed. At some point the bus begins to move so fast the landscape blurs as one thing merges into another.

As the bus approaches the speed of light, a new level of perception arises. You realize that you are part of a whole connected landscape. Suddenly it dawns on you that you could never have made this journey alone. You understand that in order to reach light speed, the bus needed the energy of every single person on board.

You and I are at the bus station right now. The ticket to board the bus requires each of us to bless ourselves and bless each other. No one gets on the bus without the blessing because it is the blessing itself that fuels the bus.

You have a special part to play in the plan of Atonement, and the message of your part is always: I am part of God and I am guiltless. You will teach and learn this in a way that is uniquely meaningful to you. But until you teach and learn this, you will suffer the pain of a dim awareness that you are not fulfilling your True Function.
– ACIM

Lesson 208

I am not a body. I am free. For I am still as Source created me.

The peace of God is shining in me now.

I am not a body. I am free. For I am still as Source created me.

Today, leave all decisions to the Holy Spirit, the Universal Communicator, the Mediator for Source. It is within you and It offers quiet guidance in peace. Ask and know you are answered. Listen with your quiet mind and open heart. Do not worry.

Lesson 209

I am not a body. I am free. For I am still as Source created me.

I feel the Love of God within me now.

I am not a body. I am free. For I am still as Source created me.

Allow the Presence of Source today, for this is the connection of manifestation. Your connection, combined with my connection, begins a chain reaction within the entire human energy field. We are part of a great change. Your willingness affects everyone around you. Are you willing to stay connected in conversation with Source? Its call to you is your call to It.

Lesson 210

I am not a body. I am free. For I am still as Source created me.

I choose the joy of God instead of pain.

I am not a body. I am free. For I am still as Source created me.

Laugh, and the world laughs with you. Weep, and you weep alone.
– Ella Wheeler Wilcox

Lesson 211

I am not a body. I am free. For I am still as Source created me.

I am an Extension of Source Itself.

I am not a body. I am free. For I am still as Source created me.

Lesson 212

I am not a body. I am free. For I am still as Source created me.

I have a function Source would have me fill.

I am not a body. I am free. For I am still as Source created me.

We find out who we are through the progressive discovery of what we are not. Once we have completely uncovered what we are not, the diamond of what we are shines.
– F. Lucille, *The Perfume of Silence*

To discover what we truly are, to see the diamond within, requires forgiveness. If I don't release through forgiveness, I hold onto something that blinds me to what I am. This is why it is our function in this world to forgive.

Here is the metaphysical equation: forgiveness = guiltlessness = invulnerability. And conversely, invulnerability = forgiveness = guiltlessness. It's a looped system. You can start anywhere on the line. When we are both equal in the knowledge of our invulnerability, we will also be equal in our guiltlessness, and the need for forgiveness will no longer exist. The diamond is revealed in all of its splendor.

Lesson 213

I am not a body. I am free. For I am still as Source created me.

All things are lessons God would have me learn.

I am not a body. I am free. For I am still as Source created me.

All things. Not some things. This single lesson learned well is a complete release from past regret and fear of the future. Learn this lesson and flow through all experiences in the knowing that that is all they are: experiences.

Lesson 214

I am not a body. I am free. For I am still as Source created me.

I place the future in the Hands of God.

I am not a body. I am free. For I am still as Source created me.

Only Source has a Mind that sees the purpose of every moment, every event, and every interaction. Only Source knows the flow of patterns through time and space within which you seem to exist in each moment. Only Source has the ability to create the lesson plan from which you are guided gently Home. Free yourself from planning because what God plans can only be Good. Your plans? Not so much.

Lesson 215

I am not a body. I am free. For I am still as Source created me.

Love is the way I walk in gratitude.

I am not a body. I am free. For I am still as Source created me.

In a word, the Kingdom of God is freedom. The Kingdom of God is freedom in a sense so free, so unbound, and so unencumbered that those of you walking this earth cannot fully comprehend it.
– Brent Haskell, *Journey Beyond Words*

Lesson 216

I am not a body. I am free. For I am still as Source created me.

It can be but myself I crucify.

I am not a body. I am free. For I am still as Source created me.

When I decline the role of victimhood, I step into alignment with my Self and my Creator, and whatever happens as a result will also be in alignment. Looking back from a place of alignment, I see that what at first seemed to be a trial was actually a gift to myself.

Only I can ignore my invulnerability by choosing victimhood. When I choose victimhood for myself, I will also choose it for others, for when I feel attacked, I will attack in return. And thus the endless cycle of crucifixion begins.

Forgiveness is the active acknowledgement of my invulnerable state. It is the place of knowing I am a co-creator of my circumstance. Forgiveness is a willingness to keep my eyes open even as things around me appear to dissolve into chaos.

Forgiveness is a willingness to step back, observe the chaos, and not react in fear.

Today, practice being in alignment. Do this simply by being aware of how you are choosing. What is the feeling source of the decision? Notice if it is fear or irritation. Notice if you are forgiving, and then choosing again, from a place of invulnerable certainty. No choice is too small to notice.

Lesson 217

I am not a body. I am free. For I am still as Source created me.

It can be but my gratitude I earn.

I am not a body. I am free. For I am still as Source created me.

The greatest gift is one I give myself. It is the realization that I am ultimately responsible for my own happiness. There is such freedom and power in this knowledge! It means in every circumstance I get to choose. Do I react out of fear, or do I allow things to unfold? Do I condemn myself with judgment or do I leave a door open through forgiveness? It is a game changer to claim this gift. It unlocks latent powers and makes us vehicles for grace.

I am the Holy Extension of God. Nothing can happen to me that is not of my own choice. And I can know the gratitude that comes from understanding I am free to choose.

Lesson 218

I am not a body. I am free. For I am still as Source created me.

My condemnation injures only me.

I am not a body. I am free. For I am still as Source created me.

Lesson 219

I am not a body. I am free. For I am still as Source created me.

I am not a body. I am free.

I am not a body. I am free. For I am still as Source created me.

In order to feel that we are not the body-mind, we have to investigate the true nature of the body, and this is done by welcoming bodily sensations. It is not enough to assume that the body is an object, or merely think it. All feelings, all bodily sensations are completely allowed in this contemplation. Allowing them to be as they are, without interference, reveals the space in which they appear and, as a result, we no longer stick to them... We are the changeless background. As long as we think we are one of them, they will take us with them wherever they go.
– Francis Lucille, *The Perfume of Silence*

Lesson 220

I am not a body. I am free. For I am still as Source created me.

There is no peace except the Peace of God.

I am not a body. I am free. For I am still as Source created me.

Part II

Focus Question 1: *What is Forgiveness?*

Lesson 221

Today begins a new series of lessons and a new way of practicing. The first six months of lessons are highly structured. Your personal mind needed to be uncovered and redirected from its habitual thought patterns. What you seek now is direct experience of Truth. You mind has been opened to receive It. Words now are guides. It is what arises between the words that will deepen your learning. Trust in what comes to you in silence. Learn to listen throughout the day.

As you go forward now, make it a habit to pause regularly (on the hour if you can) and become aware of the contents of your mind. If your personal mind is directing the show (and it probably will be), ask for help from Source. Make communication with Source habitual. You cannot ask enough, and it is not weakness but strength that seeks connection.

The daily practice shifts now from contemplation to open awareness. You can read more about open awareness meditation in the chapter on meditation. There will be a central question around which ten lessons are framed. For this series of lessons the central question is: What is Forgiveness?

To practice, read the lesson in the morning and end your day with it. There is no specific duration to your practice but I urge you to give at least one half hour each day to sit in silence. This is the thing: if you develop a practice when things are calm, you will be prepared when the inevitable challenges arrive. As the Buddha said, you have to build your boat before the rains arrive. You are wearing a path through the uncharted territory of your heart/mind. Get to know your way around.

Be assured as you sit in silence that what you sense, what you feel, what you know, is real. There will be some days when your mind is like a wild horse you must tame and ride. Other days, when you least expect it, your meditation will be effortlessly deep and insightful. A good rule is to expect nothing but be open to anything. Allow and allow and allow. Connect with the Holy Spirit. Ask for guidance and watch with loving kindness all the things your mind gives up to you.

Your next ten lessons focus on the question, "What is forgiveness?" Here are some pointers:

Forgiveness recognizes that what the "other" did to you has occurred only in illusion. Illusions are merely creations, they themselves cannot create. Seek not to make the illusion of sin real by thinking it needs forgiveness at all! Forgiveness sees the falsity of projection and lets it go. What replaces the illusion of attack will be the Will of God grounded by your own invulnerability.

Behind every unforgiving thought is unquestioned judgment. The thought, hidden by unconscious judgment, is then directed outward, tightening its chains by hiding and obscuring its source. Thus a vicious cycle of attack and counter-attack begins in the personal mind. What can come between a fixed projection of the personal mind and its chosen goal of separation from the "other," and from Source Itself?

To ensure its goal of separation, the unforgiving thought seeks frantically to survive deeper questions, or contradiction. It twists and turns to avoid anything it perceives as interference with its chosen path of projection. It distorts, lies, and attacks all who doubt its point of view.

Forgiveness is still and quiet. It allows. It waits before speaking. The one who cannot forgive must judge, for he or she must justify the failure to forgive. (I hit her because she hit me first.) To learn forgiveness Truth must be welcomed exactly as it is. You cannot attack Reality. It is. But you can perceive without judgment.

Allow all things. Forgive all things. Even your lack of

forgiveness. Do nothing and let the moment show you what it truly contains. Wait and ask Source, the Holy Spirit, your Guide, to show you how to forgive. Persist in the awakened consciousness with which Source created you, and is your own inheritance. It is your light and strength. Forgiveness is your function, given you by Creator. Remember this and your Innocence, also assured by the One Who made you Whole, Safe, Invulnerable always.

To recap: Each morning read and contemplate the core question and its answer that forms the foundation for the following ten lessons. Then read the particular lesson for the day. Then take your seat and spend at least fifteen minutes in quiet meditation. You know how to do this by now. Sit and place awareness on the breath. Breathe in peace and exhale any tension in the body. Take as long as you want to do this. Then repeat the lesson for the day in your mind, invite the Holy Spirit's assistance, and let everything go. Allow the breath to anchor your mind. Watch thoughts and feelings as they arise. Trust. Expect nothing and allow everything. Play. Be courageous. Explore total nonresistance. Forgive and know your Innocence.

Be mindful throughout the day. Practice forgiveness. Allow direct experience through conscious awareness. On the hour, remember the lesson. Use it throughout your day.

In the evening, read the lesson only. Let it guide you into sleep where it will inform the other world of dreams until you waken to this one.

Today's lesson is:

Peace to my mind. Let all my thoughts be still.

Let this lesson be an introduction to your contemplation. Let it be the send-off for your inner voyage. Leave the world with it and let its frequency inform your mind. Sit in silence, watch the breath, and allow. Go as deep as you can into inner space, guided by Source. Forgive everything that needs forgiving, for in forgiveness lies the key. The key to what? The key to the only door that takes you deeper and deeper into Peace. Ask for help if you need it.

On the hour, take a moment of silence for yourself. Let peace come to your mind. Let all your thoughts be still.

Go gently today. There is nothing you can ever do that will make you unworthy. This is true for you and everyone around you. No exceptions.

Lesson 222

Source is with me. I live and move in It Always and Everywhere.

Heaven is not a physical place, but a state of mind. The Kingdom does not exist "out there" somewhere, far away. Its presence is effortless; reached by going within. When I sit in silence I am sending an invitation to the Kingdom to come into my awareness. Or, perhaps more accurately, I am adjusting my own internal frequency to the vibration of the Kingdom.

We usually think of vibration or frequency as a measure of light or sound. But thoughts and emotions have frequencies of their own; we just haven't figured out how to measure them yet. Love is usually associated with the highest frequency, which makes sense. When something vibrates at a high enough rate, it begins to lose the appearance of vibration at all. It becomes one, which is what many people believe Love is.

The lesson for today has a frequency – as do all the lessons of ACIM. As you read the lesson for today take time to feel the words. Notice their resonance within your mind and body. "My Source is with me. I live and move in It. It lives and moves in me." How does it feel to say this? Or, how does it feel to feel this?

Take time to look around today and see beyond three-dimensional limits of the body's eyes. Look for the light vibrating in everything. It is there. Practice looking on your lunch hour, in a meeting, or waiting in traffic. Extend your feeling sense and use the words of the lesson: "Source is with us all. We live and move in Source. It lives and moves in us." Try to notice any sensation you experience when you say the words of this lesson. If it feels good, it is a reminder that goodness is your natural state. Do take this in.

Lesson 223

God is my only life. I have no life but God's.

If you were not a Thought in Mind of God, you would not be here. It's as simple as this.

> *You are not the Word as much as you are an aspect of the Word, and the energy of the Word moves through you. So, you are an amplifier, and you are a transistor, and a receiver of the Creator.*
> – Paul Selig, *I Am The Word*

There literally is no life but that of the Prime Creator. Yes, we are unique. Yes, we are our own, but we are always, at the same time, part of the greater Whole. We never think or move apart from the Whole, which contains us. Nothing can stand in isolation from Mind of God.

Today, remember on the hour that you are part of a greater Whole. Turn your mind to the great Mind that is yours when you decide to claim it. It waits for your acknowledgement. Every loving thought you have is a claim on your true identity. Every thought of forgiveness, and every thought of peace joins you with Source Mind.

Lesson 224

God is my Source and God Loves me.

The Source of life – the Source of all things is Love. The Source of the plant kingdom, the animal kingdom, the water kingdom, the kingdom of stones, the kingdom of the wind, the sun and the earth, all the stars, the kingdom of dark energies, the kingdom of the fairies, the two-legged, and the four-legged, the winged ones, kingdom of the angelics and the ascended masters, the kingdom of the atoms, the quarks, and neutrinos, the kingdom of matter and anti-matter, all of these are Source Love.

My true Identity is so secure, so lofty, sinless, glorious and great, wholly beneficent and free from guilt, that Heaven looks to It to give it light. It lights the world as well. It is the gift of Source to me; the one as well I give the world. This is the truth. This is reality and only this. Our true identity is the only gift that can be given or received.
– ACIM

On the hour today claim your identity. Claim it over and over again. Can you believe you are loved to this degree? Can you let guilt go and trust in your own divinity? There is no punishment for claiming it, only freedom. The biggest lie of this world is that we are not the light. That lie must end now, today.

As you sit in silent contemplation today, repeat the lesson in your mind. Be happy as you pause a while from the world. Prosper in your awareness of being loved. Accept the peace of Source. You are not a body. You are free. You are as God created you. Swim in the crystal clear, warm waters of divine Love.

Lesson 225

God is my Source and I Love God.

Yesterday's lesson was "God is my Source and God Loves me." What did you think of this lesson? The rational mind does not understand or believe it. The thinking heart does understand it and finds peace in it.

It is through effortless knowing that our relationship with Source is understood. Aside from not thinking, there is absolutely nothing that needs to be done to know Source. It is there and has always been there. It is not earned and it needs no maintenance to be sustained. The thinking mind, the rational mind, will tell you this cannot be. Our experience in this world says there is nothing that does not need effort and maintenance.

Source has given all Its Love to you and because giving and receiving are the same, you reflect Source's Love back to It. There is no effort in this. Love loves Its creation, and Love's creation loves its Creator. Giving and receiving are one in truth. Reciprocity is a feeling, the experience of which teaches peace, guiltlessness, and happiness. Feel your way through the day today. No effort required. Allow yourself to imagine Love for your Source.

Lesson 226

My home awaits me. I will hasten there.

In this very moment, as you read these words, you are perfect. Your perfection may be obscured by "circumstances" that seem to diminish or hide it, but it is there, bubbling just below the surface. It is your own clear and perfect self, undaunted by the visions of this world.

If I am still, I can feel the perfection that lies within. If I stop thinking and take a breath, it rises to greet me, even if only for an instant. This is what peace is: instant after instant, breath after breath of choosing to feel the silent awareness that is always there.

Peace and Home are the same thing, and both are a decision only I can make. They seem to require intention, but there is no effort required. Allowing requires nothing but getting out of your own way. Peace is waiting always. I only need to ask myself whether I so value the world of form that I cannot allow myself to stop, even for an instant, to return to the silent peace that is my origin.

Give up trying to achieve perfection. It is not achievable! It is already yours and it is free! Effort thwarts the very thing we seek. So, relax about it. Stop trying to do something about it. Close your eyes and feel your way toward home.

Practice today by giving up your practice. Don't do anything today but take a moment each hour to close your eyes and take a breath. Relax your heart and let all effort go. Just feel whatever you feel. Home is being in touch with yourself. "My home awaits me. I will hasten there." Actually, don't hasten. Just allow, and in the instant of allowing, there you are. Be pleased with yourself today.

Lesson 227

This is my Holy Instant of release.

Today's lesson is about not thinking. It is about noticing what you feel and allowing your feeling/knowing to guide you moment to moment. Let thinking be what you do in between feeling/knowing, instead of the other way around. Each moment spent in conscious awareness of feeling is a release from the problem of thinking.

While you walk this earth you cannot go to the realm of knowledge. So let it be sufficient now to realize that your thinking is not the answer. Indeed it is the source of the problem. Your feelings are much closer to your reality.
– B. Haskell, *Journey Beyond Words*

The Holy Instant is nothing less than an exercise in self-awareness. Self-awareness is by far your best teaching tool. Your thoughts and feelings are reflected back to yourself. Then you begin to understand them. You begin to assess their value. This is where release becomes real.

On the hour today, take a moment to be conscious of what you are feeling. Allow the feeling to be whatever it is. Experience its vibration – for it has a frequency that affects the body and mind, whether you recognize it or not. Feelings are multidimensional packets of information.

As you sit in contemplation today, place awareness on the feelings that arise. Notice their energy. How does joy feel different in the body than frustration or worry? Get to know these frequencies. During the day, the body is constantly sending signals through its knowing sense. With practice, listening to them becomes a conscious choice. Things begin to flow and intuitive knowing increases. This is how we get closer to the realm of knowledge.

Lesson 228

Source does not condemn me. I need not condemn myself.

In my dream I am on stage with a group of other actors. We are preparing for a performance when suddenly I realize I don't know my lines! How can I not know my lines? Have I been sleeping through rehearsals? A feeling of panic arises.

In the play, I am a young princess from a royal household. Yet

I see that I'm wearing work boots and my socks are dirty. This is a disaster! I'm not even dressed for the part! I begin to ask others, "What about my lines? Why don't I know them?" Then, someone kindly tells me, "Don't worry about it. When the time comes, you'll remember them perfectly."

With great relief I accept the sage advice. "Okay. I won't worry about it then. I know I'll know. And by the way, I'm also liking these work boots." All my unease vanishes in the trust. Being in the play can be fun!

The wisdom of this dream shows me something the personal mind very much does not want me to know: I don't need to know my lines. When the time comes, it will all be okay. There is nothing to fear.

The thinking mind (the personal mind, the ego) wants to be in charge of the play. It wants to know every single line before it's even uttered and it uses fear as a means of control. It wants me to believe I will be condemned for forgetting my lines.

Fear is how the ego attempts to maintain control. Even though it didn't write the play, and is not equipped to understand its meaning, the thinking mind wants to hand my lines out to me, one by one, while I wait in guilty fear of forgetting the very thing it has not allowed me to see in the first place! Oh, how controlling and afraid the ego is! It knows it is not the author of the play. The requirement of fear is to create more fear and it will breed itself forever until we listen to the voice that says, "It's okay. Don't worry about it. When the time comes, you will remember your lines perfectly."

Do not condemn yourself in fear. Source knows your lines because It is the creator of the play. It wrote the words, set the stage, gave you your role. Source knows your Wholeness together with It in the play. Would you deny Source's total confidence in you? Source does not condemn you. What makes you believe you should, or even can, condemn yourself?

Today, when you notice feelings of guilt, or fear, say to

yourself, "Source does not condemn me. I need not condemn myself." Mistakes about yourself are dreams. Let the dreams go today and stand in your knowing, ready to receive the Word that tells you who you are and what your lines should be.

Lesson 229

Love, which created me, is what I am.

Love is how you were made from a Mind that is Love Itself. Your body's creation is merely a temporary vehicle for the expression of a Love so large it is almost impossible for you to imagine. Only the personal mind can dream of a reality in which Love is absent, half-formed, or besmirched in any way.

The foundation question for these ten days is "What is Forgiveness?" Remember, you cannot give what you do not already have, nor can you receive what you do not give. So know yourself Love today. You seek your identity. Find it here, in these words, for they are the Truth of What you are. You are worthy. You are good. You are capable of knowing your Self. Love, which created you, is what you are.

Your job today is to stand in awareness of this feeling. On the hour today, stop whatever you are doing to align your inner knowing with this Truth. Say to yourself, "Love, which created me, is what I am." Notice what happens when you allow this thought. Do you feel the slight shift in energy? This is your alignment.

Love is what is holding every cell of your body in place. Every single cell. As you work today, know that you are not alone. There are many there to assist you. That is their job. "God, I embrace the Truth of my Self. You have kept my Identity, untouched, pure, balanced and aligned in Love. I remain as you created me, an extension of Peace, connected always with Your Mind."

Lesson 230

Now I will seek and find the peace of God.

Belief systems are, by their very nature, bound and limited. That is why they are systems. In order to transcend or understand a belief system that is not congruent with your own, forgiveness is often required. The last ten lessons have focused on the question, "What is forgiveness?"

Forgiveness is not some lightweight answer to the indignities of this world. It requires graceful strength and deep intelligence. It is a courageous presence in the face of chest-thumping swagger. Those who know their true worth are forgivers, and those who forgive know the peace it brings.

An unforgiving thought is a judgment against something in conflict with your belief system. The mind that holds an unforgiving thought twists and turns in a frantic effort to justify its choice within whatever belief system is in operation at the moment. It suffers offense at any contradiction to its point of view. Its rightness is held in a closed mind, limited by its beliefs.

Forgiveness, on the other hand, stays open to potential even as it looks upon a situation begging for the closure of judgment. Forgiveness merely assumes a watchful stance and waits in peace for guidance. Guidance will come in many forms: a word, an experience, or a simple neutral thought. Forgiveness lies outside belief systems.

Make no mistake: Source is within all situations that seem to require forgiveness. It holds to no belief system except Love, which is not a belief at all, but Truth. Source is within each and every situation as an Offering to be in alignment or not. Do you see why forgiveness is a practice? There is nothing outside of Source. Forgiveness is the choice to see that this is true and allow the option of peace.

Peace is not so much found as rediscovered. It is who we are.

We were created in peace and we remain there, beneath the foot stomping and frantic making-of-judgments about what should or should not be. Source waits for us to choose peace. It will wait without judgment for us to cease our judging. It will never deny us.

Know your self-worth today. Make it your practice to notice each moment in which something disturbs your peace. What is it? What was its origin? Is your mind open or closed around it? How does it feel to resist the moment? Know the things that take your peace away by using the intelligence with which Source has gifted you.

Step up to the plate and notice the choices you are making. Observe and remember: the first person to forgive is yourself. The belief in guilt is a belief system! Seek and find the peace of God today.

Focus Question 2: *What is Salvation?*

Lesson 231

Today you undertake deeper learning around a new theme: Salvation. "What is Salvation?" This is the core question that underlies your next ten lessons.

Salvation is a promise made by Source that the dream of separation will end. Salvation is guaranteed because it is the Will of Source. All aspects of this reality will be enfolded into the higher Reality of Source Mind because illusion cannot last forever. What dreamer never awakens?

The Thought of Forgiveness was given to the personal mind the instant it conceived of guilt. Thus, there can be no "problem" that does not also contain its solution. The problem of the split mind is belief in separation, but illusion must give way to Truth, for nothing stays in darkness forever. The Thought of Unity will return to the Mind that conceived of separation as a thing to be played with, to be experienced, to be dreamed of at all. Salvation will end the dream of the split mind and the personal mind will itself be absorbed into Truth. Salvation is "undoing" in this sense. It withdraws the illusion that is the foundational thought behind the personal mind's very existence.

Your mind is moving even now toward Salvation. You are sharing in the final dream as you extend Salvation in your perception of this world and all it contains. In your extension of Salvation, you receive It. As you remember Who you are and extend your Knowing into the world, the Light shines brighter on the path toward Home. All of us return to the Light through your Salvation.

Here is how to practice for the next ten days. Read the central question and the daily lesson in the morning. End your day by reading the daily lesson. On the hour, take a moment to stop and reflect upon the message of the central question.

There is no specific duration to your seated practice but I urge you to give at least one half hour each day to sit in silence. This is the thing: if you develop a practice when things are calm, you will be prepared when the inevitable challenges arrive.

Be assured as you sit in silence that what you sense, what you feel, what you know, is real. There will be some days when your mind is like a wild horse you must calm and ride. Other days, when you least expect it, your meditation will be effortlessly deep and insightful. A good rule is to expect nothing but be open to anything. Allow and allow and allow. Connect with the Holy Spirit. Ask for guidance and watch with loving kindness all the things your mind gives up to you.

Today's lesson asks you to remember the Thought of Peace:

My will is to remember my Source.

What more can you will for yourself than to give your mind to Peace? The Love of Source is the only thing you have ever sought, no matter how many names you've given It, or forms you've sought to see It in.

Today, remember your will. See that it is a will you share with your brother and sister, even if they have forgotten it. Remember it for them. You seek it together. Only this is what you have been given to find.

Lesson 232

Source be in my mind all through the day.

"What's in *your* wallet?" the credit card company asks. "What's in your mind?" is what I'm wondering.

At any given moment in time you have but two choices about where to focus your mind: fear or Love's freedom. An unquestioned mind will almost always avoid fear. It will bury anything that feels like fear before it even rises to the surface. A mind that seeks to know itself faces fear over and over again until all its forms are experienced.

Fear takes many, many forms. The consequence of knowing your mind means you will have periods of discomfort, sometimes a lot of discomfort. So it is, but this is how Love's freedom is chosen.

When you decide to know your own divinity, you have to plow through lots of stuff that isn't you first. That is why when something comes up in your consciousness, you must have faith that it is coming up to be addressed and cleared. All of us have created many things in fear. This world is an embodiment of it. Fear perpetuates itself in the collective unconscious of humanity, and it has become the silent motivator behind almost all of our creations. Our greatest fear is that we are unworthy of love. "Who is God to love me when I am so bad?" Oh, how the ego loves this question!

To think, "I am not worthy of Love," is insane and it produces insane behavior. It produces thought systems that say you can be worthy of Love only when you do penance; when you have the right knowledge; when you behave only in certain ways; and most of all when you have been forgiven by a source that lies outside yourself. Entire systems have been built upon the idea that it is not okay for us to claim our own divinity. These systems want us to stay in fear of our power, of our innocence, of our direct and unlimited connection to Source.

But Love speaks freely and directly to us all the time. "Communication between what cannot be divided cannot cease." Nothing outside yourself can give you Love or take It away.

"Source be in my mind all through the day." Remember on the hour who you are, what you are, and how you serve. Know yourself as a divine aspect with all the power and goodness that is yours through knowing yourself. Ask this: "Let all my fears be shown to me so I can face them each in turn and give them up to my knowing." Let Source be in your mind all day today.

Lesson 233

I give my life to God to guide today.

It is here that we are reminded that in each and every moment there are only two teachers to choose between: the personal mind, or the Voice for God. Your mind needs practice to keep its attunement to the Voice for God constant. Attunement is the practice for today.

We each have a choice, in any moment, to go with the lower attunement of the ego, or the higher attunement of Source. The results of your life are a reflection of the choices you make. Understand that most of us, most of the time, have chosen the lower attunement. It is time now to shift into higher gear.

This is how: make it a practice to be conscious of your thoughts and the choices you make from those thoughts. If you are thinking in the mode of fear, your choices will reflect your fears. If you are open to the Voice, if you stand in your knowing that you are, in reality, the higher attunement, you will make choices that reflect greater flow. Flow is freedom. Flow is not attached to outcome so much as how it feels to be free of the fear of ego. Flow comes only from conscious trust in the Guidance of Source.

"I give my life to God to guide today," is nothing more than being in a state of trust in flow. It is a statement that says, "I consciously choose to observe and act only after I have observed. I consciously choose to stand back and allow things to unfold rather than react. I literally give the moment over to a Mind I trust, Whose observation point is high above my own."

Make this commitment to yourself on the hour. You are not giving your life away; you are taking it back. Step aside from acting unconsciously and ask for guidance with an open mind. Walking with consciousness is walking with God. Trust in an open mind that allows the infinite wisdom of Universal Mind to touch it gently and inform it of Itself. It will be the perfect gift of knowing you receive.

Lesson 234

I am aware that I am One with Source.

Source, I am One with you in Truth today. I stand in my knowing of my own true nature. I recognize my Self as the Light born of my Creator and nothing, nothing takes precedence over this knowing of my Self.

Today, I see that all of us are unique aspects of the perfect Whole, and we are perfect in our uniqueness. I will take no one's perfection away today, nor will I allow my perfection to be diminished.

Today, on the hour, stop what you are doing and remember, "In this moment, I am aware that I am One with Source."

Do take time to sit in silent contemplation today. Fifteen minutes of silence belong to you. Let nothing take them away.

Lesson 235

Source, in Its mercy, wills that I be saved.

Each of us comes to know Source in his or her own way. Your path is unique and it will often seem lonely. When we chose separation, we walked a long way from Center Field and didn't look back. For most of us, the decision to stop and turn around is made miles and miles from Home Base.

The desire to explore is what started us on the path away and it is also what prompts us to return. It's a funny thing, but the return is filled with just as much uncertainty as the leaving. The journey Home requires the same bravery as the decision to go. It requires us to trust our inner guidance system. We hope someone has left the lights on for us so we will know when we've arrived.

Humanity has walked just about as far from Home Base as it can. The lights of Center Field are dim on the horizon. But they shine on. If you are reading this, you're on the path Home. And here's the thing; you are not alone on the path no matter how solitary it feels. Did you really think Source would just let you take off unaccompanied? Source is everywhere all at once. It's impossible that you could be alone.

You've done nothing that needs "saving" in the traditional sense. Being saved is but the recognition that you already are. There is no punishment for choosing to see what lies beyond the Ball Park and getting lost along the way. Only a glad welcoming Home. God is merciful. You are merciful. We are One in our mercy.

I need but look upon all things that seem to hurt me, and with perfect certainty assure myself, "God wills that I be

saved from this," and merely watch them disappear. I need but keep in mind my Creator's Will for me is only happiness, to find that only happiness has come to me.
– ACIM

Lesson 236

I alone rule my mind.

Source knows no fear and doesn't recognize ours. Why give credence to something that doesn't exist?

We believe in fear because we created it. Fear is a product of the collective mind and each mind in the collective must unmake it. Source will not remove something from your mind that It knows isn't real. Only you believe in fear and only you can remove it.

Each of us has a mind that we must rule. At times it seems our mind is not our own. But the mind serves whatever purpose we set it to. To what service do you direct your mind? Do you put it into the service of collective fear? Or do you free it from fear, raise your head up, and look around? "I rule my mind, which I alone must rule."

An open mind is free to perceive. Freed perception is the beginning of confidence, and confidence is the beginning of the end of fear. Be confident you can rule your mind! At times it may seem impossible, but in truth your mind is there to serve you and not the other way around. If you cannot make your mind serve you, then give it over to the Holy Spirit and ask for help. This request alone takes the mind back to its rightful place, which is in alignment with Love that knows no fear because it knows no death at all.

During the day today, stop often and ask yourself, "Am I choosing freedom or am I choosing the illusion of fear?" Everyone around you may be choosing fear in the moment. If you choose freedom, it will not only be a choice for yourself, but for them as well. Stop. Take a breath. Notice and make your choice. This is the place where miracles occur. Even if those around you never "know" it, they will benefit from your choice. You only have to worry about your part. Source will take of the rest.

Lesson 237

Now I am as God created me.

Each moment is like a mirror that allows all things to be reflected in it. What is reflected is what is in me. I tighten at the onset of winter only because my mind holds a judgment about something that has not ever even happened. I have given up the freedom of the now.

Do not name your moment. Observe what it holds without attaching anything to it. This is how a child experiences the world before she has learned to make problems with her thinking. Now you are as God creates you. You are not creating yourself. Your job is simply to have the experience of being in the now. Relax and let each moment come to you. You need not go to it. Do you understand this difference?

Be present in the now as often as you can today. Take at least fifteen minutes to sit in the perfume of silence. Understand each moment with your heart. Let the mind be quieted by directing its attention to the breath.

Welcome whatever appears in the now from moment to moment. Allow whatever arises spontaneously in the now to flow through you without trying to grasp it, resist it, or memorize it. That which comes unexpectedly in the now always comes from grace, from silence. That which comes from silence resonates within us.
– Francis Lucille, The Perfume of Silence

Lesson 238

On my decision all salvation rests.

I cannot remember my beginning. I do not know my future. Only what I see before me right now seems real. And even this is questionable. I have to trust. At some point even the most experienced explorer arrives at the place where trust is the only thing left. Poised on the edge of not knowing, one must choose. The thing is, when the choice is made, new doors either open or close.

What is this decision? What is the illusion? How can I know? ACIM does not ask for blind faith. It asks only that we have our experience and then decide. Open your awareness, notice what you experience, then base your decision on trust in yourself. Trust yourself to know your Self.

Open awareness will show you where your illusions are, but it is a decision only you can make for yourself. Imagine the force of a group of individuals who practice open awareness together. Collective awareness magnifies the creative force of each individual and the whole becomes greater than the sum of its parts. This is how we lift the collective fog of the personal mind.

Group thought is real. Everything you see is a product of group consciousness. When left unexplored, the fog of illusion settles in and we do not recognize that we have created our world. But one open mind can bring massive change. This is why all salvation rests on your decision.

Illusion's end requires seeing that we create our reality. Once this is recognized, a new reality, based on a higher level of knowing, becomes inevitable. The end of illusions is the beginning of new knowledge – that we are beloved, whole, and safe far, far beyond the borders of our own limited awareness.

Practice open awareness today. If you stay in the moment,

if you refrain from skipping over the now, you will see things about yourself and about others. Source trusts you to know your Self, so why do you not trust? Your Self is in everything you see and all you cannot yet imagine. It lies there, just beyond the fog.

Lesson 239

God's glory is my own.

What is so different and so compelling about ACIM is its logical emphasis on the recognition of our own magnificence. It acknowledges God's glory but asks us to focus upon it in ourselves, and thereby end the illusion of separation from the radiance that is our Creator.

This is your task today – to feel the glory within yourself and see it in each other. Glory is walking this world, living this life, in the freedom born of assuredness of your true Identity. Do not accept false humility today. Instead, be thankful for the gifts of Source.

On the hour today take a break and go inside yourself. Close your eyes and say, "I accept my glory. I am worthy of it. I honor myself as a creation of God. I am glory through my love of myself and I allow this love to extend to all that I see before me. The glory of my Creator is my own."

Lesson 240

Fear is not justified in any form.

Any form of fear that you can imagine is a lie. It is a lie because it requires you to see yourself as you can never be – capable of death, deceit, shame, guilt, temporary, and vulnerable. You are not one of these things except in dreams. This world is a dream. It is your own movie. It is your own computer program, if you will.

Imagine the hard drive of a computer. The Hard Drive, in which all programs run, is Mind of God. There are only two programs that run off the hard drive: computer programs A and B.

Program A has self-awareness. It knows it is just a program and remains connected to the Hard Drive even as it runs. It plays with all the attributes of itself, but never mistakes them for anything other than what they are – a program within the Hard Drive.

Program B has become confused. It has lost self-awareness and believes it actually is the Hard Drive. It has now lost most of its computing ability and is running off very limited capacity – even as it remains attached to, but unaware of, its original Source. The Hard Drive is invisible to program B.

You and I have been operating in program B for thousands of years, but it no longer functions smoothly. We are now being rebooted to program A. Program B is becoming aware that it is not the hard drive. All that remains is to let go of fear, for fear is one of the main operating mechanisms of program B. Fear gunks up the program.

Fear is not justified in any form. It is an impediment to healing. Like guilt, fear obscures our connection to each other and Source. Fear cannot coexist with Love because they are polar opposites and only one is true. We either operate from fear or from Love. Program A is Love.

The thought system of program B is finished. It is self-destructing and we can all feel it. We can hold onto fear and hit the wall, or allow program A to be our guide and awaken to self-awareness. It is a choice we all have now.

Fear comes in many, many forms. Learn to recognize the form fear takes in you today. A slight discomfort, a minor upset, an instant of repression, a distressful thought, a moment of anxiety, or embarrassment, or self-judgment – all of these are forms of fear. It is painful to see them and feel them. Can you see how fear perpetuates itself? We fear and we repress. We fear and then attack. Attack in the form of self-defense is now justified and the cycle begins again. This is how program B has run for eons.

The body is a wonderful messenger for the presence of fear. It will tell you which program is in control. Program B causes illness, stress, tension, aches, and pains. Become aware of what your body is telling you.

"Fear is not justified in any form." Today, on the hour – or more often if necessary – bring this lesson to mind. It offers comfort and assurance that is more real than anything the illusion of form can provide. Program A is running now. It has never, not been running.

Here is the challenge: you must shift to program A while program B is still running. This is why you are asked to stop on the hour and reboot. Rebooting means seeing which program is in control. If it is B, then shift to A. Simple to say, but it requires programming skills. Don't worry. They're built into the Hard Drive, which means they're built into you.

Focus Question 3: *What is the World?*

Lesson 241

Today begins a new series of lessons with a new central theme. The theme for the next ten lessons centers around the question, "What is the World?"

Is this not a most important question? Indeed, for its answer underlies everything we perceive about ourselves and our place in the scheme of things. For many, it seems this world is descending into chaos.

This world is an "out-picture" of inner mind – a movie projected onto a screen of consciousness. Its content is as real as any movie, which means it is false. It was born of a desire to play in the fields of separation, and when we decide the game has been played out, we will begin to see the world in another light. Knowing the world is illusion is the beginning of the end of the projection. Why? Because the source of the projection – the mind – will be corrected. A corrected mind projects the Truth.

This world is not your Home. How can an illusion be Home to anything? But even as a movie can point to Truth, so the images we have made can be given a new purpose, a new interpretation. Look to the Holy Spirit's interpretation. Hear Its Voice, for Its is the only Voice that can interpret the Truth in the illusion.

You have been told forgiveness is your function in this world. It is only through the practice of forgiveness that the screen of consciousness is able to reflect the Truth. As you practice forgiveness the act itself becomes more habitual. This is when the screen clears. Clarity begets more clarity and the experience of Knowing dissolves the screen.

The lesson for today is:

Salvation is Now, in this Holy Instant.

Experiences of Knowing are often instantaneous. ACIM calls them "miracles" or "Holy Instances." We all have these moments. I know I have experienced one when my perception of a troubling situation lifts effortlessly. There is a feeling of certainty. Often, this certainty exceeds anything I alone could create. The signal is clear, the feeling is Whole, and no doubt is present. All of us are fully capable of these experiences but we have to pay attention.

What is this world? Are we living in the worst of times or the best of times? Is this world imploding or being born anew? Wars, natural disasters, and social disruptions abound. And yet, at the same time, fantastic new discoveries are being made – discoveries that are opening up the way we think about space, time, and the nature of the mind. As we explore the furthest reaches of our galaxy and find yet another nearly massless particle, our ideas about reality will have to shift.

We were once fully convinced the world was flat. That it was the center of the solar system. Now we know this entire world is a product of our perception. In this Holy Instant, this perfect moment, you are here having an experience. But you are so much more. There is nothing beyond your capacity. Stop for a moment and experience the miracle of your own consciousness. Look around. The light is shining in everything. And it is all you. In this Holy Instant.

Do not rest until the world has changed its perception. Do not attempt to change your function. You are vital to salvation of this world. We are the mind projecting. We must behold our projection through the eyes of Christ Consciousness so that the illusion we have made can die to everlasting life.

To recap: Each morning read and contemplate the core question and its answer. Then read the particular lesson for the day. At some point in the day devote at least fifteen minutes to quiet meditation. You know how to do this by now. Sit and place awareness on the breath. Breathe in peace and exhale any tension in the body. Take as long as you want to do this. Then repeat the lesson for the day in your mind, invite the Holy Spirit's assistance, and let everything go. Allow the breath to anchor your mind. Watch thoughts and feelings as they arise. Trust. Expect nothing and allow everything. Play. Be courageous. Explore total nonresistance. Forgive and know your Innocence.

Be mindful throughout the day. Practice forgiveness. Allow direct experience through conscious awareness. On the hour, remember the lesson. Use it to anchor your day.

In the evening, read the lesson only. Let it guide you into sleep where it will inform the other world of dreams until you waken to this one, and finally to Reality.

Lesson 242

Today is my gift to God.

Have you ever considered there are other dimensions above the third? I say "above" but, in reality, dimensions above three encompass and contain it. Our perception is limited by our three-dimensional mind-set.

It is in three-dimensional consciousness that contrast and separation prevail. Here, we are limited to a choice between contrasting alternatives, and a price must be paid for each limited choice you seem forced to make.

Three-dimensional thinking is a teaching tool. We choose it and we experience it as we choose. Thus, this existence can be either a jewel or a prison. It is either a place where Love is found or where Love is lost. The choice is yours and it is the most important choice you will ever make, for it shapes the very fabric of your Soul.

The Soul is both multidimensional and unified. Your Soul encompasses many experiences in form, of which you are one. You might even say, your Soul is part of a more significant Soul Group, which is part of an even more significant Group, all of which are contained within the One, Source, the Prime Creator, God. This is why, when you choose to focus on the separation of three-dimensional form, you seem to be separate from your Soul and from Its Source.

Do not lead your life alone today. You do not see above this three-dimensional world yet. Accept that you are not leading your life unguided by One Who knows all that is best for you; Who sees you are part of Itself, even as you wander blindly. On the hour today, release the outer, three-dimensional world, and share a moment of contentment with the All. Look around and consider that everything you see is connected. Nothing is left out of One Mind. Form may change; time seems to pass. But it is all a creation of One Love that has never left its Source.

There is no need to understand the complexities of this world for they are beyond our understanding until Wholeness Itself is understood. For now, rest in the quiet giving of yourself to Source.

Lesson 243

Today I will judge nothing that occurs.

Imagine, if you will, an infinitely complex piece of fabric. It has every color imaginable. It is beautiful and magnificent, but this is not all. This fabric is ten miles wide and a mile thick, and it is floating in space. Now imagine you are a single piece of thread buried deep within this enormous cloth – and you have formed an opinion about the thread beside you.

"It's the wrong color. I don't like its texture. It doesn't match its surroundings." You go on and on about it. In fact, you'd like to move to another row, where the threads appear to be more compatible. You work yourself into a tangle and even get your neighbors involved. Now they want to move too.

Now imagine that in a single flash you see the whole cloth in all its aspects. You see the thread beside you is golden at each end, and that its color brings out all the other colors around it in the most perfect way. You see that the thread you didn't like is actually the strongest in the line. It holds all the other threads in place, and it is the perfect complement to the pattern. You realize you have misjudged and caused yourself all kinds of needless trouble.

The thread, of course, is you and me. We judge, we complain, we blame. This is the job of the personal mind. But honestly, how many times has it been wrong? The personal mind is incapable of understanding anything beyond its limited perception. Yet we act as if it is the sole arbiter of reality. Isn't this the definition of insanity?

Today, do not think you already know what is beyond your present understanding. Be willing to put down the burden of judgment this day. You do not know. That which appears unfavorable in the moment may, in fact, serve a purpose greater than you are able to perceive with the personal mind. Relieve yourself of the responsibility to assess, measure, and compare. Leave creation free to be its self.

This lesson is about ultimate freedom. If you feel relief in the lesson, you are on the right track. If you notice resistance to the lesson, this is good information also. There is a difference between judgment and discernment. Discernment says, "I notice it is hot in here. I'll open the window." Judgment says, "I think so and so is an idiot for not noticing how hot it is in here. She should have opened the window an hour ago."

Today, give yourself the gift of quiet contemplation. Sit in silence. Review the judgments you have made and let them go. Quiet the mind. Watch the breath, and open to flow. Feel your way into peace. Expect nothing. Allow anything. Breathe. Connect with the Weaver in Whose Mind the fabric was conceived.

Lesson 244

I am in danger nowhere in the world.

Oftentimes, fear sneaks up on me. It begins as a tiny, anxious voice I try to ignore. I cover it up, especially when it seems to be about something small. But fear has a way of snowballing, especially when it doesn't get my attention. What might start as a concern about having enough firewood turns into worrying about whether I've budgeted enough to snowplow our driveway this winter. Then I check the long-term forecast, as if anybody has any idea about what the weather will be three months out.

The worst of my fears are usually either monetary or bodily

based. When my chronic dry eye acts up, all hell breaks loose. The treatment for dry eye is very expensive, and I can't go without the drops. Even with them, it is one of the most annoying conditions – like driving 65mph in a desert wind, with toothpicks holding your eyes open. I get cranky, irritable, and fearful that I'll have to spend the rest of my life putting drops in my eyes every hour, and maybe even losing my eyesight.

When I become fearful like this, I know I've lost my center. I've forgotten and veered off course. I've believed my fear. Later, when things have calmed down, I wonder how I could have ever gotten so lost.

If you have just lost your house to floodwaters, or realized your homeowner's insurance doesn't cover hurricanes, this lesson might feel like a lie. It might even make you angry. But it's the truth. This lesson is an anchor in a storm. It will be what gets you through. There is nowhere and nothing in this world that can destroy your spirit but first you have to remember who you really are.

We find out who we are by surviving the storm. We find out who we are by rebuilding the house, making sure the kids can get back to school, remembering to take the cat or dog when we are forced to leave the high waters. We remember who we are when we've gotten through the pain.

If you are not in pain today, be thankful and practice this lesson. You will need it when the storm does come. The time to practice is before you need the lesson. The knowing has to be automatic. If you are in pain, forgive yourself for all your fear. Let it be what it is. Breathe and look around. You are still here and will be well in time. Isn't it always well in time?

How do you find out who you are? Become a student of your mind. Where has your mind been? Are you in bed with your fear? Or are you in your knowing of your Self?

As often as possible today, say to yourself, "I stand now, knowing myself as one who is safe, as one who is eternal. I am loved and I am in love with all that is before me and of which I am a part – even the parts where I am afraid."

Give yourself the gift of silent contemplation today. Take your seat and relax. Place your awareness gently on the breath. Repeat in your mind, "I am in danger nowhere in the world." Now allow the meaning of this idea to settle in. How does your body respond to this thought? Say the lesson again and feel its effect within your being. Take your time. This practice, over time, becomes a memory that lives in every cell. It melts the snowballs of fear that settle in the belly. Practice this lesson. Make it your friend.

Lesson 245

Your Peace is with me, God. I am safe.

Remember, the lessons for this week address the central question: "What is this world?" Here is ACIM's answer:

> *This world is a false perception. It is born in error, and it has not left its source. It will remain no longer than the thought that gave it birth is cherished. When the thought of separation has been changed to one of true forgiveness will the world be seen in quite another light, and one that leads to truth, where all the world must disappear and all its errors vanish. Now its source has gone and its effects are gone as well.*
> – ACIM

This is the great secret. Once uncovered, your true power becomes available. The secret is this: the world exists in your mind and not the other way around. And we have fear in our world only because we have fear in our mind.

Each of us is an aspect of consciousness identifying in physical form. But form is not our natural state. Form is limited and vulnerable. Form cannot contain all that we are – and on some level we recognize this is so. The challenge is to move beyond the identification with physical form. But this challenge requires us to face our fear while in form. We are moving to computer program A, while program B is still running. We must experience form to understand it is not what we are.

We are free to fear and we are free to completely identify with the body. No one can alter the perception we choose. But Truth is true and it is always true; we remain always as God created us: formless, timeless, peace, creators, sovereign, capable, majestic.

We have trained our minds to believe fear is real. We alone can train our minds to live without it. On the hour today, remind yourself that safety, and the peace that comes with it, is your natural state. When I know my own peace, I share it with you and thus double my safety and yours. We are safe at Home, in Mind of God. It is fear that is the stranger here.

Give yourself the gift of silent contemplation today. Take time to sit in peace with the idea of complete and total safety. Safety lies within, which is where everything begins and ends. Relax the body. Be mindful of the breath. Say as often as you need to, "God's Peace is with me. I am safe." Feel this feeling in your body. Let every cell bathe in the energy of peace.

Go in peace today. Share your peace and safety, not by speaking it but by living it.

Lesson 246

For me to love God is for me to love the Whole of God's Extension.

I am going to explain this lesson, but first I have someone to thank and a dream to share. Don't worry. It will all connect at the end.

Yesterday, I had the gift of a good listener and it reminded me again how vital being heard is to the soul. A good listener asks helpful questions that point to something you cannot see in yourself. They don't preach or make you feel a burden. Listening is a lesson in reciprocity, for the good listener has been well listened to himself. That is often how the craft is learned.

A good listener bears witness as you listen to yourself explore and express. How simple. What a gift to sit with another in this way. But what happens when a good listener cannot be found, when there is no one there to listen? This is when being a good listener to yourself comes into play. How many of us are good listeners to ourselves?

Last night I lay in bed unable to sleep. Realizing sleep had left and wasn't coming back any time soon, I decided to watch my breath and go into meditation. I hadn't thought of it this way before, but meditation is another way of being a good listener to yourself. So I listened, breathed, and listened. After a while I began to recognize the voice. It was the old voice of victimhood, a lonely, vulnerable victim demanding to be recognized. So I opened the door and showed her in. I heard her out. After a while I gently reminded her that no one can be a victim unless she has forgotten her sovereignty. We discussed this and then, feeling much better, I fell asleep.

I dreamed I was in a world at war. There were about 50 children in my care and it was my responsibility to find them safe passage out of the country. The enemy was everywhere, and yet I had no doubt about my mission. When the signal came from a sympathetic guard, I whispered loudly to the whole crew, "Now! Get moving!" and we snuck from our hiding place onto a waiting train. Just before waking, I was on a train with 50 kids headed for freedom.

This was a lovely little dream and I could have been content with it just as it was. I went to sleep feeling like a victim and awoke having rescued 50 children. But I knew there was something more, so I continued to listen. Suddenly, a voice reminded me that every dream character is an extension of myself. The children, the enemy, the rescuer – all of these were me. But there is more, for I also understood that my personal dream was a mirror of the group dream we are all sharing right now.

"For me to love God is for me to love the Whole of God's Extension." For me to love myself, I must love all of my extensions, not just the ones I like. I am a fractal of my Source, so it follows that for me to love my Source, I must love Source's Whole Extension, not just the ones I like. I don't have to love their behavior or their actions, but I am required to honor the story of each one.

Without passing any self-judgment, can you sit in meditation today and listen to yourself? Is it the victim who asks you to bear witness? Is it the perpetrator? Is it the rescuer? Can you see how each role requires the other to justify itself? A victim is impossible without a perpetrator. A rescuer has no job to do if there is no victim. And a victim always becomes a perpetrator when she feels attack is justified.

This world is a group dream. Our Oneness with Source cannot be known through the personal self, who is dreaming of separation. We can know it only through our Whole Mind. This is the Mind that has transcended the triad of victim, persecutor, and rescuer.

As long as we are in the dream (and we are until we aren't), we will be required to listen to things, people, situations, and voices that seem separate, angry, uncomfortable, and downright wrong. How ironic it is, that in listening without judgment, we help each extension loosen its hold on its role, and then peace comes.

All of us are playing a role. We are much more likely to give it up when we receive the gift of being listened to. Because we are each Source's extension, when I listen to you, I am listening to myself. Today, practice listening to yourself, and to the self sitting next to you.

Lesson 247

Without forgiveness, I will still be blind.

An unforgiving mind contracts. It doesn't know what it doesn't know because it has already decided. A forgiving mind is open. It isn't threatened. It allows new information, new perceptions, different points of view to inform it. It says, "I don't know. Let's see. How can I better understand this?"

Even the most advanced ACIM student can be challenged by forgiveness. Lack of forgiveness almost always involves attachment to an emotion. Emotion is itself a teaching device. To learn from emotion requires that I first acknowledge what I am feeling, allow it, and let it move through me. This is called "emotional flow and integration" and it is a key ingredient of forgiveness.

For individuals moving along the path of spiritual knowledge and expansion, it is very important not to associate negative emotion with failure. It is, however, critical to notice, feel, and allow emotion to flow through you. Burying, ignoring, glossing over, or projecting negative emotion will stall your progress. Do not allow guilt to hijack your integration! Without forgiveness, you will be blind to the original emotion and its integration will be impeded.

When an emotion rages through the body without recognition, acknowledgement, and integration, its energy is diverted, scattered, or buried, and it will lodge in unexpected places. When an emotion is recognized, acknowledged, and allowed to flow, its energy becomes a signal, a match, for more energy. But the energy match will be a neutral one, rather than an unconscious match for the original emotion. With negative or uncomfortable emotion, the first step almost always requires forgiveness of the original feeling.

Every situation, every person, you encounter that raises "negative" emotions is part of your teaching experience. You will attract "negative" teaching experiences until you have fully "moved," processed, or accepted the original emotion.

Don't allow guilt to blind you to your feelings. They are only feelings! They are there to be felt. "See" them. Watch them arise, peak, and flow through you. Have your experience with them. Today, acknowledge all "negative" emotions (and positive ones as well!). Let them move through you without attachment. Simple acknowledgement of an emotion sets it in flow.

Make no mistake: emotional energy is just as "real" as anything you perceive in your physical environment. In fact, it is more real. You may leave your physical environment, but emotions stay with you wherever you go. So which is actually more real, the physical or the emotional? You do not want to be blind to your physical environment. Nor do you want "unseen" emotions to be your source of motivation. See, forgive, and allow. Remove the blinders by forgiving – first yourself and then the one who "caused" the emotion.

Lesson 248

Whatever suffers is not part of me.

I regard consciousness as fundamental. I regard matter as derivative from consciousness. We cannot get behind consciousness. Everything that we talk about, everything that we regard as existing, postulates consciousness.
– Max Planck, Nobel Prize winning originator of quantum theory, as quoted in the *Observer* (25 January 1931)

"I regard matter as derivative from consciousness." Nearly one hundred years ago Max Planck let us in on a secret of such

majestic proportion we still have not caught up with it. Matter arises from consciousness. Thought creates things. The physical arises from the nonphysical. Yet, we still behave as if it is the other way around – that physical matter exists and we exist in it. Metaphorically speaking, we still behave as if our earth is flat and that the sun revolves around it. We have not yet invented the spiritual wheel. We still walk when we could fly.

We have disowned the truth. So long as we choose to operate in a reality that denies our connection and power, we will suffer. We will suffer because we are living with an outmoded operating system. We cannot get to Mars without the use of highly sophisticated computers. We cannot achieve ascension consciousness with an outmoded thought system. We must change the way we think about what we think.

"Whatever suffers is not part of me." What suffers is the illusion of form believing itself to be more real than the consciousness that creates it. Today, be as faithful in disowning falsity as you have disowned this truth. What grieves is not you. What pains is not you. What suffers is not you. This is the ancient truth.

Today, forgive your suffering. Wish yourself well. Love yourself in spite of your confusion. But decide against disowning the truth. You are as Source created you and you remain so forever. Settle for nothing less than this.

Lesson 249

Forgiveness ends all suffering and loss.

This lesson is so misunderstood it has wreaked all kinds of havoc. In fact, it has held many students of enlightenment back. Forgiveness is not about not feeling negative emotions. You have not "failed" when you experience negative feelings.

Emotions are a form of energy. They are energetic spiritual teaching tools.

When an emotion rages through the body without recognition of what it is or why it is there, it becomes a free-floating signal that attracts mirror energy. The individual who does not feel, acknowledge, and move difficult emotions unwittingly asks for more of exactly what they do not want. This results in a spiraling cycle of confusion and pain.

When you feel an emotion, especially a painful one, sit with it. Do not act out, ignore, bury, gloss over, or project it. For individuals seeking a path of enlightenment, the sense of failure about "negative" emotions can be a serious handicap to their progress. You do not fail when you feel anger, shame, rage, jealousy, depression, or fear. Again, you do not fail! Anger is as much a teaching tool as laughter. The point is to be present with both. This is forgiveness.

It can be a profound relief to know that "negative" emotions are not to be interpreted as "bad."

When I feel a negative emotion and then feel negative about it, I create a cycle of despair. The only way to end the cycle is to acknowledge the feeling, be grateful that I have acknowledged it, and let it move through. This automatically releases my unconscious attachment to it.

What happens when you can't forgive? Indeed, there are times when wallowing in what I feel, feels really good. For me that sometimes means believing I've been wronged and thinking I am justified in being upset about it. In the back of my mind I know I will get over it sooner or later. But in the moment, releasing all guilt about feeling angry is exactly what is needed.

When you suppress a negative feeling it is like telling Source, "Don't worry. I can take of this myself. You just go about your business and let me do my thing." But the truth is my business is Source's business. If I can't bring the bad stuff to Source, then what's the point?

Source is not undependable. But I am. Source has unlimited patience. I do not. When I limit Source by not asking for help or withholding my "bad" feelings, I am just adding time to my own healing. So when I can't forgive, and I can't forgive myself for not forgiving, I hurt only myself and deny Source the opportunity to be helpful.

Forgiveness ends all suffering because it allows everything. But it does require openness and honesty in the moment. It is also very helpful to invite assistance by asking Source to your emotional party. Remember, it is the energy you allow yourself to feel and flow through you that becomes the signal for your next energetic attraction – not the original emotion itself. Said another way: it is the flow of emotional energy that is the signal you send outward, not the emotion itself.

Bring your mind Home. You can sustain no loss. Today, make it your practice to notice and allow all you feel about everything Source brings to you.

Lesson 250

Let me not see myself as limited.

Are you willing to sacrifice your soul's growth for an investment in a belief system that says you cannot know your Self? A system that not only tells you it isn't possible to know your Self, but is also willing to punish you for questioning and learning? Take a day off from work to meditate and it will cost you. Question the religious teachings that condemn you as born in sin, and risk being called more sinful. Step back while others judge and risk attack for not being part of the group.

How can I not see myself as limited when I operate from "truths" that are misaligned to my requirements for growth? I think I am supposed to behave in a certain way, have a certain kind of spouse, job, education, skin color, political or religious affiliation, or nationality. When I am invested in a system that defines itself through separation and limitation, I will be limited and separated from my Self, for my Self includes everything and everyone.

Most people today act on an inherited belief system based on fear. They unconsciously comply to gain approval. How many of us live unquestioned lives of moderate discomfort simply because we cannot imagine a life outside the inherited system of belief?

We are in a group agreement on this planet. The agreement says we are diminished, vulnerable, sinful, aggressive, selfish… you can fill in the blanks. But it is time to stop playing dumb. Empowerment is not about false gaiety. It is real. It is active and it requires us to act – on the soul level. The actions that are required demand courage and trust in our own and others' divinity. It is only darkness that wants us to feel inferior.

Fear creates fear. All belief systems created out of fear, scarcity, or sin, are made in darkness and they keep us there. Can you step out of fear today? Can you notice when it has become your belief system? This is the first step toward creating a new belief system based on divine knowing. It is evolving now, with you.

Devote this day to your own freedom. On the hour, remind yourself, "I am not limited. I choose now to acknowledge myself as an aspect of Source. I am One with Source and with all my brothers and sisters, seen and unseen." Then look around at all that is in your view and feel the truth of your words. Be in attunement to them even if just for a moment because attunement to the feeling is a way of knowing the truth.

Remember, these past ten lessons have asked, "What is the world?" The world we seek is unlimited. We seek it because somewhere, in our minds, we know we are unlimited. Practice hourly today and sit in quiet contemplation of your unlimited beingness.

Focus Question 4: *What is Sin?*

Lesson 251

We move now into another ten lessons with a new question. The core question for these ten lessons is: *"What is Sin?"*

> *Sin is insanity. It is the means by which the mind is driven mad, and seeks to let illusions take the place of truth. And being mad, it sees illusions where the truth should be.*
> – ACIM

Sin is the belief that we can separate from God. It is a mistake, not an unforgiveable crime.

ACIM is very clear that all form, including the body, is the creation of a mind that believes sin can be real. Form is an instrument created by a mind to deceive itself. Its purpose is to contain and limit what is unlimited and cannot be contained. The idea of "sin" is the home of all our illusions. It is "proof" that what is not real is reality. You are not your body. Even this universe will disappear. It is after all our creation, made in fear of sin.

The idea of sin is frightening because the root of sin is fear itself. What a childish game! We who are One with God are playing in a body, imagining its decline and decay, its vulnerability and degradation. What littleness. How long will we, who are Source Itself, be content to maintain the game of sin? There is no sin. Source remains unchanged and we are One with It.

The lesson for today is a direct answer to the question, "What is Sin?" It tells you there is no original sin but there is a mistake that needs correction. The correction is simply the acceptance of the Truth. This is today's lesson:

I need nothing but the Truth.

There is no sin. This statement is nothing but the Truth. The belief in the reality of sin is a form of Self-deceit so great it has almost stolen our Identity. It is no longer acceptable to accept the idea of sin, for the Truth is, Creation remains Pure and unchanged. You have sought many things and found despair. Now, seek only for One Thing, for in that One is All. You need nothing but the Truth about your Self: you have everything you need in It, everything you could ever want.

Here is how to practice the next ten lessons:

Each morning read and contemplate the core question and its answer. Then read the particular lesson for the day. At some point in the day devote at least fifteen minutes to quiet meditation. You know how to do this by now. Sit and place awareness on the breath. Breathe in peace and exhale any tension in the body. Take as long as you want to do this. Then repeat the lesson for the day in your mind, invite the Holy Spirit's assistance, and let everything go. Allow the breath to anchor your mind. Watch thoughts and feelings as they arise. Trust. Expect nothing and allow everything. Play. Be courageous. Explore total nonresistance. Forgive and know your Innocence.

Be mindful throughout the day. Practice forgiveness. Allow direct experience through conscious awareness. On the hour, bring the lesson into your awareness. Use the lesson as a way to anchor your day.

In the evening, read the lesson only. Let it guide you into sleep where it will inform the other world of dreams until you waken to this one, and finally to Reality.

Lesson 252

I am a Holy Extension of God.

I awake from a dream. I have been swimming with a seal, but it wasn't like any seal I've ever seen or read about. The seal and

I knew each other well. We played in the water without a care. Being in a human body, I couldn't swim as effortlessly, but that didn't matter. As my dream ended, the seal swam to me and rested its head on my shoulder. I wrapped my arms around its warm body and felt its fur. In that moment I knew a love so deep and grand I can only say it was unearthly. I awoke knowing I had been somewhere very special and connected deeply with a fellow soul as real as any human I have ever known.

ACIM teaches that we reach the end of illusion through layers of dream worlds, each of which brings us closer and closer to Reality. The journey through these worlds brings the discovery of our true nature. Our true nature isn't human. It isn't in a body. Some call it Buddha Nature. Some call it Christ Consciousness. It has been known as El Shaddai, Brahma, the Tao, Allah, Mother Divine. These are just names for the un-nameable.

Our true nature is beyond anything we know in this worldly dream. We can only touch the edges of it, yet even that evokes feelings of wonder and awe. Gift yourself today with the discovery of your true identity. See it in the person next to you. On the hour, remember you are the Whole Aspect of an even Greater Whole. Your identity is Source Itself. You are Star Dust. You are Diamond Light. You are Golden, Shining Perfection. See it in the eyes of your neighbor, your partner, your dog or cat. Feel it in the wind and hear it in the leaves rustling in the trees. It is everywhere all at once.

Extend your gift to yourself by sitting for 15 minutes in peace. Can you watch your breath and quiet the mind so that even for a brief moment the true nature that is You arises and touches you? Take a seat. Listen. Feel. Breathe. Quietly begin to watch. Extend your awareness by going deeper. Then deeper still. Let it touch you, this thing called Source.

Lesson 253

My True Self is the ruler of the universe.

Notice what is capitalized. What is the True Self? It is Who and What you really are. Our True Self is the ruler of the universe because our Self is the creator of it.

It is impossible for anything to come to you that you have not asked for. Even in the world that you perceive, you are the ruler of your destiny. What happens is what you desire; what does not occur is what you do not want to happen. You must accept this, because this is how you go past the world to know your Self, Which is your True Will, in Heaven, Where your Holy Self abides.

What is Sin? A lie. We have lied to ourselves about What we are. To reverse this denial and undo the lie, we must forgive ourselves.

Without forgiveness, it is too painful to look at the world we have created, and we fall back asleep, believing someone or something else is responsible. Thus, the thought system of denial sets in: "If we are not responsible, then something else must be. And that something else clearly does not have our best interests at heart." This is how fear and death become "real."

Realize today that to stand in judgment is to relinquish your own authority. You relinquish your authority because you are denying your own power of creation. In truth, you are judging against your True Self! All forms of judgment are always against the Self. It cannot be otherwise!

The true understanding of this lesson is akin to a spiritual doctoral degree. But there is one more piece that is critical to understanding the True Self: Only what is created in Love is Real. Nothing that is not created in Love is Real. This is why all creations born of fear are easily forgiven and set aside: they are not Real. They do not exist in Mind of God. Source is Love and

True Creation occurs only through It. This world, born in fear of separation from Source, is a DREAM.

This lesson is for grown-ups. Be kind to your small self with it. On the hour, remind yourself of your Self. This is where our Oneness remains waiting to be rediscovered. Your True Self is the ruler of the universe. You are powerful, good, kind, capable, sovereign, indestructible, unlimited, and gracious.

Find fifteen minutes for contemplation in silence today. Sit in quiet and repeat this lesson to yourself. Then let all things go. Watch the breath and allow your True Self to guide your mind. When the personal mind begins to speak up, and it will, go back to the words of the lesson. Before sleep tonight, repeat this lesson to yourself and ask your True Self to guide you in your dreams. Notice what happens.

Lesson 254

I quiet all but the Voice of Source within me.

There only two stations I can tune my mind to: personal mind, or Voice for God. This would seem to make choosing fairly simple. But all too often, my mind catches a train of thought, and before I know it, I'm off and running. "What if this or that happens?" "What should I do to prepare for this outcome or that one?" My personal mind is loud and insistent. It is the reflexive, "go to" choice in most situations. It always originates from a place that says I need to be in control.

On the other hand, the Voice for God is very quiet. It lives silently in the background, deep below the superficial machinations of the personal mind. It holds a grounded quality of peace. It views the universe as fundamentally benevolent. All that is required is done without planning or effort. Indeed, it has already been done for me.

The voice of my ego feeds itself on fear. The Voice for God

tells us we are absolute, untouchable, and unchangeable. Which voice is the sane one?

Today you will experience more deeply how to distinguish which station you are tuned in to at any moment. Practice today by being continuously aware of the contents of your mind. While this may seem simple it is the work of higher learners.

On the hour, stop and seek inner silence. Become aware of your breath, and gently place yourself within this thought: "I align my senses with the Voice for God. I have a choice. I am making the choice now to align with my Self. I can distinguish between the voice of ego and the Voice for God. I am choosing now, in this very moment, the Voice for God."

Today you will be well served by taking at least 15 minutes in silent contemplation. Listening to the Voice for God is a practice. But it's also like riding a bike; once you learn how, the ability never disappears.

You are a higher learner now and very capable. Give yourself permission to know your own excellent abilities. You will know the Voice for Source through your senses. Your mind will quiet. Your heart will slow. A sense of peace will envelop you. There will be a sense of space. This is what we are learning to cultivate in all situations. This is mastery of the moment.

Lesson 255

I choose to spend this day in perfect peace.

Do I actually have the choice to spend all day in perfect peace? Aren't there are far too many competing voices, demands, and interests that insert themselves into any given moment? Source assures me that I am free to choose and I have faith that this is true. So, what would happen if I simply tried to keep this thought in my mind today? How would it affect the outcome of my day?

Can you make this day an experiment? Find a way to keep this thought foremost in your mind. Driving the car to work. Parking the car. Walking into the building. Sitting at your desk. In that instant before answering the ringing phone. In a conversation. Sitting in a meeting. Standing in line at the store. During your workout. Walking down the street. Make this your constant thought, repeat it all throughout the day, and see what happens. That is your choice.

In the middle of total chaos, peace waits. Wherever there is inner silence, whenever we direct our hearts toward the great quiet that remains forever in the background – there is perfect peace. It never truly leaves. It waits for us to notice.

Peace is a choice and choice is power. Knowing you can choose is a most powerful realization. You may first choose to explore your power because you have faith it is there. Once you choose to explore and have your experience with it, faith becomes certainty. Choose today. Quiet all but Source within yourself. Attune the heart and mind to peace as often as possible – even if those around you are tuned to noise and mindlessness. The power of your choice teaches silently that they have the same power to choose.

Today, greet with peace all that plays out before you on the screen of consciousness. Project the peace that belongs to you. Only you can decide to choose it. Watch what happens when this lesson is simply applied to each situation.

On the hour today, remember peace is a choice. Peace does not have to be a state of perfection or passivity. Peace can be a sense of knowing your own power, of standing in silent acknowledgement of your perfect safety, even as the world around appears to spin out of control.

And, of course, if you forget to remember this lesson – be at peace with yourself about it. Just pick up where you left off and continue on. Do this as often as you need to. Sit for fifteen minutes in silent contemplation of this idea. Peace be within you this day.

Lesson 256

My only goal this day is Source.

You will not waste this day if you should choose to make forgiveness your goal. What is forgiveness anyway? First, and foremost, it is the end of seeing anything in this world as separate from Source.

You will not waste the day if allowing is your goal. On the hour, take a moment and reflect upon the last 60 minutes. What has been left unforgiven? What is your pain in the moment? What has caused you any discomfort whatsoever? See it. Feel it. Go through it. Give it up to Source. Make this your goal.

The way to Source is forgiving every thought you have that this world is real. That it can harm you. That it can judge you. Every thought, every perception that there could be a world apart from Source needs forgiveness. There is no other way. If you did not believe the idea of being separate from Source, then you would have no need to find the way back to Truth. You would not be uncertain or confused. You would feel no guilt or powerlessness. Forgiving, allowing without fear, this is the means by which your mind is healed. This is how you learn to trust your Self again. There is no other way.

Lesson 257

Let me remember what my purpose is.

One night I awoke and sleep would not return. My habit when this happens is to lay in bed and place gentle attention on my breath. On this particular night I also used a mantra: "I know what I am. I know who I am. I know how I serve." The words come from *I Am The Word*, a channeled book by Paul Selig.

Staying with the words and the breath takes focus in the beginning. Attention ebbs and flows. But I have learned over the years to stick with it. Slowly the body relaxes, but is also energized at the same time. Sometimes it feels so full of electricity that it seems impossible to contain it all. I have learned fearlessness in these moments. I tell myself over and over to allow, have the experience, and just see what happens. This is how the inner journey always begins.

The inner journey starts along a narrow path, guided on either side by the breath and the words. I discover that each word has its own unique resonance. "I know who I am." I breathe in. It comes to me that I am not the person known as Amy. I breathe out. I am neither the mother nor the wife. I breathe in. I am not the daughter or the sister. In truth, I am none of these things. I breathe out. I am, and that is all I can know.

"I know what I am." I ride on the in-breath. Gently the knowing comes: I am not a body. I ride far, far out on the out-breath. Then I know: I am not a human being. The subtle question arises, "If I am not human, what am I?" I am weightless. I am no thing. I am the space between the particles themselves. How far out can I go on the out-breath? I can go forever into this bliss.

"I know how I serve." I breathe in and feel the word serve. "I know how I serve." I breathe far, far, far out on the out-breath. And then, I am in a place so peaceful, so wonderful, so real, and so full, that I know without any doubt whatsoever what it is to serve. To serve is simply to be. There is absolutely nothing else required. To be in service is simply to have the experience of being. There is nothing to earn, nothing to do, nothing to accomplish, nothing to strive or account for. Just being is more than enough. And I feel such gratitude to know it is enough, more than enough to simply be, that I begin to cry.

Is this possible? Are we loved so much by Source that just being is more than enough? I believe so. And yet to just be in this world seems not enough! I must obtain this title, this degree. I must earn this amount of money to pay these bills. I must have this kind of body, and these kinds of friends. I must please this person or that. This is where we veer off the path – where we get lost on the journey. We have forgotten this whole experience is just an experience. We believe it is reality and to be taken very, very seriously! This is why forgiveness is required. This is so important it bears repeating: This is why forgiveness is required.

To forgive is to allow, and nothing more. It does not excuse or condone. To forgive is to step into the river and flow with it. To forgive is to enjoy the ride as it is perfectly presented to you. This may include feelings of anger, resentment, or disappointment. There is nothing wrong with these feelings! Experience them! Why not? I do not present my moment to myself. I choose only to accept it or not, along with all the rush of emotion that accompanies it. My purpose is to have the experience. I serve Source by having my experience.

This does not mean I act out my anger. It doesn't mean I am correct in my feelings that so and so is an idiot. It means I allow myself my moment, and then return to the truth – that all of this is experience and I am in service through it. Only I am responsible for it and, at the same time, it is my gift to Source. So what do I choose? If I am sane in the moment, I will choose to allow it, and in so doing, it is forgiven. Then I will choose my next moment. I will not act as if it's Reality because it isn't.

Forgiveness is the universal Key Code on the journey through this world. Learning it is how we serve. In my late night (or early morning) meditation I knew the vast power of just being. In just being, which is forgiving, which is our purpose, we are serving Source. And being in service to Source brings a joy and gratitude that is truly beyond this world, for what more could I ask for than to be in service to Source?

Today, remember your purpose. Your purpose is to forgive, which is to allow without fear or judgment. To allow is to be.

And to be is a gift to God, to Source, and ultimately to your own Self.

Lesson 258

Let me remember that my goal is God.

ACIM places great emphasis on mind training yet it offers little advice about the actual practice of meditation. This is a bit odd given the student is asked to sit twice a day, for at least fifteen minutes, in silent contemplation.

"All that is needed is to train our minds to overlook all senseless aims and to remember that our goal is God. The memory of Source is hidden in our minds, obscured by our pointless little goals which offer nothing, and do not exist."

How easy to say, "All that is needed." Mind training takes persistence! But it is well worth it.

There is a magnificent splendor that awaits the silent mind. I know because I've seen it. That is the only basis by which I can say this is true. If I have any inkling about the peace of God, it's because I've sat in silence and followed my mind into the deepest corners I could find. And I know I can go even further, and I will go further as time passes and the Holy Spirit guides me. The Holy Spirit is my Self – the Self I give myself over to as I sit and watch, and allow all things to arise and fall away within.

How can I remember what I have forgotten I know? Sit in silence. How can I know what level of fear and discomfort I am capable of facing? Sit in silence.

The magnificence of silence requires nothing. It only asks that we allow ourselves to touch it. It waits and knows Itself and is content. Sit in silence. Let the burdens of the past arise before you and watch them until they have exhausted themselves. Let all fears of the future arise before you and watch them until they have exhausted themselves. Sit and breathe. Empty your cup of the past and future. Watch the breath and allow all things that arise in your mind to rise, peak, flow, and ebb. Allow and allow and allow. Sit and trust and stay with it until there is only the breath and then even that is gone.

Each of us will have her own experience with sitting. The point is: have your experience. Don't allow the world to steal your peace from you. The path to your Self is built over time, with practice. Our experience in meditation is the way we learn what is possible while not sitting. Meditation is a primer for daily living.

Today, be mindful of your goal. Source is your goal. Remember it today by using your power to choose. Overlook all senseless, little goals of this world, for they are but trinkets that please for a little while and vanish into disappointment. They hide the Grace of Source from your mind. Sit in silence for at least fifteen minutes today. Build the path that will become the road Home. Sit and breathe. You can do it anywhere.

Lesson 259

Let me remember there is no sin.

This whole idea of being separated by time and space is a big lie. Love cannot be separated from itself. Just because I can't see you or feel you, doesn't mean we aren't together. My attachment to my body and to your body reinforces the big lie, but it cannot make it real. Sin is the belief that separation could actually happen. Sin is the belief that death ends communication. Sin is the belief that fear is stronger than love. Sin is the insane idea that I should withhold my love from anything or anyone because I fear its loss.

"Let me remember there is no sin." Sin is nothing more than a belief that Love could separate Itself and not be everywhere. Sin is a big fat lie. Love is all over the place, even in the dimmed and hardened spaces of this world. Fear only wins when I fear to love.

Mindfulness is a form of prayer. May you be mindful on the hour and remember there is no sin. Only the belief in sin is the source of fear. It obscures your Oneness and makes you fearful of Love Itself, because you are afraid It may be given and then taken away. Indeed, you fear it has been taken away, or you would not see this world at all. Make today a prayer. Remember we are never separated from each other or from our Source. Love cannot separate from Itself and not be everywhere.

Lesson 260

Let me remember God created me.

Have you ever stood in front of a mirror and looked into the eyes of your image? It's a little uncomfortable. What you are seeing is a reflection of a reflection; the out-picturing by a mind that has no form itself.

We who have thought the body into form did not create our Self. We cannot give ourselves the power of Creation. But the personal mind believes it has done so. It exhibits this belief every time it resists what it doesn't like. Every time you perceive sin is real, helplessness is your condition, attack can kill you, or that you can attack and kill, it is the personal mind speaking. The personal mind cannot create. It can only deny. It can only say, "I do not like. I want differently. I am unhappy with this. This makes me angry. It must go away." The personal mind is limited in every way because it created itself limited through its belief it can create at all.

"Let me remember God created me." I did not create my Self, nor did you. Our Identity is beyond this world. It is fine to be here in this place, out-pictured from Mind, but it isn't fine to believe the dream. Like all dreams some moments picture happiness. But some can revert suddenly to fear, where every dream is born. If it is lasting safety and happiness you seek, it is time to remember you are dreaming.

Only Love creates what lasts because only Love truly creates. Fear cannot create in Truth. The way out of this dream is to begin to see the Love that lies beyond the shadows of our fearful projections. Behind every living thing is an aspect of Source. Stand in front of the mirror today and look at the image of your Self out-pictured. Ask the question, "Who am I? Who is looking back at me?" Feel the answer. Imagine your Self the Love that lies behind the dream image.

On the hour today, remember your Source. Feel your way into your True Identity. You are as Source created you, nothing more, and most certainly, nothing less.

Enjoy the mirror today. In truth, everyone you meet is a mirror of your Self.

Focus Question 5: *What is the Body?*

Lesson 261

Today you will engage in another set of ten lessons centered upon the question, "What is the body?" This is a most important question. It affects absolutely everything you think about yourself and the world in which you seem to exist.

The last series of lessons centered upon the question, "What is sin?" Sin is the thought you can be separate from your Source. The body is the physical manifestation of this thought.

Recall the quantum fact that matter is derived from consciousness. Thought creates form. The body is a thought in a consciousness that believes separation from Source is possible and that it has, in fact, occurred. The body is a fence we imagine we've built to separate parts of our Self from other parts of our Self, and from Source. We live within this fence and believe it keeps us "safe" from Love's Oneness. We identify with what we believe keeps us safe, so we identify with the body.

Unfortunately, the fence is neither permanent nor impermeable. It is subject to constant threats. And yet, rather than see its impermanence as proof the body is not real, we see it as evidence the body must be further protected. We treat the threat as real and the body's vulnerability as confirmation of it.

What an amazing idea! The body is a thought manifested in form we have become lost in. Is it not interesting that the mind appears to be trapped in a limited physical body by an idea created by an unlimited, nonphysical mind? Do you see why this world is a dream? Do you see why the body is a symbol of fear? It's actually rather funny, except when the body is in pain and decay. Then it sure feels real.

The body is the means by which you have become lost but it is also the means by which you can return to Sanity. You have the power to choose. You can choose to exchange the idea that created the body for an idea that is True. You can hide behind the fence of the body or can use it for a Holy purpose. What might that Holy purpose be? It is to leave the false sanctuary of the body and return to the Home that is in your mind. Stop identifying with what is not you, has never been you, and never can be you.

Does this mean you sleep outside now? Does this mean you give away all your clothes and go to work in the altogether? No. But do recognize your identification with the body is the source of all your fear. Recognize that as you seem to live and move about in a world with other bodies, you will be presented with teaching moments. These are moments that challenge you, that will seem to confirm your fear, that push your buttons. These represent false beliefs you still hold. Each one is an opportunity to allow, to forgive, to recognize, and rise above bodily fear. By overlooking the appearance of separation and embracing Oneness, you will end the dream by ending the thought that separation from Source could ever happen – even in the dream of being in a body.

Here is how to practice the next ten lessons. Each morning read and contemplate the core question and its answer. Then read the particular lesson for the day. At some point in the day devote at least fifteen minutes to quiet meditation. You know how to do this by now. Sit and place awareness on the breath. Breathe in peace and exhale any tension in the body. Take as long as you want to do this. Then repeat the lesson for the day in your mind, invite the Holy Spirit's assistance, and let everything go. Allow the breath to anchor your mind. Watch thoughts and feelings as they arise. Trust. Expect nothing and allow everything. Play. Be courageous. Explore total nonresistance. Forgive and know your Innocence.

Be mindful throughout the day. Practice forgiveness. Allow direct experience through conscious awareness. On the hour, remember the lesson. Use it to anchor your day.

In the evening, read the lesson only. Let it guide you into sleep where it will inform the other world of dreams until you waken to this one, and finally to Reality.

Today let go of the body as your refuge. Instead, place your identity in Source who is the Origin of All Things, including your unlimited mind. Today's lesson is:

Source is my refuge and my security.

What we first imagine, we may later know as truth. What we can imagine, we can experience. There is not one physical manifestation in this dream world that was not imagined first. So imagine yourself as not a body for a little while.

I once heard a woman tell of her near death experience. She spoke of falling to the floor and floating above her body. She realized she had "died" and her first thought was, "Well, how nice that I don't have to take care of that anymore. I was sick and tired of all the time it took. Thank goodness! No more brushing my teeth!"

You do not need a near death experience to experience the value of this lesson. You need only imagine how it might feel to be truly free of that which you have falsely believed has kept you safe. Only Source is your Safety. Only Mind of God is your Security. It is the only place that is not a dream.

On the hour today, look at all the bodies around you. Look at the one next to you, the one in front of you, the one behind you. She is not her body. He is not his body. Who or what might be within that body? Their Real Identity lies beyond their body, as does yours. Play with this. Imagine it.

The body is merely a way station, a temporary storage unit. It does not last but your True Identity does. It will follow you out of your body when you lay it aside one day.

As you sit in meditation today, notice how easy it is to let the body go. There will be times in your contemplation when you forget the body is even there.

Lesson 262

Let me perceive no differences today.

The perception of no difference arises from the understanding that Source is One and we originate from It. The One extends Itself infinitely. It creates ten thousand extensions with ten thousand names. Whole universes of matter and antimatter are extended. We perceive them all as waiting to be "discovered," like they're somehow new, but All come from the Original One and contain the One for there is nothing but the One. There is really nothing to be discovered and there really is nothing new if you understand the One.

I dream I am in a movie theater watching a man on the screen. He is sitting in a chair beside me, watching me watch him on the screen. Is it just a dream or is it real? I see you, seeing you see me, on a screen we have created together. We are each the actor, the watcher, and the one who perceives them both.

How far can you go with understanding? Does it seem silly? Is it too confusing? No matter, just go with it as far as you can. What is essential is your goodwill toward yourself, and all the various forms your perception shows you. Go as far as you can with your goodwill. If we all can go as far as we can with our goodwill then it is the same, for all practical purposes, as going all the way Home – to the One.

From moment to moment today, make it your play to look at all the bodies you see – young, old, big, small, dark, light, female, and male. Look at the trees, the flowers, the birds, the dogs, and cats; all of these are part of the Oneness, expressing Itself in a wild variety of form. If you are so inclined, take a moment to look up. See the clouds and know that beyond them extends a space so vast you are but a tiny speck in a tiny corner of a tiny neighborhood in a whole universe of stars.

What does it feel like to practice looking beyond the physical – even for an instant? In that instant you are born into a new knowing. You have pulled the curtain back and taken a peek behind the screen. This is all that is required – this willingness is sufficient, for the instant you have taken will reverberate through all of time.

Take fifteen minutes of quiet contemplation upon this idea today. As you close your eyes and place awareness on the breath, allow thoughts and feelings to arise. Notice them. Follow the thought or feeling from the time you're first aware of it until it slips away. Stay with the breath as an anchor. There will be a time when even the body seems to slip away and you will become one with something beyond the breath, beyond the body. Even if only for an instant, you will perceive no difference between your mind, your body, and all that surrounds you. You will touch the face of Oneness.

Lesson 263

Through my Real Perception, I see all things as Pure.

Nothing I see is not myself.
I am the tree, the rock, the wind, the rain, the falling leaf.
I am the child on the beach and I am the thrower of stones.
I am the son of the mother, and I am the daughter who chooses.
I am the dying man and she who even now is coming into the world.
I am the one who stands alone in the storm and I am the wind
    howling.
I am the fish afloat in the pond and
I am the mountain stream that feeds it.
I am the light of stardust and I am the breathing of the universe.
All of these I am. And I am none of them.
I am that, and I am that, and I am that, and I am none of that.
Unnameable, I am. More vast than any part of it alone or put
    together.
– AN Haible

Unnamable is what we are. What can be the name for Everything? Nothing we perceive would be unless it arose first in our Mind, which is Pure, and contains the All. And so today's lesson.

What is "real perception?" It is Whole Perception. Whole Perception is the realization that all things are encompassed by Mind of God, in Whose Mind our Mind resides. My mind, together with your mind, and all other minds, are the extension of the One Mind, the All That Is. Our minds together extend All That Is because that is what All That Is created us to do. How can anything be impure that has arisen out of Purity Itself?

All that is alone, penetrable, sacrificed, hardened by failure and doubt, sick and suffering, is but a dance of shadows across a screen. All that is separated, all that appears alone, penetrable, sacrificed, hardened by failure and doubt, sick and suffering, is

Purity Itself.

Today, be willing to observe the dream. Be willing to be one of the actors on the screen in the movie of life. But know your freedom, for in your knowing that even as you play yourself with all intensity and passion, it has nothing to do with what you really are. You are Purity Itself. Remind yourself of your purity and the purity of all around you today. Nothing you see is not within your Self and your Self is without blemish of any kind.

Gift yourself today the gift of meditation. As you sit, invite yourself to feel the dignity, the courage, the brilliance, the magnificence that you are. Be happy with yourself. Know yourself. Your knowing is the ripple in the pond that extends boundlessly outward.

Lesson 264

I am surrounded by the Love of God.

Even as you read this, you stand within The All, beside The All, and as The All. There is no place The All is not. You are as a wave in an ocean of Love. Your experience in this body, this time, this space and place, is but an infinitesimally tiny moment in Mind of God. Yet you do not go unnoticed or unvalued. Indeed, you are wanted, you are welcomed, you are held in the gentlest embrace. Nothing in Mind of God would be the same without you.

Take a moment on the hour today. Draw your awareness within. Silently, without words, focus your mind on the thought that you are surrounded by the Love of Source. Feel this Love, this safety, this peace, through your Holy Perception. It will change your day.

Sit for fifteen minutes in silent meditation today. Take your seat and relax. Place awareness gently on the breath. You might wish to begin your meditation with the following prayer:

Love before me.
Love behind me.
Love to my left.
Love to my right.
Love above me.
Love below me.
Love unto me.
Love to all that surrounds me.
Love to all beings, everywhere.
Love to the Universe.

Sink into the peace of this prayer. Breathe in love and let go of all that is not love on the out-breath. Invite the Holy Spirit to guide your mind.

Lesson 265

Creation's gentleness is all I see.

Is gentleness valued in this world, or is it reserved for the sick, the helpless, infants and young children? Gentleness is often associated with the vulnerable, the childish, the docile, the feminine, the weak, but rarely is gentleness associated with power. How we undervalue the power of gentleness! No one is here who has not benefitted from it!

Fear begets fear just as gentleness begets gentleness. When the barriers are down and defeat is at the door, we all call for gentleness. We hope for it. We pray for it.

I have misunderstood the world, because I have laid what I thought were my sins on it, and I saw them looking back at me. How fierce they seemed! How deceived I was to think that what I feared was in the world instead of only in my mind.
– ACIM

Gentleness is in your Mind because it is joined with the Creator's Mind. Creator's Mind perceives only gentleness. How could Source not love what It has created with the power of Its own gentleness?

On the hour, look around at all that is before you. Let your heart relax with the knowing it is all One, all your one Self, born in gentleness and held by Love in the Mind of Source. Nothing but fear can disturb the gentleness of Love, and fear is illusion. Only Love is Real because only Source exists. Find time for quietness today. It is in the quiet mind that Creation's gentleness is known.

Lesson 266

You are my Holy Self.

When I was in my early twenties I had a minor epiphany about the purpose of family. Like most families we had our share of ups and downs. There were times in my teens when I felt I never wanted to speak to my mother again.

Families often offer the first place in life we learn the lessons of forgiveness. But there is one rule: you cannot abandon the relationship. You may close your heart for a while. You may cease speaking to or seeing each other. But there has to be a mutual willingness to open again.

Our "real" family includes everyone with no exceptions. The absence of a blood relationship is merely a perceptual illusion. Until we understand the true depth of our connection with each other, until we live in willingness to be connected, heaven will always be just the other side of the mountain. This is today's lesson.

You are not being asked to love everyone today. Honest disagreement occurs in all families. In fact, family is where we are allowed to show our vulnerability and confusion. But we are still required to acknowledge that each person we meet is a part of our Self. We who did not create the Self cannot change this truth.

This is a lesson for the park bench, or any place you can sit in awareness and look around. Allow your gaze to rest softly on each person in your field of view. Say to yourself, "You are my Holy Self, and so are you, and you." Look upon each person with an open mind, an open heart. Acknowledge their sovereignty. Each person you see is wholly sovereign as part of the One Self of which you are included.

Do not fool yourself. There will come a time for each of us when we will be in the presence of our "enemy" and reconciliation will be required for both to move forward. But what will be forgiven? It will simply be the unwillingness to see our Oneness in the Love of Source. Each enemy you have is, in truth, your savior. For if you are willing to perceive them as Source does, your learning will advance.

Forgiveness is the lesson of this world. Beyond this dream of separation, where Oneness is perceived without effort, what need of forgiveness could there be? So, this lesson must be learned here, where the need for it was born. It can be learned now, or later. But the curriculum is set. If you are ready to learn the curriculum now, you can begin today simply by looking upon all you see and gently offering them the silent truth: "You are my Holy Self."

Lesson 267

My heart beats with the Peace of God.

There are those who will read this lesson and say, "Yes. This is true for me. Today, I am at peace." And there are others who look at the words on the page and think, "No, I am not at peace. And the fact that I am not, when the words say I should be, makes me even less so."

If today's lesson is easy for you, then relish it. Remember the way peace feels, for there will be other days when you will forget. But if you are among those who don't feel the Peace of God today, then know this lesson is for you. Above all, do not feel guilty that you are not at peace. Do not make the achievement of peace a burden.

We are meant to be happy but this does not mean we have to put on a happy face for God. Do you think Oneness doesn't know all Its aspects? Our calling here is not to hide but to devote ourselves, with active willingness, to the bringing forth of guilt and shame in all their forms. To achieve our calling, we must bring all to Light. So, if you are not at peace, it is a clarion call that something hidden wishes to come forth and be seen. Your job is to bring it forth to be healed with forgiveness. Place all of it on the altar of the Holy Spirit and let It take it from there.

"My heart beats with the Peace of God." I am free to let go of guilt and fear. I am free to see my hidden belief that I will be lied to or betrayed if I offer myself to God. I am free to see this fear in all its forms and forgive it.

"My heart beats with the Peace of God." I am free to release all that lies between myself and peace. I forgive myself and all around me in my awareness that this world is healed in Love and only Love is Real.

"My heart beats with the Peace of God." I am free to take time today in silence. I am free to go inward and feel my heart. I will breathe. I will sit in quiet and allow the Peace of God within my body, within my breath, within my mind. I will forgive all that is not at peace, and in forgiving, peace will be free to enter.

Lesson 268

Let all things be exactly as they are.

I am free to walk upstream if I want to. I can enjoy the feel of the water moving against my legs with each step. This might give me the feeling of being in control, of knowing where I am in the flow. How often we equate struggle with control! But it's tiring, and in truth, I'm just seeing the same old landscape I saw when I was coming downstream.

I am also free to lie down in the stream and let the water carry me where it will. I can float like a little twig in the currents. Sometimes I might bump into another twig or have to move around a stone. I can merge with other twigs and float side by side. I might move faster as streams converge and the waters get bigger. Eventually, I may come to the ocean and float there – who knows?

I can walk upstream if I want to. But this assumes I know that what is downstream is something I don't want. And really, I don't know what's downstream. If I choose to become the twig, I have to trust. Today's lesson says, "Yes, choose TRUST!"

This is all we have to do, really – trust and allow. See what happens. This doesn't mean we don't prepare or think ahead. The chickadees have been hiding seeds since July. In June, I bought our winter wood. The hummingbirds recently decided to head south. I miss their chirping and mid-flight antics, but they do this every fall. In every moment I am choosing, as they do, to resist or allow.

What will you allow today? What will you resist? Can you stop on the hour, look around, and be conscious of what you have just allowed or resisted? Or better yet, can you sense into your resistance while it is happening? And if so, can you take a breath and relax into whatever it is?

Give yourself fifteen minutes of silence today. Take your seat, get comfortable in your body, and place awareness on the breath. Notice what you feel in the moment. Allow it. Notice what happens when you allow. Is there a little more peace?

Watch the breath. Repeat the lesson in your mind. "Let all

things be exactly as they are." Sit in silent allowing of all things and just notice. Remember only one thing: forgive all things that arise in resistance, for the only thing that truly ends resistance is the forgiveness of it.

Now, everybody, get this: You don't have to fight. You can allow. Allow, allow, allow.
– Paul Selig, *The Book of Love and Creation*

Lesson 269

I look upon Oneness and I am Love.

The lessons of the last week have centered on the question, "What is the body?" Most of the time what we see with the body's eyes forms the basis of our reality. And yet, over and over again, ACIM teaches that the body is a completely unreliable tool of perception. In fact, you rely on its unreliability.

The lesson for today asks you to look beyond the physical for the Truth about Reality. True Perception is not of the body! The physical eye perceives, but the invisible mind of the heart knows. "My sight goes forth to look upon Christ's face." True vision leads with the invisible mind held in the heart. The Christ is in everyone you see.

As you move through your day, stop hourly to remember that regardless of outward appearance, the one you see before you is part of your Self, the Self you are in Truth. "I look upon Oneness and I am Love. I am Love through the act of knowing myself as Love."

A major impediment to Knowing is the inner belief we do not deserve to Know. The belief I do not deserve to know Who I Am must be put aside now. You will not Know yourself as Love without everyone around you. You will not Know yourself as Love without extending the thought that the Christ, Love, or

Source if you prefer, is in every face you see, including the one that appears to stare back at you in the mirror. Practice True Perception today. Go forth and look upon the One before you as the Christ Itself. You are Love through the One you see before you. You become Love through this recognition.

Gift yourself with at least fifteen minutes of silent contemplation today. Take your seat and relax. Let the breath come naturally and place your awareness on its constant flow, in and out. Say to yourself, "I am Love through the One I see before me." Feel the words. Your identity as Love cannot be taken from you. It is as sure as the morning sun and the evening star. Surer than these in fact, for both will fade away in time, but your identity as Love is your eternal inheritance.

Lesson 270

I will not use the body's eyes today.

Perhaps you will remember the first three lessons that began this year's exploration of ACIM? They are worth remembering. Indeed, they are always worth applying to anything that causes discomfort, wounding, or anger:

1. *Nothing I see in the room, from this window, in this place, means anything.*
2. *I have given everything I see all the meaning it has for me.*
3. *I do not understand anything I see.*

And here we are, 270 lessons later, continuing to explore the nature of "sight." Okay, this lesson does not ask us to walk around blindfolded. But it does ask that we remain willing to question the fundamental reality of what our body's eyes perceive.

Perhaps you will remember that all you see is nothing more

than the tiniest particles vibrating at a speed that makes them appear solid? Perhaps you will remember that most of what you perceive to be solid is mostly empty space? Perhaps you will consider that everything is light? Or, even more important, that Love is the underlying foundation of all you perceive because Love Light is creation Itself and nothing exists that is not a part of It?

Let yourself see beyond the superficial today. To see deeply, you will need to use your heart. You will need to sense and feel. You will need to extend your mind in peace. On the hour, remember to stop and look. Be curious! Be playful! This is not some serious game we are involved in here, no matter what the headlines say. See beyond the news of this world! Look at what lies beneath the chatter, fear, and chaos. There is so much around us that is full of life.

Remember this today: "The whole world is inside my mind and there is nothing outside of it. I give it all the meaning it has for me. Let me know it as the Light Love from which all things are Sourced. Never ending. Always changing. All One."

Begin your fifteen minutes of silent contemplation with the words of today's lesson. Then relax into the breath. See with the inner eye. Ask for assistance and allow it to come. Know that whatever arises in your mind is perfect. Receive it gently and let it go like the tide. Be at peace and worry not about the things outside the room. All you do in peace ripples out, changing things you cannot imagine, much less see.

Focus Question 6: *What is the Christ?*

Lesson 271

"What is the Christ?" This question and its answer form the theme for the next ten lessons.

To understand what the Christ is, it is helpful to revisit ACIM's teaching about how the world was "made" because the world and the "Christ" are fully entwined.

ACIM teaches that the world is a thought projection created by our own collective unconscious mind. At some point, the collective mind chose to have the experience of being like its Creator. In other words, it wanted the creative powers of the Creator on its own. It wanted to feel what it might be like to actually be the Creator. In Reality, this was impossible, of course. Still, it could be "imagined." So, having been granted total freedom by the Creator, the collective mind's desire became "real." The result is this universe, all universes in fact.

As you have heard many times over, the universe is a massive projection. And since nothing can occur without an effect, the effect of this imagined separation from the Creator was the idea of guilt. Of course, separation from Creator is impossible, so guilt is also impossible. But the guilt over having the thought seemed real to the mind that made it. Appearing to be real, the guilt was unbearable and so it was projected outward. Now, when you deny something in yourself, it has to go somewhere. Where did it go? Into the world we see around us.

When something is denied and projected outward, it is forgotten. This is why we do not recognize the world and all that is in it as our own creation. The simple truth is, we actually made what we're looking at, forgot we made it, and are now sitting in the belief it is reality.

This is where "the Christ" comes in. Christ is the Creator's Real Extension. It is like God DNA that is in every single thing – even our projected dream. The Christ is in total alignment with the Thought of God. The Christ is Source's correction to the massive, metaphysical, unconscious thought of separation, and it is the only part of each of us that has any basis in Reality. The Christ is the Source DNA memory of Oneness.

The lesson for today is:

Christ's is the vision I will use today.

Each day, each hour, every instant, we are choosing. We have spent lifetimes making the choice for separation. We have grown so used to it that it is no longer questioned. We "see" separation as real. We take it for granted. We have forgotten our true origin. It takes practice to look at the world as One. But recognition of Oneness is the only way out of this world, because it is the only Truth. The illusion of separation cannot be cured by other illusions.

The recognition of Oneness reverses all the laws of the world. When you "see" with the eyes of Christ, the insanity of our value system becomes obvious. Christ's Vision turns this world upside down, challenging the very core of its beingness.

Holiness is beyond all time and space, distance and limits of any kind. Christ Consciousness is transcendent. It is so beyond the rules that created this world that it encompasses and corrects them. It retranslates the entire language of the group consciousness that imagined it could separate from Source. Yet it is within each and every one of us. You are a Whole I Child of God.

Today, you are asked to use your Christ Mind. Use it first to forgive yourself for imagining the world is real. Then use it to forgive everyone else who is still living unconsciously in the dream. This is how to reactivate your Source DNA. Spiritual sight, done at the level of the mind, sends a signal that matches the one sent by Source.

On the hour today, stop and look around. As you have done before, in other lessons, look with new eyes on the world around you. There is not one thing you see that is separate from you. Not one person, not one living thing that is not a part of your Mind. Use your mind to remember. You need to do this as often as possible. You are reactivating a form of perception that has long been dormant. That is why we keep repeating this idea in the lessons.

As you sit in silent contemplation, call upon your Christ

Mind. It is there, waiting for you to "see" it within yourself. It is the place in your mind that is still within Source. It is what created you. You cannot lose it, but you can forget it is there. It is time to remember.

Lesson 272

How can illusions satisfy God's Creation?

There is a legendary story about the moment in which Indian guru Ramana Maharshi gained enlightenment. At the age of sixteen, he lay alone on the floor of the family home overcome with fear at the thought of his own mortality. Suddenly, he asked himself, "Who is having these thoughts? Who is the 'I' who fears death?"

Today's lesson is virtually the same answer Ramana Maharshi received in his moment of enlightenment. You are not the one who is afraid. You are not the one who suffers, and you are not the one who dies. You are the one experiencing the feeling. You are the one observing the thought. Neither the thought nor the feeling is who or what you are. It is your feeling and thought that are the illusion. It is the observer of both that is real.

Ramana Maharshi taught his students to see beyond the illusion. ACIM calls this seeing with the Christ Mind. It matters not what it is called. The point is to answer the question, "Who is experiencing this thought? Who is believing it is true?" The Maharshi advised his followers to habitually ask, "Who is having this experience of anger, fear, injustice, rejection, cowardice, remorse, loneliness?" "Who is the I who is perceiving?"

I am free to feel whatever arises in the moment. I am also free to ask, "Who feels this feeling?" Is it the daughter who was told she needed to improve herself to be accepted? Is it the employee who fears his boss's criticism? Is it the one who believes his bank account is a measure of his worth? Is it the one who believes she is a sick body? Who is behind the thought? Is the thought true or is it an illusion? Imperfection is always the illusion.

Ask yourself often today, "Who am I that is having this experience, this thought, this feeling?" Do not be content with superficial answers. See beyond the illusion of form. Use your inheritance, Christ's Perception, to "see" beyond the image on the screen of life.

As you sit in silent contemplation today, ask yourself, "Who am I?" That which arises as the "I" is in your mind and especially in your heart. The heart is the origin of "I" for it is the seat of knowing. Feel your way into the answer to the question, "Who am I?" Be kind with yourself. Who is the "I" that remains after all the questions have been asked? In the deep peace of stillness, what is left that still perceives? This is what you are.

Our deepest fear is not that we are inadequate. Our deepest fear is that we are powerful beyond measure. It is our light, not our darkness, that most frightens us. We ask ourselves, "Who am I to be brilliant, gorgeous, talented, fabulous?" Actually, who are you not to be? You are a child of God.
– Marianne Williamson, A Return to Love: Reflections on the Principles of A Course in Miracles

Lesson 273

The stillness of the peace of God is mine.

There is a tendency to think the world can offer consolation and escape from problems that its purpose is to keep. Why should this be? Because it is a place where choice among illusions seems to be the only choice.
– ACIM

This world cannot offer anything except temporary respite

from its relentless expression of separation. This is because the purpose of this world, which is an outward projection of inner mind, is to show you what separation looks like. Therefore, do not expect this world to give you what you really want. You want the lasting peace of God. It will not be found here, but only in your mind, joined with Source. Do not take this on faith! Open the door, step in, and have the experience of it. Only then will you know.

The stillness of the peace of God is yours. Only you can claim it for yourself. Take it today. If you cannot, be content and even more than satisfied to learn that such a day is yours anyway. It is yours through your own knowing. Make this day your minion!

This world has no real or lasting value because it is not real or lasting itself. But the beauty of this world is a reflection of the magnificent abundance that lies within you. All that is good in this world echoes the Reality of Source. This is lasting. This has value.

There can be no guilt whatsoever in loving the stillness of the world today. Take the opportunity to remember the unending peace of God within. Come to it from a place of love and experience it in love. It is an outer reflection of an inner state that is your inheritance unlimited by anything but your own willingness to remember.

On the hour, stop what you are doing and listen. Open the window of your mind to the silence that lies beneath all the overlying noise and clutter. See and listen with the eyes and the ears of the heart. Take this gift. If you feel any disturbance, let today be the day you learn how to dismiss it and return to peace. Any uncomfortable feeling is the same as any other uncomfortable feeling, no matter how big or small, because it's not peace.

Find time to sit in silence today. Slowly, say in your mind, "The stillness of the peace of God is mine. I need not fear its loss, for what can rob me of the gifts Source gives? I cannot lose what is mine by right, and so I seek and know in quiet and stillness the Love that is My Self in Truth."

Real choice is no illusion. This world has no real choices to offer. Do not take it seriously. Remember, this world was formed when we forgot to laugh at the tiny, mad idea we could be separate from Source.

Lesson 274

Today belongs to Love. I will not fear.

Love includes everything because it fears nothing. Fear, on the other hand, excludes all but that which is acceptable to it. It perceives vulnerability as the truth about itself. Fear and Love. Love and fear. Can it be true that fear is nothing more than the wisp of illusion? When you are sitting in the peace of silent contemplation, is fear present? When you are in the midst of a fearful situation, can you even remember what peace feels like? Both seem to be true, but in Truth, only one is Real.

Nothing real can be threatened. Nothing unreal exists.
– ACIM

If you know one thing, know it is fear that is unreal. Hold fast to this Truth in moments when it appears night has fallen permanently.

Do not feel guilty if love is difficult some days, for guilt is a waste of time. It just gives the ego's voice more power. Forgive yourself for not feeling love in the moment. This opens the door guilt has slammed shut.

In your time, do what you can to love. We must know our own invulnerability to feel only Love's presence. But be aware, even if you do not love fully in the moment, Love is always with you. Be willing to look with diligence at the thoughts that keep the fear alive. Ask, "What is it I value here? What am I afraid of? Why am I unable to allow this moment?" Allowing and Loving are not so far apart. Allowing what is, is a form of Love.

Love sees through the illusion of fear. When I am certain of Love's presence I stop reacting to the world as if it is real. Today, step out of fear as often as you can. You are Home now, in this moment. Fear is the stranger here.

On the hour, take a break. Ask yourself, "What have I been fearful of in the past hour? How has fear motivated what I said or how I responded to someone or something?" Let go of any guilt around what you discover and move on.

Those who succeed in Love are persistent about removing the barriers to It. They are both honest and forgiving at the same time. Over time, they see Love's power to reverse all the laws of this world. We who are born of Love cannot fail to find it.

On the hour today, remind yourself, "Today belongs to Love. Let me not fear." Fear is the stranger here, not Love. Do what you can today. Love is the end of separation. The end of separation is the end of fear. Forgive and know Love for yourself and for the world that is in such need of It.

As you sit in silent contemplation, you may well reach the state where fear is a distant memory. Keep this feeling close as you rise from your seat and go about the day. It is your gift to yourself. If you lose the gift, or forget it, re-gift yourself with the memory of its presence.

Lesson 275

God's healing Voice protects all things today.

The personal mind believes reality is found only in this world. Whatever form the idea of "heaven" might take is so far beyond as to be all but unavailable. You have to die to get there. The personal mind holds out heaven like a carrot on a stick, just beyond reach. We spend lifetime after lifetime walking in the endless cycle of the personal mind's thought system. "Seek for eternity, but do not find it." This is a thought system that consumes hope to feed itself.

The kingdom is not of this world because it was given you from beyond this world.
– ACIM

The alternative to this world cannot come from this world! The definition of insanity is to repeat the same thing over and over, expecting the result will change. Stop looking for Love in a world that was made to show us what Love is not.

There is a "Voice" for Love that is beyond this world. It tells us things we cannot understand alone nor learn apart from It. It takes willingness to hear this Voice. It takes faith at first to be assured that the Voice is not a projection of your own mind. It may come as a synchronicity, an image, an animal, or a sudden thought that seems to arise out of nowhere. Often the Voice is felt in the heart.

How will you recognize the Voice? It will always be kind. It will never judge or punish. It will be inclusive, instructive, gentle, patient, quiet, and totally affirming. It will call upon you to lay aside your anxiety and be present in the moment.

It often takes practice to hear the Voice. It takes trust and courage in a world that seems to thrive on not hearing. But honestly, what greater skill could you cultivate in this life than the ability to hear and follow the Voice for Source? The Voice is Love Itself. On the hour take a moment and be still. Before deciding anything, take a moment. Just listen and trust what you feel. Know your listening is protected.

As you sit in silent meditation today, trust yourself to hear. Place your attention on the breath and leave all things to that which created your mind and sustains it in waking and sleeping.

You will hear. Every peaceful or forgiving thought is hearing. You will hear because a mind in concert with its Source is capable of understanding.

Lesson 276

The Word of God is given me to speak.

In the beginning was the Word, and the Word was with God. Through Word all things were made. Without Word nothing was made that has been made. In Word was Light and Light is in all things. The Light shines and there is nothing that can overcome It.
– John 1:1–14

What is the Word of God? The Word is Light and all things are contained in It. The Word is you and It is me, and It is only both of us together. And the Light of Word has been given to us and nothing can overcome It.

Source extends Itself and we are Its Holy Extension. Deny that you were created in Source and you deny your Self. Deny your creation in Source and remain unsure Who you are, What you are, and Why you are here. You are Word Itself and you are here to Know your Self as Word.

The Word of God is given you to speak. You did not create It, but you are free to extend It. This is your task today: extend the Light that has been given you. Know your Self as Word and share It with the one next to you. You Know your Self as Word through your powers of extension. All that you give, all that you extend, will be received and returned to you. This is the Law of Love. It is how Source receives through extending Its Self to us.

Lesson 277

Let me not limit Oneness with laws I have made.

In Oneness we are limitless. All that Is becomes ours in Oneness. It is separation that requires a thousand different laws to keep each separate part safe, alone, defined, and confined.

There really is only one law needed in this world. It is called the "golden rule." It is known as, "Love your neighbor as yourself." It is known as, "Do unto others as you would have done to you." The Law of Oneness extends outward infinitely. Treat the planet as you would be treated. Treat animals with loving kindness. Treat your body with the dignity you wish to experience. Allow all other beings the respect you would like extended to yourself.

When we abandoned the Law of Love, we created a thousand other laws to take Its place. Unable to love equally, unable to be fair, unable to remain awake, unable to consciously control our bodies or our minds, unable to see the other as our Self, unable to stand together in recognition of our Oneness, we created entire libraries of laws, supposedly adaptable to every situation. In the confusion of laws we forgot the Law of Oneness, which really is the only Law that applies equally to all things, in all situations. "Would I want what I have done, or am prepared to do, done to me?" "Would I want him or her to say to me, what I am prepared to say to her or him?" "What would it if feel like if I were in her/ his shoes?" Answered truthfully, the Law of Oneness suffices in every situation.

> *Limbs are cherished because they are parts of the body. Why then are other people not cherished because they are parts of humanity?*
> – Shantideva

The Law of Oneness has been abandoned for the law of "what's good for me." As we devolved from limitless to limited, our view of the world descended into single bodies from which each of us alone now views creation. But all illusions must end.

This world's laws are clashing against each other. Just for today, try practicing with the Law of Oneness. But do remember: simplicity does not always equate with ease. The personal mind creates a thousand situations that seem to demand a different law for each. It takes diligence to practice the Law of One. Forgive yourself when you fail; forgive others for not trying hard enough. The purpose of this world is to be the place where we relearn the Law of One.

If it helps, remember this: we did not make the Law of One, nor can we unmake it. Like it or not, it is a Law that supersedes all others. This is why, in one form or another, you also always "reap what you sow." This is not a punishment. It is a teaching device. Give what you wish to receive. Give all to have all.

Lesson 278

If I am limited, so is Source.

A spiritual teacher of mine was fearless in her quest for truth. Blessed with a quick mind and a photographic memory, Dr. Zoe Marae was truly a force to be reckoned with.

When she first began to hear her "guides," Zoe thought she was losing her mind. With a doctorate in bio-physiology, she had all kinds of tests done, thinking she might have a tumor or some other brain disorder. Nothing turned up. One day, fed up with sharing her mind, she demanded the voices stop. "I have the right to my own mind!" she declared. "You cannot come in uninvited!" Suddenly she "heard" a thunderous applause. "It was like Yankee Stadium," she said. Her guides roundly approved her declaration of her independent will, and the voices quieted down a notch.

Zoe was a difficult teacher, in part because she expected us to be as talented as she was. She accepted no limitations for herself and none for us. It is Zoe I think of now, when I stretch my mind out as far as it can go in deep meditation. "What is behind that thought?" I ask. "What lies beyond this fear?" "Bring it on," I tell the universe, just as she did. And I feel heaven's answer back, a resounding, "Yes!"

And so the lesson for today, which reminds us yet again that we are not limited by the physical any more than is our Creator. The laws of this world do not apply forever and forever. There are worlds beyond this one that abide by rules we have not yet even imagined. Each time we state our declaration of independence, our willingness to explore, heaven applauds us for it.

> *If I accept that I am a prisoner within a body, in a world in which all things that seem to live appear to die, then Source is prisoner with me. And this I do believe when I maintain the laws the world obeys, must I obey; the frailties and the sins, which I perceive are real and cannot be escaped. If I am bound in any way, I do not know my Creator or my Self. And I am lost to all Reality. For Truth is free, and what is bound is not a part of Truth.*
> *– ACIM*

Know yourself capable. Your fears are dreams, born in a world of dreams. But you are the living Template of Heaven Itself. You are as unlimited as the One Who created you.

Lesson 279

Creation's freedom promises my own.

My freedom is wholly dependent upon yours, and yours is also dependent upon mine. Freedom is an all or nothing deal.

Freedom and limitlessness have much in common and both are ours by right. The instinctive desire to be free is a yearning with which we are born. Yet, in this world we are all too willing to ignore the slavery of others so long as we think it will not impede our own freedom. The instant I compromise your freedom to enhance my own, both are lost. Why is this? To understand the answer you must know what limitlessness is.

Limitlessness is achieved naturally in Oneness. This is why all things are of the Creator. It is also why you do not have to imagine what it would be to play like Mozart, to write like Shakespeare, to paint like a master, or to know mathematics with the mind of a Nobel Prize winner. Your mind shares all of these minds.

Some children are born with a certain skill far in advance of their age. Some hear voices. Some know things before they happen or can communicate with those who have passed out of the physical realm. This is not far-fetched stuff; it happens because minds are always in connection with Mind. We should get used to it. We should explore the hell out of it! Instead, we limit ourselves to the voices that say, "No. It cannot be so." Make no mistake – these are same voices that tell you it is possible hurt another and remain free yourself.

We are limitless because we are Oneness extending Itself endlessly. We do not need to understand all the details, but we do have to be open to possibilities – which requires a certain amount of fearlessness. We stand at the threshold of a room, the contents of which we are unaware. Should we open the door or not? What will happen if we open it? Forgive your fear and open the door. It is the act of opening the door that is the teaching itself. It is the act of opening the door that extends freedom.

How have you limited yourself? What is it that has been limited? And whom have you limited in the hope of expanding your own freedom? Has it given you what you wanted?

Today, take your freedom and share it with those in your

presence. Source does not withhold anything, because It knows that in giving, It is receiving through you. Do the same for those in your presence today. Here's a little secret: we become the Creator when we act like It.

Lesson 280

I cannot limit the Creator's Creations.

You were given everything when you were created, just as everyone was.
– ACIM

On the face of it, this statement sounds absurd. It seems perfectly obvious that some have more than others – more wealth, more intelligence, more physical attributes, more capability, more resources, more talent, or more beauty. Yet, if the common denominator of all this "more" is taken into account it becomes apparent that the "more" always has to do with the body and the needs it has. Only the body wants more. Only the mind that believes it is a body wants more.

When Source created you, It did not "gift" you with a body. It gifted you the power to create one for yourself. And herein lies all the difference. You are not the body you created and now seem to inhabit. You are so much more. Lack, or its perception, is always of the body. I lack warmth, clothing, food and shelter, other bodies to keep me company, a job that pays enough to keep the body healthy. The limitations of physical form and the accompanying belief it is what we are, and only what we are, are almost beyond your comprehension. Today's lesson requires you to drop the limitations of the body and begin to comprehend your Self.

It is the personal mind – the mind that identifies exclusively with the body – that perceives limitation of God's creation. The absolute belief in limitation by the personal mind is an attempt to undo Creation Itself.

The whole idea of lack is this: I would be better off in a state somehow different from the one I am in. But if I was truly created without lack, where did the idea of lack come from? It comes from the separation. Before the fall into separation, nothing was lacking. There were no needs at all. Need has arisen because we have deprived ourselves.

The sense of separation from Source is the only lack you truly need to correct. Undo the separation from Source in your mind, and all else will follow. Let go of the idea that you are your own teacher. The personal mind teaches only lack!

You are unlimited in Truth. All aspects of lack and fear are untrue because they do not exist at the level of creation!

Perfect Love casts out fear.
If fear exists,
Then there is not perfect Love.
But:
Only perfect Love exists.
If there is fear,
It produces a state that does not exist.
– ACIM

If you would spend the day in contemplation of this simple statement it would take years off your learning. You who did not create yourself, but were created to create, have created the illusion of fear in all its forms. Today, accept the truth about yourself: you are unlimited by anything. Look beyond the face of fear. Look beyond the body. Use the sense that transcends all bodily senses and know this about yourself.

Focus Question 7: *What is the Holy Spirit?*

Lesson 281

"What is the Holy Spirit?" This is the foundation question for your next ten lessons. In all likelihood, the Holy Spirit has never been adequately explained to you, which has hindered Its ability to heal your mind. The Holy Spirit has many names but Its function does not change. Let me explain.

It is true that you have been told Source does not know fear. You have also been told Source does not experience guilt, confusion, or doubt. Yet we seem to live with all of these. They form our "reality." How does Source, Which Knows only Reality, speak to illusion? How does Source, which sees us as only Whole, within Itself, reach out to a split mind that has created a dream and is now lost in it? This is the Holy Spirit's function.

The Holy Spirit reaches through the dream to the dreamer. It is the Interface between the All and the illusion. It is the Universal Translator that speaks the Language of Source and the language of the dream. The Holy Spirit brings the Voice for Source to the mind asleep.

When the Holy Spirit shares its Perception, your mind is called to recognize and forgive its illusions. If you do not recognize and forgive your illusions, they will remain to terrify you. Fear and guilt shield your mind from the Truth of Love. The Holy Spirit is Light. It is the Voice for God that speaks quietly in your mind, turning it from illusion to Knowing. It is That within you that seeks for and recognizes the miracle. You could call It your gift of Source DNA. You could say, It turns your Source DNA on.

Learn to listen for the Holy Spirit in your mind. You will know It through experience. Through experience you will learn to recognize Its Voice. It will never speak harshly to you. It will never offer judgment. It is the Call for Love to be Love Itself. It is your Homing Beacon for Wholeness. You will know It through a sense of Completion and Peace. It is always there to help you fulfill your function.

Here is how to practice the next ten lessons. Each morning read and contemplate the core question and its answer. Then read the particular lesson for the day. At some point in the day devote at least fifteen minutes to quiet meditation. You know how to do this by now. Sit and place awareness on the breath. Breathe in peace and exhale any tension in the body. Take as long as you want to do this. Then repeat the lesson for the day in your mind, invite the Holy Spirit's assistance, and let everything go. Allow the breath to anchor your mind. Watch thoughts and feelings as they arise. Trust. Expect nothing and allow everything. Play. Be courageous. Explore total nonresistance. Forgive and know your Innocence.

Be mindful throughout the day. Practice forgiveness. Allow direct experience through conscious awareness. On the hour, remember the lesson. Use it to anchor your day.

In the evening, read the lesson only. Let it guide you into sleep where it will inform the other world of dreams until you waken to this one, and finally to Reality.

Your lesson today is:

I can be hurt by nothing but my thoughts.

Understand that the finite is created by the infinite, and this lesson will become perfectly obvious. But for those who still believe the world begins and ends with form, it will be difficult, if not impossible, to grasp. This is a lesson that must be experienced to be understood.

Thoughts are formless, multidimensional energies. They arrive from and extend beyond this three-dimensional world of form. The physical brain is not the origin of knowing. Its function is to receive, compute, and transmit. Each of us holds individual thoughts as well as collective thoughts. Both are immensely powerful. They create our world.

For thousands of years we have held a collective agreement with a thought system that values the material body above all else. What we value is what we consider truth. Hence, the body becomes our obsession and the measure of our worth. If it is sick, "we" are sick. If it is beautiful, "we" are beautiful. If it is comfortable, "we" are comfortable. If it is having any experience at all, so too are "we." If we imagine it dead, "we" must be also. How odd it is that some of the most intelligent minds cannot conceive of a consciousness that lives beyond form!

Our collective agreement is completely in error. What we have valued must be released and a new agreement made. Indeed, this is happening. If you are reading this, you are part of the new agreement. And when you know the truth about who you are, you bring all things with you into the new contract.

You are here. In the face of all challenges and despair, you are here. In the face of all the fear we have created that has made this world, you are here. Claim this truth for yourself. No one else can do it for you.

Love requires no sacrifice. This is the truth of the new agreement. I cannot build my house on the bones of my brothers, nor can I build it on the ashes of my own guilt. We are here now to stand in our truth and declare ourselves free of the myth of death. That is the truth. When I know my truth, my thoughts change. When my thoughts change, my world changes. This is a lesson that must be experienced to be understood.

"I can be hurt by nothing but my thoughts." In the face of fear and uncertainty, claim your sovereignty! Trust in your own virtue. Know that behind his or her fear, your brother and sister are also virtuous in Truth. When you make the claim, "I am here! Nothing can hurt me," you are pronouncing the Love of your own creation. And your thought is your creation. Know this: "All healing is essentially a release from fear."

Create in Love or create in fear. Fear begets only more fear.

Love extends Love. Only one is real. Guess which one it is? Here's a clue. Love is infinite. Fear is limitation itself.

Lesson 282

I will not be afraid of Love today.

The vast majority of us experience love as something that must be earned and is always susceptible to withdrawal if conditions are not met. We want love but fear its unwillingness to stick around.

No love in this world is without ambivalence, and since no personal mind has experienced love without ambivalence the concept is beyond its understanding.

Your confusion of sacrifice and love is so profound that you cannot conceive of love without sacrifice. And it is this that you must look upon; sacrifice is attack, not love. If you would accept but this one idea your fear of love would vanish.

A God that demands sacrifice for love must be feared. Is this not true? If you believe you are a body, made by God, then you will fear love. For what kind of God would condemn its creation to live out life in a body? The body is a symbol of sacrifice and separation from God, not Its Creation.

Frail, susceptible, alone, needing other bodies to survive, the body gives nothing without getting something back. The body perceives love as a bargaining tool whose sole purpose is to purchase its fragile safety. We cannot conceive of Love that asks for nothing and endures, regardless of anything we do or don't do for It. If you don't believe this, ask yourself if you have ever experienced this kind of love. Or, better yet, ask if you have ever given it and if you are still giving it. No personal mind has experienced love without ambivalence. The concept is beyond it.

Love's Unity requires a mind that sees beyond the body because the bodily experience emphasizes separation. Separation induces fear and love becomes only a temporary respite from "reality."

There is nothing outside ourselves that demands sacrifice. We demand it only of ourselves in our ignorance of what we are. Love created you and has never left. Indeed, the Love that created you is the one Love you can rely upon. Your relationship with your Source is the most truly meaningful relationship available to you. Do not fear it is illusion and do not accept anything less for yourself.

"I will not be afraid of love today." This is your declaration of sanity. It can only be sane to accept yourself as Source created you: your True Self, which is One with Source, and Which is your One Identity.

As you sit in silent meditation, begin with this idea: "I am the Self that God created as the Aspect of Itself which is Love. I will release my fear of love. I am worthy. I am willing to know myself as Love. I claim myself as Love because I am allowed to Know Who and What I am." So be it.

Love me when I'm bad. That's when I need it most.
– a 4th grader

Lesson 283

My True Identity was given me by God.

When you are born you were given a name. You learned to write it in school and say, "This is who I am." Your identity may arise out of personal traits. For example, you may be the one who pleases others, or the one who is angry. You may be the one who wins praise and adulation, or the one who does not. Perhaps your identity comes from your professional status. "I am So and So. I am the one who has accomplished X."

The identity we take on can make us feel safe and secure. "Yes. This is who I am. I am the one who makes others laugh. I am the one who is always first in the race." Or, it can erode our inherent dignity. "I am the one who always sits in the back of the class. I am the addict, the failure, the one who has not lived up to my potential."

Your identity can always be amended. One day you may be the doctor. Then you receive a diagnosis and become the patient. The lesson today asks you to think about your sense of identity. It asks you to consider the layers of masks you have taken on to shield yourself from the world. You don't need to become a stranger to yourself, but you can deepen and expand what you know yourself to be.

Your True Identity is not of this world. It is none of the masks you have ever worn here. They are temporary shields that only obscure. When you know your True Identity, you can be wholly certain of yourself. When you know who you are, you also know your purpose, which is simply to be your True Self. For in being your True Self, you show others they are also free. In being your True Self, you proclaim your worth regardless of any identity this world has placed upon you.

You are a Creation of Source. Your True Identity was given at the moment of your creation and it has never changed. But being an extension of One Mind doesn't mean you are not unique. Sharing a True Identity isn't a requirement for blandness, but rather an expression of expansiveness and limitless proportion.

On the hour today, stop and consider, "Who is present now?" "Who is having this experience?" "Who is speaking?" "Who is listening?" Sit in silent meditation and ask, "Who is thinking these thoughts?" The answer will be, "I am." "I am." "I." The one without a name. The one who simply is. The Silent One who sits in Peace, and Is now, and always will be.

Lesson 284

I can choose to change all thoughts that hurt.

I'm going to quote directly from ACIM's *Workbook* for this lesson, and then I want to say what it means and what it doesn't mean for me. What it doesn't mean is as important as what it does. Here is the quote:

> *Loss is not loss when properly perceived. Pain is impossible. There is no grief with any cause at all. And suffering of any kind is nothing but a dream. This is the truth, at first to be but said and then repeated many times; and next to be accepted as but partly true; with many reservations. Then to be considered seriously more and more, and finally accepted as truth.*

"Loss is not loss when properly perceived." What does "properly perceived" mean?

Few of us have the kind of major epiphany required to perceive the illusion so completely it becomes powerless. Indeed, most of us learn in stages. But here is the key point: while free will allows us to take time with the lessons, the curriculum itself is not up for debate. It is not up for debate because we did not write it.

The thought system that got us here cannot be used to get us out. The illusion we have accepted as "reality" does not contain the information that enables us to free ourselves from it. This is the miracle of the teachings – they are a gift from a source beyond the illusion. So, we can choose to change our thoughts and we can take our time with it. But the illusion must be seen for what it is and pain is an illusion.

However, just because I am told pain is an illusion doesn't mean I should jump from the highest floor of the nearest building and expect to fly. It does not mean I should put my fork through the hand of an unruly dinner guest or run in front of an automobile shouting, "Pain isn't real!" And I most certainly should not respond to a friend in need by telling her, "Your suffering is an illusion. You'll get over it."

There is nothing in ACIM that asks you to deny your feelings. There is nothing in ACIM that suggests you should deny the feelings of others. In fact, the opposite is true. All feelings and all thoughts must be brought to light and treated with kindness and compassion. Do not forget your function is forgiveness. The decision to change all thoughts that hurt requires me to know what those thoughts are – not bury them in false progress and call myself spiritual.

"I can elect to change all thoughts that hurt." What are those thoughts? Know yourself! Know yourself, for you cannot elect to change what you have not been willing to look upon. What we do not see, we cannot change. What is not brought to Light cannot be brought to Love. This is the meaning of today's lesson. Do not repress, stifle, or fear the contents of your own mind. Choose to become awakened to your Self by awakening to what is not your Self. This is the lesson for today.

On the hour notice your feelings and thoughts. What has hurt you? Whom have you hurt? Are you impatient or mildly annoyed? Any feeling but peace is calling for your recognition. Your thoughts are a choice you make. If you need to make a correction, it is in your power to do so. Notice and take responsibility.

Lesson 285

My holiness shines bright and clear today.

My husband is one of those people who wakes up bright and cheery. He's ready to get out bed before sunrise and he's usually in a pretty good mood. He has the whole day in front of him and he's ready to "do" things. On the other hand, I love my sleep and take my waking slow. Sleep is where I feel most free. How do you wake up? Depending on your waking mood today's lesson can feel like a reflection of your own joy or a request to stay a while in bed.

> *Today I wake with joy, expecting but the happy things of God to come to me. I ask but them to come and realize my invitation will be answered by the thoughts to which it has been sent by me. And I will ask for only joyous things the instant I accept my holiness. For what would be the use of pain to me, what purpose would my suffering fulfill, and how would grief and loss avail me if insanity departs from me today, and I accept my holiness instead?*
> – ACIM

"For what would be the use of pain to me?" What is the use of pain? Its presence is, at least in part, to serve as a reminder that I can change my thoughts about it. I have learned this lesson and forgotten it so many times it would be boring if it weren't so essential. When I remember my inherent goodness, my invulnerability, that I am not my pain, I come closer to feeling less of it.

When I awake, I take my waking slow. Before I put my feet on the floor I decide in my mind to allow things to unfold – whatever they are. I give the day up to Source and let it go. This thought, held throughout the morning, is often enough to make the day.

What I do know is this. My day is always best when I am along for the ride. I'm only in charge of the basics. I take it one step at a time. Now, I put my eye medication in. Now, I make the bed. Now, I feed the dog. Oh look, he's thrown up again! Now, I get the paper towels and clean it up. Now, I brush my teeth.

Now, I keep my appointments. And I am certain, based on my own experience, that if I ask for the day to shine bright and clear, it will. However, in order to make this happen I have to do my part, which means I accept what comes to me as in my highest good – whatever it is. And I take nothing at all personally.

This is the truth, which I will first say, then repeat many times. Then, I will partly accept it as true, with many reservations. But I will seriously consider it more and more. Finally, I will accept it as truth.
– ACIM

You are Whole, as Source created you. Nothing can impair your happiness unless you allow it. All of us allow until we don't. But take nothing for granted – even your own unhappiness. Try on your holiness today, and have your own experience with it. Be your own judge. Only then will you know the truth of it.

Lesson 286

The quiet of Heaven holds my heart today.

What is the quiet of Heaven? It is the vast silence, the ever-present stillness, the magnificent peace that underlies this world and worlds beyond this one. It is the Ground of All Being. Today's lesson asks you to connect with It through your heart. Put down the phone. Turn off the television. Sit and feel the soft texture of silence. There is nothing to do. No effort whatsoever is required. Know yourself capable, sovereign, certain, gracious and commanding. You are the Ground of Being.

The lesson today asks the question, "Do you believe you can control the thoughts in your own mind." If your answer is "No," you may wish to consider then, who does? If your answer is, "Yes," then consider if you are at peace now, in this moment.

Today is a day to claim your right to peace. The mind that is in discernment knows itself and is willing to say, "Yes, peace is something I want. Yes, this is something that is possible. I can claim it for myself."

Conflict is possible only in doubt. We doubt ourselves and seek control. We doubt each other and seek control. We doubt our Source and do not trust Its presence in all things, and so we seek control. Can today be a day where you allow and trust? Let Source direct your mind.

Practice today through discernment. Check in with your heart frequently. Go slowly even if others around are in a rush. Watch and breathe. Everything you seek has been given to you already. Peace is yours if you will but choose it.

Above all, take the time to be kind to yourself and others. Do not punish yourself for lack of peace! Notice, breathe, and go into the stillness of forgiveness. Make no decision out of haste. Center yourself and ask what the decision should be. Let the answer come to you in silence. It is already there, for no question can be asked that doesn't have the answer contained within it. Whatever path is taken, be at peace with it.

Lesson 287

Source is my one true goal.

It is justifiable to ask the question, "How is peace possible in this world?" If the question is worthy of being asked, then it is worth an honest answer. Peace seems impossible here. Still, ACIM is adamant that it can be found if only because Source has promised it. What Source wills must not be impossible, yet here we find ourselves.

If we are to love this world as Source does, then we must look at it the way Source does. We did not choose this fact, but we can choose, indeed we must choose to learn Source's Way of

Perception.

It is here that the question of judgment arises again. Source offers this world Oneness, Peace, and perfect safety. But we see only divisiveness, war, and endless recriminations. Only one of these views can be true. Which is right? One of them is wrong and only one is right. Peace cannot coexist with war. Oneness cannot coexist with separateness.

Everyone believes in what he made, for it was made by his believing it. Into this strange and paradoxical situation – one without meaning and devoid of sense, out of which no way seems possible, Source sends Its judgment to answer yours.

How is peace possible in this world? In your judgment it isn't and never can be.
– ACIM

Peace is impossible to those who look on war. Peace is inevitable to those who offer peace. We must be peace to know it. We must practice peace to understand it. We must share peace to see it returned to us. Does this mean the body will never suffer? No. Does this mean those around you will instantly know peace? Probably not. But all peace, every single speck of it, comes from within. If you are peace within, then peace is not absent from your world. This bears repeating. If you are at peace within, then peace is with you and nothing can undo it except yourself. This is why today's lesson asks that you make Peace your only goal.

Your goal above all else – is to know yourself as Source knows you: eternal, loving, kind, patient, sovereign, dignified, radiant, brilliant, masterful, enduring, expansive, peace. Even God comes next, for God can come only to those who know themselves.

Sit in meditation today and ask yourself, "How do I feel when I hold the thought that I am unworthy?" "How do I feel when I am in judgment of myself?" "How do I feel when I am at peace and can say to myself, 'I like myself. I'm happy with myself. I am certain about myself'?"

"What could be the substitute for happiness? What gift would I prefer before the peace of God? What treasure would I seek and find and keep that can compare with my Identity? And would I rather live with fear than love?"

Today, bring the quality of peace into every possible moment. Make this your goal. We are born with the ability to know our True Self, and no one does not possess it. Make this your goal. As often as you are able, be the peace you seek. Oneness or separation? Endless war or eternal peace? Loving kindness or cruelty? Only one can be Real in Mind of God. Which do you choose? Which do you see? Which do you believe in, and which do you offer? Source knows only peace because It Knows there is nothing else.

Lesson 288

Let me forget my brother/sister's past today.

Imagine you are in a balloon and your greatest wish is rise as high as possible, so you can explore the whole world. You see yourself floating easily above the highest peaks, flying with magnificently-colored birds, through soft, warm cloud banks. You can reach out and touch the tops of the highest trees. It is perfectly safe in the balloon and the journey beckons, but there is a problem. A number of sandbags are attached to the basket and they are holding it down.

All of us have sandbags attached to our balloons. The sandbags holding us down are guilt, shame, and judgment – all of which are heavy, low-frequency bundles of thought and emotion. You cannot rise in spiritual frequency as long as you identify with these thoughts and emotions. You want to rise. What do you do? You take a leap of faith and let them go.

You cannot rise with ancient fears. You cannot ascend with hatred. You cannot know Mind of God if you carry guilt across the threshold. Allow yourself to know you do not know. Your thoughts of fear, hatred, and guilt are meaningless because you do not know.

The rage I hold against my sister is not based on truth. In fact, the concept she holds of herself isn't either, as long as she believes her guilt and fear are real. Her actions against me, which I believe I hate, arise out of ignorance. She does not know who she is. As long as I don't know either, I will believe she can act against me. Is this too complicated?

I have created all the illusions about myself, and my brother. I have made every sandbag holding us down. Today, I cut the ties by forgiving my sister, my brother, and myself, for not knowing. I take the leap of faith for all of us.

If you cannot take the leap today, try again tomorrow. It isn't always easy, and this lesson is not meant to gloss over anything. Do not bury your grief, your rage, your fear, but do bring them all up to be recognized and seen in the light.

If I want the freedom to explore the whole world I cannot be weighted down. If that means giving up thoughts about my past, so be it. All of this I do for myself now. I do it in stillness and quietness. I wrap my brother's past and place it on the altar of the Holy Spirit. What happens next is not my concern. I have taken the leap of faith and I will take it again and again until I am weightless, free of all the burdens I have made and believed, in ignorance, to be real.

Each one you see in light brings your light closer to your awareness.
– ACIM

Lesson 289

The past is over. It cannot touch me.

This lesson harkens back to the first week of lessons in which you learned, "I don't know the meaning of anything I see." You don't know the meaning of anything you "see" because everything you "see" is informed by the past.

We are taught to value the past as a learning tool, and it is true, we can evolve through this learning. But it is also true that the past holds us back. It prevents us from being present now. It literally steals the present moment and all its potential for new creations. How often have you called upon the past to predict your future? Each time you do so, you guarantee an outcome that is the same as it was before.

Has the Middle East evolved beyond its thousand-year wars over the same original argument? Are you still grinding over something someone said, or didn't say, a decade ago? Are you preparing for an uncertain future because of some ancient hurt?

Holding to the past is how we stop learning anew. It is why we stop seeing. It forms our safe identity and is the reason we repeat old hurts, generation after generation after generation. If one person tries to move beyond the past, there will always be several around to call her back to it.

Only if the past is over in my mind can I be free to use my Real Perception, because otherwise I perceive nothing. I perceive what is not here. I allow something that is not here to arise out of nothing and make it real. This is an enormous burden.

The "real" world, seen from a mind that holds to its past, is colored by memories of moments that no longer exist. How can I then perceive the openings to forgiveness that are gifted to me in the now?

The past cannot touch me unless I allow it. Sometimes it takes days or even years to let it go – and that is okay. The purpose of time is to learn forgiveness. The point is to be conscious of whatever is being carried forth into the present. Know how it serves you. Take it out regularly and look at it anew. Ask if you still want to keep it. Be the one who chooses. Stand in your power to choose and move into the present from your choice.

Today, be aware of what you are dragging with you into the present moment. As you sit in silent contemplation, be mindful of your thoughts. How many of them arise out of the past – a past that exists only in your perception? True Perception is of the moment, viewed now, with an open heart: guiltless, willing, open, safe, in the presence of eternal mind. True Perception opens doors the past doesn't even know exist!

Lesson 290

My present happiness is all that I perceive.

The present moment is the clear space out of which all life unfolds, fresh and new, now. It is most precious because it is as close to truth as I can get. If I bring the past with me, it colors my entire perception. The past brought into the present becomes a lens through which I view the world, and nothing I see is seen anew.

How are you right now, in this moment? How do you perceive yourself? If you are reading this, then in this very moment you must be safe. You must have all you need right now. "Unless I look upon what is not there, my present happiness is all I see."

This lesson is not new. Most of us have heard of it in one form or another. We just don't practice consistently. We are well intentioned, then things happen and we forget. A strong emotion, an uncomfortable thought, or simple boredom can pull us right out the present and into the past or future. For most of us, futility sets in, as we seem to fail again and again. We give up on ourselves.

Being present in the moment requires both persistence and forgiveness. There really are no substitutes. There are lots of ways to remember to remember. One student I heard of put something in his pants pocket. Every time he reached for something he was reminded to check in with himself. Another student wrapped a rubber band around her wrist. I use my emotional body as a reminder. If I feel discomfort, I am pulled into the present moment.

This quote from Daniel Scranton explains perfectly the importance of being present.

The relationship that you have to Source Energy is the exact relationship that you have to life. If you don't think about your relationship to Source Energy at all, then you probably do not think about the purpose of your life. You are probably not asking the big questions. If you are afraid of Source, and are afraid of the judgment of Source, then that is probably how you face your fellow humans, as if they were representatives of Source. If you are seeing Source as a benevolent being who loves you unconditionally, is infinitely wise and expanding, then that is how you will view the other humans that you encounter and your life in general. You see, Source really is all that is. And so, how you approach all that is will reflect how you approach Source, and how you approach Source will reflect how you approach all that is. If you want to change your life, you can change your relationship to Source.

Take up the practice of being aware of your relationship to Source by being aware of your thoughts and of yourself as the witness. Over time, you will notice a new dimension of consciousness within. You will sense yourself behind or beneath the thoughts. The thoughts will lose their power over you because you are no longer energizing your mind through identification with them. Freedom from compulsive thinking is within your reach as thoughts of the past and future are recognized for what they are and put aside for presence in the now.

The past is not there. The future is a guest that never arrives. The present moment – as it is – is all there is. Let it be. Your relationship to it reflects the one you have with Source. Nothing is required but that you have your experience with it. Watch it as it unfolds. Flow from one moment to the next. This is how acceptance begins and with acceptance comes peace.

Sit in silent meditation today. Get comfortable, place your awareness on the breath, and let thoughts arise. Notice your relationship to them. Are you letting them carry you away into the past or future? If so, just notice and bring the mind gently back to the breath. Are you safe now? Do you have all you need now? Are you present with your happiness, your contentment, just sitting? "Unless I look upon what is not there, my present happiness is all I see."

Focus Question 8: *What is the Real World?*

Lesson 291

"What is the Real World?" This is the subject of the next ten lessons and they are happy lessons indeed. They are happy because they speak directly of a World that is not of our invention, but is a direct extension of the Creator's Mind.

The Real World is "seen" only through the use of Real Perception. Real Perception surpasses the personal mind's projection of separation and its ensuing guilt and fear. Real Perception sees beyond the illusion of separation projected by the personal mind through forgiveness.

This next point is important. The Real World has a greater significance than this world. By greater significance I mean it encompasses and supersedes this one. Think of it this way: a one-dimensional point is superseded by a two-dimensional line, and a two-dimensional line is superseded by a three-dimensional form. The point and the line are superseded because both are contained within the form. Thus, the form has greater significance than either the point or the line.

The Real World encompasses and has greater significance than ours. The Real World contains the idea of form but supersedes it. Remember, immaterial mind creates material form. Mind is the builder. As long as your mind believes that only form is real, the Real World will remain beyond its grasp. The mind that perceives separation as the sole arbiter of reality cannot see Oneness. How can you Know the Reality of Oneness when you have separated from It?

This world is based on the idea that events and things exist outside us, and that we can only observe them as apart from us – "out there." ACIM teaches the opposite is true and more Real. There is nothing outside – it is all inside. This world is a projection onto a screen of consciousness. It is a movie we have taken as reality.

Projection makes perception. Perception is a mirror, not a fact.
– ACIM

The personal mind perceives through the fear of separation. Real Perception allows and blesses through forgiveness. It does not perceive through fear because it does not project it. This is why forgiveness is your function. You must perceive through it to perceive the Real World – a world that supersedes fear through the knowing of True Identity.

The Real World, which holds your True Identity, is endless, loving, creative, and expansive. It transmutes and transcends. It easily transitions in and out of form, and light, color, thought, feeling, sound, and deep silence. The Real World has limitless variation because all is contained within It. The Real World cannot be held back from the Love that is Itself. We are the Real World but we must use True Perception to Know It. The Real

World is your True Home and you are at Its Doorstep.

Here is how to practice the next ten lessons. Each morning read and contemplate the core question and its answer. Then read the particular lesson for the day. At some point in the day devote at least fifteen minutes to quiet meditation. You know how to do this by now. Sit and place awareness on the breath. Breathe in peace and exhale any tension in the body. Take as long as you want to do this. Then repeat the lesson for the day in your mind, invite the Holy Spirit's assistance, and let everything go. Allow the breath to anchor your mind. Watch thoughts and feelings as they arise. Trust. Expect nothing and allow everything. Play. Be courageous. Explore total nonresistance. Forgive and know your Innocence.

Be mindful throughout the day. Practice forgiveness. Allow direct experience through conscious awareness. On the hour, remember the lesson. Use it to anchor your day.

In the evening, read the lesson only. Let it guide you into sleep where it will inform the other world of dreams until you waken to this one, and finally to Reality.

Your lesson today is:

This is a day of stillness and peace.

Stop often today – on the hour at least – and look around. Even if your environment is in chaos and turmoil, know Real Perception is yours by choice. Hold It in your mind as you survey your kingdom. Use your Real Perception to see it with forgiveness and peace. Place your heart in the hands of the Creator whose power to hold it safely is beyond your imagination.

Gift yourself with fifteen minutes of complete stillness and peace today. Do not try to figure this out. Do not sit and reason with your thoughts. Do not think at all! Open your heart and listen without effort. Be available and witness what arrives at the doorstep of your peace. Breathe, be present, and repeat the lesson in your mind. Allow all thoughts that come, to come. Forgive all ideas of pain, judgment, or worry. Allow them to arise and place each one on the altar of forgiveness. What happens to them is not your concern but that of the Holy Spirit.

Lesson 292

A Happy outcome to all things is certain.

Happy is capitalized here because it is God's Happiness, which is the final outcome of all things. Source promises only Joy and there are no exceptions to what is promised by Source. We can, however, take all the "time" we want to accept the promise.

> Those of you who cling to the earth and the belief it is real are doing nothing more than cherishing your own creativity... Form itself is nothing but an echo of your Spirit, and that is the reality of what you are.
> – Brent Haskell, PhD, DO, *Journey Beyond Words*

To be in this world and imagine a World beyond this one, more real than this one, is to stand on the edge of a precipice. It is to stand on the edge of all I have believed to be true and say, "Yes. I am willing to know my limitations. I am willing to face my fear. I am willing to step off into the unknown. And I am willing to do it not once, but over and over again until I learn that there is nothing to fear at all."

To be in this world, and let go of its valuing, to be curious without fear, this is the lesson. When I allow the day to ebb and flow without need to control it, or manage it, or fear it, I find freedom. And when I practice this day after day I begin to know with a knowing that is beyond thought: all is well.

Being free, I can choose to experience this lesson whenever I wish. But the outcome of all things is certain beyond my will.

So long as I perceive myself to be in this world, I am in learning mode. What am I learning? I am learning that all of my defenses are vain attempts to control what is beyond my control. Thank God for that, for when I face the fear and recognize its illusions, I will end my need for defenses.

Rest in this lesson today, even as you face self-doubt, disappointment, or pain. This is not a silly promise. You cannot know ahead of time how things will be. But how many times have you faced fear in this life, and yet, here you are! Fear is in the moment. Pain is in the moment. It cannot last because it arises from an alien will, and Source does not will it. What Source wills is certain and Source wills only your Happiness.

As you sit in silence today, rest in the peace of these words. Breathe and allow thoughts to arise. Watch them come and go. Every thought you hold is held in Mind of God. You will seek and find as directed by a Will far superior to your own. Fear not, you will be sent every experience you need to learn this lesson. And again, fear not, you will learn it.

Lesson 293

All fear is past, and only Love is here.

Over 50 years ago a young psychologist named Helen Schucman was "instructed" to write the words, *"Projection makes perception."* The "instruction" came from the same voice that scripted the entire 669 pages of *A Course in Miracles*. In the years since, quantum physics has confirmed that quantum particles are altered through the simple act of observation. This has fundamentally changed our perception of how the material world works. Most of us just don't know it yet.

"Projection makes perception." This is what makes today's lesson so important. "All fear is past. Only love is here." If I can perceive this lesson to be true and daily act from its truth, my world cannot not change.

Consciousness has consequence! It has creative potential in the material world. When I think with fear, I create with fear. When I think with love, I create with love. Awareness of my thoughts and feelings is the first step in the creation of a different life.

Fear is outside Mind of God. How could something that is One with Everything fear Itself? When I choose to align my will with Divine Will, I come into agreement with It. When I choose to allow the day's unfolding and watch from a place of knowing I am perfectly safe, the power of fear is greatly diminished. To be known this has to be experienced. It can't be learned from reading a sentence or a book.

In seeing my fear I am willing to know it. In knowing it, I am willing to release it to Source. In releasing it to Source I am accepting the power of my choice to align with Divine Will and I cannot fail.

"Projection makes perception." When I create in fear, I create more fear. When I create in alignment with Source, no matter what happens I am moving toward greater safety and that is what I will experience.

"Only love is here. All fear is gone." This is today's lesson. Allow yourself to feel its power as you move throughout your day today. Notice what happens when you align with its words. Just have the experience and pay attention. Be a willing learner. Be a happy learner. Enjoy.

Lesson 294

My body is a wholly neutral thing.

Today I will feel my body. I will experience it, but I will be continuously mindful that it is not what I am.

My body is a symbol I have created. It seems solid. It appears to contain me. It seems to be me. But I am dreaming this body. Its form is my imagination and I am sleeping still, even as I seem to awaken from a dream and move my body into a "new" day.

My body is not "good" or "bad." Only my belief it can contain all that is me has consequences that seem hurtful. I stub my toe and call out in pain. The effects of aging seem reflected in the mirror. The truth is, my body is a wholly neutral thing. I am simply projecting an imaginary form and calling it myself. Myself, as spirit, is vastly more real than any form could possibly be.

Source did not create this body, but Source is in it because Source is in me. God is in every thought I have. I am an Aspect of the Mind of All. Not one thought I have does not contain some reflection of my Source.

The body is a wholly neutral thing. It lives and passes away. I am not wedded to it but I will care for it as long as the dream seems real. I know it is a reflection of my thought so I will not debase it or treat it carelessly. My body is useful as a tool of communication with the unseen, unformed world beyond this one. I can listen to my body with respect and it will tell me many things. My body is a receiver of information beyond words and I can feel its connection with other bodies even when no words are spoken.

It will be my practice today to listen to my body. I will tune into it like a receiver. What channel is it receiving? Is it open to love or fear? Does it feel in flow or is it guarded against the world? If my personal mind tells me one thing and my body tells me something else, I will trust my body's truth. I am listening. I am open. I am not my body. I am free and my body is a wholly neutral thing.

As I sit in meditation today, I watch my breath. I become my breath. I am the breath. I breathe in love. I exhale all doubt and worry. I breathe in love. I exhale all things that burden me. I empty myself into the universe, and what am I then? I am consciousness, in form as an experience now, but the form is nothing more than a temporary container. It cannot hold all that I am. I breathe in love. I exhale all that I am not. I feel my mind expand beyond my body and taste the freedom of pure being. I breathe in love. I exhale myself into eternity and I am Home.

Lesson 295

The Holy Spirit looks through me today.

You have never given any problem to the Holy Spirit It has not solved for you, nor will you ever do so. You have never tried to solve anything yourself and been successful. Is it not time you brought these facts together and made sense of them?
– ACIM

ACIM is nothing if not logical. Is it not time to "bring the facts together" and realize separation is misperception? The search to know myself must end in knowing I am part of a whole.

We have more than a little tendency to fragment and focus only on the parts, thinking it a better way to understand the world. We separate and name, we take apart, and put together, believing this means we know the truth of a thing.

But Spirit knows Itself whole. It sees both sides of the equation and so must I if I am to know my Self. Source needs me to see my wholeness and speak for it. When I see it, I can teach it. In teaching it, I learn it.

Let the perception of wholeness be my unconflicted goal today. Let me teach peace to know it. Let me remember I can use my mind to recognize when even the slightest form of fear or pain crosses the threshold into my awareness. And I can know this is a signal to refocus my perception and begin again.

The Holy Spirit is immanent within me. The more I am

conscious of Its presence, the stronger my connection with It is. The Holy Spirit, the Universal Communicator, is my direct connection to Source. I see through Its presence today and fear is gone. Nothing is apart from me and nothing can truly hurt me because nothing hurts Itself.

Lesson 296

The Holy Spirit speaks through me today.

Yesterday's lesson asked you to see through the eyes of the Holy Spirit. Here is what I discovered when I worked with the lesson. How does it compare for you?

First, I practiced seeing openly. I tried to look at everything as it was exactly in the moment. I noticed any judgment that attached itself to what I saw. It was surprising how quickly judgment and comparison arose in my mind and how much lighter it felt when I set them aside. Color was more intense and little things I normally wouldn't see became apparent. How casually my eye usually falls upon the things within its view!

When I saw with the Holy Spirit, the world moved as if in a dance! The birds flew from the tree, to the feeder, and back again. All of it was a play of light, shadow, and movement. I looked more closely at each person I encountered, trying to feel beyond their outward appearance. "Who are you, really?" I asked myself. I remembered the words of someone who told of her near death experience. Everything she saw, including the little dog who'd died with her, had been made of visible light. I practiced seeing things as light.

I noticed, too, that my eyes softened when I looked this way, and when my eyes softened, my heart responded somehow. It felt comfortable and natural to see this way. I enjoyed my day more and felt connected to things. How was it for you?

Today, we are asked to speak without rushing. "The Holy

Spirit speaks through me today."

I have a feeling this lesson will greatly decrease the number of words I use today. If I practice speaking from my truth, which is love itself, I will think before I open my mouth. I will say only what I would want said to me, for the person to whom I am speaking truly is me. How will I treat myself? How will I use words that show I know myself? Will I free the one in front of me with the words I use, or will I judge her, compare her, and use her to satisfy some momentary need I think I have?

How will it go for you? You will never know unless you try. Have the experience yourself. See what happens. Then know it as your own truth.

Lesson 297

Forgiveness is the only gift I give because it is the only gift I want.

The acknowledgement that forgiveness is a gift you want makes this lesson an event. It is not something you understand and then nothing happens because it changes your perception of everything you experience.

When you know you are forgiven, you are free to awaken to a deeper sense of accountability. This idea is so important, I will restate: when you can rely on total forgiveness, you are free to accept responsibility and accountability for every choice you make. Every experience you have is of your own choice. When you forgive your choices it opens your awareness. When you become aware of what you did not know before, doors open and the path to Love widens. Forgiveness is like lifting a weighted veil.

Forgiveness is the only gift worth having in this world. When you know you are allowed to receive it and give it back in endless variation, transformation has begun. Salvation's simple formula is this: everything you give, you give to myself. Learn this simple lesson and your alignment with Love begins in earnest.

When I know I am the one who is allowed to forgive, who is able to forgive, who is able to transform her history through a new idea, then I will say, "I can be free," and I will lift my consciousness above the wall that has created the separation in which I exist.
– Paul Selig

Make this day a gift to yourself: notice when you forgive and when you don't. The act of forgiveness includes both the smallest and largest events; there is no order of miracles. Don't worry if you find yourself unable to forgive; just notice!

Give yourself fifteen minutes of contemplation on this lesson today. Sit in peace, watch the breath, and when you are in the stillness of silence, feel your way into what absolute forgiveness feels like. If you are fully present, you will sense a burden has been lifted. This is your natural state. This is the miracle of forgiveness. It is real. And it is yours.

Lesson 298

I love my God, and I love God's Creation.

Do you feel just a bit of resistance to these words? If so, simply acknowledge the resistance. The words are less important than the claim you are making. The claim you are making is for yourself. It is a way of saying, "I am in agreement with the Divine Love that has created me."

When I claim my Love I also claim my inheritance. I do not know my inheritance through thinking about it. Thinking is a way of managing information and it is useful. There are many, many ways to process information and some are cleverer at it than others. But knowing is not mental, it is intentional. You could call it a form of inherited wisdom we all share. There is no cleverness about it at all.

No one does not have full access to the wisdom of knowing, but it must be claimed. I have to agree to accept it. When I have accepted it for myself, when I embody it for myself, I affect everyone around me because giving and receiving are one in Truth.

"I love my God," means, "I am willing to know the Love from which I was created." It does not mean I love some antiquarian in the sky. "And I love God's Creation," means, "I am willing to use my inherited wisdom to know the presence of Love in everything."

When I allow Love, and that which Love has created, it is a signal that draws things to it. It does not mean life becomes rosy and peaceful. It means I have stated the intention that I am ready to draw to me that which serves my highest potential for growth. The declaration to Love is a call that will be answered.

Love is a conscious choice. Today, give yourself permission to receive and know the gratitude of It without fear. Be prepared to receive that which you have given. Its forms will differ, but you will know It in your wisdom.

As you sit in silent contemplation today, begin with this thought: "I know who I am. I am here to claim my Self." Be mindful of the breath. Relax into the silence. You have chosen to sit in silence, and you are in your authority. You are claiming yourself for your Self. Indeed, you are proclaiming your Self. Your Self will hear and respond. Look for it. Wait and watch. Listen and hear. Love your Source and Its Creations. All of it is you.

Lesson 299

Eternal holiness abides in me.

Today's lesson is a wonderful example of scientific support for a spiritual truth. The support comes in the form of a discovery, made by researchers at the Delft University of Technology, which confirmed the theory of quantum entanglement.

Quantum entanglement occurs when two separated particles of light communicate faster than the speed of light, regardless of their distance. When one particle of light is spun clockwise, its partner's spin is instantly altered, even when they are thousands of miles apart. It is if the two separated particles are one – as if they have the same "mind."

Quantum entanglement opens whole new areas of thought. It gives scientific credibility to one of the oldest spiritual ideas of humanity – Unified Consciousness. What was created from One remains One even as It is expressed with unlimited variety across vast distances. Nothing is not entangled with the One from which all things arise. Oneness is immanent in everything.

We are born of Light and like It our eternal Wholeness is unending, unlimited by time or space. We are entangled with Source, and with each other, in such a way that no amount of time or distance can impede our Union. Source wants us to know our Oneness and Its Will cannot be denied. We are instinctively guided toward It. The pain of believing we are separate drives us to know ourselves as Spirit.

My holiness is far beyond my ability to understand or know. Yet Source, Who created it, acknowledges my holiness as Its Own. My holiness is not of me. It is not mine to be destroyed or suffer from attack. It stands forever perfect and untouched. Holiness Itself created me and I can know myself Whole because it is the Will of Source that this be so.

Our Oneness stands forever perfect and untouched. In it all things are healed. We live in exciting times, healing times. Science is beginning to speak the language of spirit. Yet, what science is just discovering, spirit has always known. What Albert Einstein called, "spooky action at a distance," is a reflection of Truth.

Today, look about your world! Know all is light, of light, and connected in the One Light of Source. Nothing is as it seems. Do not accept the illusion of separation today. Know What you are: light, in light, with light. The dross of all humanity is an illusion, waiting to be seen beyond itself. It may feel spooky, but it is all One.

As you sit in silent contemplation today, begin with the words of the lesson. Relax into the breath. Say to yourself, "Eternal holiness abides in me," and know the truth of it. Feel the truth of it. Your joy lies in the truth of it.

Lesson 300

Only an instant does this world endure.

Again, quantum physics helps explain today's lesson. It says this: our perception of time is an illusion at both the scientific and metaphysical levels. Linear time is the perception of three-dimensional space, but it is not a universal truth. This is not a new idea but one that was first proposed by mathematician and physicist Hermann Minkowski.

In 1907, Minkowski discovered a mathematical model that combined space and time into a single continuum. He called his model "space-time" or the "space-time continuum." It has been used ever since to accurately describe and predict the uniform workings of the universe at both super-galactic and subatomic levels. In space-time, all possible events exist concurrently, side by side. Space-time is Now.

For Now is the closest approximation of eternity this world can offer. It is in the reality of Now, without past or future, that the beginning of the appreciation of eternity lies.
– ACIM

Eternity cannot be understood at the level of the personal mind. The personal mind does not question linear time. It agrees wholeheartedly with the idea of a past and future. The personal mind's agreement that linear time constitutes "reality" is a major impediment to healing.

Healing cannot be accomplished in the past. It must be accomplished in the present to release the future.
– ACIM

All healing happens in the Now. Healing begins with the decision to step outside of linear time and release the past to the present moment. The present moment is almost always better than any past the ego can devise. In this instant, I am alive. In this instant, this world is perfect. In this instant, all is well and nothing needs changing to be better, safer, "more" of anything. It simply is as it is and all eternity lies within it. It is the zero-point in which I can pivot in any direction I choose.

We are not our bodies and we are not "stuck" in linear time. This earth does not sit and contemplate its past. The clouds that move upon the face of the earth, come and go. They do not contemplate where they came from or where they are going. The truism that "those who forget their past are condemned to repeat it" has limitation, for it is just as true that "those who will NOT forget their past ARE condemned to repeat it."

"Only an instant does this world endure." It is in the reality of Now that we begin to appreciate the idea of eternity. Can you stop whatever it is that you are doing and look around? Take it in? Smell it? Feel it? Listen to it?

Today, release yourself to the healing of the present moment as often as you can. Now is the zero-point and it is the only point in which you are free to choose. If a problem presents itself to you today, take a breath before you act. Choose from the conscious awareness of the Now.

As you sit in meditation today, reflect on this idea. Breathe in Now. Breathe out Now. String together as many Now-breaths as you can. Remember, the breath is your own personal, portable centering device. When I string together a day of zero-point moments I begin to see the face of eternity.

Focus Question 9: *What is the Second Coming?*

Lesson 301

The next ten lessons deal with one of the most significant questions in Christian thought: "What is the Second Coming?"

ACIM waits to address this question because all prior lessons lead up to the answer, which is both simple and profound. The Second Coming is "an event as sure as God." There is no doubt about it happening, yet, what is it that will happen? And will it be for everyone? The Second Coming does not happen so much to you, or for you. It happens because of you.

Each of us is asked to hasten the Second Coming by making the decision to lift the veil of judgment and separation from our own eyes. It is almost as if a tipping point is reached; a moment in which sufficient numbers of humankind realize the Reality of Oneness with each other, all things, and Source. It is the moment in which a majority sees clearly that what we do to others, we do to ourselves. The Second Coming is the knowing beyond doubt that we receive all that we give. This knowing will end the world as it is now. It will turn it upside down – or right side up, if you prefer.

The Second Coming is assured as the one event in time which time itself cannot affect. It is, quite simply, the return of Sanity, for every mind that ever came to lose itself in fear and separation will be equally released from illusion. In this equality is our Christ Consciousness restored as One Identity.

The Second Coming is the correction of the projection that made this world. The projection arose from a mind mistaken in its belief that separation from Source could be accomplished.

"Forgiveness lights the Second Coming's way because it shines on everything as One. And thus is Oneness recognized at last." Accept forgiveness as your function and you do your part to assist Source. Your willingness builds upon Its Will only to the degree that you have free will to See the Truth.

The Second Coming is the day you make your Last Judgment. It is not the return of Reality, but it is your awareness that It has been here all along. You are an integral part of the Second Coming because, in a very real sense, you are it.

Here is how to practice the next ten lessons. Each morning read and contemplate the core question and its answer. Then read the particular lesson for the day. At some point in the day devote at least fifteen minutes to quiet meditation. Sit and place awareness on the breath. Breathe in peace and exhale any tension in the body. Take as long as you want to do this. Then repeat the lesson for the day in your mind, invite the Holy Spirit's assistance, and let everything go. Allow the breath to anchor your mind. Watch thoughts and feelings as they arise. Trust. Expect nothing and allow everything. Play. Be courageous. Explore total nonresistance. Forgive and know your Innocence.

Be mindful throughout the day. Practice forgiveness. Allow direct experience through conscious awareness. On the hour, remember the lesson. It should be the foundation of your day. In the evening, read the lesson only. Let it guide you into sleep where it will inform the other world of dreams until you waken to this one, and finally to Reality.

Today's lesson is a metaphor for forgiveness, which is the single most important ingredient for The Second Coming, also known as the Ascension. It is:

And Source Itself shall end my need for tears.

Only if I judge will I weep because only if I judge will I know judgment. This world can be my home when I do not judge it, because only then will it become a reflection of the Will of Source. I do not know enough to judge! My judgment is a distortion that reflects only my own limitation. Do not judge the world today. See it with the eyes of God. Do you think this is impossible? If so, you must still be in doubt about who you are.

In Hinduism: "The truth is that you are always united with the Lord. But you must know this. Nothing further is there to know."

In Christianity: "In the beginning was the Word and the Word was with God and the Word was God."

In Eastern thought: "The Tao is everything."

In Arabic: "Tawhid is the oneness of God."

The knowing of our Oneness is a universal. You are the Second Coming and I am with you in Its arrival. We are on the path together and its end is inevitable because separation from Source is illusion. All suffering is but a temporary insanity. Let us help each other end the need for tears. This is the Second Coming and It is happening now. It has never, not been happening.

"And Source Itself shall end my need for tears." Today, place your faith in Source. See through Its Eyes. Do Its work.

As you sit in silent meditation, allow your awareness to rest on the idea of Oneness. Do nothing. Simply be. Breathe. Watch what arises in the mind. Notice the sounds around you; the sensations you experience; the feelings that come up. Notice how they change constantly. There is only one thing that doesn't change, and that is the ever-present I Am, which is You, which is One, which is also me.

Lesson 302

Where darkness was, I look upon the Light.

Like many people, I often find myself awake in the wee hours of the morning. I used to lie there, frustrated, until I understood it wasn't a punishment, but a blessing. I decided to use my early mornings to meditate and they have been some of the most rewarding inner journeys of my life. I forgive my sleeplessness and place awareness on the breath. I usually have to go through layers of thought and feeling but it is so worth it. These meditations are a wonderful reminder that my mind belongs only to me.

The Second Coming is not about the arrival of some spiritual superhero. It is about finding the superhero that lives in myself. "Looking upon the light" is about finding the light in my own mind. It's about keeping the flame of mindfulness alive and immanent within.

Lying awake in the darkness I am moved to find the light inside. When I do I am grateful to remember yet again: the light is the gift I give myself. Because no one gives it to me, no one can take it from me either. I wouldn't have rediscovered my light if I hadn't been woken from sleep. I wouldn't have made the journey through my own breath, going deep down into the inner silence so pervasive that nothing can intrude upon it. The gift of knowing is often packaged in strange ways.

Where darkness is, the light is also. The light lies in a bed of forgiveness. It walks beside us. It is who we are. We forget and then we remember. We remember, and then we forget. Each disturbance today contains the same gift, which is the opportunity to remember the light again. There is no guilt in forgetting and there are no limits to remembering. Where darkness is, there is light, seen through the perception of forgiveness, which is allowing, which is trusting, which contains curiosity, which is itself a form of devotion.

Lesson 303

Christ Consciousness is born in me today.

Your awareness of your Christ Consciousness does not come

from cognitive effort. It is not an intellectual achievement. The intellect was given as a tool. It was never supposed to be your master.

It is in the heart that awareness of Christ Consciousness is realized. The heart embraces all things, allows all things, and trusts all things. The intellect wants to be in charge. The heart trusts its connection to Mind of God because it knows God is in charge.

You cannot force your awareness of Christ Consciousness but you can allow it. It is like a little bird you learn to feed by hand. You stand, with arms outstretched, quiet, and open, offering yourself in peace. Christ Consciousness will always enter a willing heart when such an offering is made.

"I hold Christ Consciousness in my awareness." Open your mind to the Thought of Source. Be unafraid to trust. Welcome with an open heart and follow the lead of the Cosmic Dancer. You need do nothing but follow. In truth, we are the little birds. It is Source Who stands with outstretched hands willing us to safely land. Take the offering. It is what your heart truly desires. Know your True Self is the Christ Consciousness.

Lesson 304

I will not let the world obscure my Christ Consciousness.

Refine your mind today. Allow your heart sight to penetrate the world of form. You can do it. The God particle is alive in you. End your false humility and the arrogance of a thought system that proclaims God is not alive and well within this world.

"Perception is a mirror, not a fact." What you look upon is your state of mind, projected outward. Forgive your projections! Nothing in the personal mind's world is not in need of it because all of it has been made with judgment!

What you experience from one moment to the next appears to

happen to you. This is because you have agreed to perceive it as a separate being so long as you are in the dream. You awaken from the dream when you realize you are free to choose the manner in which you respond to what is presented! Your response changes its feeling, its meaning, its shape, and ultimately it even changes the next moment you draw to yourself. Your response to the world you see has enormous value. Outer experience is altered internally! This is a paradox, but it is vital knowledge.

Today, practice your inner awareness. View the external condition of the world through your Christ Mind. What is the external world mirroring for you? Is it doom and gloom or can you see beyond it? Can you see more deeply into it? Are you in love with the projection on the screen, or are you in Love as you view something that appears to be outside you?

Find the place within yourself today that still knows the perfect purity of your brother, your sister, and this whole world of form. See that all things are either the extension of Love, or a cry for Its help and healing.

Lesson 305

There is a peace my Christ Mind bestows on me.

The Christ within each of us knows its Origin and finds peace in the knowing. It does not waste time disputing the fact that there is only the Will of God. Unlike the ego, which claims a will of its own, the Self knows it is enhanced through Source. It doesn't see Oneness as a threat to Its uniqueness.

God is not a product of *our* will, but we are a product of God's. There exists no opposite to God no matter what our perception, wish, device, or denial might be. There is only the will of God and we are It. All the time.

The Christ within each of us is a channel tuned directly to the Ground of All Being. Knowing the Christ within requires me to face my resistance to the fear of losing my "self" in the vastness of the Will of God. The ego cannot envision anything but itself. The Self knows it retains its unique qualities but the Whole is the Source of those qualities.

Step back and let Source lead today. It is ironic, but that is the only way to move forward. In every moment of contention, dispute, fear, anxiety or tiny speck of discomfort, take a step back. Ask, "What is this moment for?" "What do I decree this moment to be?" "Will I allow it or fight it?" "Will I meet it in peace or resistance?"

Then listen through your heart center. Touch the delicate awareness that floats beneath the cacophony. Step out of the circus and go behind the tent. Walk in the silence and darkness the players have abandoned and see the peace and glory there.

Lesson 306

The gift of Christ is all I seek today.

Imagine you have the power to create whatever your idea of a beautiful world might be. It is full of fragrant flowers, green meadows, and its waters are crystal clear. Everyone you love is there. The idea of conflict does not even enter your mind.

Imagine being able to change your body. You may alter its shape, its size, its color, or its gender until you find the perfect fit for the day. Imagine being able to communicate with anyone, at any time, across any distance. Imagine having the answer to every question simply by connecting your mind to the one who knows. Imagine knowing you are never alone, and nothing can harm you ever at all.

Buried deep inside each of us is an ancient memory of such freedom. We can feel the truth of it. If we can imagine it in our mind it has to be possible, for imagination is creation.

We yearn for freedom because it is our natural state. But here's the kicker – the source of freedom and the power of creation is Love. Love holds the power of creation because only It can draw upon the unlimited potential of the universe. Love has access to everything because It perceives itself as everything.

The gift of Christ is this: Love's True Perception of Oneness with each other and All That Is. The gift of Christ is freedom from fear. The gift of Christ is the ability to remember the ancient memory, which is the call of freedom to create with Love.

The gift of Christ today is the release from being satisfied with small things. We are the wind, we are the stone, and we are the man on the street. There is no end to what we are, or can be, because there is nothing in God's creation to limit us at all. We are freedom itself.

But we do not know what we do not know. So when you imagine yourself the king of the world remember, you cannot do so and be separate from anything else. You cannot be king of the world and not be in love with all that is around you. And when you are in love with all that is around you, your perception of everything will change, and so your choices will change, and your imaginings will evolve, as you know yourself without fear.

What I value, I make real. What is the "best" you can imagine? Here is how to use today's lesson: Take five minutes and go outside. Is raining or cold? No matter! Just put on your shoes and coat and go. Stand there and look around. Feel your feet on the ground. Now close your eyes and breathe in. Smell. Listen. Say hello to Mother Earth and all Her children. This is the gift of Christ Perception. This is your Second Coming. It is beginning now.

You might imagine that someone comes up to you and says, *"You know, you are just so stupid. You believe that this wall is not real. Look, when I push against the wall, it's hard."* And you say, *"Yes, right now it is, but in my knowing, I can change that. I can walk through the wall. What is a wall? It is energy that has been brought together. What are you? You are energy. In my knowing, it is possible to make my energy compatible with the wall and walk through it. You expand the molecules."* So, you will find ones who will come up to you and say, *"You're crazy."* And you will reply, *"Yes, but I'm having fun with it."* That is the answer. *"Yes, but I am having fun with it."*

Accept the gifts of your Christ Mind. Take five minutes on this morning, and choose anew, so that you can go out and *see* the tree, *hear* the songbirds, *smell* the morning air, *feel* your way into the day. Allow yourself to know, *"I am One with everything I create."* Create happy.

Lesson 307

Conflicting wishes cannot be my will.

Unhappiness with "what is" is a sure sign my will is in conflict. This doesn't mean I should not try to change things I don't like – it just means I don't take it personally when presented with an obstacle to my happiness. I don't see my will as being at war with what is. I don't see it as an attack I need to defend against.

Source is change Itself. Source moves, expands, and evolves. It is completely free to fearlessly experience all It can imagine. I am continuously motivated by Mind of Source to do the same. While I cannot always see it, my will to be free is a perfect match for God's.

This means I am in a constant dance with the present moment in complete safety. The only thing that can throw me off balance is my fear, which morphs into a desire to take the lead. My deepest desire is really to allow and move with what flows toward me, letting it touch me, having my experience with it, then letting it touch me again. I am dancing. I am always free, even when I decide to resist. I am free to be in resistance and have my experience with it.

Today, pay attention to your will. What is it you truly desire?

How smoothly can you dance with Will of Source? What happens when you make changes while still remaining in the dance? Can you feel the difference?

Lesson 308

This instant is the only time there is.

The idea that our thoughts create our reality is still in its infancy. When humanity assumes responsibility for individual thought as well as group thought, the result will be revolutionary. The same is true regarding our concept of time.

Our experience of time relies heavily on the belief that what happened in the past controls the present and will affect the future. The things that have already happened, that have brought us to this point, will now have an effect on what will happen down the road. ACIM calls this idea a wolf in sheep's clothing for it steals from you the only thing that is real: the present moment.

The idea of time robs the present moment of all its joy, all its freedom, and all its gifts. The idea of time blinds you to the Reality of Now. We use time as a form of judgment in that we judge the present by the past. The idea for this week is The Second Coming. The Second Coming is the end time or, more accurately, the end of time.

I can hear you asking, "How can I live without time?" First, you can begin by giving up ideas about what should be or what should have been. Second, you can release yourself from guilt and fear because both serve only to carry the past and future into present time. A guilty past creates a fearful future. Third, you can recognize and release the desire for judgment, for judgment is based on the idea of what "ought to be" rather than acceptance of what is now. The "Last Judgment" is nothing more nor less than making your own last judgment in time. Your last judgment will be the end of the conflict you experience.

We live in a world that believes the creation of time is real and good. We think it's the only way to keep our commitments and follow up on things. We take pride in being able to measure time in the smallest instant and use it to make predictions about the behavior of atoms and molecules. What fun this can be! But it is also an illusion of perception, for time is within us, not outside of us. The construct of time is an unconscious group agreement and this is where it gets its power over us. We have forgotten we created it.

Perception of time requires choice. Can you choose to step outside the group agreement today and allow the experience of pure being? Can you feel the present moment within? Can you agree to bypass time just for an instant, and then another, and then another? What happens to your moment when you do this?

> *The only interval in which I can be saved from time is now.*
> *All love is ever-present now, here and now.*
> – ACIM

Lesson 309

I will not fear to look within today.

You have probably noticed that when sitting in meditation, you often have to pass through a war zone to get to fields of inner peace. Unfortunately, for many, many people, this inner journey is too fearful to undertake. We dip our toe into the pond, think it too deep and cold, and here we remain, perpetually skimming the surface of a quiet mind.

I have a friend whom I dearly, dearly love. He is understandably upset with the current state of the world. He sometimes gets angry that I am not as concerned as he is. He wants me to rise up in indignation and combat the evils of the world. "If we don't, who will?" he asks. He has a point, but it is also true that if I believe I am at war with evil, I make evil real. Fear feeds itself. Left unattended, it has nothing to feed upon. This is where "being in the world, but not of the world" comes in.

Perhaps you remember lesson 130? "It is impossible to see two worlds." This lesson is as direct as it gets. I cannot see two worlds. I cannot believe that fear and Love can coexist in Mind of God. They cannot and do not. Only one is real. Yet, in this world, we do believe we can keep both fear and Love alive at once. We believe we have not chosen one and cannot truly keep the other. One seems to be imposed and the other is beyond our grasp. This is the insanity of the personal mind that refuses to take responsibility for what it has created through its perception. And this is what makes this world.

Fear has made everything you think you see. All separation, all distinctions, and the multitude of differences you believe make up the world. They are not there. Fear has made them up. Yet love can have no enemy, and so they have no cause, no being, no consequence. They can be valued, but they remain unreal.

– ACIM

I can believe I do not value fear. Indeed, I can hate it. I can rage against it. But this only makes it real. It is impossible to hate something or someone I have not made real. What I make real is what I value. Do you see this? We must place value on fear or we would not continue to see it. The question is, why?

Fear is the foundation of the personal mind's perception. Fear is the natural outgrowth of a mind that believes it has split from its Source. It is a paradox, but in order to understand the unreality of fear I have to go deeply into it. I have to confront the fact that I have valued it. So long as I am afraid to see that I have valued fear, I will continue to make it real. I must be willing to let fear die for Love, and that means crossing the war zone of fear itself.

What doesn't exist in Mind of God is not. And yet, until I recognize the impossibility of fear I will believe it can coexist with love. I will choose to believe that fear and love have equal power and blind myself with illusion. It is impossible to see two worlds. The real and the unreal are all there are to choose between and nothing more than these.

Today is a day to examine your fear. Take it out and play with it. See where it comes up and how it motivates you. What does fear make real for you?

Take time for quiet contemplation. Rest the body in a comfortable position. Follow the natural breath. Repeat the lesson in your mind and allow all that arises to float across your mental screen. Do nothing with it. Especially do not fear it. Forgive it. Enjoy it. Stay focused on the knowledge that only Love is Real because that is all that exists in One True Mind – which created you, in which you still abide.

Lesson 310

In fearlessness and love I spend today.

Most people believe they want love. We want its good parts, the special warm and fuzzy parts. But love demands courage too. In this world being vulnerable is associated with love. Many never fully benefit from the experience of love because they wish to avoid the vulnerability. Love needs fearlessness for its full expression.

Our idea of love is only a partial reflection of a Whole. "I love you so much I would never be with anyone else." This kind of love is what ACIM calls "special love." It is reserved for a single person or group of persons. Its hidden function is to separate through specialness. Even this special love is only temporary. We have all experienced how love falters when the other does something unacceptable.

But the Love that created us is a steady state. It never falters and is never at risk. Its expression is full acceptance without vulnerability, and with no expectation of return. When I can look at someone and know she is an expression of Love, regardless of her external presentation, I am in Love, and I am transformed by it.

When we can collectively look at each other and see how we are all expressions of the same eternal Love, there will be a collective transformation. But this requires fearlessness and trust. The trust itself inspires the fearlessness. Once experienced, it is known as the Truth.

You could say Love is a field of frequency within which we coexist in consciousness. All things vibrate in It naturally. Not to recognize Love is simply to mistake yourself. It is a form of denial.

In truth, who are you to decide you are unworthy, or that your sister or brother is unworthy of Love? Your authority does not extend to devaluing yourself or others. You cannot differentiate yourself by saying, "I don't deserve the Love within which I was created." Truly, you are not so special you can deny the Love that created you.

Still, our sense of separation from Source makes us fearful. The powerful, who would have us believe our unworthiness, benefit from our fear. But when we know ourselves as Love, we will become fearless, for we will recognize nothing can stand between Love and each of us.

In fearlessness and love I spend today.

Sit in silent meditation today. Place your attention on breathing naturally. Allow the breath to settle into its own symmetry. When you are ready, imagine a clear bubble of Love surrounding your body. It can extend as close or as far as you wish.

On the in-breath, inhale the Love/Light. It flows into your lungs, your heart, and extends into every single cell and the spaces between the cells. No effort is required. Your willingness is all it takes.

On the out-breath, visualize all that you do not need leaving with the breath. Every particle of fear, loss, guilt, or pain – all of them move effortlessly out of the body, passing though the bubble of Love to the ends of the universe. Do not worry about what happens to the particles. The Holy Spirit will take care of it for you.

Sit, breathing in this pure bubble of loving light for as long as you wish. Breathe in Love/light. Breathe out all that is not Love/ Light. Watch it flow into you. Feel it move out of you. Your body is becoming Love/Light. Allow yourself to receive this blessing that requires only your permission, your acknowledgement of your own worth.

Take time during the day today to visualize the bubble of light around you. It is always there. It is your own personal container of safety. Breathe it in, and let all that is not Love be released. In moments of stress or mental agitation, try to return to the Love/ Light. Even if you only visualize it for a moment its effects will be there. This is not some fantasy. It is sanity restored.

Focus Question 10: *What is the Last Judgment?*

Lesson 311
The next ten lessons deal with the question, *"What is the Last Judgment?"* Here is how ACIM describes it:

The Last Judgment is one of the most threatening ideas in your thinking. This is because you do not understand it. Judgment is not an attribute of God. It was brought into being only after the separation, when it became one of the many learning devices to be built into the overall plan. Just as the separation occurred over millions of years, the Last Judgment will extend over a similarly long period, and perhaps an even longer one. Its length, however, can be greatly shortened by miracles, the device for shortening but not abolishing time. If a sufficient number become truly miracle-minded, this shortening process can be virtually immeasurable. It is essential, however, that you free yourself from fear quickly, because you must emerge from the conflict if you are to bring peace to other minds.

The Last Judgment is generally thought of as a procedure undertaken by God. Actually, it will be undertaken by my brothers with my help. It is a final healing rather than a meting out of punishment, however much you may think that punishment is deserved. Punishment is a concept totally opposed to right-mindedness, and the aim of the Last Judgment is to restore right-mindedness to you. The Last Judgment might be called a process of right evaluation. It simply means that everyone will finally come to understand what is worthy and what is not.

The Last Judgment is the decision to end all judgment. It is the understanding that judgment is above my pay grade. The personal mind cannot see Wholeness, so its judgment is unreliable. The Last Judgment recognizes that in Oneness there is no benefit to valuing one thing as better than, worse than, or lesser than. The Last Judgment arrives with a sense of humor. It carries the laughter that comes from drawing aside the curtain of perception and seeing the entire world has been one big passion play.

Here is how to practice the next ten lessons. Each morning read and contemplate the core question and its answer. Then read the particular lesson for the day. At some point in the day devote at least fifteen minutes to quiet meditation. You know how to do this by now. Sit and place awareness on the breath. Breathe in peace and exhale any tension in the body. Take as long as you want to do this. Then repeat the lesson for the day in your mind, invite the Holy Spirit's assistance, and let everything go. Allow the breath to anchor your mind. Watch thoughts and feelings as they arise. Trust. Expect nothing and allow everything. Play. Be courageous. Explore total nonresistance. Forgive and know your Innocence.

Be mindful throughout the day. Practice forgiveness. Allow direct experience through conscious awareness. On the hour, remember the lesson. Use it to anchor your day.

In the evening, read the lesson only. Let it guide you into sleep where it will inform the other world of dreams until you waken to this one, and finally to Reality.

Today's lesson draws aside the curtain of the passion play. It recognizes that judgments are always against one's self, made with the limitations of the personal mind.

I judge all things as I would have them be.

"As I would have them be." The I here is your personal mind.

Consider that two people can see the same event and come away with totally different perceptions of it. Each of us literally has our own reality. There are billions of different realities in existence on this planet. This is a problem when we disagree amongst ourselves. Peace dissolves. Wars are waged. But this is nothing compared to the decision to disagree with All That Is.

All That Is IS all that is. It cannot be judged. Every personal mind's judgment becomes a weapon against the Truth of Oneness. Our decision to perceive ourselves as only bodies, with separate interests, competing needs, and conflicting goals is a judgment against Love. The perception that I can benefit even as you fail is to judge separation as Truth.

The belief in separate interests puts us in constant confrontation with each other and All That Is. Even when it all seems to be going "my" way, I am rarely ever satisfied for long. If I judge the moment as "good," I fear it won't last. If I judge it as "bad," I need to know when it will be over. The final judgment is not the end of creativity. It is not passive acceptance. It is the willingness to remain open in the present moment without fear.

I cannot count the number of times I've been wrong in my perceptions. I'm sure you've had the same experience. We will always make mistakes because we cannot see the Wholeness of all creation. Every judgment is only a reflection of our own internal perception. So really, why not give it up?

Rest your mind from judgment today. You'll realize that what appears to be a passive thing actually requires your full participation. I have my moment. I accept it on its face. I allow it. Then I decide with total freedom how to move out of it. I have my next moment and I am free to choose again. I enjoy seeing what happens. I play with the moment, not against it. This way of being is much less tiring than struggling against what is.

As you sit in silent meditation today begin with this idea, "I wait with an open mind. I am willing to listen for the Voice of my True Self. I am a conduit through which the Mystery lives Itself. My mere existence is a service to the Mystery. I have nowhere to go and nothing to achieve. I am here. Empty. Spacious. Receiving."

Lesson 312

I see all things as I would have them be.

You have learned the personal mind is incapable of seeing Wholeness. You know that failure to see Wholeness results in judgment, and it is always against one's self.

To understand today's lesson, one must know the fundamental

Law of Cause and Effect. The Law of Cause and Effect is entirely logical, but you must understand this: form is always an effect of thought. Thought is causative. Material form is its effect. In other words, everything that appears in form must first have appeared in thought. The Law of Cause and Effect applies at both the individual and group mind levels.

"I see all things as I would have them be." Change my mind, and what I see is affected. We see all things as we would have them be. Change a sufficient number of minds and the effect will be to change the world. Again, ACIM's words on the Last Judgment say, "If a sufficient number become truly miracle-minded, this shortening process can be virtually immeasurable."

Our full realization of the power of thought is just beginning. Science and spirituality are merging their knowledge and wisdom. The fact that consciousness alters reality on a quantum level is now beyond doubt. The future application of this knowledge might seem miraculous but it will be nothing more than an advanced application of the Law of Cause and Effect.

An advanced application of this Law requires me to be continuously aware of the content of my thoughts – for my thoughts have effects. They are how I create. The mind never loses its creative force because that is its purpose, its gift, from Universal Mind. But remember this: True Creation comes only through the power of a mind whose thoughts are Whole in Love. We can Truly Create only with what Source uses to Create. Illusions are not True Creations, which is why this world is illusion. An advanced student creates through Love only.

Creation does not happen in isolation because minds are joined above the level of form. In a very real way, this makes individual creation critical because each of us contributes to the whole. A major goal of ACIM is the liberation of the individual in order to liberate the whole. The whole is more significant than the sum of its parts. Each of us is part of a creation that is beyond our individual imagining.

How would you have things be? You will know through what you think you see. You will know through your judgment of what you see. Perception is everything. Is a stone just a stone? Or, is it a glowing collection of atoms and molecules vibrating with its own uniqueness? Is the man in the mirror an aging body made of flesh and bone? Or, is he a perfect, eternal being of light experiencing itself as form in time? What is the truth of it? What is the truth you see?

Today is a day to be perfectly aware of how you are creating. There will come a time when you will be so in touch that each thought you have will contain the power to pull the building blocks of form together and take them apart. We start today with baby steps. It is enough to just be aware of what is happening in your mind.

Stop often today and listen to your inner voice. Is it anxious? Is it sad? Do you believe these thoughts are true? How does each thought feel in the body? Do you believe you are capable of choosing your own thoughts?

Begin your seated meditation today with the words of the lesson. Say the words slowly in your mind. As you say the words, take in the meaning of each word. For example, "I see." What do I see? "All things." Yes, this lesson includes *all things I see*. "As I would have them be." How would I have them be?

You are a Holy Fragment of Source. You have been gifted with all Its creative power. It is time to understand that you have a right to ask and receive what you would have Be. In fact, this is what you have been doing all along.

Lesson 313

Now let a new perception come to me.

This lesson is an obvious progression of the ones before it: "I judge all things as I would have them be," and therefore, "I see all things as I would have them be."

When I come to the realization that my judging and seeing are based on a very limited perception, I have stepped through a door into new territory. But what is this new territory and is there a map to help me navigate within it?

There is a map of the new territory, but to read it I am required to perceive anew. To understand the new map I am no longer allowed to abnegate my own authority as the one who can know, who can perceive rightly. I must acknowledge myself capable!

Fear and uncertainty keep me from stepping into the new territory. The fear is that there will be nothing there, that it will be empty space. The fear is that what lies ahead might not sustain me. I might fail or be disappointed. Things might be worse in the new territory. Oh my!

The new perception, the new territory, is not a lie. But it does require commitment. I cannot step in and out of the new territory and then complain that I am still seeing the same old thing. When I step out of the old territory I have to leave it behind.

The perception of God within myself, and all things, requires me to know my own worth. For a while, this may mean I have to have faith. There is nothing wrong with faith if it gets you over limitation. Many false limitations have been imposed upon this world. Faith is often the first step toward Knowing through experience, and thus releasing false limitation.

At first, your experiences with new perception may be fleeting. But over time, and with persistence, your experiences of True Perception will become increasingly frequent. The space between True Perception and false limitations will grow smaller and smaller. Yes, you will have setbacks and relearning. But this is what will sustain you on your journey into the new territory. Once you have stepped in the new, it becomes more difficult to revisit the old place because you know what awaits you there and it cannot suffice.

True perception sees that Love is excluded from nothing. It

may only go unrecognized. The one who does not perceive Its presence must be forgiven. Today's lesson requires that you know your worth as the one who sees with new perception because in your vision the world is changed.

True perceptions looks on all things as sinless, so fear is gone from the mind. Where fear was, I invite Love to be. Love will come wherever I ask.
– ACIM

Stop often today and say in your mind, "Now I behold all things in Love. I am capable of perceiving Love in everything, and I am capable of forgiving those who have forgotten What they are."

As you sit in silence, begin your meditation with the statement, "Now let a new perception come to me." Expect your will to be fulfilled for you are a divine being. Your will cannot remain unfulfilled once stated. But the statement is only the first half of the equation. The second half is to remain open to new perceptions – which will come. Sit in silence and allow all things. You have stepped into the new territory and your new perception awaits.

Lesson 314

I seek a future different from the past.

The bottom line of this lesson is this: The way I respond to my present moment has everything to do with the moment that follows it.

I am a walking antenna. I both send and receive energy. For simplicity's sake let's call it electromagnetic frequency (EMF). When I experience a strong thought/feeling, I send out a signal and the universe responds by sending something back. What comes back is reflected in my next moment in the form of a person, event, or thing. Whatever it is, it will be a "match" for the original signal I sent out.

If I am unaware of my thoughts and feelings, I will also be unaware of my broadcast. Thus, I will fail to recognize anything that comes back to me as "mine." But if I'm present in my moment, aware of my feeling/thoughts, the EMF I broadcast will be clear. When I broadcast from a clear state, I am literally tuned in to a different frequency – a higher frequency, and the response will match it. This is how I create a future different from the past – I attract it from my present moment.

If I stand in my moment unafraid, willing to let it touch me, and knowing I am completely safe, then what I get back will be very different than something unconsciously created from a fearful past. I let the next moment touch me, whatever it is, and the next, and the next. As I practice this, every new attraction is of a higher vibration. It cannot be otherwise! But I cannot carry the past into the present moment. Each moment must be free, open, and willing without judgment.

Do you begin to see why continuous consciousness is a requirement? This is why ACIM calls it the Holy Instant! It is why we are so strongly advised not to be in judgment. It is why we are told our only function on this earth is to learn forgiveness. Every future moment we "attract" is a reflection of what we've broadcast. Sometimes it comes in the form of an event. Sometimes it is a person or a thing. But it's always a match.

We cannot see inside ourselves so Source kindly sends us a mirror. This is what our "moment of attraction" is – a mirror of what we hold within. Because we live in linear time, it is often difficult to match the thought/feeling with the attraction. But the more we pay attention, the easier it is to see the connections. The key is to recognize the future is an extension of the present moment. Past mistakes, judgments, fears, anger, shame and blame carried into the present moment will affect the future. This is the Law of Cause and Effect!

Free your present moment, and you begin to free yourself. Does this mean you will never experience loss or pain again? No. But it will change the way they are experienced. We'll talk about this more in upcoming lessons. For now, be in your moment. Let it touch you. Then respond consciously, without fear. Have your experience and notice what happens. Pay Attention and It will pay you back a thousand-fold!

Today, make it your intention to maintain a moment-to-moment awareness. This is an advanced technique. It may feel impossible at first. However, if you make it a practice, you will begin to notice, over time, that it gets easier. You will move in and out of awareness, but the gaps between being awake and asleep will shorten. If you practice this, your life will change. This is how you create a future different from the past. It is your job to stay present in the moment. Leave the future to Source, Who will reflect it back to you.

As you sit in silent meditation today, place your awareness on the breath. Experience your bodily shifts and changes. Watch the images and feelings that arise and float away – moment by moment. You will begin to see that every emotion carries a bodily sensation with it. Stay with it. Do nothing except have the experience. Give yourself at least fifteen minutes. Thirty would be even better.

From new perception of the world there comes a future very different from the past. The future now is recognized as but an extension of the present. Past mistakes can cast no shadows on it, so that fear has lost its idols and its images, and being formless it has no effects.
– ACIM

Lesson 315

All gifts my brothers/sisters give belong to me.

This lesson, and the one that follows it, speak to the metaphysics of Oneness. But do not think the broad scope of this lesson makes it untrue or some kind of dreamy hopefulness because it isn't.

When you read of a community that offers warmth and welcome to refugees, does your heart not open? Do you not settle a bit more comfortably in your seat? When you watch a video of a child laughing, or an animal being rescued, does it not feel good inside? Call it empathy or sympathy. Quantum entanglement would not be far off the mark. We are entwined with each other across space and time. The reverse is also true. When we see a photo of a child crying or an animal in fear our stomach tightens, the heart contracts, we want to look away.

The invisibility of our connection does not make it less real. Thought and emotion reside at a level above form and our minds are joined there. So not only do I receive what I give, but what others give as well. There are not six degrees of separation – there is no separation whatsoever. The gifts my brothers give to me are unlimited. When one is joined in Love then I am also joined. And as we join, the circle widens exponentially.

The thoughts I hold about what may and may not be are what tether me to what may or may not be. Do I believe these connections can be real? Or are we all separate bodies with separate minds? Is it possible that kindness shared across the world can affect my day? What thoughts and beliefs tether you? What "proof" do you need before your heart will open?

There are those who would keep us powerless by saying, "No. It may not be. You are not me, and I am not you. Anything meaningful beyond that is merely imagination."

This is a belief system that keeps us small. The gifts my brothers give are mine and within this knowledge is all the power of the world. What I give I receive, and I receive only by giving that which I would have myself. There is no end to giving and there is no end to our connection. We did not create the connection; Source did. But we are the ones who may choose to know it or not, and the knowing changes everything.

On this day use your perception in play with this idea. Give something away – a smile, a kind word, a thought of peace. See what happens in the next moment or the one after that. Yesterday you were asked to be aware of your thoughts continuously. Today you are asked to choose thoughts of loving kindness and play with extending them beyond yourself.

As you sit in silent contemplation today, spend a few moments in review. What has been given to you? What have you accepted? What have you given to your sister or brother? How was it received? How would you choose now knowing that all you give comes back to you? It may not be in the same form, but it will be an energetic match. The Law of Cause and Effect requires it.

Lesson 316

All gifts I give my sisters/brothers are my own.

The Law of Cause and Effect requires that I will always receive what I give. It may come later, obscured by the illusion of time. It may arrive in a different form and my personal mind may very well not perceive it. It almost certainly won't if I am not mindful. But it is the Law. All the gifts I give my sisters/brothers are my own.

The decision to receive is a decision to open. We could also say it is the decision to allow. The gift I accept, or allow, is whatever is in front of me. I receive my jealous coworker and I accept her as she is. This doesn't mean I let her walk all over me, but before I cast her aside I use my will to look inside. She is either projecting something onto me, or I am projecting something onto her and she has picked it up. Either way, at least one of us is projecting something, and it may very well be me.

Here is the pivot point for this lesson: When I respond to something negative outside me, I am making it real. I am saying, "Yes. This person, event or thing has the ability to ruin my day." Thus, their bad temper becomes my reality. But when, in my freedom to choose, I decide that nothing outside me can affect my inner peace, I am teaching her that I am free and she may also be. Thus I give her the gift of peace and I will receive it in return.

I will not know my own Wholeness until I see It everywhere – even in my coworker who has not yet recognized it in herself. Can I allow her mistake, knowing that if I respond to it in kind, I will only make it real? When I make it real for her, I am making it real for myself. Therefore, the gift of forgiveness is really my own as well as hers.

So many gifts go unrecognized. It isn't easy to accept unkindness, pain, or disease as a gift. It is easier to simply remember that I am invulnerable in Truth, and every attack is a call for love – whether it is an attack by another human being or the body's attack against itself.

I cannot know how Oneness is unfolding in my moment. The only sane response is to receive through acceptance and forgive if necessary. In the act of forgiving, the recipient of forgiveness will always include myself. All the gifts I give my brothers are my own: the moment of eye contact, the offer of assistance, the willingness to listen fully, the decision not to judge.

As every gift my brother/sister gives is mine, so every gift I give belongs to me. With each one I allow a past mistake to go, and leave no shadow on my Holy Mind, which Source Loves. The Law of Love is Wholeness and Timeless. Thus it is that every gift anyone has received throughout all time is also mine.

– ACIM

No gift is ever lost. It is simply not perceived. If it is Love you seek today, then give it. If it is forgiveness you need today, then give it. Give all to all to receive All from All.

As you sit in silence today, begin by repeating this lesson in your mind: "All the gifts I give my brothers (sisters) are my own." Then place awareness on the breath and settle into the body. Slow down. Stay with the breath. Say again to yourself, "All the gifts I give my sisters/brothers are my own." Then ask, "Who gives?" Answer: "It can only be that I give." Now ask, "Who receives?" Answer: "I do. I do. I receive." Sit in silence and receive. Allow receiving to come. Every gift you've ever given is returning home to you.

Lesson 317

I follow in the way appointed me.

Your way is appointed already. It is unique to you. You did not create your way, nor did you create That Which you are following. You may choose to follow or you may choose to resist – for those are the only two choices available to you. There are only two choices. Recognize this, and you are on your way.

To follow in the way appointed is very much like surfing. For example, you did not create the wave or the ocean from which it arises. But once you are on your board and catch your wave, a flexible stance is imperative if you want to stay on. Those who stiffen in fear, those who resist the motion, will not stay on the board for long. Those who relax and sink into their body, bending and aligning it with the movement of the wave itself – those are the ones who will ride far in to shore.

Contrary to most people's thinking, following in the way that is appointed me is not giving up or being passive. It is the opposite. When I know the truth that I am not the one in charge of everything, I become free to use my power in alignment rather than in resistance. Does the surfer tell the wave which way to go?

Every wave is unique. There has never been one wave created in the whole of time that is exactly the same. Your role, which is unique in this universe, is to move with what is offered, not stiffen against it. This makes all the difference. You didn't create the wave, but you find yourself upon it. Can you work with it, go with it, and ride it all the way in?

Until I make the choice to see this world as my own dream and forgive it and all it contains, I am in resistance to the wave and Ocean from which it arises. I have limited myself to linear time and human destiny. There is another way, but it does require me to let go of the personal mind and follow a Mind that Knows. This means I have to trust the wave will not purposely throw me or dash me upon the rocks. "There is no cruelty in Source, and there is none in me." Trust. You are an eternal being.

While on the wave, it is perfectly reasonable to ask for assistance. It is not passive to ask, but it is highly interactive. The Ocean of Source wants to interact! Ask Source to show you how to ride the wave. Ask your higher Self to show you how to stay on the board. Trust It will take you into something else, something more desirable. Then let go and surf from one moment into the next.

Your way is certain and secure. You are not wandering alone. You are in flow with the Great Mind, your most willing Partner, Who is most easily accessed when you surrender to Its lead. When you do this, you will catch a wave that will take you to places you never could have dreamt on your own.

Let go of your thought processes today. Try following and see what happens. Watch the world and step in when it feels right to do so. Step lightly in and out. Everyone around you is surfing too, whether they know it or not. Your flexibility on the board shows them how to lead by following. It may feel like you are falling in at times, but do know this: someone is watching you from the shore. She sees your grace and she is picking up her own board to get in.

Lesson 318

In me salvation's means and ends are One.

The path of creation includes the experience of extreme separation and polarity. Source fragments and compartmentalizes Itself as innumerable selves in order to understand Itself and know Itself. Once known, each fragment begins its return journey back toward integration, unity, and Wholeness. This cycle of Wholeness, fragmentation, and return to Wholeness allows Source to know Itself in unlimited ways.

It is difficult for the personal mind to grasp this. But Source both Knows Itself and seeks to Know Itself, all At Once, At the Same Time.

Perhaps it's now clearer why we are asked to "follow in the way appointed." The personal mind did not create the path outward. It is the end result! The personal mind has no idea how it got here nor can it find its way Home. It seeks continuously, but never, ever finds. However, the part of your mind that has remained in connection with Source does know. As a fragment of Source you can never not contain this connection, also known as the Holy Spirit.

The Holy Spirit (or Whole I Spirit) is alive in each of us. It is rekindled when the dominance of the personal mind is recognized as the illusion it is. It blossoms with acknowledgement of your eternal divinity. It flowers when you recognize fully that there is not a single part of you that stands alone.

When apparent opposites – male and female, dark and light, up and down, good and evil, matter and antimatter – are seen as polarities of Source, we can say "singularity is experienced." Singularity does not happen "out there." It is an inner knowing. The absence of singularity is an illusion. The recognition that opposites and polarities are part of Source is our salvation.

You were created as the very thing you seek. The world is searching for what it already possesses but does not see. The Oneness of Source can be realized from an individualized expression of choice – indeed it must be. Each unique aspect of Source must realize its Oneness from its perspective of uniqueness. There is no contradiction between uniqueness and Oneness. This realization is a fundamental underpinning to seeing beyond the limits of this world.

I am the means by which God's Creation is saved, because salvation's purpose is to find the sinlessness that God has placed in me. I was created as the thing I seek. I am the goal the world is searching for. I am a Holy Creation of God, Its one eternal Love. I am salvation's means and end as well.
– ACIM

Today, maintain awareness of the Oneness around you. Know in your mind that the man or woman next to you is part of your Wholeness, even as he or she seems to be having a separate experience. It is only separate at your current level of awareness. Above that, somewhere in your mind, the apparent separation is reconciled. Feel your way into that reconciliation as often as you are able to do so, for as long as you can.

Take time for contemplation with this lesson. Sit for at least fifteen minutes in silence. Thirty would be even better. Go to the quiet place where you will not be disturbed. Sit and get comfortable. Breathe normally and close your eyes. Watch the breath and notice any bodily sensations. If there is tightness, breathe into it. When you are calm and still, repeat the lesson in your mind: "In me salvation's means and ends are one."

Slowly say each word. "In me is salvation. In me the means and ends are One. In me is the very peace I seek."

Continue to breathe and watch thoughts that arise. If your

mind begins to wander, repeat the lesson slowly and purposefully in your mind. Turn the words slowly over and feel each one. Stay with the breath. Who is speaking? Who is listening? You are; the part of you that is always there beneath the noise; the part of you that arises from the singularity of Source.

Lesson 319

I came for the salvation of the world.

Here is a thought that has no arrogance, no self-deception, or exaggeration. Your purpose, and your capability, is to save yourself and the world. It is the only reason you are here. You are the very one you have been waiting for.

You came to know your Self. It is one of the least egotistical journeys you can make. Only the ego limits itself. Only the ego would seek to curtail your journey by redirecting your mind to fearful, guilty, judgmental, egoic efforts. It is not selfish, useless, or impossible to seek your True Identity, for there is no other task worthy of you.

How many lifetimes have you spent seeking experiences of fame, fortune, guilt, retribution, loss, power, or helplessness? How many moments in this lifetime have egoic concerns outweighed any effort to go within and face all that you are not, to know all that you are? You are given all Power of Source and you cannot constrain your Self forever. You have drawn the veil over your mind and you must lift it.

As you sit in silent contemplation, begin in the usual way. Relax the body and place awareness on the breath. When you are ready, repeat in your mind, "I came for the salvation of the world." Watch what comes up. Does this feel like a burden or an opening to something greater you have not yet imagined? If you feel burdened or constrained by this world, it does not mean you are. It means only that one tiny portion of your mind is still willing to believe in limitation. Forgive yourself. But do not believe it. Your light has never dimmed.

Lesson 320

My Creator gives all power unto me.

What is this power Source has given us? Like the power of Thought, it is unlimited, unbounded, and unrestricted. It applies equally and universally to everything and everyone in Creation Itself. An unforgiving mind is a separate mind, but a forgiving mind is united in its creation. Until I understand the truth of Oneness I cannot use the full power I have been given.

Today, open yourself to your own power through alignment with the Will of Source. Say, "Yes," to the moment, whatever it brings. Do not waste your power in resistance, but be one with it, dance with it. The power of Source is playful and takes itself lightly. Yet it is mighty enough to bring forth an entire universe of stars.

As you sit in meditation today, begin with the idea of this lesson. Repeat the lesson in your mind, "My Source gives all power to me." Notice how it feels in the body to say these words. Is it a little intimidating? If so, it is because the personal mind is elevating fear above joining. A mind that purposefully joins with Source in creation need not fear its creations.

As you sit, take time to imagine what you might create if you knew your power to be unlimited. Watch your thoughts. Feel your way into the truth of your creation. Use the breath to anchor your mind. Be playful and enjoy yourself. If you could create with the Love of Source, what would it be? Desire is powerful. There is nothing wrong with it! Do you think Source did not have desire when It created you? It desired to Know Itself through you! Trust in your desire for it is the beginning of knowing your powers of creation. But do remember, only Love creates in Truth.

Focus Question 11: *What is Creation?*

Lesson 321

The foundation question for the next ten lessons is, *"What is creation?"*

Here is how to practice the next ten lessons. Each morning read and contemplate the core question and its answer. Then read the particular lesson for the day. At some point in the day devote at least fifteen minutes to quiet meditation. You know how to do this by now. Sit and place awareness on the breath. Breathe in peace and exhale any tension in the body. Take as long as you want to do this. Then repeat the lesson for the day in your mind, invite the Holy Spirit's assistance, and let everything go. Allow the breath to anchor your mind. Watch thoughts and feelings as they arise. Trust. Expect nothing and allow everything. Play. Be courageous. Explore total nonresistance. Forgive and know your Innocence.

Be mindful throughout the day. Practice forgiveness. Allow direct experience through conscious awareness. On the hour, remember the lesson. Use it to anchor your day.

What is Creation? Creation is the sum of all God's Thoughts, which are limitless and infinite across all time, space, dimensions, and beyond even these. Only Love Creates and only like Itself. Creation is you. Creation is beyond the ability of the personal mind's understanding except in the most general terms.

Only Love creates and only like Itself. There was no time when all that It created was not there. Nor will there be a time when anything that It created suffers any loss. Forever and forever are God's Thoughts exactly as they were and as they are, unchanged through time and after time is done.
– ACIM

There would be no need for the concept of Creator and Creation if not for our perception of separation from Source. We participate in creation only through thoughts we share with Source. When our thoughts are in alignment with Love, we create. When our thoughts can imagine nothing opposite to Source and the Will of Source, we create. We create when our thoughts join with Thought and extend in Love.

In this world of illusion, creation appears as an expression of freedom: freedom from fear, freedom from guilt, freedom from shame, and freedom from judgment – in short, freedom from anything that is not Love. This is why nothing created in fear is real. Nothing created out of guilt is real. These creations only limit; they do not extend.

All our power to create comes from Source and we can create only in the manner of Source. So it follows, all that you do not create out of Love is unreal. It will not last. It has no true effect at all. It is like mist in the wind. Creation is the opposite of illusion and happens only in complete Wholeness with Source.

Of myself, I do nothing. But my Source, through me, does all things.
– ACIM

Who conceives an idea of beauty and creates it in form? Who writes the book that tells the story of courage and redemption? Who paints the image of light and color that calms the heart and mind? Who thinks at all? Oh, how the egoic mind rails against this question! It wishes to be the sole originator of all creation, all idea, and all thought. But hear this: only the thoughts you think with God are real. All creation comes from union with Mind of God. We are the extension of Creation and we extend in Creation only with Its Will. Make your creations in this world through Source and know the freedom to create. This is your lesson today:

Source, my freedom is in You alone.

When do you create without doubt? When do you create wholly confident in yourself? When do you create and truly love what you have made? Create in shared consciousness with Source and you will not doubt your creation. Ask Source to create with you and then open yourself to Its Influence. You will be amazed at the scope of work you are capable of without the ego's doubting influence.

Today, remember to ask yourself often, "What am I creating in this moment?" "What is sourcing my desire? Is it fear? Is it in conscious alignment with Love?" You will know the answer immediately through your heart. Let this be clear to you – creation with Source begins the instant you cease your resistance to what is in front of you in the moment. This is why the Holy Instant is now. This is why you cannot create out of a guilty past or a fearful future. Creation is free from both of these limitations. Your lesson today is experiential. Notice how you create today. What is the source of your creative desire? Is its fulfillment dependent upon your will alone?

Begin your silent meditation with the idea behind these words, "Source, I did not understand what made me free, nor what my freedom is, nor where to look to find it. I have searched in vain until I heard your Thought directing me. Now I would guide myself no more. For I neither made nor understand the way. But I trust in You Who endowed me with my freedom in Oneness with You. It is my will to return to Love."

There is a reason for the deathbed adage, "You can't take it with you." You can't take your house, your belongings, your job, your fame, or that special piece of jewelry when you pass on. Only the Love you have created is free to cross the boundaries of this world because only It has the Creative Power of Source to do so.

Lesson 322

I give up only what was never real.

Yesterday, you learned your freedom comes only from Source, Which granted it in the first place. But, when told it cannot truly create and freedom is found only through giving up its will to a greater Will, the personal mind will rebel. It will reject true freedom for false sovereignty because it perceives a requirement of sacrifice. There is no sacrifice in accepting the freedom of Source because the personal mind's kingdom is a dream.

> *I sacrifice illusion; nothing more. And as illusions go I find the gifts illusions tried to hide awaiting me in shining welcome.*
> – ACIM

The "freedom" offered by the personal mind is so limited and so parochial it is really only a form of imprisonment. Face your fear of loss and give it up. You are completely capable of joining your mind with Source in creation. In fact, you are already doing so, for your Self has never left It. Every moment of peace you experience is in alignment with Mind of God. Peace is a creation. The decision to give up illusion is a form of creation. The decision to return to Love is creation of the highest order.

What do your creations express – Love or fear of loss? What do your creations convey about yourself? Do they express trust in your Self, or in the personal mind?

Your creations are a feedback loop for yourself so you can witness the effects of your choices. Every choice you make is a creation, born of a mind that anticipates fear of loss or the loss of fear. To Source, all sacrifice remains forever inconceivable. You cannot suffer loss except in dreams. What loss can you anticipate in joining your mind to Source except the loss of fear and the return to Love in your mind?

Lesson 323

I gladly make the "sacrifice" of fear.

This world is awash in fear. It was created from a thought of separation from Source, so how could it be otherwise? What has left its Creator is alone. Me, my, mine. You, yours, its. This language is produced by perceptions that arise out of the personal mind. They aren't bad; they are just incorrect for they perceive only a partial truth.

The sacrifice of fear means giving up the predominance of me, my, mine. It requires us, we, ours. Us, we, ours is much, much closer to the truth. It speaks to the diamond web of consciousness that holds all of us together in One Mind.

The world of me and mine is sparsely populated indeed. The world of us and ours is richly appointed. The truth of Oneness does not require the demise of individuality, for Oneness is expressed infinitely! The personal mind would make us choose either mine or yours, but the choice of Love is to say, "YES," to everything because Love knows no scarcity. It is endlessly varied and yet... One.

As you reach toward the end of your lessons, you will be increasingly asked to let go and trust. Isn't it strange to call the end of fear a "sacrifice"? But ask yourself, what you have sacrificed in the name of fear? The sacrifice of fear is the only sacrifice Source will ask of you.

Today, allow yourself to become aware of the fear you hold within. This may feel uncomfortable or even unreasonable. It will probably require you to let go of the rational mind. Notice your fears and consciously give them over to the Holy Spirit. When fear is gone, peace fills the space. When we are at peace, love returns to our awareness.

Notice every moment of fear today. Your body will always let you know when fear is present. It makes a gift of tension, tightness, and discomfort by saying, "Stop! Pay attention to your mind!" Step into your fear. Look clearly but do not attach to it. When you have moved the feeling through, let it go by giving it up to the Holy Spirit.

Take at least fifteen minutes for silent contemplation. Sit and get comfortable. Watch the breath. When you are ready, say in your mind, "I gladly make a sacrifice of fear." Hold your mind in the silence and stillness of calm awareness, with just the breath to anchor. Trust and allow what arises. If feelings of fear come up ask, "What is this fear? How has it tempered my existence?" Feel your way into these questions. Breathe. Every bit of fear you notice and release pays a debt to truth – a debt that is merely letting go of self-deception and images mistakenly treated as real.

Lesson 324

I merely follow for I would not lead.

If you interpret this lesson as a demand to give up your power, know it is your personal mind speaking. The Whole Truth is a series of nested truths but the personal mind's perception doesn't even make it out of the box.

I cannot give up what was never real, and I gladly sacrifice my fear for what is. What is fear but the trepidation of not knowing what is to come? The personal mind, which lacks all trust in Source, wants to know. It wants to lead the way, to plan and to explain. It will happily make up stories that offer comfort, but they will not be Truth. The Truth is, there is never a moment outside God's presence. You need do nothing to lead the way because it has been made for you already. No instant in this universe lies outside Mind of God. This realization is not giving up your power; it is taking it back.

This is a lesson in flow. It asks you to jump in the river and trust the current to take you where it will. Certainly there will be times when the current feels too fast. And there will be periods of stagnation. This is where trust and flexibility come in. But you will never be lost when you step back and ask Source to take the lead because Source is both the river and the current.

Not one of us can see the whole of the river in our mind. But you know part of the river and I know another part of it. When we jump in together, joining our minds and sharing what we know, the way becomes less confusing. We can hold hands as we flow together. That's part of the plan anyway and it makes the journey Home so much more fun.

Your ending is assured and safe harbor guaranteed. Today, allow yourself to be the watcher. Choose silence instead of opinion. Quiet the heart and mind and take a look at the river flowing all around you. Where are you in it? Are you resisting the current in this moment? Whose hand are you holding, or are you floating alone?

Take at least fifteen minutes for silent contemplation today. Settle in and become aware of the breath. Sense your way into the body. Breathe into any tight spots. Notice what feelings are there. Breathe into them as well. Breathe in light. Breathe out all that is a barrier to light. Do not worry. Ask Source to lead your mind for a little while. Then relax and notice thoughts and feelings that come up. Make peace with yourself. Flow.

Lesson 325

All things I think I see are reflections of ideas in my mind.

This is salvation's keynote: What I see reflects a process in my mind, which starts with my idea of what I want. From there, the mind makes up an image of the thing the mind

desires, judges valuable, and therefore seeks to find. These
images are then projected outward, looked upon, esteemed as
real and guarded as one's own.
– ACIM

You have heard this over and over again because it is so critical
to your enlightenment. This is why you must become conscious
of your thoughts. It is why you must become aware of and
relinquish all perceptions that obscure love and stand in the
way of knowing yourself worthy of it. It explains why you must
make a sacrifice of fear.

All things you think you see are mental images projected. In
essence, they mirror the contents of your mind. As you believe,
so you will perceive. If you are unhappy with your creations you
must attend to the things that limit you in your own mind. You
attend to them by first forgiving them. Do not crucify yourself
for any creation you think you have made. Illusions require
forgiveness, not punishment.

Here's the deal: when you understand today's lesson your
life has to change. It doesn't mean you will now manifest that
mansion you've always wanted. But it will change what you
experience going forward. It must be so because in making the
decision to be in charge of your own mind, you raise the quality
of every thought you have.

The world we see is a projection upon a screen. Your thoughts
are the projections, expanded outward and made into an image
that appears real. Change your thoughts and the images on the
screen will begin to shift. When enough people change their
thoughts, the whole movie is altered.

Forgive your personal mind. It is your creation. You have
given it its power. Put it to bed kindly. Its insane thoughts
have produced an insane world. From its judgment comes a
world condemned. And from forgiving thoughts a gentle world
emerges with compassion for all of God's Creations. Only then

will this world be a place to rest on the journey Home together.

Today, renew in earnest your commitment to observe continuously the contents of your mind. It is not too much to ask that you stop every fifteen minutes and review your thoughts. It is not too much to ask that you remain a constant observer. You have the power over your mind. If not you, then who does?

Sit in contemplation today. This practice is a transition into more continuous awareness. Sit. Breathe. Settle into the body. Let thoughts and feelings arise without judging or holding onto them. Practice being still and watching your own mind at work.

Lesson 326

I am forever an Effect of God.

Now we come to the final truth, the answer to every question you could have about what you are. All of the remaining lessons rest upon this fundamental thought. Faith and knowing speak to this idea but science is now crossing a spiritual boundary that shows its Reality in a new way. Welcome again to spiritual quantumness, or more precisely, quantum entanglement.

As described in an earlier lesson, recent experiments have now confirmed the existence of quantum entanglement. This means particles created by the same action remain connected across time and space. Actions performed on one instantly affect the other no matter how far apart they're separated. They are forever an effect of each other.

Albert Einstein wasn't convinced about quantum entanglement. He called it "spooky action at a distance." My guess is he would be thrilled with the discovery. And while it is true that some of today's quantum physicists decry the use of their work to support spiritual claims, the cat is now out of the bag.

We are quantum beings and we are entangled with Source

and with each other. Yes, Source is far beyond science. Still, what has been created by Source must point to It. There are a thousand languages to explain the presence of God. Science is only one of them. But the language of science is persuasive for us, so this is important. We are a Thought forever entangled with First Thought, or Mind of God.

Source, I was created in Your Mind, a holy Thought that never left Its home. I am forever Your Effect, and You forever and forever are my Cause. As You created me, I have remained. Where You established me I still abide. And all your attributes abide in me, because it is Your Will.
– ACIM

We are a Thought of God and we have never left God's Mind, nor have any of Its creations. There is nothing in your mind, in this world, in this universe, nor in any of the multiple universes that exist or are yet to come, that are outside Mind of God. No thought or feeling you have ever experienced is yours alone. This recognition is your grace. It is your liberation from the personal mind that is so convinced of its unrelenting loneliness. You are imbued with all the attributes of your Creator. As you move through your day, take on this cloak of grace. Wear it. Own it. Share it.

Give yourself at least fifteen minutes to sit in silent contemplation of this lesson. Get comfortable and place gentle awareness on the breath. Settle into your body and notice any tension or tightness. Breathe into those places. When you are ready, say the lesson slowly in your mind: "I am forever an effect of God." Now, simply hold the phrase in your awareness and be still. Let the words resonate. Watch the breath. Then bring the words into awareness again. Hold them in stillness for a time, then let go and place awareness on the breath. Find your own rhythm now. Allow that part of your mind that knows its connection with Source to disclose the deeper meaning of this lesson for you. You are opening space for intuitive wisdom to arise. Trust and allow. You cannot fail.

Lesson 327

I need but call and You will answer me.

I step aside and let Source lead, using my energies not to resist, but to interact creatively with what rises to greet me. In doing so I give up nothing but the illusion of control and gain the awareness of freedom without fear.

Each moment I remember that everything outside of me is a mirror of what is inside, I become more curious and more willing to know the contents of my mind. I do this so I might begin to understand the process of co-creation with Source. I am a co-creator because I have been endowed with all the attributes of my Creator.

As I develop self-awareness I begin to notice things. Connections between my thoughts and events that follow become more apparent. Perhaps I even see how frequently I have allowed the past to influence the thoughts I hold now. With this, the present moment is freed and its full potential is released in a new way.

As I deepen self-awareness I remember to ask for help. Each time I remember to ask, and then relax into silent awareness, my own strength is reinforced. It's paradoxical but it's true. My increase in confidence comes from the direct experience that no request for assistance is ever denied. It may come in a form I do not immediately recognize or didn't expect. But I know what was given was exactly what I needed at the time of the request.

We are not asked to take our Oneness with Source on the basis of unsupported faith. Source has given us the intelligence to determine for ourselves what is true. All that is required is a little willingness. Faith in the beginning becomes knowing through experience.

Truth is here to be known and permission has been granted to know it. As I allow myself permission to ask for help and to receive it, the truth of its presence comes into my awareness. This is the alchemy of creation with Source. I transform the landscape of my world through awareness that I do not do so alone because I am entangled with Mind of God.

Today I give myself permission to ask for help and know it has arrived. I will not judge the form it comes in. I will not judge myself for asking. I use the gifts Source gives me to see and hear and know that all I ask for, I receive.

Lesson 328

I choose the second place to gain the first.

The personal mind fully believes it has a will separate from Will of Source. It perceives time, space, powerlessness, suffering, hierarchy, judgment, and death, as its reality. None of these exist in Mind of God, thus the personal mind's will is in conflict with Will of Source.

The personal mind wants what it wants, when it wants it. It resists what is right in front of it! If the will of the personal mind desires only its will and resists all else, then it must place its will first, and Will of Source second. Thus the personal mind believes in its own illusion of primacy. God is dead.

The personal mind considers autonomy to be its salvation. It perceives its autonomy as "freedom." Yet, what this "freedom" really brings is loss of meaning and confusion about purpose. The personal mind did not create Source, and yet it seeks power over It. It perceives a reality different from Reality – even at its own expense. What could be a greater sacrifice than death?

We choose the second place by realizing our mistake and

putting the personal mind to bed. It can teach us nothing. There is no Will but God's. There is no "one" and "two." There is only One. Source is Creator, not the personal mind. The personal mind aligns with nothing but itself.

It is only in separation that hierarchy appears real or even useful. There is only One, and It holds both similarity and uniqueness together without any conflict. Forgive the personal mind and its rules about reality. Forgive all past thoughts of separation. Choose the second place to see the Reality that you are One – that there is no second place at all.

This world is upside down. There is no punishment for knowing your own worth and there is nothing but freedom when you recognize mine. Seen right side up, all is One. When power is not over something or against anything then no defense is necessary. Sanity is restored. When I know this in my own mind, I set myself free, and the world with it.

Today is a day for liberation. It may seem paradoxical, but when you choose to follow, you become the leader. The personal mind would have you choose your place in its hierarchy and then imprison your mind within it. But when you use your will to align with Will of God, all Its power becomes yours.

Lesson 329

I have already chosen what You Will.

Yesterday's lesson was, "I choose the second place to gain the first." The lesson for today is its companion. It has similar qualities to a Zen Koan, an exercise in non-dual thinking. Here is an explanation.

You have free will. You may choose to follow the will of God, or that of the personal mind. Source does not limit Itself or Its creation. However, in Truth there is only One Will and your mind has already chosen It. This is because the will of the personal mind is not really a choice at all. There can be no real choice among illusions.

> *As you look upon yourself and judge what you do honestly, you may be tempted to wonder how you can be guiltless. Yet consider this: You are not guiltless in time but in eternity. You have "sinned" in the past but there is no past. Always has no direction. Time seems to go in one direction, but when you reach its end it will roll up like a long carpet spread along the past behind you, and will disappear.*
> – ACIM

Can you imagine everything in time being rolled up like a long carpet and disappearing in an instant? Time is an illusion. Choice among illusions is illusion. There is no "out there" out there. The choice for Love or fear seems to be made in every second, every hour, of every day. Yet decisions are required only in time. Beyond time, and there is an awareness beyond time, we have already decided for Love. Eternity is forever. The choice for Love cannot be taken back. God has lit our minds and keeps them lit by Its Light because Its Light is what our minds are and always will be.

We cannot destroy our inheritance of Light, but we can turn our mind from awareness of It. The cost of sleeping unaware is time and space, and all that they entail. This universe will disappear from our mind. Its carpet of stars rolled out and right back up in an instant of thought; the time it took to hold and release one tiny mad idea about the possibility of being separate from Source. We walk now upon a field of dreams.

It is not our task to make Reality, but we can choose to remember it. Make this a day of remembering your Self. Hold to the light that is already there: endless peace, an untroubled mind, serene in its knowing it is One with Source.

Sit in contemplation today. Hold the knowing of your choice

in your heart's awareness. Breathe. You need not analyze or philosophize, but be still. Feel your way into each word of the lesson and allow it to inform you. Then come back to the breath. Bring the lesson back into awareness and allow whatever arises to come. Then go back to the breath. Be at peace. God's will is done.

Lesson 330

I will not hurt myself again today.

A woman with a long spiritual practice confided to me that there was one person she could not forgive. A practicing yogi, with much knowledge of spiritual things, she wanted to forgive but feelings of anger kept coming up. I suggested she might begin the process of forgiveness by forgiving herself for not being able to forgive.

Too often it is ourselves we don't forgive. We hurt ourselves over and over again. Unable to heal within, we are unable to extend true healing to others. Self-forgiveness doesn't let me off the hook, but it often begins the end of a vicious cycle.

How often have you felt guilty, ashamed, or stupid because you allowed someone to hurt you? Forgive yourself. Then focus on the other with a clear heart.

Forgiveness is an act that frees both the forgiver and the hostage. Accept forgiveness as your only function today. End the war of attack and counter-attack in your mind. Do not teach it that it is powerless, for Source holds out Its power to you in endless Love. Accept Its gift. Once accepted, extend it to your sister and your brother, for neither you nor they have ever "sinned" except in illusion.

Only you can deprive yourself of peace. This realization is the dawn of light. It can often feel painful to realize at first, and denial takes many forms. But you cannot blame your sister or your brother for any deprivation without blaming yourself. You cannot enter God's presence if you attack another. There is no hate in Heaven and there can be none in you to get there.

Make today the day you begin to fulfill your highest function – indeed your only function. Notice the slights, the grudges, and the angry thoughts. Just notice them, without any judgment. Ending the war against yourself requires knowing that forgiveness is unlimited and continuous. Extend compassion to yourself. Take it in and then share it from the fullness of your own Innocence.

Take time to sit in silent contemplation of this lesson. Take your seat and get comfortable. When you are ready, say in your mind, "Source, I am One with You. I cannot fail to know the Identity I share with You. I cannot be hurt, nor can I hurt another. If I think I can suffer, it is because I have forgotten my Self, which was created by You and abides within You now. I will not hurt myself again today." Then sit in silence. Allow what arises. Let thoughts and feelings parade in front of your awareness. See them and gently set them aside by going back to the breath. Start your forgiveness practice now.

Focus Question 12: *What is the Personal Self?*

Lesson 331

Today begins a new set of lessons under the rubric, *"What is the personal self?"*

The personal self is called the "ego" in traditional psychotherapy. A "balanced" ego is considered a necessary component of a healthy psyche by most psychotherapists. But ACIM takes a totally different view. ACIM teaches that the ego is merely the creation of a mind that has obscured its own Oneness. The ego is:

A wrong-minded attempt to perceive yourself as you wish to be, rather than as what you are. The ego is a product of separation and is capable only of asking questions, but not of perceiving meaningful answers. A separated, or divided mind must be confused because only One-mindedness can be without confusion.

The personal mind, or ego, cannot be truly healthy. It was created to stand "beyond the Everywhere, apart from the All." It perceives itself limited amidst the Limitless. It is the "will" that sees the Will of God as a foreign thing, capable of being resisted, challenged and overcome. The egoic mind recognizes only itself and lives in a terrible autonomy in which death is the final reprieve. The personal mind is insane.

The personal mind has built a castle of sand and moved in. It lives now in fear of the very paper dragons it has made. You are not your personal mind. However, you cannot fight illusion by making it real to you, so do not hate and do not fear your personal mind. You are fully capable of using your higher mind, your heart center, to forgive its perceptions and render it without effect. This is why forgiveness is the key to happiness. This is why forgiveness is your function here. Forgiveness is the only sane response to the insanity of the personal self.

It is sobering to hear that we must release the personal mind's thoughts, actions, dreams, aspirations, powers, and plans for its own salvation. Yet the price we have paid for our faith in its perception of separation is a history of suffering so immense it is almost beyond imagining. Faith in the personal mind, the ego, offers only daily crucifixion in exchange for a temporary fix of diluted pleasure. See it, call it out, and replace its thought system with one of forgiveness. This is how light is brought to darkness.

Here is how to practice the next ten lessons. Each morning read and contemplate the core question and its answer. Then read the particular lesson for the day. At some point in the day devote at least fifteen minutes to quiet meditation. Sit and place awareness on the breath. Breathe in peace and exhale any tension in the body. Take as long as you want to do this. Then repeat the lesson for the day in your mind, invite the Holy Spirit's assistance, and let everything go. Allow the breath to anchor your mind. Watch thoughts and feelings as they arise. Trust. Expect nothing and allow everything. Play. Be courageous. Explore total nonresistance. Forgive and know your Innocence.

Be mindful throughout the day. Practice forgiveness. Allow direct experience through conscious awareness. On the hour, remember the lesson. Use it to anchor your day.

Reality lies beyond the limits of the ego's ability to perceive alone. This is the lesson for today:

There is no conflict, for my will is Yours.

Today's lesson is a call out for the personal mind. The conflict between it and will of Source must be resolved. It cannot be evaded or set aside. The end of conflict is the recognition that the personal mind wishes to be "first" and therefore triumph over Reality. We choose the second place by realizing this can never happen and it is a mistake to think so. Then we realize there is only Unity, so there cannot be a one or a two. There is only One.

Conflict arises from the limited perception of the personal mind. The source of conflict must be seen exactly as you think it is, where you think it is, and in the form you think it is real, and with the purpose you've given to it. Only then can you bring it to the Light of Truth and undo it. Your forgiveness is the Light. It allows you to see the threads of original conflict and unwind them.

Practice self-awareness today. Notice when the personal mind is directing you. It will make itself known through feelings of resistance, irritation, judgment, denial, depression, conflict, and fear. Notice it. Forgive it. Then move into the next moment. Trust Source even as you feel discomfort or fear. It is ironic, but the personal mind will use discomfort to keep you from ending the conflict it perceives! This is your only task for today. Do not allow the personal mind to be in conflict with Reality.

Do not hesitate to stop often today and ask for direction. Find the quiet space in your mind and ask Source what It would have you do. Then wait to feel Its response in your heart.

Lesson 332

Fear binds the world. Forgiveness sets it free.

The personal self makes illusions of fear and an unquestioned mind believes in every one of them.

Who is it that is afraid? Who lives alone and vulnerable in "my" little body, separate and isolated from all other life? Who needs preservation and defense from all the other "I's" who also believe they are separate and alone?

We believe in the personal mind. We perceive separation as a fact. We wallow in our specialness and want it even as it promotes our dreams of isolation. You are you. And I am I. It is impossible that we could share a mind. And if we could, I would never want you to see what it is in mine. Nor would I be able to stomach what might be in yours.

The grand illusion that it is desirable to be an "I" is the source of all fear. It is the "I" that needs control over "my" own life. It is the "I" who lives in "my" body that must be defended against weather, time, illness, and death. Every single thing we "work" for in this life is a defense against the loss of "I."

It can be confusing to pull aside the curtain of illusion. If I am not this "I" then what am I? I am rudderless without my sense of self! And yet, if I accept the notion that everything is an idea, a product of my own thoughts, then a small sense of freedom creeps in and sits down beside me. What if we really are all a single Mind at peace with its Self? What if I am you, and also me, in love with our togetherness?

The personal mind is a mere collection of thoughts that shift and change depending on time and circumstance. We are not our bodies and we are not our fears. We can and must forgive ourselves for the believing in this lie.

As long as I awaken every morning on this earth, in this body, forgiveness will be my function. What am I forgiving? Every single thing the personal self tells me, and I choose in the moment to believe is true. I live in the act of forgiving and I never tire of it.

The hot water heater breaks down and I forgive myself for believing its demise could ruin my day. My boss yells at me and I forgive him for trying to pass his fear to me. I forgive the "terrorist" who lives in terror himself and wants me to believe his own illusion even as he pulls the trigger in front of me. I am driven by memories and expectations, until I forgive both and return to this moment, this exact moment, in which the past does not determine the future and I am free of it.

There is no conflict in the present. It simply is and I create it as I wish now. I give up nothing but fear. The only sacrifice is illusion, but I have to face my fear in every moment to see it and know the freedom that lies just beyond.

The personal mind creates illusions. Truth undoes them. Fear holds your mind prisoner. Forgiveness sets it free. Illusions attack. Truth never attacks. It simply is as it is.

Take at least fifteen minutes in silent contemplation today. Imagine the end of fear. See yourself free of doubt, completely certain of your safety. Hold this feeling in your heart. Get to know it. Allow it to inform your moment. Wear a path to it.

Lesson 333

Forgiveness ends the dream of conflict here.

Wisdom is the ability to hold two or more conflicting ideas at once and know the truth of each, without attachment. Wisdom recognizes that conflict is born in fear, often a fear of scarcity. "If you win, I must lose. There is not enough for us both. You do not deserve, but I do. Your freedom will limit mine. I do not trust you but I want you to trust me so I can get what I want from you. I will regret it later if I give up now."

We all have these thoughts. They speak of duality and opposites. They speak of suffering and loss. They reflect the personal mind's perception of lack. It is these that must be brought to light day after day. Shame and guilt too often keep them hidden. In effect, fear keeps fear from coming to the light.

Face your conflict to escape from it. You cannot project your conflict, rationalize it, or call it by another name. You cannot deflect it, set it aside, or hide from it. You must see it exactly as it is. Paradoxically, once you see it, you are free of it. The will to see begins the act of forgiveness.

I cannot take my seat at the bargaining table without first claiming my own fears. Once claimed in truth and forgiven, I am free to see yours and hold both at once without sacrifice of any kind. In truth all conflict is a dream. We are only arguing with our self, projected as the "other." There is no "other!" There is nothing to win or lose and there is no sacrifice except the belief that sacrifice is real.

Today, experience the certainty of safety, freedom, and the truth of what you are. What you are in Truth cannot be in conflict with its self. If you desire to end the conflict in your life, this is where you must start.

As you sit in silent contemplation, allow thoughts to arise. Be mindful of the breath. Sense into the body. It will tell you where conflict is being held. Breathe into any places of stress and let them go on the out-breath.

You may wish to contemplate a particular conflict now, or one may arise on its own. Either way let the conflict show itself clearly. Look at it from your own point of view. Don't attach to it. When you are ready, breathe into it and let it go. Now pick it up again. Look at without fear or attachment from the "other's" point of view. When you are ready consider this: there is no such thing as one absolutely true point of view. Each one claims authenticity by the viewer. Both are "true" at the same time. And both are also illusion. Can you see this? Can you hold this greater Truth and forgive them both?

Lesson 334

You have entered the final month of lessons. Today's lesson asks us to make a claim of freedom, which is gift of forgiveness.

Today I claim the gifts forgiveness gives.

What are the gifts I receive through forgiving? I know them most often through the daily experience of allowing. The act of forgiving shares many qualities with the act of allowing. So often, when I cannot do the deeper work of forgiving, I step back and allow. Only later, when I see what simple allowing has done for me, I realize forgiveness was truly warranted and would have been the bigger gift.

There are three basic ways most of us respond to a situation. The first is to go into "Tupperware" mode in which I curl up and suck it in. This is not allowing. This is a form of resistance through denial and shutting down. It has many negative repercussions that often come up later in unconscious behavior or bodily illness.

The second response is to "kick ass." In this mode I resist by throwing my energy back at the other person. This is not forgiveness or allowing – it is a form of attack and I will almost certainly be attacked back. Often things escalate and the original issue is lost in the chaos of unconscious emotion.

The third way of responding is to notice, stay open, trust, and allow. I take the moment in. Only then do I respond, which moves me into the next moment. This is the way I claim the gift. The gift lies in the pure potential of the next unscripted moment. By allowing, by not reacting, I get to sit back and see what comes up next. Often the gift is revealed in the moments that follow and it always contains the element of peace.

A friend told me of her experience with this lesson. She had texted her former husband a kind note about an upcoming event with their children. He had not read her text, so he approached the event with defenses up. But my friend chose not to react. She stopped, thought, and realized he was uninformed. She suggested he read her earlier text. Her former husband went back and read the text. He arrived at the event and warmly told her how much he appreciated her parenting skills, her presence, and her patience with him. None of this would have happened had she responded with anger. She paused, allowed, noticed, and forgave, opening the door for a new opportunity to present itself.

Forgiveness is the grease in the machinery of life. It is the only response that doesn't shut things down and bring them to a grinding halt. Forgiveness keeps all the balls in the air. The gifts are unknown until they are received – sometimes at a later date. Forgiveness is not a linear thing – it defies time. I can forgive something in the past and it can change my experience of the present moment, thereby also altering the future.

Today, claim the gifts forgiveness brings. When you learn what they are, you will find yourself content with nothing less.

Lesson 335

I choose to perceive only Innocence.

Sin is a false perception of the personal mind. It is false because the world in which you have imagined yourself sinning is false. Illusion cannot make other illusions Truth. You were created from Innocence and will remain so forever.

The Innocence of our creation lies far beyond the memory of the personal mind. Yet it is there, within our very cells. We must come to the point where we can say, "I do not know what I do not know." And from there, a door opens and we can step through.

When I say without fear, "I do not know," I am really unburdening myself. When I unburden myself, I am allowing something new to arise. When I witness what arises and I allow it, I am reborn in that instant. And this is true not only for myself, but also for my sister and my brother. When I can say, "I do not know," about her or him, I am allowing some aspect of their being I may previously have denied. And when it does, I free them and I free myself of the burden of denial I have placed upon us both.

Forgiveness is a choice. It is a choice made more easily when I have experienced the state of "I do not know." I cannot see my sister as she is. How do I know her life, her dreams, her loss, and how she protects herself? Her experience is beyond my own unless I am willing to forgive – and then I see that everything she is, is also within me.

The Innocence of Source in me is made known through my experience. This is not known in the body or through thinking but through direct understanding. It takes thought only in that it requires attention. I get to choose in every instant and it so often begins with, "I do not know."

I do not know the lessons my brother and sister have for me, and I never will so long as I am content to sit in judgment. Judgment is fear in disguise. Ask what you judge and you will know this in your heart. Everything I judge, I fear, because I have an investment in a certain way of thinking, believing, and seeing. Judgment will never, ever allow me to know what I do not know. Judgment hides innocence behind a veil of fear.

Today, notice what you judge. What is the feeling attached

to your judgment? And when you choose to see your brother's Innocence, what then? How does that feel? Just notice and leave the door open. You may find it opens for you, and if you step through, you may catch a glimpse of something you have not known before. It may change everything. Can you allow yourself to know that you do not know? Your decision to perceive the Innocence in others can only restore Its Presence in you.

Lesson 336

Forgiveness allows me to perceive Oneness.

Forgiveness removes the veil of separation from perception. I will tell you over and over, forgiveness is alchemical. Like the philosopher's stone it changes base metal into gold.

Perception is a mirror of my internal state. To repeat physicist John Gribbin, "Nothing is real unless we look at it, and it ceases to be real as soon as we stop looking." In other words, what I see is what I have already created in my mind.

Have you ever considered that every single person on this planet is having his or her own experience? No one ever has the same day. Even if we share the same space, each aspect of our sharing is unique. Or so it seems.

Here's another way to think of it. We are in the same theater, watching the same movie. We've entered the theater along with our own histories and expectations. Not one of us experiences the same movie. But we are all in same theater at the same time, and we agree a movie is being shown on screen. Such is our group consciousness, also known as "reality."

In the theater we watch all sorts of mayhem but realize it is not true because we understand the actors are just images on a screen. This is the alchemy of forgiveness. Source reaches beyond the projection, past perception's highest reach. It sweeps away the distortions on the screen. We see behind it and know all is light and shadow only.

What can harm the Holy Thought of God created in Innocence? Nothing except a lesser thought which has no power at all. The thought you can be hurt is illusion. The thought you can die is illusion. Forgive your belief in the illusion. Rise out of your seat, open the door of your mind, and step into the day. The theater itself is illusion.

Forgiveness is the means by which perception ends and Knowledge is restored. Knowledge is restored after perception is first changed, and then gives way entirely to what remains forever past its highest reach.
– ACIM

Practice today with your perception. Look around at all you see: the different people, the moving cars, the trees swaying in the breeze... and know all of it as theater. A wild and wonderful theater it is, but nothing more than that. Forgive the theater and all the actors in the play.

Begin your contemplation with this: "In this silence may the Voice for God guide my mind so that I may perceive the Oneness around me. Innocence remains in my mind. The Love that created me abides in my heart. Let me be still and know it."

Lesson 337

My Innocence protects me from all harm.

Innocence was given us by Source and we cannot take it from ourselves except by denying the Truth. We have never "sinned" but in imagining we have, Source seems far, far away. We blame ourselves twice: first, for imagining the "original sin" of separation, and second, for believing it to be true.

Our True Identity is not ours to give away. We did not create it, nor did we create the One Who gave it to us. We are free to create the theater of this world. We are free to try on all sorts of costumes and believe they are who we are. We are even free to confuse the play with Reality. But we are not free to wipe away our Innocence or make real what is not.

Our Innocence protects us even from illusion. Born of Happiness, created out of Happiness, only Happiness is our True State. That is why we love it so. That is why we are drawn to it, and that is why we are out of sorts when we do not feel it. Learn this today: you need do nothing yourself but accept your Self, Innocent and Pure. Know your Self, the Holy Thought of God, loved forever and always. Source is not mistaken about What you are. It holds the Truth for you even as you wander, seemingly lost.

Sit in contemplation of this thought today. Wrap yourself in its perfect peace. Accept your Self in thought for that is where your Self was born and still resides. You are Presence Itself. You can never be harmed except in dreams. You are not your body and its vulnerabilities. You cannot be extinguished.

Lesson 338

I am affected only by my thoughts.

Nothing affects me except my own mind. My thoughts determine all I perceive down to the very last detail. Does this seem too radical? Too far-fetched? Impossible? The truth is, you need only this thought to save your entire mind, for in it you are released from all your fears.

We were created through Thought and we create through it as well. The only Thought we did not give ourselves is the original Thought with which Source created us. This Thought resides within each of us still. To know It requires us to remember we are loved by Love Itself. If we can believe this even for an instant, it creates an alignment with the Thought of Love that sustains our very being.

The beginning of the journey is the hardest part because it requires the undoing of layers of doubt and guilt. Courage is required to face frightening thoughts long buried. But when we rise, new vistas will appear that pull us forward even as we seem to march across heavy terrain. Change your thoughts; change your mind. Change your perception and change your reality.

The decision to know "I am affected only by my thoughts" has consequences. It marks the end of your small self and its plans built on fear. It moves you into spiritual maturity because it requires responsibility on a level you have not considered necessary or even possible before. Remember this along the way: all thoughts except Love are illusions of the small self. There is but One Thought that promises to lead Home, and that is the memory of your Innocence given by Source.

Know your Self Love today. Stop often and remember What you are. What is in your mind now, and now, and now, and now? If it is not a thought of loving kindness, allowing, or even simply calm abiding, then forgive it, and move on. Begin to be aware and notice what happens when you are.

Sit in silence today. Stay with the breath and sense into the body. The body is a barometer of your mind. Breathe into any tense places and let them go on the out-breath. Don't rush; do this as long as you need to. Thoughts will arise. Receive them with gratitude, without holding onto them. Bring everything into the light and let it go. If at some point all thoughts fade into pure silence, know you have discovered the territory of pure being. This is spontaneous. Allow it. It too will pass and return again on its own.

Lesson 339

I will receive whatever I request.

If wishes were horses, beggars would ride.
If turnips were watches,
I'd wear one by my side.
If "ifs" and "ands" were pots and pans,
There'd be no work for tinkers' hands.

The first time I heard this 17th century English nursery rhyme I knew it wasn't true. I just didn't know why. Today's lesson explains.

What we wish for is often merely resistance to what is. I want a million dollars in the bank because I don't have it. I want my body to be healthy because it's not. I want so and so to be nicer to me, but I want it without introspection on my part. In these instances, what I'm really paying attention to is my lack, and the signals my heart sends out are vibrations of scarcity and fear. I want what I already believe I do not have. Let me repeat: I want what I already perceive I do not have.

I was once in a course that supposedly taught us how to "manifest" our desires. We were instructed to walk for an hour in an enclosed paddock, repeating our desire like a mantra. One hundred students gathered in the early hours of the morning and began to pace back and forth.

I considered my desire carefully. What did I really, really want? Around me, people were choosing all kinds of different things – vast sums of money, power, houses, fame, healing. After some consideration I decided upon the idea of knowledge, specifically the knowledge that I have always been blessed. Up and down I walked repeating, "I have always been blessed. I have ALWAYS been blessed."

It wasn't that I didn't want a million bucks. But something told me if I wanted peace and safety, knowing I was always blessed offered the best foundation. I could gain and lose a million dollars but nothing could steal away the blessing. It was immutable and applied to every situation. It felt like a fortress in a storm.

The *Song of Prayer* in ACIM describes the ultimate prayer not as an entreaty, but as acceptance.

> *Prayer is a way offered by the Holy Spirit to reach God. It is not merely a question or an entreaty. It cannot succeed until you realize that it asks for nothing. How else could it serve its purpose? It is impossible to pray for idols and hope to reach God. True prayer must avoid the pitfall of asking to entreat. Ask, rather, to receive what is already given; to accept what is already there.*

It's a paradox but the first step in getting what you want is to be content with what you currently have. You have it now because you wanted it. If that desire has changed, it can only be manifested from a place of strength and willingness. Wishes do not manifest from the energy of resistance or lack.

We are all creating, all the time, and at both an individual and group level of thought. Much of what we create arises from a thought system of limitation and scarcity that has been imbedded for many, many lifetimes. Limitation does not resonate with the energies of true creation. Make no mistake: this world has been our desire. We wished to experience separation from Source. It is time to wish for something else but only from a place that knows separation has never occurred at all. You are already Whole. Abundance is already yours.

Today, wish not for small things of this world, but to awaken to the truth about your Self. It is not an idle wish to know one's Self. Wish for this. Wish to know your whole being in the Light of what you are. Then work on the bank account.

Lesson 340

I can be free of suffering today.

This is a world in turmoil. The weather is changing. War is everywhere. Species are dying. The planet is dying. Despots are in power and political leadership is failing. Never has this world seen so many challenges at so many levels. And every bit of it is self-imposed.

A mind in turmoil creates a world in turmoil. But a healed mind also creates healing. And while images of war, decay, and death seem to overpower, there is also something new taking place. Never before has the old power structure of fear been so exposed. And the transparency is everywhere because our connectedness is also unparalleled.

We are in the midst of enormous change and the old must go before the new can arise. The old dominates through fear. The old gains its power by separating and dividing. The old values service to self above service to others and mocks those who disagree, calling them weak and stupid. The old does not want you to understand this lesson.

When I suffer it is because I have failed to recognize my Identity. I have placed my value in external things. I have given my will to sources outside myself and called their judgment real. But when I realize my mistake and stand certain of myself as Holy, as One with Source and all of humanity, I will cease to judge, nor will I accept judgment. I will be free of suffering and my freedom will free others.

Do not be dismayed, but stand certain of yourself. Let your light shine, for there is nothing you can ever do that can separate you from Source. Nothing can take your Oneness, your beauty, the fullness of what you are. End your imagining of guilt and fear, and then extend your light to one next to you. This is the resurrection. This is what you came here for – to save the world, first by saving yourself and then your brother and sister.

Know yourself capable today. Even in the face of what appears insurmountable. It is all a dream. It is time for a new dream; a dream that is closer to Reality. For that is how we reach

Reality – by dreaming new and better dreams until we awaken and dream no more.

Sit today in silence. Begin with gratitude for the freedom Source has given your mind to perceive the truth about your Self and this world. Use your freedom as it was given. Know yourself capable, sovereign, senior, gracious, and gifted. Be certain of your own light. There is no room for anything else in you but light. Open your heart, breathe it in, and on the exhale share it with the world.

Focus Question 13: *What is a Miracle?*

Lesson 341

As we begin our last month of lessons for the year, we turn to the topic of miracles. The foundation question for the next ten lessons is, "What is a miracle?"

ACIM defines a miracle as a correction of perception. Remember, the personal mind, the ego, perceives only through the veil of separation. But the mind at one with its Source connects with Truth through knowing. Miracles are an instantaneous expression of knowing. You have experienced many miracles but your personal mind may not have recognized them or may have chosen not to remember.

Miracles come in a thousand different forms, yet each one has a similar attribute. A miracle momentarily lifts the veil of egoic perception. A miracle is a correction of perception. You know a miracle has occurred when you look upon fear, guilt, ugliness, and death, and recognize what you see is not the whole truth.

A miracle allows the personal mind to receive what it cannot understand alone. Miracles contain the gift of Grace. They illustrate the Law of Love. A miracle turns perception from upside down to right side up. Miracles end the distortions created by the personal mind so that you see forgiveness is totally justified and the only sane response to anything.

Miracles are like water. They purify the sight. Miracles extend forever and are never lost. They touch people you may never meet and produce undreamed-of changes in situations of which you are not even aware. Forgiveness is the home of miracles. Miracles happen all the time. If you will allow it, you will experience one today.

Here is how to practice the next ten lessons. Each morning read and contemplate the core question and its answer. Then read the particular lesson for the day. At some point in the day devote at least fifteen minutes to quiet meditation. Sit and place awareness on the breath. Breathe in peace and exhale any tension in the body. Take as long as you want to do this. Then repeat the lesson for the day in your mind, invite the Holy Spirit's assistance, and let everything go. Allow the breath to anchor your mind. Watch thoughts and feelings as they arise. Trust. Expect nothing and allow everything. Play. Be courageous. Explore total nonresistance. Forgive and know your Innocence.

Be mindful throughout the day. Practice forgiveness. Allow direct experience through conscious awareness. On the hour, remember the lesson. Use it to anchor your day.

Today's lesson realized can be a miracle for you. This lesson contains healing beyond any that medicine can offer.

I can attack only my own Innocence, and it is only that which keeps me safe.

Created out of Innocence, you are incapable of sin. You can only attack your sinlessness. And even that is an illusion. You cannot be separate from the Light. You can only hide It from yourself. You remain Innocence Itself even as you play in the illusion of dirt.

You cannot attack your brother or your sister, for they are sinless too. You can only imagine you harm them, even when they share the dream of attack with you. And when you attack them, you are always also attacking yourself for they are you.

In truth, you are never not safe. You are the Word of God made manifest. The Word is and will always be. How can the Thought of God be diseased, shot with a gun, told she is no good, denied what is rightfully his, or made less than? Only in a dream can this be so and the miracle comes in knowing this.

At first, you may take the miracle on faith. But through your faith, you will call to yourself experiences that justify it. The miracle is the experience and your conscious recognition of its presence. The miracle is your call, your faith, your awareness, and your experience. Often they all happen at the same time.

The false perceptions of the personal mind can and will be released through the grace of miracles. Their surety comes through experience. Miracles end the conflict of trying to imagine that we are what we are not – separate, alone, guilty, and vulnerable. The miracle pulls the curtain back and shows the stage for what it is – one big fantasy – not to be valued but to be enjoyed with laughter and a chuckle, nothing more.

Today, end the attack on your own Innocence. Be mindful of all self-denigration in any form. And do remember, denigration of the other is denigration of the self.

Sit in silence today. Take this lesson in. Begin with the idea that you can attack only your own Innocence and it is this Innocence Itself that keeps you safe. You cannot undo your Innocence. It contains the Light of God in you.

Lesson 342

I let forgiveness rest upon all things,
For thus forgiveness will be given me.

Do these words make you feel weaker or stronger? Do they apply in today's world or have we entered a time now where forgiveness needs to be reevaluated? There are many who would agree we should set forgiveness aside and perhaps bring it out later when circumstances are more suitable.

We can let anger hijack peace but it is peace we want. Even those who deal in death really want peace but they would steal peace to make it, and that is gross confusion. It is a form of insanity and we are poised at its edge if we let fear win.

The opposite of illusion is Truth but to the personal mind Truth is meaningless and weak. So it responds to the illusion of threat with threats of its own and this is where we seem to be. Anger responds in anger with words of "strength." "We will carpet bomb them into oblivion," sound like words of strength. "I don't know if sand can glow in the dark, but we are going to find out," makes the threat sound reasonable and justified.

Such words are meant to be a rallying cry for strength. There is not one shred of forgiveness in them. In fact, to speak words of forgiveness now, in some circles, would be an invitation to be attacked. And so insanity seems to win the day.

You do not have to accept attack, but if you respond with hatred it will only add to the energy of fear. It is possible to forgive and exhibit strength at the same time. Remember there are but two emotions: love and fear. One takes many forms but its effect is always loss. The other is changeless but continuously exchanged. It extends because it increases as it is given. This is how love always wins.

All attack is a call for love. The end of illusion is seeing this truth. When have you ever attacked another and not really wanted love? When have you struck out when what you wanted was acceptance? See this in yourself, then understand it in your brother who is yourself. Forgive your own attacks, then step it up and forgive your sister too.

Live these words today: "I let forgiveness rest upon the world and I am stronger for it. What I forgive in you is forgiven in myself for we are One and invulnerable together. What is a miracle but the instant this truth is recognized? Let us make miracles together today."

Spend your silent meditation with the words of today's lesson. "I let forgiveness rest upon all things. For thus will forgiveness be given me." Breathe the words in as you say them slowly in your mind. If your mind wanders, come back to the lesson and the breath. Savor this meditation.

Lesson 343

I am not asked to make a sacrifice
To find the mercy and the peace of God.

This is another lesson about guilt and its impediment to growth. How often do you feel you must sacrifice peace to gain it? We make war to "end" war. If we want to "get ahead" we must forgo the pleasure of leisure time. Learning is "hard work" and often occurs in the school of "hard knocks." Sacrifice to gain is ingrained in the thought system of the personal mind. But Source requires nothing of you except that you allow. Source only gives and does not take away. Forgiveness cannot result in any loss. It can only be a gain of peace and mercy.

There is no judgment for not forgiving. We can take all the time we want with it. But at some point the effects of holding grievances become obvious because our thoughts are always projected back to us. We are our own teachers in this way. If I teach peace, I feel it. If I teach judgment, I will feel that too. If I hold hate, it will be reflected back to me. Emotions and thoughts are energy forms, and like attracts like.

The ego would have you suffer rather than learn. It would have you strive for the illusion of victory, a victory that never lasts if it ever comes at all. The ego would have you believe that forgiveness requires sacrifice of yourself; that it makes you weak and liable to be hurt again.

Accept the truth that there are no limits of any kind to the mercy and peace of God. Think of every kindness you would give yourself or another, and it will be the truth of what you are. Imagine the greatest mercy you could bestow, and you will be in alignment with Source. How do you know this is truth? It feels good and right. If it is certain for Source, it is certain for you.

Today, be aware of your hesitancy to forgive. Simply pay attention to unforgiving feelings. Be aware of their impact on the body. Notice how it feels in the heart to create and sustain a grievance, even a small one. Then make the choice to let it go. Or not. The choice is up to you. But do be aware that if you choose not to forgive now, you will be asked again and again. Why? Because your freedom is assured and you cannot carry the energy of judgment Home because it is not in alignment with Source.

Sit in silence with the words of this lesson. Breathe in and settle into the body. Notice any areas of tension and breathe them out. Then allow your mind to notice the grievances it holds. How old are they? Are there any you are ready to let go? Ask for guidance and assistance if you need it. You might imagine laying each one at the altar of the Holy Spirit. Place it there and lift the burden from yourself. The Holy Spirit will transmute it into something far beyond what you can imagine.

Lesson 344

Today I learn the Law of Love; that what I give my brother/sister is my gift to me.

Oh, what a lesson this is! If you learn this lesson you will add immeasurably to your own joy.

There are laws that govern spiritual reality – a reality that is more "significant" than the one we take for granted here. Remember, what exists in two dimensions (a line and a point) is contained within three (a line, a point, and height and width).

What exists in four dimensions contains the three below it, and what exists in five contains the four below that, and so on. As you go up the dimensional scale, the higher dimension encompasses all those below it, like a series of nesting dolls.

But what is the reality of these higher dimensions, and what are the laws by which they function? Certainly the laws must be different than ours and yet they must also contain ours since each higher dimension contains the ones below it.

Today's lesson deals with a fundamental spiritual law that applies here and in the dimensions above it. Its language is simple, direct, and there is no getting around it. The Law of Love states I must always receive the gifts I give away. Give away love and it must come back to you. Its specific form might change or it might arrive from a source different from the one you originally gave it to. But it must return to you, and when it does, it is multiplied.

The one who can share love through forgiveness receives everything she has given and more. Love multiplies in the giving because as it is received, it is reflected back to the giver. The gift of love I give my brother is my gift to me. This is why fear will never triumph over love. Fear limits; love extends. Isn't this a grand law!

We live in physical reality that is linear and limited. We do not often "see" the effects of our actions because time seems to separate one action from another. Thus, I can steal from you and believe myself free of the consequences. But above this dimension, time is not linear. All of now is accessible now. Cause and effect are immediate above this dimension.

There are many who have crossed the boundary beyond our physical world and they return with the same message: Love is the ground force of the universe. Know this today. Practice, play, experiment today with this Law! Give love and see what comes back. But give without any expectation of return, for that is the caveat: Love is given freely or it is not Love. Extend your love as Source does – because it is your True Nature to do so. Be a blessing for someone.

Take time for silence today. Settle in and place awareness on the breath. Repeat the lesson in your mind. Then wait in silence for the Voice for God, the Holy Spirit, to arise in your thoughts. Whatever comes through is perfect. Simply watch. You may wish to specifically contemplate times when you have given love freely and seen it returned to you. Remember the feeling. Breathe into it. Feel good about yourself.

A Course in Miracles: Lesson 345

> *I offer only miracles today,*
> *For I would have them be returned to me.*

Have you ever awoken with the feeling that the day would unfold effortlessly? It is as if the happy dream carries forward, even as sleep ends. You feel no resistance. You experience everything in flow and nothing can steal your peace. Such mornings are gifts.

I have found I can carry these mornings right through the day. In fact, I can even create such mornings myself if I take my waking slowly and decide that whatever happens I will meet it with patience and peace. The coffee maker might not be working. Last night's dishes might still be in the sink. The dog might have made a mess. I refuse to take any of it personally. Everything slows down, it all works out, and I see very clearly the "little" miracles that are happening all around me.

Today is a good day to slow down and receive the gift of the moment. Source is constantly sending Its miracles. They will always take a form you can recognize if you but allow yourself to see. Receive in peace and then extend the miracle forward to whomever or whatever comes along. What might the miracle be? A thought of peace. A gesture of kindness. Patience with one who needs it. Gentleness and loving kindness with the car that won't start, the toilet that has backed up, the dog that threw up last night's dinner on the new carpet. It really doesn't matter what the miracle is but it will always contain peace.

It is a privilege of high order to be able to think and then act on what you know.
– bell hooks

May you know yourself on your journey today. May you feel your full power as a Holy Thought of God. Stand firm in your authority. Be good to yourself. Allow nothing to intrude upon your peace. Know yourself worthy of all miracles that come your way, and fully capable of offering them in return to all who need them. Be yourself a blessing to all you encounter.

Sit in silence for at least fifteen minutes today. Begin with the words of the lesson and then spend a few moments in contemplation of the miracles that have been offered to you. They might be "big" or "small." There is no order to miracles. Each one is a maximum expression of the Love that is Source. Give yourself the gift of basking in whatever miracle has been received, and remembering the feeling of extending a miracle to another.

Lesson 346

Today the Peace of God envelops me, and I forget all things except Its Love.

If you awoke in peace, be glad and take these words in fully. But if your day began in turmoil, sickness, or fear, you may well find yourself in resistance to these words. If so, stop now and offer forgiveness to yourself. Forgive your pain. Forgive your lack of peace. Forgive your resistance. Breathe and rest a moment in stillness.

This is a lesson in loving kindness to the self. Peace is the natural state of a mind in alignment with All That Is. It doesn't believe the critical inner voice. A mind in alignment with its Source observes in stillness. It speaks only when necessary and never with hostility to itself or other minds.

What you seek today is transcendence of this world, its time, its laws, and its upside-down values. Observe, but do not subscribe to the insanity that chose to make this world separate from Source. Let miracles correct your perception this day and live with the perfume of peace. Gift yourself with many, many moments of stillness. Quiet your mind. Look around with soft eyes and a soft heart. Forgive all things that are hard, loud, thoughtlessly rushing from one thing to the next. Step back and let Source lead in peace.

Take time for an extended period of silence. Sit and get comfortable. Place awareness on the breath and settle into the body. Notice any places of stress and breathe into them, letting the tension go on the out-breath. When you are ready, repeat the lesson in your mind. Spend the remainder of your contemplation simply watching the breath. Surrender. Offer your mind to Source. Receive whatever comes. Watch the thoughts that arise and let them go. Be the peace you seek. Be a blessing to yourself.

Lesson 347

Anger must come from judgment. Judgment is
The weapon I would use against myself
To keep the miracle away from me.

Your first judgment is always against the truth of your own invulnerability. This is why any reactivity indicates the need for self-forgiveness. Each time you react in anger to another it is a signal that something has been presented in your awareness that you have not forgiven in yourself. You will continue to project onto others what remains unhealed within yourself until you see that this is true.

You are the source of your own disturbance. Consider a circumstance in which you have been angry. Is it really the other person who has stolen your peace? "Well, I am angry because they are angry," you might say. In effect, you have chosen to match their anger. Do not convince yourself that it was not your choice.

Today, drop your weapons. Step back inside the circle of Oneness. Give all judgment to the One whose Thoughts see the Great Pattern of Existence. Count it as a blessing when you recognize your disturbances. You have been given a miracle of right-mindedness. Take the opportunity to see your belief that attack or counter-attack can solve your problem. Ask yourself, "What is this disturbance in them masking? What are they really crying out for?" Then take a moment of silence. Ask the Holy Spirit to help inform your mind. Allow the miracle of compassion.

When I am able to see that every single instant of anger, fear, or irritation in another's behavior always stems from their immaturity, or my own, rather than their unkindness, or mine, it becomes much harder not to learn the lesson of forgiveness.
– TUT

There is nothing real that needs the protection of your judgment. There is nothing your criticism can heal. There is nothing your argument with Reality can change for the better. Seeing this is your miracle.

As you sit in silence today, begin with those who need your forgiveness. Your freedom from guilt depends upon theirs and only you have the power to give it. Begin your contemplation with these words, then sit in silent contemplation of them: *"I give you the Holy Spirit as part of myself. I know that you will be released, unless I want to use you to imprison myself. In the name of my freedom, I choose your release because I recognize we will be released together."*

Now spend a few moments with someone you have judged, or whom you believe has unfairly judged you. Ask yourself, "What is it in them that is a mirror for me? What fear might they be masking? Can I release them and feel the release extend to my own heart?" If you feel it, you will know. This is how you discover the power of your choice for healing. This is how you change your creation.

Lesson 348

I have no cause for anger or for fear,
For You surround me. And in every need
That I perceive, Your grace suffices me.

This lesson requires a certain spiritual maturity. It asks initially for faith. Through experience it evolves into certainty. Faith is required in the beginning because the personal mind will most certainly reject the premise that it can receive grace at all.

Young souls believe the thoughts of the personal mind are always true. Older souls have learned to question their thoughts. And really old souls know thoughts are the building blocks of this entire world, and none of them that are not sourced from Love can suffice.

You have no cause for anger or for fear because you not your body. You exist beyond time. Your true nature is Grace Itself. Yet so long as you perceive yourself to be a vulnerable body only (and we all do until we don't) fear will be present, and grace will be forfeited for mere survival. When you choose mere survival this world becomes your master. You will bow to it when it should be in awe of you.

This lesson asks you to be still and feel your way into the field of grace that surrounds your every cell, every molecule, and every atom. You may experience this field as an inner vibration. It may present itself as heavy or dull, or as a tingling feeling – almost like an inner champagne bath. It may be experienced as a sort of electricity. Do not analyze or judge your experience. Just be aware of it and know there is a connection between your inner field and the one that surrounds it.

As you sit in contemplation, visualize your inner field expanding outward on the out-breath. Let it form a bubble of perfect protection that surrounds you. What is in the bubble? Source energy. The power of grace. Breathe it in and let it out. Feel its vibration. It is alive with life! Yet it is also a womb of dark, soft, rich, velvet peace.

The grace of God surrounds you always. It is what created you. It is your desire because it is the only thing that suffices. It suffices because it is Real, and somewhere in your being, you know this to be True.

Lesson 349

Today I let the perception of my Christ Mind look upon all things for me. I will not judge, but extend to each one a miracle of Love instead.

How is this lesson to be experienced? It's not so hard, but it does require you to allow yourself to give everything the freedom to be itself without judging it. "Thus do I obey the Law of Love, and give what I would have to make my own." Give freedom to receive it.

I give freedom to have my own. I give light to know light. I am free to skip down the street if that is what's called for. I am free to decide nothing that happens can harm me today. I am free to ignore my neighbor's angry mood or the fact that all hell seems to be breaking loose in the world. It's not that I don't care, but I am seeing it all through eyes that know none of it makes any difference because it's just a passion play. Does that sound naïve or unrealistic?

Christ's vision is not some magical thing that is unavailable except in my imagination. Seeing is a decision based on knowing what I am: not this body, not this guilt, not of this world, but free and fully connected with you. What are you? What more important question is there?

I love the fact that you are me. I love that your experience is also mine. How intelligent I will become when I can join my mind with yours! How free I am when I know freedom is my birthright. Words cannot describe it and nothing in this world can touch it. I simply know that I am safe and free together with you.

Christ's vision looks upon a world playing with form and sees the light within each mind. Everything is light, swirling, merging, sparkling, and spinning together in one big dance. No light ever goes out; it simply changes color or shape. Every imagined trial and circumstance has been designed to light us up. We are all together, moving higher and higher on this journey we have created for ourselves. We are all light emerging. Do you see it? Can you feel it? Extend the inner sight of your diamond mind. It is a perfect fragment of the Great Diamond Mind.

Lesson 350

Miracles mirror the eternal Love of Source.
To offer them is to remember Source,
And through my memory of Source, to save the world.

Now we are called to remember the great power in the miracle of forgiveness. Forgiveness is remembering that no harm can be done to you for you are the Holy Word of God.

We are eternal creators and nothing happens without our consent. You have created your life and your circumstances down to every last detail because you are Word of God in form. Nothing that happens to you has not been created by you and does not have your approval, because you are Word of God in form. You are asked to sacrifice nothing in your learning that you are Word of God in form. And everything you forgive is returned to you and that is how you remember you are whole and free and you are truly Word of God in form.

> *What we forgive becomes a part of us, as we perceive ourselves. The Son of God incorporates all things within himself as You created him. Your memory depends on his forgiveness. What he is, is unaffected by his thoughts. But what he looks upon is their direct result. Therefore I turn to You, my Source. Only Your memory will set me free and only my forgiveness teaches me to let Your memory return to me and give it to the world in thankfulness.*
> *– ACIM*

I awaken to my Holiness when I extend the power of forgiveness. When I extend it, I receive it also and thus double the miracle. Know your power today. There is nothing that has happened without your consent. Forgiveness is an art. It is a skill. It is your resource and it will pay you dividends beyond anything this world can offer. It will never cease paying you forever and forever, even beyond this dimension.

As you sit in contemplation today, find the memory of someone who needs your forgiveness, for you benefit from it as much as they. Say to yourself, "I do not judge you. I extend forgiveness to myself for what I have created. I embrace you and I free you to be yourself for there is nothing in your freedom that can deny me mine. I bless you as myself and wish you only well."

Focus Question 14: *What am I?*

Lesson 351

You are almost to the end of the curriculum. The remaining lessons for the year center around the vital question: "What am I?" What question could be more important to you? How many of us spend our entire lives trying to define who and what we are?

You may define yourself by your profession, your status in life, by your bank account, or by the friends you have. Perhaps your accomplishments or level of education define you. Perhaps it is your family relationships or your children who give your identity. Yet none of these point to what you truly are. Are not all of these temporary? And are not all of these external projections only? What things in this illusion of a world could possibly tell you what you are?

What you are is one thing and it is the foundation from which all other temporary identities arise. You have only the identity your Creator gave you. It is all you need for it suffices in every situation and under every condition. No other identity is worthy of you.

"I am God's Holy Creation, complete and healed and whole, shining in the reflection of Love. In me is Creation sanctified and guaranteed eternal life. In me is Love perfected, fear impossible, and joy established without opposite. I am the Holy Home of God Itself. I am the Heaven where Love resides. I am Innocence Itself, for in my purity abides the Innocence of Source."

If this is the only thing you learn in your year of lessons, it would be healing enough. What Christ is, you are also. The Truth of What You Are cannot be described in words but you can realize your purpose here in this world when you exemplify the power of forgiveness. With the Christ in you, you are your own savior. You are God's Holy Messenger, extending peace to every mind through the peace you are.

When I know what I am it changes everything. When I know what I am I see the whole world differently. When I know what I am I accept responsibility for myself. I know what I am and I see who you are.

Here is how to practice the next ten lessons. Each morning read and contemplate the core question and its answer. Then read the particular lesson for the day. At some point in the day devote at least fifteen minutes to quiet meditation. Sit and place awareness on the breath. Breathe in peace and exhale any tension in the body. Take as long as you want to do this. Then repeat the lesson for the day in your mind, invite the Holy Spirit's assistance, and let everything go. Allow the breath to anchor your mind. Watch thoughts and feelings as they arise. Trust. Expect nothing and allow everything. Play. Be courageous. Explore total nonresistance. Forgive and know your Innocence.

Be mindful throughout the day. Practice forgiveness. Allow direct experience through conscious awareness. On the hour, remember the lesson. Use it to anchor your day.

Today's lesson is a statement of your own power:

My sinless sister/brother is my guide to peace.
My sinful sister/brother is my guide to pain.
And which I choose to see, I will behold.

We remain Love in whatever form our expression may take. So long as I know you are worthy of Love, I confirm that I am also worthy. How I am willing to see my sister and my brother is a direct reflection of how I am willing to see myself.

How I treat you reflects the way I wish to be treated. This does not mean I have to sing your praises if you've just stolen my car. It does mean I have to honor your Source Innocence. I have to know what you are, even if you have forgotten, and even if your actions speak otherwise, and this makes all the difference. I must hold the knowledge of your worth no matter what your outer expression may be.

We are on a new road that can only be travelled together with recognition of our joint worth. Our awareness is changing and we are claiming new possibilities. What has not been valued is being questioned and new values are arising. We are lifting the veil and we are asking, "What are we? Why are we here? How should we live?"

When I know who I am I also know my service lies in knowing who you are. We both serve together by remembering for each other. Practice today's lesson through the remembrance of your Innocence. The Innocence you perceive is your guide along the road to peace, just as the guilt you perceive is the guide along the road to pain. What you choose to perceive, you will experience.

As you sit in silence today, begin with this idea: "My mind is part of Source's Mind so I can use my mind to perceive as Source does. If I perceive myself alone and friendless in a fearful world, that is what I will experience. But this perception is a choice that I make, so I can relinquish it and see the Innocence of all things, as Source does. Let me know my Innocence and my everlasting Purity. May the Holy Spirit, which is in my mind, inform me now."

Lesson 352

Every thought I have is like a pebble dropped into a still, clear pond of consciousness. If I hold to thoughts of judgment, I drop that pebble into the pond and certain ripples are formed. If I hold to thoughts of allowing, flowing, ease, and non-judgment and I drop that pebble in, very different ripples unfold.

Judgment and Love are opposites. From one
Comes all the sorrows of the world. But from
The other comes the Peace of God.

In every moment you are standing in your own pond of

consciousness. It reflects your every thought. Today, can you stand on the shore and say, "I will use my will to remain aware of the ripples my thoughts create? I am willing to begin now to drop a different pebble in."

Your pond of consciousness is an infinite pool of creative awareness. It vibrates with your thoughts and feelings. It is how you create. When you judge a thing unworthy of yourself, it will be unworthy of you. But when you cease resisting it, when you allow it to be, you step into the clear pond and something else unfolds around you.

Today, use the power of your awareness to choose. Your choice is a creation that affects the quality of vibrations all around you. Do you choose judgment or Love? Your choice begins a series of ripples that moves out from the center of your consciousness, intersects with the ripples around you, and then returns to your field. What returns to you will always reflect what you've extended outward. This is how you create. Know this and you will master creation itself.

Spend time in silence today. Begin your contemplation with the thought, "Judgment is the opposite of Love. One brings only sorrow. The other brings the Peace of God. I am redeemed when I redeem." Then look within and notice, without any judgment whatsoever, the thoughts of judgment you have been holding. Feel the vibration of judgment. Sense its ripples in the body. Breathe. Then bring thoughts of peace to mind and feel their vibrational quality. Notice the change. Which is preferable? Which do you wish to send out to the world?

You get to choose, and you are always in choice. You are a Holy Child of God. You are a Perfect Fragment of Diamond Mind. Play with your choices. Have your experience. Then you will be free to say, "I like this creation." Or, "I do not like that one anymore. Good to know. I'll get rid of that thought. What would I like to replace it with?" Then choose and watch what comes back.

Lesson 353

Today's lesson is an exercise in using the physical to go beyond it. The language is a bit obscure but look for the meaning behind the words:

> *My eyes, my tongue, my hands, my feet today*
> *Have but one purpose; to be given Christ*
> *To use to bless the world with miracles.*

We add to Source through our experience. And whether we know it or not, our experience is always in movement toward happiness. Yet, in this upside-down-mirror-of-a-world, our idea of happiness seems to be in conflict, because the personal mind defines happiness as getting solely what it wants.

Source wishes us to be happy as It is, and this is also your will. Can you imagine your unhappiness being the will of Source? "Your function is to add to God's treasure by creating yours. You cannot find joy except as God does." So, yes, Source wants you to be happy but your joy comes through extending it as Source does. You cannot secure lasting happiness at the expense of another.

Today's lesson speaks to using the body for joy. Paradoxically, this is accomplished through the recognition that the body is not what you are. When a Child of God sees herself and others as a body only, she makes herself small. The body cannot hold all that you are! Yet the body can be a messenger that extends the bliss of Spirit. To do this, we must look at the body very, very differently.

Spirit cannot be made physical but it can be made manifest through the physical. Remember, Spirit created the body and can join through Its creation. To accomplish this joining, one must look at the Spirit in the body and not simply at the body itself. This line of thought is uncommon now but in the future it will be seen as obvious.

Let me offer an example of how this works.

Imagine a group of people gathered to hear a singer. She has a beautiful voice and is a gifted performer. Now imagine someone in the audience has brought his harmonica. He steps forward and joins the singer on stage, accompanying her softly at first. After a bit, she steps back and invites him to play a solo. When he is finished, the singer invites the whole audience to join them and the room fills with the sound of voices. Feet tap in rhythm, hands clap, voices rise and fall. The performers and the audience now have but one purpose: the joyful sharing of each song together and not one person is left out.

This is how we use our eyes, our tongues, our hands, our feet together to bless the world with miracles. This is how we give in service to each other. Some create the beauty and others partake of it. Then those who partake create and others get to enjoy. Nothing is ours alone and everything is more when it is shared. This is how we use the body to bless the world. This is how we rise above the limits of aloneness. This is how we add to Source through our experience and know joy as God does.

Today, use your body as a means to communicate Source's Love. Reach out and touch the person you are talking to. Give a hug. Share the Love of Source through your own presence.

Sit in silent contemplation today. Settle in and place awareness on the breath. Sense your way into the body. How does it feel? Breathe into any tight spots and exhale it all out. Allow the breath to be the focus of your gentle attention and then go deeper into awareness of the body. You may hear your heart beat. You may feel a kind of aliveness, a sense of space, a frequency, or a vibration. As you breathe out, sense the space around your body. Your consciousness extends beyond its form. This is your light body and it is as real as your blood and bone.

Sit for a while like this. Use the breath as your anchor. On the out-breath, ride the exhale to its edge. Where does it go? Feel the response in your body as you explore this outer space. As you breathe in ask, "What am I breathing? What is in the space between the molecules I inhale?" You cannot do this wrong. Just play with it and notice what happens. You are using your body to perceive the world beyond it.

Lesson 354

I stand within the All, beside the All, and as the All. God is in Christ and Christ is in me. I am in God and God is in me.

The words of today's lesson establish us as One. In this world we are challenged to remember we are wholly free, and beyond time. Forgive yourself for forgetting you have no self except the one that is together with all other selves in Mind of Source.

We can lose sight of Oneness but we cannot make it unreal. It is the one thing that is real and Its expression is lasting and deep. We know It when we experience It. We love it because it feels good, and what feels good is a pointer toward truth.

The world you see is based on "sacrifice" of oneness. It is a picture of complete disunity and total lack of joining. Around each entity is built a wall so seemingly solid that it looks as if what is inside can never reach without, and what is out can never reach and join with what is locked away within the wall. Each part must sacrifice the other part, to keep itself complete. For if they joined each one would lose its own identity, and by their separation are their selves maintained.
– ACIM

"By their separation are their selves maintained." We have known ourselves only as separate. But the walls so seemingly solid are coming down. This world is full of turmoil because they are coming down. Some would have the walls remain, but many others are reaching up and pulling out the mortar.

Our shared reality requires no loss. We are both One and a unique expression of One at the same time. We are One! It's a beautiful day. We are unlimited forever. We are free. You stand today, right now, within the All, beside the All, and as the All. Source is in you and you are in It. This is Truth. Separation is not. There is no sacrifice in knowing Truth.

Lesson 355

There is no end to all the peace and joy,
And all the miracles that I will give,
When I accept God's Word. I accept it now.

You can only accept the Word of Source now, in this present moment. The past is gone and the future not yet arrived. Sit for a moment in your seat and understand this: you have manifested yourself as physical form! You have created the chair your form is sitting in. Your heart beating, the sound of birdsong outside the window – all of it you have called to yourself to experience! What a miracle that is! You are an amazing creator!

When I choose to know myself as Word of God, I begin to sing a different song. I begin to know myself in new ways and new perceptions come to me. I share my new perceptions through my new expression. I am singing this: "I am Word of God in form and I am in service to Word through my willingness to know my Self."

Accept the Truth of yourself as Word of God. When I hear you singing your song, I sing with you. Together, our voices rise and we stand steadfast. We wait together and listen for the others to join us. We keep the lights on. We know who we are and what we are – all of us, singing together, free, and without limit.

Sing the song of your Self today. You may sing quietly, or you may broadcast your song and knowingly join with others.

Source will conduct the orchestra, but you must sing. Your song is a claim of your inheritance. It says, "I am one who may choose in freedom and without limit, and I rejoice in knowing What I am."

Be your authentic self. There is only one of you and your uniqueness is no threat to the Unity of Source Who only rejoices in your full expression. Sing your authentic song and be happy for the song your sister/brother sings. Forgive those who are not yet singing or who are out of tune. They will hear your song and it will remind them. It is a miracle that you are here, together with them, all part of Christ Mind together.

Look upon the world today with your Christ Mind. Drop a pebble of light into your pond. Watch it ripple outward, touch all in its path, reach the far shore, and bring the light right back to you.

Lesson 356

Sickness is but another name for sin.
Healing is but another name for God.
The miracle is my call and God's answer.

There is no sickness in me at all except when I believe myself to be separated, alone and abandoned by Source. When I see beyond my personal mind and answer the call of my Self to listen for the Voice for God, healing comes. This is the miracle: that I am motivated to seek a vision beyond the illusion, that I can perceive the Presence of Source, and accept the power of Source's Answer.

It does not matter where I perceive myself to be. It does not matter what condition my body is in. I am One with Source and when I call on the Name of Source I call on my own True Name.

Lesson 357

Truth answers every call I make to God,
Responding first with miracles, and then returning me to full
awareness of Truth.

You stand on the shore of your pond and drop a pebble of thought into its still waters. This is your call. The ripples extending outward are a perfect vibrational match for your pebble of thought. They reach the farthest shore of the pond, bounce off it, and flow back toward to you. What returns is a perfect match of your original call.

Every pebble of thought you drop into your pond is either a call to Source Truth or the illusion of personal mind. Source will match your call to It with miracles, each containing an aspect of True awareness within.

Forgiveness is Truth's vibration. It is a match for Source in this world. As you look upon your brother and sister today, drop only pebbles of forgiving thought into your pond. Behold their sinlessness and miracles will be yours, for what you extend to them can only be returned to you – a perfect match.

Sit in open silence for fifteen minutes today. Breathe your way into calm awareness. Expect nothing and be open to anything. Forget ACIM. Forget this lesson. Simply notice thoughts as they arise in the still pond of your awareness. Respond to each one with gentle acceptance and then let it go. Notice what comes back to you.

Lesson 358

No call to God can be unheard nor left
Unanswered. And of this I can be sure;
God's answer is the one I really want.

Yesterday's lesson asked you to remember, *"Truth answers every call I make to God."* Today you are asked to consider how often you make your interpretation of the truth a requirement for happiness. Is it possible that your preconceived idea of truth has ever gotten in the way of receiving it?

When I think a fat bank account is what I need, is that the truth? The bank account is just a symbol of security, which is what I'm really looking for. And is it true that my body requires healing for my happiness? The truest healing is my remembrance that I am not my body at all. Do I need the special love of another to make me feel complete? No, for special love never lasts. It is the everlasting Love of Source that fills the heart and never wavers.

You are free to ask for anything but you may not insist on interpreting its fulfillment. God's answer may come in a form you do not recognize at first, but the answer will be given. The miracle will be when you hear it, see it, allow it, and know it is yours.

Today as you sit in contemplation begin with this prayer. "You, Who alone remember what I really am, Know what I really need. What You offer me is in the form You choose. Let me remember all I do not know and let my voice be still. Let me not forget myself is nothing, but my Self is all." Now consider what it is that will give you comfort. What is it that would satisfy your need to feel safe, loved, and secure? What would complete you and make you whole? Send your request from a place of peace. Know that what you truly need is already yours. Now stand back and be ready to receive from a place of abundance. It will arrive in whatever form Source knows you need.

Lesson 359

Yesterday you learned, *"No call to God can be unheard nor left unanswered."* Today you learn what form God's answer always takes.

God's answer is some form of peace. All pain
Is healed; all misery replaced with joy.
All limitations are removed. And all sin
Is understood as merely a mistake.

You were born Innocence, Whole, and Pure. Give up all mistaken perceptions of yourself as anything less. Be happy with yourself. Like yourself. Stand in certainty of your Self. Accept this blessing, for we have all always been blessed and there is nothing else.

When you see with the eyes of Christ it is a new day. All things are possible. Today, give up to the Holy Spirit all that obscures Love from your sight. Relinquish what limits you. Make it your purpose to see yourself as the Love you are.

I forgive the world and all Extensions of Creation that have seemed so separate from me. I have misunderstood everything but I have not made myself separate from You. I am still as You Created me. There has never been a sin that is Real. There has never been anything that can truly disturb my peace.
– ACIM

Lesson 360

Peace be to me, the Holy Child of God.
Peace be to my brother and my sister, who are One with me.
Let all the world be blessed with peace through us.

"Peace be to me, the Holy Child of God." I am Wholeness Itself. I am a Holy Child of God. I am vaster than vast, immortal, All Knowing, Innocence Itself, and powerful beyond measure. I am without fault of any kind. I am a Creator Being. I Create in Peace because Love is my entire Mind.

"Peace be to my brother and my sister who are One with me." I am One with All Things, and no one is not my Self. We are all of us made of Light, and nothing is not all of us joined together. Peace be to me and peace be to you. The Law of Love knows no distinctions and surpasses all other laws.

"Let all the world be blessed with peace through us." In Whole I Ness, we were created. In Whole I Ness, we remain. Let me demonstrate my holiness through the recognition of our Oneness. Together, let us renegotiate the ancient agreement that we would forget our Oneness. Let all the world be blessed through our remembrance. When you forget, I will remember for you. When I forget, I am grateful that you remember for me.

May you know loving-kindness.

May you know an end to suffering.

May you know peace.

Final Lessons 361–365

The final five lessons of ACIM are as free of words as possible because you are no longer in need of them. What is unlimited cannot be described and you are on the path to the unlimited. Leave these lessons to the Holy Spirit, which abides within and is never apart from you. Listen to Its Voice. You are perfectly capable. If you have any doubts about your ability, remember it is only the personal mind that doubts. You are here, reading these words. You have brought yourself to this place of healing.

What a gift you have allowed yourself to receive and what a gift has been given you. You know what you are! You know your function! You have been shown the way to the Peace of Source. Let nothing else direct your journey from now until your journey's end. The illusion of time will be with you. Its end may seem far off. But its end is already here, in the Holy Spirit, Which Lovingly guides you on your path. You do not travel alone.

Dedicate your mind to your salvation. Remember your function is forgiveness. Look softly upon yourself and the world. Do not rest your eyes for long on anything in judgment. Make it a habit to ask for help when the illusions of pain, disease, suffering, attack and counter-attack, destruction, and death seem to overload your senses. They are part of your perception that you are in the world, and for so long as you seem to be, it will be your function to forgive them. Extend your Memory of Source to all that you perceive.

Remember that all giving is receiving. This is why loss is not possible and why death does not exist. God, Which you are, can transmute only into Itself. Continue to perfect your ability to release resistance to Creation's flow. Practice showing up as a Fragment of Diamond Mind in individuated form. Enjoy your time here. Be at peace with yourself. Play. Love. Listen. Be your authentic self. Drop your pebbles of thought into the Pond of Creation and have your experience with them.

Now go in honesty with God. The end of the dream is certain and the means as well. Trust in Source. Wait in confidence. The Love of Source surrounds you and will never leave you comfortless.

Here is how to practice the next five lessons. Begin and end your day with the thought behind the lesson. Practice mindfulness throughout the day. Mindfulness should be your companion now. Use the breath as a portable centering device. Stop often and breathe into peace. Know the contents of your mind. React as little as possible but act often from a place of calm awareness. Practice forgiveness. Allow direct experience through conscious awareness.

Give yourself the gift of contemplation for at least fifteen minutes each day. Find a regular place where you will not be disturbed. Sit and place awareness on the breath. Breathe in peace and exhale any tension in the body. Take as long as you want to do this. Invite the Holy Spirit's assistance, and then let everything go. Judge nothing. Allow everything. Be present and watch all thoughts, feelings, and sensations as they arise, peak, and then fall away. This will be your practice now although you may always return to a specific lesson when you need its wisdom.

Begin and end each day with this lesson:

This Holy Instant I would give to You.
Be You in charge. For I would follow You,
Certain that Your direction gives me peace.

"This Holy Instant I would give to You." I now make the conscious choice to open my mind to the Mind of Source.

"Be You in charge. For I would follow You." I am here to have my experience. I am here to let this moment touch me, and when it does I will allow it. I am open to what I did not see before. I know that I do not know. I step aside and let You lead.

"Certain that Your direction gives me peace." You Who created me like your Self know Peace is what I seek. If I have a question, I will know You have answered because peace will be the result.

Chapter 7

Continuing the Ride

What you have done this year cannot be overstated. ACIM teaches that the application of these lessons will reduce your time spent in the illusion "by thousands of lifetimes." You have devoted a full year to your Self and Source but what you have accomplished in this training will last you forever.

Perhaps you have already experienced the life-changing nature of the lessons. Rest assured, they will continue to shed light on situations, events, and relationships in ways you cannot imagine now. Learn to expect moments of insight, clarity, and release. Your journey has begun. You will also continue to peel away the layers of your resistance and blocks to Love's Presence. But you have tools and experiences to draw upon that you did not have a year ago. And remember, you do not journey alone.

If you are like me, you will appreciate the structure the daily lessons have offered. So here is what I encourage you to do: begin them again. Why? Because the knowledge contained in each lesson is holographic. When you spiral back to each lesson again it will be from a different vantage point. You will see things, know things, and experience things with a perception that was unavailable to you the year before. Make no mistake: the energy within each lesson is layered and multidimensional. It is worth repeating them once or even twice. Trust your inner voice to instruct you about it and be at peace with whatever you choose.

Whether you begin a new round of lessons or continue your journey in another way, here are some suggestions to assist in you on your path:

1. Begin and end your day with the thought of Source. Try not

to get out of bed without making a connection with God. Choose whatever method works for you, but make space for Source as you begin the day. You may awaken with a dream to ponder. You may gently focus on the breath and open your heart to whatever guidance comes. Source is already there but you must be open on your end to receive. When your day is over, consider what you have been grateful for that day. Ask for guidance to continue in your sleep state. Then let go of the day completely. Carry no guilt or remorse with you into sleep. If it helps, consciously turn it over to the Holy Spirit.

2. Create a daily practice of contemplation and meditation. Choose a convenient place and time to devote at least fifteen minutes of your day to it in whatever form works best. The more you practice, the more comfortable you will become with your own mind. In time, you will be able to practice anywhere, any time. You may choose a lesson, a phrase, or sit with empty mind and ask the Holy Spirit to be your guide. But do sit and do not feel guilty when you can't.

3. Make awareness habitual. Use the Holy Instant. During the day stop often and ask yourself, *"What am I feeling now? What is in my mind?"* Thoughts and feelings create your reality. Know what your building materials are.

4. Listen to your body. The personal mind cannot hide from the body. It will tell you when your mind has been consistently holding stressful thoughts because it will feel tense, tight, and contracted. Use your breath to soften areas of tension by breathing into them and letting go on the out-breath. The breath is your personal, portable centering device. Cultivate it as a form of mindfulness and use it to access the Holy Instant.

5. Give all to all to receive all from All. The Law of Love requires you will always receive what you give. Try to remember that every attack is a call for love and therefore every situation can be a reminder that you are free to extend the miracle of God's Love. Forgive yourself first and then extend your forgiveness to the other. You have created every moment of your reality. Use what you have brought to you to heal yourself through the extension of the miracle. If you forget, and you will, forgive.

6. Cultivate trust in Source. The practice of trust takes practice. First I trust with faith. When I see what trust produces, I know. Trust that Source will send you whatever you need. Be confident in this for there is never a problem sent to you that does not also contain its solution. Mind of God is Whole.

7. Play often. Then play more. ACIM says this world was created when we "forgot to laugh." Enjoy yourself and play with the experiences Source sends. Let go of your mistakes. They are nothing at all but learning devices! You will learn to fly when you take yourself lightly.

8. Above all: Forgive. Forgive. Forgive. Allow. Allow. Allow. This is your function for so long as your journey on this earth lasts. Forgive yourself first and then extend your forgiveness to the world. Mistakes are a crucial aspect of learning. Nothing does not warrant forgiveness for in truth:

Nothing real can be threatened.
Nothing unreal exists.
Herein lies the peace of God.
– ACIM

BOOKS

O-BOOKS

SPIRITUALITY

O is a symbol of the world, of oneness and unity; this eye represents knowledge and insight. We publish titles on general spirituality and living a spiritual life. We aim to inform and help you on your own journey in this life.
If you have enjoyed this book, why not tell other readers by posting a review on your preferred book site?

The Holy Spirit's Interpretation of the New Testament

A course in Understanding and Acceptance
Regina Dawn Akers
Following on from the strength of *A Course In Miracles*, NTI teaches us how to experience the love and oneness of God.
Paperback: 978-1-84694-085-9 ebook: 978-1-78099-083-5

The Message of A Course In Miracles

A translation of the text in plain language
Elizabeth A. Cronkhite
A translation of *A Course in Miracles* into plain, everyday language for anyone seeking inner peace. The companion volume, *Practicing A Course In Miracles*, offers practical lessons and mentoring.
Paperback: 978-1-84694-319-5 ebook: 978-1-84694-642-4

Rising in Love

My Wild and Crazy Ride to Here and Now, with Amma, the Hugging Saint
Ram Das Batchelder
Rising in Love conveys an author's extraordinary journey of spiritual awakening with the Guru, Amma.
Paperback: 978-1-78279-687-9 ebook: 978-1-78279-686-2

Thinker's Guide to God

Peter Vardy
An introduction to key issues in the philosophy of religion.
Paperback: 978-1-90381-622-6

Your Simple Path
Find happiness in every step
Ian Tucker
A guide to helping us reconnect with what is really important in
our lives.
Paperback: 978-1-78279-349-6 ebook: 978-1-78279-348-9

365 Days of Wisdom
Daily Messages To Inspire You Through The Year
Dadi Janki
Daily messages which cool the mind, warm the heart and guide
you along your journey.
Paperback: 978-1-84694-863-3 ebook: 978-1-84694-864-0

Body of Wisdom
Women's Spiritual Power and How it Serves
Hilary Hart
Bringing together the dreams and experiences of women across
the world with today's most visionary spiritual teachers.
Paperback: 978-1-78099-696-7 ebook: 978-1-78099-695-0

Dying to Be Free
From Enforced Secrecy to Near Death to True Transformation
Hannah Robinson
After an unexpected accident and near-death experience, Hannah
Robinson found herself radically transforming her life, while a
remarkable new insight altered her relationship with her father, a
practising Catholic priest.
Paperback: 978-1-78535-254-6 ebook: 978-1-78535-255-3

The Ecology of the Soul

A Manual of Peace, Power and Personal Growth for Real People in the Real World

Aidan Walker

Balance your own inner Ecology of the Soul to regain your natural state of peace, power and wellbeing.

Paperback: 978-1-78279-850-7 ebook: 978-1-78279-849-1

Not I, Not other than I

The Life and Teachings of Russel Williams

Steve Taylor, Russel Williams

The miraculous life and inspiring teachings of one of the World's greatest living Sages.

Paperback: 978-1-78279-729-6 ebook: 978-1-78279-728-9

On the Other Side of Love

A Woman's Unconventional Journey Towards Wisdom

Muriel Maufroy

When life has lost all meaning, what do you do?

Paperback: 978-1-78535-281-2 ebook: 978-1-78535-282-9

Practicing A Course In Miracles

A Translation of the Workbook in Plain Language and With Mentoring Notes

Elizabeth A. Cronkhite

The practical second and third volumes of The Plain-Language *A Course In Miracles*.

Paperback: 978-1-84694-403-1 ebook: 978-1-78099-072-9

Quantum Bliss
The Quantum Mechanics of Happiness, Abundance, and Health
George S. Mentz
Quantum Bliss is the breakthrough summary of success and spirituality secrets that customers have been waiting for.
Paperback: 978-1-78535-203-4 ebook: 978-1-78535-204-1

The Upside Down Mountain
Mags MacKean
A must-read for anyone weary of chasing success and happiness – one woman's inspirational journey swapping the uphill slog for the downhill slope.
Paperback: 978-1-78535-171-6 ebook: 978-1-78535-172-3

Your Personal Tuning Fork
The Endocrine System
Deborah Bates
Discover your body's health secret, the endocrine system, and 'twang' your way to sustainable health!
Paperback: 978-1-84694-503-8 ebook: 978-1-78099-697-4

Readers of ebooks can buy or view any of these bestsellers by clicking on the live link in the title. Most titles are published in paperback and as an ebook. Paperbacks are available in traditional bookshops. Both print and ebook formats are available online.

Find more titles and sign up to our readers' newsletter at http://www.johnhuntpublishing.com/mind-body-spirit

Follow us on Facebook at https://www.facebook.com/OBooks/ and Twitter at https://twitter.com/obooks